MW0103130

PHIL ROBERTSON

with Mark Schlabach

HOWARD BOOKS
A DIVISION OF SIMON & SCHUSTER, INC.
New York • Nashville • London • Toronto • Sydney • New Delhi

Howard Books
A Division of Simon & Schuster, Inc.
1230 Avenue of the Americas
New York, NY 10020

This book is based on *The Legend of the Duck Commander*, as written by James F. Robertson.

First Howard Books hardcover edition May 2013

HOWARD and colophon are trademarks of Simon & Schuster, Inc.

For information about special discounts for bulk purchases, please contact Simon & Schuster Special Sales at 1-866-506-1949 or business@simonandschuster.com.

The Simon & Schuster Speakers Bureau can bring authors to your live event. For more information or to book an event, contact the Simon & Schuster Speakers Bureau at 1-866-248-3049 or visit our website at www.simonspeakers.com.

Designed by Stephanie D. Walker

Manufactured in the United States of America

30 29 28 27 26 25 24 23

Library of Congress Cataloging-in-Publication Data is available.

ISBN 978-1-4767-2609-0
ISBN 978-1-4767-2611-3 (ebook)

To my four sons: Alan, Jase, Willie, and Jep

"Let them revere nothing but religion, morality and liberty."

—Excerpt from letter to Abigail Adams
from her husband John Adams regarding their two sons,
April 15, 1776

Contents

HAPPY, HAPPY, HAPPY™

HAPPY, HAPPY, HAPPY

When A&E TV approached us about doing a reality TV show based on our family, I was somewhat reluctant and wasn't quite sure if it would work.

"Let me take a guess here," I told the producers.

I told them that there was probably a boardroom meeting at the A&E headquarters in New York City, where all the suits, yuppies, and best creative minds were kicking around ideas for a new reality TV show. At some point during the meeting, someone probably spoke up and said, "Uh, Bob, I know this might sound weird, but why don't we try portraying a functional American family?"

And I'm sure the guy sitting across the table shouted, "Now, that's a novel idea!"

Everything else on TV nowadays is dysfunctional and for the most part has been that way for forty years. The last TV shows we saw that featured functional families were *The Andy Griffith Show,*

The Waltons, *The Beverly Hillbillies* (don't laugh), and *Little House on the Prairie*. That was a long time ago!

I'm sure someone else in the A&E board meeting probably then asked, "Bob, where do we find a functional family in America?"

For whatever reason, they looked for one in West Monroe, Louisiana.

To be honest, our family isn't much different from other families in America. There's a mom and a dad, four grown kids, fourteen grandchildren, and a couple of great-grandkids. We started a family business, Duck Commander, which turned into a pretty lucrative enterprise with a lot of elbow grease, teamwork, and God's blessings. But as you'll find out by reading this book, we've had our share of trials and struggles, like a lot of other families. We've battled alcohol and drug abuse, sibling rivalries, and near poverty and despair at the beginning of our time together as a family. It wasn't always like what you see on TV. So except for our very manly appearances, it might not seem that we're all that different from everyone else.

But I think what separates the Robertsons from a lot of other families is our faith in God and love for each other. It's unconditional, and it has been that way for as long as I can remember. For me, the most dramatic part of every *Duck Dynasty* episode comes at the end, when our family gathers around the dinner table to eat one of Miss Kay's home-cooked meals. You don't see families gathering up like that anymore. Everybody in America is so busy, busy, busy. Americans are too preoccupied with their cell phones and computers, so they don't take the time to sit down with their spouses, children, grandchildren, aunts and uncles, and grandparents to eat a meal together. The family structure is slipping away from America, but not in our house.

Thomas Jefferson, the third president of the United States, probably said it best. Shortly after our founding fathers left the large cities of Europe for the wide-open spaces of America, Jefferson said of the American people, "When they get piled upon one another in large cities, as in Europe, they will become corrupt as in Europe." You'll never find me living in a city, folks. Where I live, I am 911. Like I say, if you spend too much time in the subdivision, you go a-runnin' when the snakes fall out of trees!

What separates the Robertsons from a lot of other families is our faith in God and love for each other.

The other problem in America today is that the young girls don't know how to cook. Their grandmothers and mamas cooked for them, but they never took the time to learn how to cook. They were more interested in other things. If you go out into the subdivisions and suburbs of America, where all of the yuppies live, you'll see the restaurants are packed with people.

They don't want to eat slop and they're looking for good food, but they don't want to take the time to make it. Dad is working, Mom is working, and so no one has the time or energy to cook a good meal anymore. So our families end up eating in restaurants, where they're surrounded by noise and clutter, instead of sharing quality time in a family setting.

When I reluctantly agreed to be a part of *Duck Dynasty,* the producers told me they were going to make a reality show without duck hunting. I asked them if they understood that I spend most of my waking hours in a duck blind or in the woods. There isn't much else I do! I asked the producers, "You know, you're dealing with a bunch of rednecks who duck-hunt. For the life of me, do you really think this is going to work?"

"Ozzy Osbourne made it," they told me.

Ozzy was able to pull it off on reality TV, so he's given hope to all of us. I'd never really watched many reality TV shows and knew nothing about them, but I was 100 percent convinced *Duck Dynasty* would never work. It just goes to show how little I know about today's world, because I was dead wrong. For the life of me, I can't figure out why people are so attracted to our family. Maybe it's because we live our lives like people really want to live, how we all used to live before everything got so busy, busy, busy.

Duck Dynasty has made us a little bit more famous, but it hasn't changed much of anything about us. Miss Kay and I still live in the same house on the Ouachita River outside of West Monroe, and I'm still driving the same truck and hunting with the same guns and dogs. Of course, we still go to church every Sunday morning and I'm still reading my Bible. If anything has changed, it's that it's a little more difficult to go places, like driving down an interstate or walking through an airport. If I'm driving somewhere, someone might drive by and recognize me (undoubtedly because of my beard). They'll get on a cell phone and call their friends, and then when I stop to take a leak, I'll have to sign autographs and pose for pictures for about thirty minutes.

When we went duck-hunting in Arkansas recently, we stopped at a Walmart to buy our out-of-state hunting licenses. We were in the sporting goods section of the store when some people recognized us, so we started posing for pictures and signing T-shirts. When it was finally time for us to leave, three African-American girls approached us.

"Well, girls, I didn't know you soul sisters were duck hunters," I told them.

"We don't care about no ducks," one of them said. "You're ZZ Top, ain't you?"

I guess not everyone in America watches *Duck Dynasty*.

Miss Kay and I haven't done too badly, and the good Lord has really blessed us. We've been married nearly fifty years and our boys have grown up to become loving husbands and fathers, the kind of men I wanted them to be. Our business is in good shape, even after I had my doubts about where it was going. But when the boys took over, they breathed new life into it, and it's still growing. Not many are as fortunate as we are, with all the trouble in the world.

Since I turned over the reins of my company to my sons, I keep busy with hunting and fishing and speaking engagements. God provided those. The appearances give me an opportunity to preach the gospel, which I feel compelled to do. I've also had a chance to learn from all the people I've met—and the chance to travel all over the country. I hope I've helped those who have heard the gospel.

Where do I go from here? The time is near when the dust will return to the earth and the spirit to God who gave it. I'm ready for that, but not quite yet. I have a lot of speeches to give, a lot of blinds to build, a lot of *Duck Dynasty* episodes to make, and who knows how many more duck seasons to hunt.

Maybe the greatest thing is that I've been able to live life the way I wanted. Following Jesus has been a blast. The Lord has blessed me mightily.

It is what makes me happy, happy, happy.

LOW-TECH MAN

Rule No. 1 for Living Happy, Happy, Happy
Simplify Your Life
(Throw Away Your Cell Phones and Computers, Yuppies)

What ever happened to the on-and-off switch? I don't ask for much, but my hope is that someday soon we'll get back to where we have a switch that says on and off. Nowadays, everything has a pass code, sequence, or secret decoder. I think maybe the yuppies overdid it with these computers. The very thing they touted as the greatest time-saving device in history—a computer—now occupies the lion's share of everybody's life.

Here's a perfect example: I owned a Toyota Tundra truck for a while, and I got tired of driving around with my headlights on all the time. If I'm driving around in the woods and it's late in the evening, I don't want my headlights on. I tried to turn the lights off and couldn't do it. I spent an hour inside the truck with a friend of mine trying to turn off the lights, but we never figured it out. So I called the car dealer, and he told me to look in the owner's manual. Well, it wasn't in the book, which is about as thick as a Bible. Finally, about ten days later, after my buddy spent some time with a bunch of young bucks in town driving Toyota trucks, he told me he had the code for turning off my lights.

Now, get this: First, you have to shut off the truck's engine. Then you have to step on the emergency brake with your left foot until you hear one click. Not two clicks—only one. If you hear two clicks, you have to bring the brake back up and start all over. After you hear one click, you crank the engine back up. I sat there thinking, *Why would you possibly need a code for turning off headlights?* What kind of mad scientist came up with that sequence? Seriously, what kind of mind designs something like that? To me, it's not logical. I just don't get it, but that's where we are in today's world.

I miss the times when life was simple. I came from humble, humble beginnings. When I was a young boy growing up in the far northwest corner of Louisiana, only about six miles from Texas and ten miles from Arkansas, we didn't have very much in terms of personal possessions. But even when times were the hardest, I never once heard my parents, brothers, or sisters utter the words "Boy, we're dirt-poor."

We never had new cars, nice clothes, or much money, and we

certainly never lived in an extravagant home, but we were always happy, happy, happy, no matter the circumstances. My daddy, James Robertson, was that kind of a guy. He didn't care about all the frills in life; he was perfectly content with what we had and so were we. We were a self-contained family, eating the fruits and vegetables that grew in our garden or what the Almighty provided us in other ways. And, of course, when we were really lucky, we had meat from the deer, squirrels, fish, and other game my brothers and I hunted and fished in the areas around our home, along with the pigs, chickens, and cattle we raised on our farm.

It was the 1950s when I was a young boy, but we lived about like it was the 1850s. My daddy always reminded us that when he was a boy, his family would go to town and load the wagon down and return home with a month's worth of necessities. For only five dollars, they could buy enough flour, salt, pepper, sugar, and other essentials to survive for weeks. We rarely went to town for groceries, probably because we seldom had five dollars to spend, let alone enough gas to get there!

We rarely went to town for groceries, probably because we seldom had five dollars to spend, let alone enough gas to get there!

I grew up in a little log cabin in the woods, and it was located far from Yuppieville. The cabin was built near the turn of the twentieth century and was originally a three-room shotgun house. At some point, someone added a small, protruding shed room off the southwest corner of the house. The room had a door connecting to the main room, which is where the fireplace was located. I guess whoever added the room thought it would be warmest near the fireplace, which was the only source of heat in our house. In hindsight, it really didn't make a difference where you put the room if you didn't insulate or finish the interior walls. It was going to be cold in there no matter what.

I slept in the shed with my three older brothers—Jimmy Frank, the oldest, who was ten years older than me; Harold, who was six years older than me; and Tommy, who was two years older than me. I never thought twice about sleeping with my three brothers in a bed; I thought that's what everybody did. My younger brother, Silas, slept in the main room on the west end of the house because he had a tendency to wet the bed. My older sister, Judy, also slept in that room.

I can still remember trying to sleep in that room during the winter—there were a lot of sleepless nights. The overlapping boards on the exterior walls of the house were barely strong enough to block the wind, and they sure didn't stand a chance against freezing temperatures. The shed room was about ten square feet, and its only furnishings were a standard bed and battered chest of drawers. My brothers and I kept a few pictures, keepsakes, and whatnots on the two-by-four crosspieces on the framing of the interior walls. Every night before bed, we unloaded whatever was in our pockets, usually a fistful of marbles and whatever else we'd found that day, on the crosspieces and then reloaded our pockets again the next morning.

To help battle the cold, my brothers and I layered each other in heavy homemade quilts on the bed. Jimmy Frank and Harold were the biggest, so they slept on opposite sides of the bed, with Tommy and me sleeping in between them. My daddy and my mother, Merritt Robertson (we started calling them Granny and Pa when our children were born), slept in a small middle room in the house. My youngest sister, Jan, was the baby of the family and slept in a crib next to my parents' bed until she was old enough to sleep with Judy.

The fireplace in the west room was the only place to get warm. It was made of the natural red stone of the area and was rather large. One of my brothers once joked that it was big enough to "burn up a wet mule." Because the fireplace was the only source of heat in the home, it was my family's gathering spot. Every morning in the winter, the first person out of bed—it always seemed to be Harold—was responsible for starting a fire. It would usually reignite with pine fatwood kindling, but sometimes you had to blow the coals to stoke the flames. Some of my favorite memories as a child were when we baked potatoes and roasted hickory nuts on the fireplace coals for snacks. We usually ate them with some of my mother's homemade dill pickles. There was never any candy or junk food in our house.

The only other room in the cabin was a combination kitchen and dining area. The cookstove was fueled by natural gas from a well that was located down the hill and across the creek. The pressure from the well was so low that it barely produced enough gas to cook. Pa always said we were lucky to have the luxury of running water in the house, even if it was only cold water coming through a one-inch pipe from a hand-dug well to the kitchen sink. We didn't even have a bathtub or commode in the house! The water pipeline habitually froze during the winter, and my brothers and I spent many mornings unfreezing the pipe with hot coals from the fire. When the pipe was frozen, we'd grab a shovelful of coals and place them on the ground under the pipe. When we finally heard gurgling and then water spitting out of the kitchen sink, we knew we could return to the fire to get warm again.

Breakfast began when Granny put a big pot of water on the stove to heat. We didn't have a hot-water heater, so we bathed in cold water when I was young. Granny used the hot water for cooking and cleaning the dishes. Breakfast usually consisted of hot buttermilk biscuits, blindfolded fried eggs, butter, and fresh "sweet milk": every morning, one of my brothers or I would take a pail of hot water to the barn to clean the cows' udders after we milked them. There were always several jars of jams and jellies on our table. Pa and Granny canned them from wild fruits that grew in abundance in the Arklatex area. Pa liked to scold us for having too many jars open at once; he said we opened them just to hear the Ball jar lids pop. He may have been right.

Nearly everything we ate came from our land. The eggs came from our chickens, the milk and butter from our cows. Bacon and sausage came from the hogs we raised and butchered. We canned vegetables from our large garden, which spread over about eight acres in three different patches. Cucumbers were turned into jars and jars of sweet, sour, bread-and-butter, and dill pickles. Our pantry shelves were lined with canned tomatoes, peppers, beets, and just about anything else my family grew, including pears, peaches, plums, and grapes, as well as the abundant dewberries and blackberries of the area. Cut-up cabbage, green tomatoes, onions, and peppers were mixed together and canned to make what we called chow-chow, a relish that was a delicious accompaniment to just about anything—especially fish.

In addition to our garden, where we also grew such things as English peas, butter and pole beans, lettuce, turnips, mustard greens, onions, radishes, carrots, Irish and sweet potatoes, cantaloupes, and watermelons, my family grew several fields of peas, peanuts, and corn. We started many of the vegetables from seeds that were planted in a hotbed (called a cold frame by some) in early February. My brothers and I gathered cow and horse manure, which, as it decomposed, kept the bed warm and enriched the soil. After the plants sprouted and grew big enough, we transferred them to the garden.

One year Pa, figuring he would get a jump on the market for the early watermelons that brought the highest prices, had my brothers and I collect manure from the cow pens to put into two hundred holes. He directed us to dig the holes two feet square and two feet deep. In early February, Jimmy Frank and Harold laboriously filled washtub after washtub with manure and then transported them on a slide pulled by an old mule to the holes that were dug. After depositing the manure into the holes, we mixed the top of it with soil and planted the watermelon seeds.

To be perfectly honest, Tommy and I didn't become too interested in the project until Jimmy Frank and Harold told us we should plant marbles—along with the watermelon seeds—in the holes. They promised us we would grow a big crop of marbles. Of course, we were young enough—and thus gullible enough—to believe them. We already had marbles running out our ears from ill-gotten gains at the schoolyard, where we played bull's-eye, cat's-eye, and hotbox for "keeps" (whoever shot best and won the others' marbles got to keep them). We won regularly and often came home with pockets bulging with marbles, which we deposited in a five-gallon bucket just inside the back door. Tommy and I grabbed our bucket and, with high hopes, planted them in the manure just like our older brothers told us to do.

It didn't take Tommy or me too long to realize we had been duped. We ended up sacrificing ammunition for our slingshots for a bumper crop that never came. There were always two things in my pocket when I was young—marbles and a slingshot. We made our slingshots from forked tree limbs and red real-rubber bands we cut from old inner tubes (the black synthetic inner tubes didn't have the necessary snap to propel a marble or small rock). We used the slingshots to bring down small birds, but Granny and my grandmothers always admonished us not to shoot the mockingbirds or "redbirds," as they called cardinals.

Our watermelons came up beautifully that year. The decaying manure heated the beds enough to sprout the seeds early, and the soil's added richness gave the young watermelon plants a tremendous growth spurt that turned the hillside where they were growing into a couple of acres of lush, verdant green vines. Pa never followed up on selling them, so we wound up giving away what we didn't eat to kinfolk and friends.

My entire family took part in harvesting fruits and vegetables. If we hadn't, we wouldn't have had enough to eat. From the beginning of May, when the mayhaws and dewberries ripened, until the end of fall, with the gathering of muscadines and pears, my family and I could regularly be found in the area's swamps, fields, forests, and abandoned home sites. With our buckets and tubs, from the youngest to the oldest, we would be stooped over or stretched upward gathering whatever fruit was in season.

The trick was to get there when the fruit was ripe—and before another family beat you to it!

Pa, who worked on drilling rigs usually located in the wilds, often discovered fruit trees and berry and grape vines as he moved about with the rigs. He also knew the locations of many old home sites with abandoned peach orchards, grapevines, and plum and pear trees. There was no shortage of places to harvest. The trick was to get there when the fruit was ripe—and before another family beat you to it!

I remember one particularly cold, wet spring when my family was wading ankle-deep (in our everyday shoes because we didn't have rubber boots) to gather mayhaws in cottonmouth-infested waters near Myrtis, Louisiana, in a swampy area off Black Bayou. Clouds of mosquitoes covered our backs, biting through our thin shirts while we stooped to gather the floating fruit we shook from thickly clustered trees. Mayhaw jelly is still my favorite, and even today my wife, Kay, and I gather the bright reddish-orange berries from the swamps around our home each spring. We make plenty of the tart jelly for our needs, usually with enough left over for our children and other family members and friends. Mayhaw jelly has a unique, delicious flavor.

One year when I was young, the wild grapes were so abundant in the old Ruby Florence field that they filled all of our tubs and buckets with rich, purple-red fruit. We could barely fit our harvest into the car, which was already crowded with adults and children. In fact, the trunk was so crammed full of tubs and buckets of fruit piled on top of each other that the lid wouldn't shut. Several large buckets and pans of grapes were jammed inside the car, on the floorboards, between our legs, and on our laps. The harvest was so great that Granny lit all four burners on the stove and had Pa and Jimmy Frank set an entire number three washtub full of grapes on top of them to render the juice.

As our luck would have it, this was also one of the years when the price of sugar was sky-high (always a consideration in canning as to whether it was worth the cost). After making a smaller amount of jelly than usual, my family simply sealed a number of gallons of surplus grape juice in quart jars without sugar and stored them in the cabinets alongside and beneath the sink—thinking we might make jelly later, after the price of sugar went down. But we eventually found that the stored juice was delicious, so my brothers and I drank a quart or more daily for breakfast and snacks. Before too long, the juice began to ferment. In only a short time, it turned into a very good wine. My parents and older relatives began to drink this, too, but couldn't finish it before it turned into vinegar. Granny used the vinegar in her canning throughout the rest of the year.

Of course, man can't survive on fruits and vegetables alone (at least not a *real* man), so we also raised and butchered our own beef, usually killing two steer calves annually that weighed about four hundred pounds each. The calves were the offspring of our milk cows, which were bred to my aunt Myrtle's beef-type bull—a runty, mostly Black Angus mix, which still sired nice calves. Pa and my older brothers would kill the calf, gut and skin it, and wrap it in an old bedsheet, which they then put into the trunk of our car. We didn't have a deep-freezer, so the meat was taken to Vivian, Louisiana, about two miles away, where it was hung to cool and age in a local icehouse. After about fourteen days, Pa brought the sides of beef home and cut them up on the dining table. Then Granny and Pa wrapped the meat in freezer paper and took it to a rental storage locker in town, where it was frozen. Granny periodically retrieved packages of beef when she was in town and transferred them to the small freezing compartment in the refrigerator at home.

Homegrown chickens were another staple at my house when I was a boy. Pa bought two hundred baby chicks by mail order each year at a cost of about five dollars per hundred—one hundred early and another hundred later, so we always had young fryers running around the yard. It was a big day when the baby chicks were brought home from the post office in a ventilated cardboard box. They were immediately moved into a brooder Jimmy Frank built with four-by-eight-foot sheets of tin. The brooder was heated by using an old washtub—with vents on the sides—and a small burner that was fueled by the natural gas well that also heated the stove.

We didn't wait too long to start eating the chickens—even if it took eight of them to make a meal! We usually kept twenty or so hens every year to lay eggs, and we dined on the older ones from previous years during the winter. Of course we cooked and prepared them the old-fashioned way: wringing their necks, plucking the feathers, and singeing them over a stove burner. Our Sunday meals in the spring and summer typically consisted of fried chicken and homemade ice cream, which was made with the rich cream of our Jersey cows. On the way home from church, we'd pick up a twenty-five-pound block of ice, and my brothers and I would make the ice cream outside. Jimmy Frank or Harold cranked the freezer, while Tommy or I sat on it to keep it steady.

The story of the Robertson family is a pretty good picture of an early American family. We didn't have much, but we loved each other and found ways to keep each other entertained. We didn't have cell phones or computers, but somehow we managed to survive. As far as I know, none of my brothers or sisters has ever owned a cell phone, and Jimmy Frank is the only one who owns a computer, because he's a newspaperman and needs one to write his stories. I've never owned a cell phone and don't plan on ever having one. I've never owned a computer, and I'm still trying to figure out what the fuss over social media is all about. I can promise you one thing: you'll never find me on Twitter or Skype. If anyone needs to talk to me, they know where I live.

GREAT OUTDOORS

Rule No. 2 for Living Happy, Happy, Happy
Don't Let Your Grandkids Grow Up to Be Nerds

The Boy Scouts might have the motto "Be Prepared," but where I grew up, you practically went straight from diapers to manhood. You had to be prepared for anything. I learned to hunt and fish shortly after I learned to walk. If you couldn't shoot and kill something, chances were you weren't going to eat. If a hurricane had hit my boyhood home and wiped out everything, I would have found a way to survive—even when I was only five years old! I'm trying to teach those same lessons of survival to my grandchildren, because the last thing I want is for them to grow up to be nerds.

Let me tell you one thing: I don't see the inherent value in the video games that kids are playing today. But that's all these kids seem to want to do. Kids in America today are overweight and lazy, and it's their parents' fault for letting it happen. Kids sit around playing video games and eating junk food all day, and when they're not doing that, they're texting on their cell phones. It's only their fingers that are moving; they're not getting out and about. Have you ever seen a macho man walking around with a cell phone, mashing it with his fingers and yakking on it all day? That's too much talking. By the time these kids are young adults, they're going to have to go to Walmart to buy a personality. Kids need to be out with nature, learning what it takes to survive in this world.

By the time these kids are young adults, they're going to have to go to Walmart to buy a personality.

When I was a very young boy, much of our food and sustenance came from the land around us. While living in Vivian, Louisiana, immediately following World War II and before we moved into the log cabin where I spent my formative years, Granny often told us, "If we have another depression, we could live off this acre." The Great Depression was never far from my parents' thoughts; they suffered through the worst economic depression to ever hit the United States when they were younger.

In those days, living off the land surrounding our house sounded feasible. Even on our limited acreage, we had a milk cow that was pastured on half the land and staked out alongside the road when grass was scarce. We had several fruit trees, which we'd planted, along with a large truck garden (it was called a "truck garden" because the overflow of what we raised in it was put on a truck and taken to town to sell), that provided abundantly from spring to fall. The garden yielded such food as turnips and greens far into the mild Louisiana winters. My great-aunt Willie Mae Irvins, who lived next door to us, kept a flock of chickens, and we purchased eggs and occasional young fryers and roasting hens from her.

As a boy, living off the land influenced my outlook on life probably more than anything else, especially after I discovered an abundance of wild game and fish that was there for the taking in the area where we lived. I always had a conviction that I could survive off the land without being tied to a regular job. As I grew older, that belief influenced many of my decisions.

I always had a conviction that I could survive off the land without being tied to a regular job.

I killed my first duck—actually, two of them—when I was eleven years old. I was hunting on the bank of a small slough when three teal and a pintail flew close enough for me to shoot. I fired three times, bringing down the pintail and one teal. To this day, I can show you the exact spot where I shot those ducks. Remember what I said about being prepared? If I ever go back there, I'll be sure to take my dog or a boat, or at least some good waders. My first kill taught me a valuable lesson—sometimes shooting the ducks isn't nearly as hard as retrieving them!

With no retriever and no boat, the only way I could recover the birds was to take off my blue jeans and tattered shirt and wade into the icy water. I returned home with them and proudly announced to my father, "I have struck!" (As you might have noticed, I sometimes speak in dramatic terms if the occasion warrants it.) It turned out the event was momentous: it shaped the rest of my life and absolutely convinced me I could live off the land.

My father always lived by that philosophy and passed it on to my brothers and me. The son of Judge Euan Robertson, longtime Vivian justice of the peace, Pa grew up a farm boy outside of town, with two brothers and four sisters. He gravitated early to a career in the oil industry, which was booming with the fabulous East Texas and Pine Island discoveries, both classified as giant oil fields, practically at his doorstep.

Pa served in the U.S. Navy at San Diego during World War II, achieving the rank of fireman first class. His familiarity with heavy pumps, which he gained in the oil fields, pointed him toward the repair base, where he fixed even bigger pumps used in warships. After returning home from the war, Pa bought a house on an acre of land just outside of Vivian with a federal homeowner's loan. It was a small A-frame house, with two bedrooms, located close to town and Highway 2. I was born at a clinic in Vivian on April 24, 1946. I was named after Granny's first cousin Phil Shores, who was killed in World War II, and my great-grandfather Lemuel Alexander Shores (my middle name is Alexander).

I think much of my independent attitude was fostered by the fine example of Aunt Willie Mae next door. She was part of the original Robertson clan that moved to northwest Louisiana from Tennessee in a covered wagon in the late 1800s. (In fact, there's a street in Nashville—James Robertson Parkway—that is named after one of my early ancestors. He was an explorer and companion of Daniel Boone and cofounded the city of Nashville.) Willie Mae was eleven years old at the time and lived long enough to tell her grandchildren and numerous great-nieces and -nephews about making the trip.

Willie Mae's husband had been dead for many years before we moved next to her, but he left her with a few acres of land and a little money, which she used to build cabins she then rented out. With that income and more from boarders in two of the rooms in her home, and with a garden, chickens, and a milk cow, she made out pretty well. She often hired my siblings and me to weed her garden, mow her yard, and complete any other chores she could think up. We were paid with a shiny dime (she saved every one she acquired and had a considerable hoard), which just so happened to be the price of admission to the picture show.

Saturday afternoon trips to the double features at the local movie theater were about our only form of entertainment. We didn't have a TV, so we crowded around a radio near the fireplace to listen to Roy Rogers and Gene Autry. I'll never forget the opening monologue of *Gunsmoke,* when the announcer would introduce "the story of the violence that moved west with young America, and the story of a man who moved with it." Then Marshal Matt Dillon, with his deep, resonant voice, would proclaim, "I'm that man, Matt Dillon, United States marshal, the first man they look for and the last they want to meet." I used to love hearing those words.

We were paid with a shiny dime, which just so happened to be the price of admission to the picture show.

After a few years of living next door to Aunt Willie Mae, my mother began urging my father to move to a larger place outside of town. Granny grew up in the country and thought it would be easier to raise her family there. There were six kids in our family after my youngest brother, Si, was born, so we needed more space in the house, too. Her biggest concern was there was a busy paved highway that ran in front of our house, and my mama always worried one of her children would wander into traffic, with the dangerous speed limit of twenty-five miles per hour. After one of my brothers was nearly hit by a speeding car, she ordered Pa to find us another place to live.

Granny wanted to buy the old Douglas Waters place, a log home that sat on about twenty acres between Vivian and Hosston, Louisiana. It was on the same road that ran in front of our old house, but the Waters home sat several hundred yards back, making it much safer for my siblings and me. But Pa wasn't interested in buying it, so we instead moved into a rental home in the middle of the Pine Island oil field. It was located ten miles south of Vivian, and we had an oil well right in the middle of our front yard. The oil field ruined our water, which stained our commodes and sinks. The water smelled and tasted bad. Our drinking water came from a cistern made from an old oil field tank that collected water off the roof. It didn't take Granny and Pa long to realize we had to find somewhere else to live.

About a year later, we ended up moving into a log home that used to be owned by the Waters family—the log home Granny had wanted to purchase all along, which was where I would spend my formative years and was the house I told you about earlier. My great-aunt Myrtle Gauss bought the house because the place adjoined her four hundred acres of land. We rented the house from her, and she put us in charge of tending to her seven cows and bull, an old mule named Jake, and an equally old (and stubborn) horse named Dolly. She rented us the house and her four hundred acres of land for the kinfolk price of twenty dollars a month.

Moving to that log home enabled my father to recapture his youth, which in turn shaped the lives of my brothers and me. The old Waters place had about twenty acres of land, only ten of which, around the house, was cleared and tillable land. A creek that flowed year-round traversed the rest of the land, meandering across Aunt Myrtle's four hundred acres and providing ample water for our stock. Our land, which included a mature growth of oak, hickory, pine, sweet gum, and a variety of other trees, adjoined Aunt Myrtle's property. On her land were two cleared, cultivatable fields of about thirty acres each. Mature woods covered the rest of the property. A wide pipeline right-of-way cut across all the land, which, because of its maintenance and mowing, grew a lot of grass that provided pasturage for the animals. The right-of-way also accommodated electric and telephone lines. A barbed-wire fence enclosed the entire four hundred and twenty acres and was a constant chore for us to repair and maintain.

Doing things the way they were done while he was growing up enabled Pa to make our farm self-sufficient in many ways—we were still living as people did in the 1800s, although it was a hundred years later. About forty acres of the land were worked with the old mule (and later a gift horse named Dan) and hand plows to produce a great deal of our food, plus grain and fodder for the horses, cows, hogs, and chickens. The fields and wooded parts of the farm yielded squirrels, quail, and doves; ducks and fish were easily obtainable from Black Bayou, only a couple of miles away. An occasional trip to Caddo Lake produced catches of white perch and bream. Our out-of-pocket expenses were minimal.

Some lagniappe came from a boom in fur pelts. My brothers and I were able to get a couple of steel traps and set them out on the creeks running throughout our land. "There's a mink walking every creek in Louisiana" was a popular saying at the time, and an extra-large prime pelt would bring thirty-five dollars—a big sum for a youth, just for the fun of trapping. We never made much money with our too-few traps, but we learned a lot about wildlife in our pursuit of mink, raccoon, and opossum pelts.

My developmental years also coincided with Pa's advancement in the oil fields as he progressed from roughneck, driller, and tool pusher to drilling superintendent for a series of small companies. He was a good hand and in his prime. His skills were in enough demand to allow him to shift from job to job easily. When a company for which he was working idled its rigs, he would go to work for another that hadn't. But he still suffered occasional layoffs—which were sometimes prolonged enough to cause hardship. Granny complained that he always seemed to get laid off during duck season, enabling him to hunt more. He took it all in stride. His attitude could be summed up in a phrase he often used: "I was looking for a job when I got this one."

There were lots of chores on the farm, with my older brothers doing the plowing and tending of the larger animals. Jimmy Frank did the milking, and Harold fed the hogs. The younger children fed the chickens and did the lighter work. Judy did most of her work inside, and the cooking experience she gained would be enhanced later with dishes such as jambalaya and white beans that she learned how to cook while living in south Louisiana.

> **Granny complained that he always seemed to get laid off during duck season, enabling him to hunt more.**

Growing up on the farm wasn't all work—we learned to have a lot of fun, too, and transformed our land into our own massive playground. In the front yard we regularly spent hours playing a game we devised using a broomstick or a broken hoe handle for a bat and several discarded socks stuffed tightly into one another for a ball. The game was a combination of baseball and dodgeball. Once you hit the sock ball into play, it could be picked up and thrown at you. If you hadn't reached base or strayed too far from it and were hit with the sock ball, you were out. The rest of the rules were those of conventional baseball.

Jimmy Frank, by virtue of being the eldest brother by four years, was umpire, coach, and general arbiter of play—not without some objections and arguments from his brothers and cousins. It was he who decided to let me bat left-handed, although I threw right-handed. He made all of my other brothers put the broomstick on their right shoulder.

Granny's once-attractive front yard, which was surrounded by several mature oak trees with rock-walled flower beds around them, was turned into a beaten-down ball field with fairly large holes in the sandy soil around the bases—the result of years of my brothers and me and our friends and relatives sliding into them. Although my four brothers and I were usually enough for a pretty good game, frequently our friends, such as Mac, John Paul, Marv Hobbs, Frankie Hale, or Kenny Tidwell, joined us. Even Pa, Judy, and Jan were occasional participants.

Our backyard served as a football field—complete with a goalpost at one end, which Jimmy Frank and Harold made from a couple of oak-tree uprights and a sweet-gum crossbar. Remarkably, that football field ended up becoming the proving ground for several North Caddo High School Rebels and later Louisiana Tech University Bulldogs players.

Our football field was bounded by a couple of big oak trees on the east, the log house on the north, the smokehouse and outhouse on the south, and a vegetable garden on the west. It was about thirty yards long and half as wide. We played two-hands-below-the-waist touch football year-round. Jimmy Frank, who played for the Vivian High School Warriors until it was consolidated into the North Caddo High School, always had a plentiful supply of footballs—old worn ones from his high school team.

Jimmy Frank played center his freshman year, making first string when a player ahead of him quit school to join the navy during the Korean conflict. Jimmy Frank was later moved to guard, then tackle (all 147 pounds of him) during his senior year, where he made second-team all-district. Jimmy Frank played linebacker all four years—players still played both offense and defense during those days—but he really wanted to be a quarterback. Since Jimmy Frank couldn't do it, he was going to make sure one of us would play in the backfield.

Since we played on a short field in our backyard, each team had only four downs to score, or the ball went over. I remember Jimmy Frank slapping our hands when we missed a pass, and then smacking the ball into our belly and saying, "Catch it." Everyone learned to throw. I started passing when my hands were so small that I was unable to grip the ball fully and had to balance it on my palm.

My brothers and our friends had varying abilities when it came to football. Tommy was the first to make quarterback, later converting to halfback to make room for me when I began playing for North Caddo High. Passing seemed to come naturally for me. Harold, who had a milk allergy and underwent two major operations while a child, suffered a broken elbow while playing freshman football and never played in high school. Silas was a hard-hitting defensive back for the Rebels. Tommy and I earned first-team all-district football honors. As a senior, I was named first-team all-state quarterback and first-team all-district outfield in baseball.

When I graduated from high school, I followed Tommy to Louisiana Tech in Ruston, Louisiana, on a full football scholarship. Tommy started as a wide receiver for Louisiana Tech but was converted to cornerback his junior year. I sat on the sidelines my first year, then earned the starting quarterback job as a redshirt freshman the next year.

Playing college football wouldn't have been nearly the same without having one of my brothers there with me. We were all intensely competitive, and this trait extended to all our activities, not just sports. We played for blood, whether it was Monopoly, dominoes, or card games. We showed no mercy, and tenderhearted Jan, who often cried in frustration, was not consoled but ridiculed. In fact, we went out of our way to tease her and make her cry.

My brothers and I were intensely competitive, and this trait extended to all our activities, not just sports.

Our competitiveness may have reached its peak in the waging of our "Corncob Wars." One side took up a position inside the barn, while the other attacked from outside. We used corncobs, of which there were plenty in the barn; feed troughs; and the barnyard during the winter months. A hit from a corncob below the waist rendered a player "dead," and he had to withdraw from the game. When everyone on one side had been "killed," the remaining players on the other side had won.

Some little quirks in the game made it noteworthy. Although you could keep playing if a corncob hit you above the waist, you had better not stick your head out from behind cover or you risked a knot on your noggin. You were fair game for a well-aimed cob, whether or not it "killed" you.

Necessity also added another messy detail. In the late spring and summer, corncobs became scarce around the barn, but there were always plenty of dried cow chips. These became legal missiles, too. If you found one that was crusted over enough to pick up but still soft on the inside, you were a force to be feared. We still laugh about a wet patty that got Jimmy Frank full in the face. Luckily, he was wearing his glasses.

We also played a game in which we would wrench old, dried cornstalks from the ground and square off like sword fighters in a duel. One would hold his stalk out, and the other would strike and try to break it. If he failed, the other was required to hold his stalk out and let it be smashed. Whoever survived with an intact cornstalk, usually after repeated smashes, was the winner.

I guess now I know why my sons are so darned competitive—they learned it from their father. My brothers and I spent our youth competing with each other outdoors; there weren't any Xbox 360 or Nintendo games to keep us occupied inside. I spent my youth exploring the fields, woods, and swamps that surrounded our home. My time out in nature shaped the rest of my life, and it's something I wanted to make sure my sons learned to enjoy. Whether it was hunting, fishing, or playing sports, my children were going to grow up outside. They weren't going to be sitting on the couch inside.

At least they didn't grow up to be nerds.

RISE, KILL, AND EAT

Rule No. 3 for Living Happy, Happy, Happy
Learn to Cook (It's Better than Eating Slop)

Here's a fact: every human being on Earth has to eat or they will die. It's called starvation. You have to eat if you're a human being, whether you live in Monroe, Louisiana, or in some foreign land, like Los Angeles or New York. There has to be a food supply, and you have to consume food or you're dead. It's an undeniable fact—look it up.

Not everyone likes to eat. These little chicks today are starving themselves to death, which is kind of ironic, but it's their choice. Since you have to eat to live, you're left with a dilemma. You can choose not to learn how to cook and just eat slop, and you'll stay alive. You can live off terrible cooking, which doesn't taste very good, but you'll somehow manage to survive. But my contention is that if you have to eat anyway, it just seems to me that you're shortchanging yourself if you don't learn how to cook. If you have to eat, why not learn how to eat well?

Of course, the downside to eating well is that if you eat too much, you can't get through the door. Well, if that happens, you might ought to cut back some. You can overdo anything, and when you can't get through the door because you're too rotund, you might ought to say, "I think I need to start eating a few salads." I'm not saying you should just shovel it in. I'm just saying if you learn how to cook, your stay on Earth might be more enjoyable.

I learned to cook when I was young, and most of my meals started with something I killed. I have a God-given right to pursue happiness, and happiness to me is killing things, skinning them, plucking them, and then having a good meal. What makes me happy is going out and blowing a duck's head off. As it says in Acts 10:13 (KJV), "And there came a voice to him, Rise, Peter; kill, and eat."

What makes me happy is going out and blowing a duck's head off.

Rise, kill, and eat—that's my modus operandi.

When I was young, heaven to me was hunting in the woods around our house or fishing on the nearby lakes and rivers. We hunted and threw lines into the Red River for catfish and white perch nearly every day. We didn't have much of a choice; it's where we got our next meal.

But when I was in high school, we were forced to move out of the log cabin where I grew up. My aunt Myrtle sold the farm, so we moved to the nearby town of Dixie, Louisiana. The town was a nice enough place; we lived on Main Street, just a stone's throw from Stroud's General Store, which was adjoined by a one-room post office. The general store and a cotton gin were the only businesses in town.

My father hoped the change of environment would help my mother, who had suffered a nervous breakdown and needed numerous trips to Schumpert hospital in Shreveport, Louisiana, for treatment. Granny was diagnosed as manic-depressive and was twice confined to the Louisiana mental institute at Pineville, where she received electric-shock therapy, a treatment in vogue at the time. At times my mother was almost her old self, and Pa would bring her home to be reunited with us. But her condition didn't stabilize until several years later, when it was discovered that lithium could control it. Fortunately, my mother went on to live a productive and venerated life until her death at ninety-five years old.

Granny's illness couldn't have come at a worse time for my family. A short time after we moved to Dixie, Pa fell eighteen feet off the floor of a drilling rig and landed on his head. The impact fractured two vertebrae in his back. As Pa collapsed forward, he was bent so severely that it burst his stomach. He also broke his big toe, which slammed into the ground as he doubled up. Telling us about it later, Pa said with a wry smile, "I've heard of people getting hit on the head hard enough to break both ankles—but not their big toe."

The vertebrae in Pa's back were fused with bone from his hip; his stomach and big toe were repaired. But he was in a neck-to-hip, heavy plaster-of-Paris cast for two years; a round opening had been left only over his injured stomach.

As always, Pa met the situation in his own laid-back manner. Jimmy Frank and Harold were in college at Louisiana State University in Baton Rouge at the time. They were sharing a GI Bill payment of $110 a month and supplementing their income by Harold's work at the Hatcher Hall cafeteria and Jimmy Frank's work on the LSU horse-and-sheep unit experimental farm. They wanted to drop out of school and come home to work to help support the family, but my daddy insisted they stay in school, remarking dryly over the phone, "We'll make it."

And we did—but not without hardship.

Pa's disability payment from the state was thirty-five dollars a week. In the late 1950s, that money went a little further than it does today, but not nearly far enough. Somehow my family coped. With our mother sometimes away in the hospital, Pa was often left on his own, with five children under his care. He was almost immobile at first, but within a few months, he was able to get around and help with the cooking.

My sister Judy was a rock and did much of the cooking, though all of us helped, and she saw that Silas and Jan got off to school in good order. Fortunately, the school bus stopped in front of our house.

To help make ends meet, Tommy and I gathered pecans and sold them for thirty-five cents a pound. In three hours, we could gather about a hundred pounds—equaling the weekly disability payment. Tommy also cleaned the church building each week in Blanchard, Louisiana, where we worshipped, for five dollars a week. With this money he was able to pay for our school meals, which were fifteen cents per day per child, thanks to Louisiana's liberal school-lunch supplement.

Our food staples became rice and beans, which we bought by the hundred-pound sack. To this we added corn bread. Our meager diet made fresh game and fish doubly appreciated. Fortunately, vegetables were cheap in a farming area, and we purchased what we could with our scanty means from the Biondos, an Italian family that had a commercial truck farm a few miles down the road.

As I noted earlier, a real man can't survive without meat, so it was up to Tommy and me to find some. It wasn't easy, because we no longer had acres and acres of bountiful land surrounding our home. There were plenty of farms around us, but the farmers in the area didn't want anyone on their land. They depended on it for their living and were diligent in warning off what they considered intruders.

Tommy, Silas, and I often led the farmers on wild-goose chases through the woods surrounding their plowed land. When the ground was wet, the red clay in the plowed fields would cling to our shoes and build up to several inches in depth and pounds in weight. My only remedy was to stop occasionally, shake my leg vigorously to dislodge the mud, do the same with my other leg, and then continue on. Progression across the thick land was sometimes nothing more than three steps and a kick!

We never considered what we were doing as poaching on someone else's land. We had our own code. We didn't bother any equipment, crops, or anything on someone else's farm. And I was always careful not to step on any young cotton or corn plants. But if it flew, grew wild, swam, or lived in trees, I figured that it belonged to whoever captured or gathered it. I might have even picked up a ripe watermelon (there were thousands of them out there) every once in a while—wouldn't have wanted it to be overlooked and get overripe!

I can still remember my first encounter with a game warden. I was squirrel-hunting out of season—my family had to eat—and

I had a mess of them. It happened before I repented and was one of the reasons I needed to repent. When I squirrel-hunted, I carried a big, metal safety pin, and I sharpened its end so it would run through the squirrels' legs right above the joint. If I saw a game warden, I'd drop the squirrels, close up the pin, and then take off running like the wind. On this occasion, I was wearing two pairs of old men's argyle socks without any shoes and had my pant legs taped so they wouldn't flop when I was running. I was trying to be as quiet as possible. I was sitting there shooting squirrels when I sensed that someone was watching me. I couldn't see anybody and couldn't hear anybody, but I just had a feeling come over me that I was being stalked in the woods.

If it flew, grew wild, swam, or lived in trees, I figured that it belonged to whoever captured or gathered it.

Suddenly I heard a stick break behind me, and I turned and saw a man standing there with a gun in his hand. He was wearing a wide-rimmed cowboy hat and identified himself as a game warden. He was standing about twenty yards from me. When I heard the stick break, I dropped the squirrels and they hit the ground.

"Hold it, son," he told me. "I'm a game warden."

"That's what I thought," I said.

I was lean and mean and could run for miles. After the man identified himself as a game warden, I put it into high gear. For the first one hundred yards, he was running with me. But I was grinning and thinking, *This guy doesn't realize that he's not in good enough shape to be running with me.* He was wearing cowboy boots and wasn't properly dressed to keep up with me. A buddy who had dropped me off earlier picked me up on the other side of the woods.

When I was in high school, our basketball coach, Billy Wiggins, asked me if we were killing any squirrels. He said he wanted to go hunting with me, as long as we weren't hunting on land that had been posted for no trespassing. "Of course not," I told him. "You'll be fine."

Coach Wiggins and I went hunting right after daylight one morning, and it wasn't long before I heard a truck coming at a pretty good rate of speed. It was coming across a pecan orchard right toward us. The last two words Coach Wiggins heard were, "Run, Coach!" I took off running in the other direction.

Moving to Dixie also introduced me to frog gigging. Some of the larger bullfrogs have legs bigger than chicken drumsticks and are delicious! We never ate frogs before moving to Dixie, but they were so abundant in the area that they eventually became part of our regular diet. In springtime, in less than an hour we could gather up a large enough bunch to make a meal, even for a family as big as ours. The slough behind our house was overrun with frogs, as were many others just a short distance across the road.

To catch them, we waited until dark and immobilized them by blinding them on the shoreline with a bright flashlight. One of us held the light and another used a long-handled, spring-loaded clamp, or "grab," to "gig" the frog. Some people called the clamps gigs—but the actual sharp-pronged gigs were illegal. The trick was to hit the frog sharply on the back, thus springing the grab and causing it to clamp around the frog, then to lift it out of the water or off the ground quickly so it couldn't use its powerful legs to leap free.

During one particularly memorable frog gigging, we caught a tow sack full of the big ones, probably thirty or forty pounds of them—so many that cleaning them was going to be a chore and take a while. So we laid the sack on the floor by the door when we went into the kitchen for a snack before beginning—carelessly leaving the top only loosely twisted to keep the frogs secure.

While we lingered in the kitchen, the frogs worked themselves out of the bag. When we returned, the bullfrogs were everywhere: leaping and jumping under the beds, tables, chairs, and chest of drawers. They were even inside our shoes—and every other place they could find to hide! One big one was in the middle of a bed!

It took us longer to find and catch the frogs the second time than it had the first.

It took us longer to find and catch the frogs the second time than it had the first. We were still finding them hours later, and when we finally went to bed, we nervously wondered if we would wake up with a cold, clammy companion.

Of course, we grew up with guns in the house. It was the era of Gene Autry and Roy Rogers. Cap pistols were always a big Christmas item in our house, and as we grew older, BB guns became our prized possessions. Shotguns and .22s for each of us were beyond my father's means, but there was always ammunition for his shotgun, and he freely allowed all my brothers and me to use it.

Every one of us learned to shoot with our father's Browning semiautomatic sixteen-gauge shotgun. We also used a Remington .22 that belonged to our uncle Al Robertson and somehow wound up in our house. It was a bolt-action with a seven-shot clip.

From the time Pa purchased his shotgun, the year after World War II ended, he or one of us boys hunted with it almost daily. It would be difficult to calculate how many shells were fired through the old gun's barrel—or the pounds of meat that were downed for our dinner table. Pa bought an entire case of shotgun shells at the beginning of each duck season—and purchased more if that wasn't enough.

The shotgun, more than sixty years old, has been retired. Silas, the last to use it regularly, still has it but doesn't shoot it. Before his death, Pa sent the gun to Browning for refurbishing and repair but received a letter back from the company saying it was "extremely abused." To repair and replace all the worn and damaged components would have cost almost as much as a new one. One of the faults, said the letter, was that the "barrel was kinked and unsafe" and would have to be replaced. Pa had always prized the hard-hitting, close pattern of shot the full-choke barrel delivered (you had to be pretty good to hit with it, as the tight cluster of shot left little room for error). He reluctantly laid the gun aside and bought a new one when times improved.

My brothers and I were all excellent marksmen. Yet my first remembered experience with guns was anything but auspicious. Tommy and I received new BB guns for Christmas one year, but one of them didn't survive. There's still some confusion as to exactly what happened. As my brother Jimmy Frank remembers it, he found Tommy and me fishing in the outhouse toilet hole with straightened wire coat hangers. One of us had been holding a BB gun over the toilet hole. I remember it being Tommy; he, of course, says it was me. Whoever was the culprit was trying to get the other to do something (what isn't remembered) and was bluffing that he would drop the BB gun if he didn't do it. Then he did drop it—accidentally. It disappeared into the mess below.

Tommy remembers that it was his gun and that I did the dropping. Harold remembers that it was his BB gun that was dropped into the hole, and he blames both Tommy and me. I don't exactly recall what happened. Regardless, the gun was never recovered—although desultory fishing operations went on for some time.

When Pa's cast was finally removed, Barnwell Drilling Company put him back to work doing light duty as a tool pusher. He recovered almost completely, and later, after I left to go to college at Louisiana Tech, he and Granny moved south of Baton Rouge to Gonzales, Louisiana, where Pa worked as a pipe fitter in the area's refinery and petrochemical construction boom along the Mississippi River.

Fortuitously, Pa had acquired a union card during the construction of a plant in Marshall, Texas, where he worked for a few months shortly after the war. The plant was under a construction deadline and was hiring anyone who could fit pipe together—particularly those in the drilling industry. Workers were required to obtain a union membership, and it was this reinstated pipefitter card from the late 1940s that later gave him the seniority to get high-paying construction jobs—if he was willing to travel to them, which he was in his later years. He worked at a particularly well-paying job in Page, Arizona, in the 1970s, where a coal-fired electricity-generating plant was being built.

Even after we left the log cabin where I grew up and the beautiful woods and swamps surrounding it, I was never far from nature. I always found a way to get back to God's most beautiful creation. Since I was a little kid, I've had this profound connection with and love for deep, dark, unmolested woods. I've always had a longing to be in the deep woods or on the water. I want to be on the lakes, streams, and rivers and be surrounded by everything that comes with it—the ducks, birds, fish, and other wildlife. I guess it's in my DNA, and I just love being out there. Even to this day, it's where I want to be. I think part of it is that there's no clutter out there—there are no computers or cell phones (at least not in my duck blind), and constantly updated information isn't being thrown at you from all directions. You might hear a train in the distance every once in a while or see an airplane in the sky flying to New York or someplace else, but your sense of peace and serenity isn't disturbed by clutter.

I've always had a longing to be in the deep woods or on the water.

I have a deep connection with what God created, and what I would love to see more than anything else is a pristine Earth, just like the one He created. There would be no power lines, skyscrapers, or concrete, but there would still be a big ol' kitchen for Miss Kay to make her home-cooked meals. Heaven to me is endless cypress swamps and hardwood forests loaded with game and ducks and not a game warden around! Now, that would be a sight!

STRANGE CREATURES

Rule No. 4 for Living Happy, Happy, Happy
Don't Try to Figure Out Women (They're Strange Creatures)

I've been on this earth for sixty-six years, and I've reached a conclusion and it's a fact: women are strange creatures. One day I went into the bedroom to go to sleep and then woke up a couple of hours later with my wife, Kay, standing over me.

"Phil, do you love me?" she asked.

"Yeah, of course I do," I said.

"Well, write it down then," she said.

"What?" I asked her as I closed my eyes to go back to sleep.

"Write it down," she said.

I turned over and went back to sleep. I woke up about four A.M. the next morning to go duck-hunting. When I looked at my chair in the living room, I saw a piece of paper with a felt pen sitting right in the middle of it. Then I remembered my conversation with Kay the night before.

I took the sheet of paper and wrote the following: "Miss Kay: I love you. I always have, and I always will."

I told Kay I loved her when she asked me, but she wanted it in writing. You know what Kay did with that piece of paper? She taped it to the headboard of our bed, where it has been for the last few years. I guess she goes to bed every night with the comfort of knowing that I really do love her. Therefore I concluded that women are very strange creatures; there's simply no other explanation for the way they sometimes act.

Miss Kay was the perfect woman for me. I was sixteen and she was fifteen when we were married. Nowadays some people might frown on people getting married that young, but I knew that if you married a woman when she was fifteen, she would pluck your ducks. If you waited until she was twenty, she would only pick your pockets. Now, that's a joke, and a lot of people seem to laugh at it, but there is a certain amount of truth in it. If you can find a nice, pretty country girl who can cook and carries her Bible, now, there's a woman. She might even be ugly, but if she cooks squirrels and dumplings, then that's the woman you go after.

I was sixteen and Kay was fifteen when we were married.

I counsel young men all the time, and I tell them to find a woman and eat six of her home-cooked meals before signing on the dotted line. If you're going to spend the rest of your life with her, you at least have to know what the grub is going to taste like. If her cooking passes the test, then she's passed the first level. Even more important, she has to carry a Bible and live by it, because that means she'll stay with you. She also needs to pick your ducks. Some of the young bucks call and ask me, "Hey, what about two out of three?" I tell them two out of three is better than nothing.

As it says in 1 Peter 3:1–6:

> *Wives, in the same way submit yourselves to your own husbands so that, if any of them do not believe the word, they may be won over without words by the behavior of their wives, when they see the purity and reverence of your lives. Your beauty should not come from outward adornment, such as elaborate hairstyles and the wearing of gold jewelry or fine clothes. Rather, it should be that of your inner self, the unfading beauty of a gentle and quiet spirit, which is of great worth in God's sight. For this is the way the holy women of the past who put their hope in God used to adorn themselves. They submitted themselves to their own husbands, like Sarah, who obeyed Abraham and called him her lord. You are her daughters if you do what is right and do not give way to fear.*

That's Miss Kay in a nutshell—she's a kind and gentle woman. In my eyes, she's the most beautiful woman on Earth, on the inside and the outside. She has a natural beauty about her and doesn't need a lot of makeup or fancy clothes to show it. The more makeup a woman wears, the more she's trying to hide; makeup can hide a lot of evil. I think Miss Kay is probably a lot like Sarah was. For some reason, we always talk about Abraham, the father of our faith, but nobody ever mentions Sarah, the mother of our faith. I'm beginning to suspect the reason the mother of our faith is never mentioned is because people don't appreciate a woman who is beautiful on the inside, who is quiet, gentle, and submissive. But God says that being a woman like that is of great worth in His eyes. I believe that Sarah, the mother of our faith, should be revered as much as Abraham, the father of our faith.

Kay and I always were the perfect match. I was our high school quarterback, and she was a cheerleader. We first started going together when she was in the ninth grade and I was in the tenth. One of Kay's older friends decided we might make a cute couple, so she told Kay that I wanted her to walk me off the football field after one of our games. Then the girl came to me and said, "You know that little cheerleader Kay Carroway? She wants you to walk with her off the field after the game." The rest is history, as they say.

Kay and I started dating shortly thereafter, but it didn't last very long. As soon as the Christmas holidays were over, hunting season started, and I was determined to spend all my free time in the woods. I didn't have time for a girlfriend, and I certainly wasn't going to take Kay in the woods with me. Women are a lot like ducks—they don't like mud on their butts. I figured she would just get in the way. But then the next May, Kay's daddy died of a massive heart attack. She was only fourteen at the time, and I knew it was going to be really hard on her. I went to her daddy's funeral, and we made eye contact. I asked her out a few weeks later, and we've been together ever since.

Women are a lot like ducks—they don't like mud on their butts.

Kay's mother wasn't thrilled when we started dating again. She told Kay, "You don't want to marry into that bunch." But Kay told her mother that even though my family didn't have much money, we loved each other and that was worth a lot more than new cars and fancy clothes.

"They might be poor, but they don't know they're poor," Kay told her mother. "They're a very happy family and love each other. They don't realize they're missing things other people have."

After Kay's daddy died, her mother started dating again and spent a lot of time away from home. Her mother started drinking heavily and became an alcoholic. It was a hard time for Kay, but she always had a safe place to go at our house. Kay is a person of strong principles—many of them learned from her grandmother, whom she called Nannie. Kay spent a lot of time during her growing-up years with Nannie, as both her parents worked full-time in the Ida general store, which was founded by her grandfather and had been in the Carroway family for seventy-five years.

Kay's father worked in the store every day, while her mama tried to do it all: cooking, taking care of the house, and working alongside her husband.

Kay learned how to cook from her grandmother, and I love the woman for teaching her. Kay can prepare anything from wild game to unbelievably good pies, biscuits, and just about anything you can name. The table she sets is renowned among our family, friends, employees, television crewmen, hunters, and others, and there always seems to be a large number of people eating at our house. For years Kay prepared a big meal at the noon hour for anywhere from six to fifteen or more people. She jokes that we could have built ten mansions with the money we've spent feeding everybody over the years. But we don't regret it one bit, and she's enjoyed doing it every day. As it says in Romans 12:13: "Share with the Lord's people who are in need. Practice hospitality."

Because both of her parents worked, Kay spent many childhood hours alone. She filled them with activities like taking in stray cats and other animals. Some of the cats were wild, and she would give them milk and tame them. Her father had bird dogs, and she made friends with them. Her family also had chickens, turkeys, canaries, turtles, baby alligators, and a pony. She likes to joke that she had her own circus while growing up, but she didn't know she was going to marry into one!

Kay's father hunted and fished, and she always loved those

things about him. When I came along with the same attributes, she was naturally drawn to me. Her love for animals also came into play in our relationship. We were soul mates from the very beginning.

It wasn't long before I started taking her with me on fishing or hunting expeditions. My qualms about taking Kay into the woods were quickly relieved. And Kay wasn't only a spectator. She helped catch baitfish, gather worms, hook them onto trotlines, and of course, pick ducks by plucking their feathers to prepare them for cooking. You know you have a good woman when you return home from a hunt and she's standing on the front porch, yelling, "Did y'all get anything?" Before I repented, Kay also drove my getaway car when I was hunting out of season. I always knew my woman was waiting for me on the other side of the woods if I got into trouble.

Before I repented, Kay also drove my getaway car when I was hunting out of season.

When I received a football scholarship to Louisiana Tech, we moved to Ruston and rented an apartment in the same complex as my brother Tommy, who had received a scholarship to play for the Bulldogs two years earlier. Tommy and his wife, the former Nancy Dennig (they were also high school sweethearts), had been living there for more than a year. With their company, the transition to Louisiana Tech was much easier for us. Kay had not yet graduated from high school, so she finished her senior year at Ruston High School. She was pregnant with our first son, Alan.

We lived in the Vetville Apartments, which the school built in 1945 to accommodate married veterans coming home from World War II. The red-brick apartments were located on south campus, about a mile from the main campus. For Tommy and me, it was like reviving old times. Tommy bought a boat, and I bought a motor for it. We began fishing and hunting in the area waters and woods: the upper Ouachita River and Bayou D'Arbonne Lake, a recently impounded reservoir just north of town. We would usually take someone fishing with us and come home with the daily limit. Kay and Nancy carried a black iron skillet between our apartments until the grease burned it from frying so much fish and other game.

Tommy and I even arranged our schedules so he went to class on Mondays, Wednesdays, and Fridays, and I went on Tuesdays and Thursdays. Tommy would fish while I was in class, and I fished when he was at school. It didn't take me very long to figure out that a few of my instructors loved crappie, or white perch, as they're called in Louisiana. A judicious gift of fresh, filleted white perch to certain instructors, particularly in subjects where I was having difficulty, greatly improved my grades.

One particular class in sports medicine—which was about

taping ankles, diminishing the effects of bumps and bruises, and such—held little interest for me. It was primarily for athletes who were planning to become coaches, which I wasn't sure I wanted to do. Those white perch allowed me to make a passing grade in the course without even attending classes. For whatever reason, the instructor only gave me a C. I thought those fish were worth at least a B. Shoot! Maybe even an A—all those fish!

Generally, I was a quick enough study that I didn't have difficulties in many classes. I basically looked for a strong C average, and I made sure I maintained it. I paid attention in class and took good notes—when I was there. Occasionally, I had to buckle down with a book to get past some difficulty, but I only spent about 30 percent of my time on college. To get better than a C average would have taken too much time and would have interfered with my hunting.

Word quickly spread around campus that I had fish. Even a prominent former Louisiana legislator, who wanted to help me while I was in school, was one of my clients. When the politician paid me, he insisted that he was not buying the fish (selling game fish in Louisiana is illegal) but only paying for me to clean and dress them—to which I readily agreed.

Not everyone on campus was fond of my hobbies. After football practice one day, one of my coaches informed me that the dean of men wanted to see me. I wasn't sure what I had done wrong, but I knew they had me on something. I walked into his office, and he asked me to close the door.

"We have a problem," he said. "Do you know what street you live on? Do you know the name of it?"

"Vetville?" I asked him.

"Let me refresh your memory," he said. "You live on Scholar Drive."

Apparently, the president of Louisiana Tech had given members of the board of trustees a tour of campus the day before.

"When he went to where you live, it wasn't very scholarly," the dean told me. "There were old boats, motors, duck decoys, and fishnets littering your front yard. He was embarrassed. This is an institution of higher learning."

"That's my equipment," I told him.

"But everybody's yard is mowed—except yours," he replied.

"At least the frost will get it," I said. "It will lay down flat as a pancake when the frost gets it."

"It's July," the dean said. "Cut your grass."

One summer the Louisiana Tech football coaches got me a job in Lincoln, Nebraska, as a tester on a pipeline that was being built. Kay loved it and thought it was the biggest adventure of her life, but I missed being in the woods and lakes back home. I could hardly stand it. We only had a company car, which I drove to work, and we lived in a tiny apartment and didn't have a TV, so

Kay woke up every morning and walked miles and miles all over town. I feared Kay was about to die of boredom, so I brought her a little white kitten I found in a cornfield. We named it Snowball, and it was a lot of company for her. When we flew back to Louisiana at the end of the summer, we hid Snowball in a basket packed with sandwiches and travel necessities that we carried on the plane. That cat stayed with us in Louisiana for the next several years and became the first of her many pets.

By then, my interest in playing football was really beginning to wane. My game plan was to hunt and fish full-time and get a college education while doing it—putting as little effort into school as possible. The reason I went into education (I wound up getting bachelor's and master's degrees in education, with a concentration in English) is because you have the summers off, as well as Christmas and Thanksgiving holidays. Consequently, I would have more time to hunt and fish. The only reason I wanted a college degree was so that when people thought I was dumb, I could whip out the sheepskins. Unfortunately, Louisiana Tech didn't offer a degree in ducks.

Unfortunately, Louisiana Tech didn't offer a degree in ducks.

My interest in football was secondary to ducks, but it was paying for my education. I remember riding on a bus going to ball games and scoping out the woods we passed as to hunting possibilities. I just didn't have my mind on football. As a result, I had a checkered playing career. In spite of my God-given talent, I was never fully devoted to the game. Even in junior high, it was merely a social event. When I was playing defensive halfback, I would lightheartedly wave to people in the crowd and grin at things shouted.

I had in my mind that football was a game, something you did solely for entertainment. You go out there and win or lose, but it's certainly not life or death. If you did well, you won. If you didn't do too well, you didn't win. But as far as making a career of football, that never entered my mind—I didn't see the worth of it. I couldn't make much sense out of making a living from work that entailed large, violent men chasing me around—men who are paid for one reason: to run me down and stomp me into the dirt. I just didn't see it.

Despite football not being my primary interest, I still had a decent career at Louisiana Tech. I played quarterback for the Bulldogs from 1965 to 1967 and was the starter in 1966, throwing for more than three hundred yards against Southeastern Louisiana University. During preseason camp the next year, I looked up and saw a flock of geese flying over the practice field and thought to myself, "What am I doing out here?" I walked off the practice field and never went back.

The coaches came to my apartment the next morning and found me cleaning a deer in my kitchen.

"It ain't season," I told them. "I had to bring the meat inside."

No matter how hard they tried, the coaches couldn't persuade me to come back. The quarterback behind me on the depth chart was a guy named Terry Bradshaw, who was a lot more serious about football than I was. Terry started the next three seasons at Louisiana Tech and was the number one pick in the 1970 NFL draft. He became the first quarterback to win four Super Bowl championships, with the Pittsburgh Steelers, and was selected to the Pro Football Hall of Fame. I still tell Terry that if I had never left, he wouldn't have won four Super Bowl rings.

The quarterback behind me on the depth chart was a guy named Terry Bradshaw.

After I graduated from college, former Louisiana Tech running back Robert Brunet, who was playing in the National Football League, encouraged me to come to Washington, DC, and try out for his team, the Washington Redskins. Vince Lombardi had just been hired as coach.

"You won't beat out Sonny Jurgensen," he told me. "But they've got this hot-dog rookie coming up, Joe Theismann. Robertson, you can beat him hands down. No problem. You make the team, they'll pay you sixty thousand dollars a year."

Some people might think that was pretty good money in the 1960s, but it sure seemed like a pretty stressful way to make a living. I told Brunet, "I don't know—you're up there in Washington, DC, and you miss duck season every year. Do you think I'd stay?" He took a long look at me and said, "Nah, you wouldn't stay."

As far as I was concerned, my football career was over. And as it turned out, my career choice of chasing ducks and whatnot turned out to be a pretty good one. Besides, at the time, I had a young wife and a baby boy. I had their future to worry about, too.

I didn't know I was about to find out how good of a woman my wife really was.

WHO'S A MAN?

Rule No. 5 for Living Happy, Happy, Happy
Always Wear Shoes (Your Feet Will Feel Better)

According to the Guinness book of world records, a police constable in India set a world record last year by running 150 kilometers (93.2 miles) in twenty-four hours in his bare feet. A couple of years earlier, a forty-one-year-old man in Oregon ran 102.6 miles barefoot on a rubberized track in less than one day. I'm not sure why Guinness World Records doesn't recognize his *feat* as the record—it seems to me the guy who ran farthest would be the record holder, but what do I know?

While I might not be Zola Budd or a world-record holder, I know neither of those cats have anything on me. When I was about twenty-five or twenty-six years old, I chose to go shoeless for about two years. I simply didn't put any shoes on my feet day after day after day. Here's what I found out: if you don't wear shoes for about two years, you develop pads on the bottom of your feet made of about a half inch of solid, thick, tough callus. You wouldn't believe how tough a man's feet can get! You can literally walk on hot coals—or briars, hot pavement, cold ground in winter—without any shoes. I went duck-hunting with no shoes at all—no waders and no hip boots—just walked out into the water like it was summertime.

We'd go duck-hunting in mid-January, and everybody would be covered up with clothes, but I would be barefoot. We would take people on guided hunts, and one of them would look down and say, "Good grief! This cat doesn't have any shoes on!" I went like it was a summer's day, even if it was only thirty-five degrees outside. I guess you condition your mind and train yourself to be oblivious to pain. On many nights, Miss Kay would have to remove embedded thorns from my feet with a long needle and magnifying glass. Of course, my hunting buddies and I were drinking whiskey straight out of the bottle, so that probably numbed the pain.

After I gave up football at Louisiana Tech, I started running with a pretty rough crowd. It was during the turbulent 1960s, when people my age questioned everything about the government and society in general. The Vietnam War was raging, and I wasn't sure why my brother Si had been sent to Southeast Asia to fight in some country we'd never heard of. It was an era of disillusionment. The status quo and old ways of doing things were being scrutinized with a jaundiced eye. Buttons proclaiming, "Don't trust anyone over thirty"—and a lot worse—were being worn in colleges and elsewhere nationwide.

I listened to the protest songs of Bob Dylan; John Lennon; Peter, Paul, and Mary; the Byrds; and others, and owned a number of their recordings. Clint Eastwood's rebel roles on the screen appealed strongly to me. Years later, when we started making our hunting movies, some of the Eastwood phrases and gritty realism still resonated with me. We had parties and everybody got drunk except for Kay, who wanted nothing to do with the tomfoolery. It went on from when I was about twenty-one or twenty-two until I was about twenty-eight. We got drunk on anything we could get our hands on—running wild and duck-hunting.

Everybody got drunk except for Kay, who wanted nothing to do with the tomfoolery.

It wasn't just beer and whiskey, either. It was the 1960s, and so usually there was a little marijuana around. We never bought any, but we'd smoke it if it was available. So between the whiskey, diet pills, and various kinds of black mollies (or medicinal speed), we were staying pretty messed up. As far as alcohol, it was mostly confined to whiskey, beer, and wine. Throw in a little marijuana and pep pills, and that was the drug scene, as far as I was concerned. I never got into any of that serious stuff like LSD or heroin; I thought it would have been insanity to stick a needle in my arm. But we pretty well stayed ripped for seven or eight years.

In a lot of ways, I was withdrawing from mainstream society. I was trying to drop back about two centuries to become an eighteenth-century man who relied on hunting and fishing for his livelihood. But I was living in the twentieth century, and everything was constantly changing around me. Hunting and fishing was no longer a way to provide food for my family's table; it was a competition between my buddies and me, and all the rules and laws regulating it were thrown out the window.

Our mantra, or battle cry, was "Who's winning? Who's a man?" We were romping and stomping! We were getting drunk, shooting way too many ducks, and catching too many fish. We were outlaws. It was all about who could kill the most ducks and catch the most fish. We didn't care about anything else.

After leaving college, I took a teaching job in Junction City, Arkansas. The guy who hired me, Al Bolen, persuaded me to take the job with what he called "fringe benefits." One night when I was at home blowing on a duck call, Bolen showed up.

"The fringe benefits are these," Bolen said as he handed me a stack of pictures of ducks and fish.

We agreed on my taking a job teaching tenth-grade English

and physical education to junior-high boys. As soon as I accepted the job, Bolen said, "Let's go get a beer." Before too long, one beer turned into a six-pack, and we became close drinking buddies. And after he showed me the game-rich Ouachita River bottom in the Junction City area, I thought, *Boy, good times are here.*

It was a riotous time. I totaled three new trucks by turning them over or running into trees. It took a good truck to go hunting because we were going into some of the most inaccessible areas of the river bottom. The winch on the front of a truck was forced into use on virtually every trip, as our truck would sink into mud holes on the rutted tracks that passed for roads. The truck would sink so deep that mud flowed onto the floorboards when the doors were opened. When we were stuck, we would stretch out the winch cable, tie it around a tree, pull ourselves back to solid ground, and continue on. It was careless, rollicking, and sometimes very dangerous.

One time, I was running a boat through a small creek with the throttle wide open. Big Al Bolen was in the front of the boat. We were jumping up wood ducks and shooting 'em, which is illegal. But that's what we were doing; we had no fear of the law. When I came around a curve, I was almost on top of a huge pin oak tree that had slid down into the creek. The bank had caved in. There was no time to stop or guide the racing boat around the tree in the narrow confines of the creek. After throttling down for a split second, I decided our best chance was to run up the trunk and sail over the treetop like Evel Knievel. So I gunned the motor.

We hit the trunk, and our boat went airborne, bouncing about three times across the limbs. It came to rest nestled in the limbs, still upright, at about a twenty-five-degree angle. We were two-thirds the way up the tree, leaving Al and me suspended twenty feet in the air above the water—the motor still running.

To get down, we selectively shot limbs off the tree, allowing the boat to slide down far enough so we could pull it back into the creek. I just fired up the motor again, and we were on our way. Big Al reached in his coat and took a swig of whiskey. We continued along, feeling no pain.

On another occasion, when I was trying to save time, I decided to run my aluminum boat up on the bank instead of going through the trouble of pulling it up to the boat ramp, backing the truck and trailer into the water, and loading the boat the usual way. Unfortunately, hidden behind a wall of reeds on the shore was a stump that I hit at full speed, head-on, throwing my passenger in the front of the boat over the stump and out onto the bank.

When the guy was thrown, his legs, which had been under the small front deck of the prow, slid under the deck and hit it with enough force to pop out the rivets that were holding the deck to the side of the boat. His momentum just peeled the deck forward. That probably saved him from breaking his legs. But it ripped the skin off his shins, and his legs immediately turned purple and puffed up. His injuries were severe but didn't incapacitate him. I was thrown from the back of the fourteen-foot boat to the completely crumpled front, breaking a finger. He sailed over the stump, hit the ground, and bounced twice. I was shook up from the collision, and he was pretty addled. When he got up, he took off running toward the lake, dove in, and started swimming away from shore. When he was several yards away, he grabbed on to a tree.

Hidden behind a wall of reeds on the shore was a stump that I hit at full speed.

I could see he was confused, so I hollered, "What are you doing?"

"I'm trying to get away from that bad thing on the bank!" he replied.

There were a lot of other unforgettable incidents. Once, Silas and I took several men on a guided hunt. I had already taken a bigger boat with some of the hunters to the blind. Si was loading the rest of the men into a smaller, twelve-foot boat. When the four men, whom Si estimated weighed at least 250 pounds each, stepped into the boat, it sank deeper into the water—alarmingly deep! The five men in that overloaded boat pushed it down to the point where the water almost overlapped the sides. But Si persevered and was almost to the blind when (maybe he was traveling a little too fast) the front of the boat dipped and started under.

Si knew the water was not deep in front of the blind and had the presence of mind to grab all the shotguns as the boat completely submerged, dumping everyone into the water. The four guests, who had no idea how deep the water was, thought they were in danger of drowning in their heavy hunting clothes and started floundering and flailing at the water.

Me and the other hunters in the blind realized they weren't in danger and started shouting, "Stand up! Stand up!" Si, holding their saved shotguns, stood neck-deep in water watching them.

Each of the Benelli and Browning shotguns I have owned has ended up at the bottom of a lake multiple times. Each of the shotguns lost during my wild years was recovered, except one that was flipped out of the boat by a limb. Sometimes, I had to resort to buying a wet suit to recover guns from icy, murky waters. Remarkably, the first shotgun I ever owned somehow survived the madness. I worked as a roughneck for a while, following my father into the offshore drilling business. I gave every one of my checks to my parents because I thought that's what I was supposed to do. But with my last check, I asked Pa if I could buy a new shotgun. I purchased a 1962 Browning Sweet 16 shotgun for $150 and still have it today; sometimes I even shoot with it.

During my outlaw years, much of our duck hunting took

place at Moss Lake, where we had a blind halfway up a remarkable cypress tree that stood on the edge of a circle of water surrounded by other cypresses. My brothers Tommy and Jimmy Frank discovered the hole on a bluebird day when they kept seeing flight after flight of ducks circling the area, dropping down into it, and not coming back up. Pa was also hunting with them that day.

Tommy and Jimmy Frank decided to investigate, although they were having a pretty fair shoot from the floating blind they were in, which was in open water about a quarter mile from where all the other ducks were going. Pa stayed in the blind.

My brothers got in their boat and motored straight at the area until they ran aground on a submerged ridge covered with buck brush. Deciding the day was warm enough, although the water was ice-cold, they tied the boat and started wading. They were without waders and just in their hunting boots, but this was the way we hunted back then.

The water was only about knee-deep on the ridge, but then quickly dropped off and rose almost to their waists as they progressed toward where the ducks were still spiraling down. They were soon among the trees and witnessed an amazing sight. It was like something out of primeval times. There must have been five thousand ducks in the opening, probably only thirty yards wide, surrounded by the trees! The entire surface of the open water was completely covered with ducks—so many that they crowded shoulder-to-shoulder, like a giant raft made of ducks. It was a year when the male-female ratio was out of balance, and most were mallard drakes, their green heads standing out sharply in the dark mass. Ducks continued to spiral down from above as my brothers watched in amazement.

Jimmy Frank got tangled in a dead tree underneath the water, but Tommy kept moving forward. The ducks spotted him. They stirred but didn't fly. When he felt he was close enough, Tommy shot them on the water, surprisingly downing only two ducks. Still the ducks didn't fly away but continued to mill around, dodging in and out among the trees. And more ducks kept spiraling down from above the hole.

By the time it was over, my brothers downed a total of ten ducks.

As amazing as the number of ducks on the water was, even more impressive was the old cypress. It was nearly twenty feet wide at the base and hollow from water level to about thirty feet up. The opening was wide enough for a man to easily pass through, and it was there that Tommy and I, along with our friend Maurice Greer, built a blind with a porch from which eleven men could shoot.

The big hollow at the water level was so large that a pirogue could be pulled into it (a larger boat was used to reach the area and was hidden some one hundred yards away, beneath some buck brush). After sinking the pirogue to conceal it, we made our way to the blind above by climbing up through the hollow on several boards that we'd nailed on the inside to form a ladder. When we got to the shooting porch, ducks that circled to look at the decoys often flew right in front of us. At times, we actually shot down at the ducks.

The old cypress tree was one of the Almighty's great creations, and it's where we spent many glorious mornings together as a family. But during my rompin' and stompin' days, I never embraced its beauty and rarely cherished the time I spent with my father and brothers.

> **The old cypress tree was one of the Almighty's great creations, and it's where we spent many glorious mornings together.**

The only things I seemed to be worried about were how many ducks I could kill and when my next drink was coming.

By then, I had a growing family at home. Our sons Jase and Willie had been born, and Kay was at the end of her rope with me. I was always out, partying with my buddies, leaving her alone to raise our three sons. I was growing more distant from everything I had known and been taught and was pulling even farther away from the people who loved me the most. Kay felt her entire life was in ruins and that she had failed as a wife. After a while, the school where I was teaching could no longer ignore my public conduct. Students and their parents were beginning to notice my boorish behavior, and my days as a teacher and coach were numbered.

Sadly, even as my life continued to spiral out of control, like a downed duck falling from the sky, I failed to realize that "callous" also described me as a man.

HONKY-TONK

Rule No. 6 for Living Happy, Happy, Happy
Put the Bottle Down (You'll Thank Me in the Morning)

After I resigned from my teaching position (before the school board could fire me), I made one of the biggest mistakes of my life: I leased a honky-tonk in the middle of nowhere. I managed the place, worked the bar, cooked for the customers, and broke up occasional fights. One of my specialties was something I called squirrel mulligan: ten pounds of freshly killed squirrels, ten pounds of onions, ten pounds of potatoes, and enough crumbled crackers to give it the proper thickness. It didn't taste too bad, and its aroma smelled better than the overwhelming scent of urine and stale beer that permeated the place. I also served fried chicken, pickled pig's feet, and boiled eggs, though most of the regulars, including me, were only there to drink as much beer and whiskey as we could.

It was a rough, rough place. I managed the place before

integration was firmly established in the South, so my honky-tonk was somewhat unusual. It was really a segregated beer joint, which you didn't see very often. The blacks drove up in the back, and we had their jive going on back there, and the rednecks came through the front. I was in the middle, serving and cooking for everyone, while trying to keep the peace.

Kay and our three sons moved out in the middle of nowhere with me. The bar was a long, low, one-story wood building, unpainted and yellowed. Our trailer home and another building were roughly attached to it, making the whole complex an irregular U-shape. It wasn't very pretty, and it certainly wasn't the proper place to be raising my boys. Kay, of course, worried about me constantly, so she worked as a barmaid most nights to make sure I stayed out of trouble. She never was much of a drinker—probably because she saw what alcohol did to her mother—but she was right beside me on most nights, watching me slowly drink away our lives.

After a while, my parents, brothers, and sisters started to hear what was happening with me. One night, my younger sister, Jan, drove out to the bar with William "Bill" Smith, one of the preachers at White's Ferry Road Church in West Monroe, Louisiana. Jan lived close by in the area, so she knew more than the rest of my family how far I had strayed from my former ways. She was determined to save me and enlisted Bill Smith to help her.

When they walked into the bar, Smith found me sitting at a desk in the connecting structure. I had a quart bottle of beer in my hand.

"You some kind of preacher?" I immediately asked him. When Smith told me he was, I added, "You ever been drunk?"

"Yes, I used to drink a few beers," he told me.

"Well, what's the difference between you and me?" I asked him. "You've been drunk, and I'm getting drunk right now. There ain't a dime's worth of difference between you and me, Jack. You ain't putting any Bible on me. That's the way I was born."

"You some kind of preacher?" I immediately asked him.

At that moment, one of my patrons stuck his head in the door and said, "Phil, your sister's running into some problems out there in the bar."

Jan was in the barroom handing out religious tracts. The patrons were cussing and carrying on as usual—getting drunk. One guy was arguing with her. "Hey! Hey!" I said as I stepped in.

They all turned around, looking at me. "This is my little sister. She's handing out religious tracts. Let her hand them out. But don't be messing with her, or you're going to deal with me."

"This is your sister?" one of them asked.

"Yes. She's going to do whatever she does here," I told him. "Leave her alone!"

Jan, now in a little bit of a dither, went on handing out tracts—in a dead quiet—until she had given everyone one. I turned around, went back to Smith, and ordered him out of my bar.

As Jan and Smith walked back to their car in the drizzling rain, with the country music wailing behind them in the front of the building and rhythm and blues blaring in the back, he exclaimed, "Whew! I don't think he's ready! Let's give him a little time. I'm glad I got out of there without getting beaten up!"

Although Smith's visit left me unmoved, Kay later began to study the Bible with him. She knew our marriage and lives were rapidly deteriorating.

A few months later, I hit what I thought was rock bottom. One night the couple that owned the bar came in and informed me they were going to raise my rent. So I decided I'd hightail it out of the place after fulfilling the last two months on my lease. An argument ensued, and I ended up throwing the man and woman across the bar, injuring both of them pretty badly. By the time the fight was over, there were four police cars out front. Ambulances were also on the way to take the bar owners to the hospital; I'd whipped both of them pretty good. I went out the back door and jumped in my truck before the police could arrest me. Before I left, I told Kay, "I'm going to the swamps or somewhere. You're not going to see me for a few months."

Of course I left Kay behind to clean up my mess. The police issued a warrant for my arrest, but Kay persuaded the bar owners to drop criminal charges against me. The plea bargain came with a hefty price: the bar owners took nearly all the money we'd saved while operating the honky-tonk. They wouldn't even let Kay get our personal belongings—a washer and dryer and photographs and keepsakes of our boys—out of a storage shed in back. Fortunately, Kay had hidden about two thousand dollars in a lockbox and used that money to move our trailer—which we were still paying for—back to Louisiana.

After the fight, I got out of Arkansas. Even though Kay paid off the bar owners, I didn't know whether there were still arrest warrants out for me—assault and all that stuff. The bar owners had a restraining order against me, so I couldn't go anywhere near them. I stayed out of Arkansas for about a decade because I didn't know whether they were going to try to get me, put me in jail, or what.

Kay moved our trailer to a spot beside Lake D'Arbonne at Farmerville, Louisiana, as she and I had discussed during a phone conversation. I eventually got a job working in the oil fields offshore in the Gulf of Mexico. In the meantime, Kay had to handle everything concerning the move back to Louisiana. For about the next year, she and I somehow endured, though our marriage was under tremendous strain.

While I was a fugitive, I kept hunting and fishing as much as I could—sandwiching the activities I loved around my offshore job. The incident at the bar didn't stop me from romping, stomping, and ripping with my drinking buddies. Kay later said I wasn't an alcoholic, only a problem drunk. But it was pretty clear I had a problem. She always held out hope that I would change my ways, and she believed that if we moved to a new location and met new people, things would get better. But they never did; things only got worse.

> **Kay said I wasn't an alcoholic, only a problem drunk. But it was pretty clear I had a problem.**

One rainy night, Kay came home late from work, and I accused her of running around on me, which I knew she would never do. It was a life-changing event for Kay, and she remembers the details and aftermath of the incident better than I do:

I think Phil's problems really started during our first year at Louisiana Tech. He was playing football but had a wife and baby at home. It was a lot of grown-up responsibility for an eighteen-year-old, and he really wasn't ready for it. He saw his teammates going out and partying all the time, and he wanted to go out, too. I think that's why he so easily got in with the wrong group—he wanted to be like the single guys who had all the freedom. He'd never really experienced the single life since we married so young. I tried to do the party scene with him, but I couldn't leave Alan, who was only a baby. I didn't think it was right. I didn't like drunkenness. I didn't think it was wrong to have a drink, but I just didn't like the whole scene.

I really thought that after Phil graduated from Louisiana Tech and we moved to Junction City, Arkansas, he would settle down. After all, he was going to be a coach and teacher, which came with a lot of responsibility. But Al Bolen, the man who hired him, was as big a party guy as Phil, so the partying and running around only continued.

When Phil leased the bar, people couldn't believe that I went out and stayed with him. I worked as a barmaid, and the people there really respected me and told everybody, "Don't you talk ugly to her. She doesn't drink and she's a nice lady." It surprised me that those people were so protective of me. They always asked me why I was in the bar if I didn't drink, but when I decided to stay with Phil and remain faithful to him, I felt it was my duty to protect him. With me at the bar, I felt he wouldn't get in as much trouble as he would if I wasn't there.

The year after the bar fight was probably the worst time of my life. Phil was working offshore and drinking more than he ever had before. When I came home one night, he accused me of having an affair, which was so stupid. I had never done anything like that, and it wasn't because his friends weren't hitting on me, either. It was because I wasn't that kind of person. I always told him, "If I leave you, I'll divorce you and find somebody else if I want to. I would never cheat on you."

I've always considered myself a good person. I don't know if it's my personality or what, but I've always been a very serving person. During all of Phil's troubles, I felt like I was operating on my grandmother's faith and what she instilled in me. I finally realized you have to have your own faith. Phil was cursing me and calling me every ugly word under the sun. It was the first time in my life that I felt hopeless. When I was younger, I read that a person can live so long without water, so long without food, but that you can never live without hope. I have always believed that hope and dreams are what keep us going. My entire life, all I had ever wanted was to be the best wife and mother I could. I didn't want riches or fame; I wanted to have a loving, good, and safe home for my boys—that's all.

"When I came home one night, he accused me of having an affair, which was so stupid."

The night Phil accused me of having an affair, I hit rock bottom. I went to the bathroom and cried. It was the first time in my life that I didn't know how to fix the problem. It's the only time in my life that I had suicidal thoughts. I just wanted to go to sleep and not wake up because I didn't know how to fix our lives and didn't know what to do. Would I have gone through with it? I hope not, but I really wanted Phil to suffer because of what he was doing to me.

But as I sat there contemplating what to do, I heard my little boys' house shoes running down the hall. Alan was nine, Jason was five, and Willie was three. Alan knocked on the bathroom door and said, "Mama, don't be sad. Don't be crying." I'll never forget what he said next: "God's going to take care of us. You'll be all right. We'll be all right. Daddy will quit drinking one day." It was like a light went off in my head. I thought, "Oh, my goodness, what am I thinking? I've got three little boys. Am I going to leave them behind to live with a drunk?" Phil couldn't have taken care of the boys in his condition.

I prayed to God and asked Him to help me find some kind of peace. Obviously, my life wasn't going right, but I knew I had to take care of my three boys. The next day, I was watching a TV show called *Let the Bible Speak,* and there was Bill Smith, the preacher Jan brought up to the beer joint. The things he was saying were what I needed to hear—what I wanted in my life. He was speaking about how to obtain peace and hope. So I called the number on the screen and set up an appointment to meet him the next day. Somebody kept the kids for me, and I went over to White's Ferry Road Church.

One of the first things Bill Smith asked me was, "If you die, do you think you'll go to heaven?" I told him, "I sure do. Let me tell you what I've been living with." I went into how bad Phil was and how I'd still been a faithful and loving wife to him. Smith asked me if I thought I'd earned my way to heaven, and I told him that I certainly had. Smith asked me if I had peace and hope in my life, and I told him, "Now, that's the problem." There was some sort of disconnect because I felt I had earned my way to God, but I didn't have any hope and didn't feel any peace.

Smith shared the gospel with me, and I became convinced that I couldn't be saved on my own good works. I was a good person, but I was a good person without Jesus Christ in my life. That's not enough. Smith told me that if I wanted to, I could leave the church that day with Jesus Christ in my life. I confessed to Jesus and made him the Lord of my life and was baptized. The best thing Smith told me that day was that when I went home, Phil would still be as drunk as ever and would still act terrible. But Smith told me I would be different because I would have God's spirit living in me. He told me that when things were bad here on Earth, I just had to think about my next life in heaven and how wonderful it would be. I left his office as a Christian and started developing my own faith.

I went home and tolerated Phil's behavior because I knew God would help me through it. I was working in the offices at Howard Brothers Discount Stores in West Monroe, and Phil wasn't doing much of anything besides drinking and staying out all night. I came home from work late one night, and Phil started in on me about running around on him again. He looked at me and said, "I'm sick of you. It was bad enough that I had to live with you before, but now you're a holy roller." He also called me a Bible thumper and a goody two-shoes. "You think you're an angel," he said. "I want you to get out and take the three boys with you. I want y'all to leave." He knew he couldn't separate me from my sons.

I asked Phil, "Are we messing up your bachelor's life?" He told me yes, and I knew there was nothing else to do but leave. Our little boys were so sad and had tears streaming down their faces. They didn't want their daddy drunk, but they loved their father. We stayed with Phil's

My parents James H. and Merritt Robertson

My third-grade picture

Playing baseball in my junior year at North Caddo High School, Vivian, Louisiana

During my playing days conferring with North Caddo coach Ed Sigrest

The Robertson men in the early 1970s in Gonzales, Louisiana. Left to right: James (Pa), Tommy, Jimmy Frank, Si, Harold, and me

Kay and me—high school sweethearts

Kay as a sophomore at North Caddo

Kay with her Papaw Carroway and miniature pony, Tony

My sophomore year at Louisiana Tech (1966). Pictured here are the backfield and receivers. Terry Bradshaw is number 12 and I am number 10, on the back row third from left.

My first year teaching English and PE in Junction City, Arkansas

Alan, Jase, Kay, and me in 1972

From left to right: Alan, Kay, Willie, and Jase, Christmas 1976

Al Bolen and me in the early 1970s

Me in front of Granny and Pa's house in Luna, Louisiana, holding catfish caught on the Ouachita River

The boys—left to right: Willie, Jep, and Jase—waiting on me to return with the fish

Me at the lathe in the mid-1970s

Still building duck calls in the 1990s

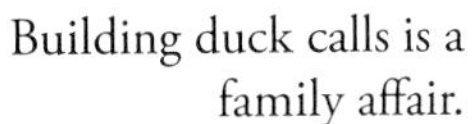

Building duck calls is a family affair.

Me with Peggy Sue out on my land

Mac Owen and me hunting among the cypress trees of Louisiana

Here I am preaching the gospel at a speaking event.

Grand opening of the new location in 2010

The Duckmen accepting our Golden Moose awards in 2010

Si and me enjoying some brother time

Jimmy Frank, Tommy, and I admire the five-hunter limit from the last hunt of 2011.

brother Harold for one night. He told us we could only stay one night because he was afraid of what Phil would do. I never held that against Harold because I didn't know what Phil would do either.

The boys and I moved into a low-rent apartment, and White's Ferry Road Church helped me pay the rent and get some furniture. We were apart from Phil for about three months; I was really hiding from him. I put everything in my maiden name, thinking he wouldn't be able to find us. I went to lunch every day with one of my girlfriends at work, and one day when we came back to the office, we saw Phil's old, gray truck in the parking lot. Phil's head was lying on the steering wheel, so I figured he'd driven there, then passed out drunk. I told my friend to go on into the office and watch out the window and if she saw Phil flashing a gun to call the police. "You can't go out there by yourself," she told me. "Let's go in and call the police." But I didn't want Phil following me into my office and hurting anybody, so I told her to watch out the window and call the police if anything bad happened.

I walked up to Phil's truck and opened the door. His face rose up, and there were big tears streaming down his face. I had never seen him cry. The macho man never cried. He looked at me and said, "I can't eat. I can't sleep. I can't do anything. I want my family back." He told me he wouldn't drink anymore and was done with partying. Of course, I'd heard that many times before. I felt God's courage inside me and told him, "Phil, you can't do it by yourself, buddy. You just can't." Phil told me he needed help and then asked me where he could find it.

"There's only one person who can help you," I told him.

"God?" Phil asked.

"Yes," I said.

"I don't know how to find Him," Phil replied.

As a boy, Phil had gone to church and Sunday school, but he had been away from God for a long time. I told Phil I knew someone he could talk to and to be back at my office at five thirty, when I got off work. I told him I'd lead him to my apartment. When I went back upstairs to my office, I was so happy I sailed up three steps at a time. I called Bill Smith, the preacher, and told him to be at my apartment at five forty-five. He said, "Well, let me check my calendar."

"I can't eat. I can't sleep. I can't do anything. I want my family back."

"What is more important than one lost soul coming back to the Lord?" I asked him. "If you have anything else, you have to cancel it."

"You know what?" Smith told me. "Nothing is more important than that."

Smith and his wife, Margaret, met Phil and me at my apartment. The first thing Phil told him was: "I don't trust you." Smith told Phil that he could understand why he didn't trust him. "Considering the people you've been running around with, I wouldn't trust anyone either," Smith told him. Then Smith held up his Bible and said, "Do you trust this?"

"Yeah, I trust that book, but I'm going to check out everything you say," Phil said. "I don't take any man's word for anything."

I went into the back room with the boys and Margaret, and Phil and Smith studied the Bible together for several hours. When they were finished, Phil told Smith he was going to check out everything they'd talked about, and they scheduled another meeting for the next night. We let Phil move into our apartment, and the first thing the boys asked him to do was bring back our big TV. The next day, the boys and I left to go to the grocery store. When we returned home, I found a note from Phil, telling us to come to White's Ferry Road Church. When I walked into the back door of the church, Phil was already in the baptistry. He's so impatient, he couldn't wait for me to get there! Smith had taken Phil's confession and was in the process of baptizing him. I looked down at our boys and they were crying. Alan looked at me and said, "I guess that devil is going to be gone now." Phil was twenty-eight years old, and our lives were starting over.

Once I make a decision, I'm all in and there's no second-guessing. After I was baptized, I attended regular church services three times a week (twice on Sunday). I also studied the Bible with someone or a group the other five nights of the week. I went back to teaching and worked for Ouachita Christian School, which had just opened in Ouachita Parish. I felt like I needed time with Christian people to get me back on my feet spiritually, so I did that for about two years. Because everything was in Kay's maiden name, my old friends couldn't find me. When they finally tracked us down after about three or four months, I told them never to come back. It was about five years after I was baptized before the pull of sin finally stopped.

Although I was healing spiritually and was beginning to earn the trust of my wife and children again, there still seemed to be something missing in my life. It's funny how things work sometimes. Even during my romping, stomping, and ripping days, when I was at my lowest point, the hunting and fishing were actually a training ground for what I wanted to do with the rest of my life. It was in my blood, and I spent as much time as I could doing it. When I was partying, we would go from the beer joint to the woods or lakes and back. Yet out of all that heathen activity came my expertise for duck hunting and catching fish, as well as my dream to one day build my own duck calls. Even as I sank deeper into that wild lifestyle and as my values and sense of worth were severely battered, there was a core of resilience inside that kept me going.

Out of all that heathen activity came my expertise for duck hunting and catching fish, as well as my dream to one day build my own duck calls.

I wasn't entirely sure where it was going to lead me—until one day Kay found something in the back of a newspaper.

SPORTSMAN'S PARADISE

Rule No. 7 for Living Happy, Happy, Happy
Buy a House Near Water (It's a Lot More Fun)

When I started my Christian walk, I began a very intensive study of the Bible. Like I said, I don't do anything halfway; it's my personality to become immersed in something once I set my mind to it. I attended services at White's Ferry Road Church at least twice a week and spent the other five days of the week studying God's Word with groups of friends or alone. I was determined to become a scholar of the Bible, to understand the true meaning of every verse of Scripture, so I might one day be able to spread His word to other people who found themselves in the predicament I once struggled through.

After a couple of years, I regained my confidence and had a new outlook on life. But in the back of my mind, I still wanted to return to hunting and fishing, which was always my consuming passion. Kay understood my struggle and was sympathetic when I told her that I could make more money as a commercial fisherman than at my teaching job. It was something I had been thinking about for a few years, as I still yearned to be in the woods, lakes, and rivers, where I was most happy and at peace.

With a lot of faith in me, as always, Kay encouraged me, saying she thought it was a good plan. Together we made a life-changing decision. We decided I would quit my teaching job at Ouachita Christian School and begin fishing. We planned to adopt a lifestyle that would involve virtually living off the land, just like my family had done when I was a child. I told Kay to search for land with water that eventually flowed into the sea. I was gambling that by doing what I wanted to do, I could make a living for my family—which was still growing. Eventually Kay and I would have four sons; Jeptha, our last, was born in 1978.

Kay found six and a half acres of land just off the Ouachita River at the mouth of Cypress Creek outside of West Monroe, Louisiana. It was at the end of a dirt road in one of the most heavily forested areas on the river. The classified advertisement in the newspaper described it as a "Sportsman's Paradise." When we drove out to see the land, I knew it was perfect as soon as we crested the hill that leads down to the house where we still live today. The place was absolutely perfect.

The real estate lady sensed my excitement and told me, "Now, Mr. Robertson, I'm required by law to inform you that this home sits in a floodplain."

"Perfect," I told her. "I wouldn't want it if it didn't."

Our land fronts a small slough, which eventually flows to the sea by way of Cypress Creek and the Ouachita, Red, Atchafalaya, and Mississippi Rivers. When we purchased the property, two houses stood on the land: one a substantial three-bedroom, white frame house, the other a primitive camp house of weathered, green-painted lumber. The latter was subject to being flooded during times of high water when the Ouachita River overflowed its banks. The front yards of both houses sloped gently down to the slough, which wrapped around the land on the north side.

When we drove out to see the land, I knew it was perfect as soon as we crested the hill.

Behind the houses, the hill continued steeply upward, making a large promontory that jutted out into the juncture of the river and creek. The land was covered with towering oaks and pines.

The Ouachita River varies from a small, crystal-clear stream flowing over the rugged rocks of the Ouachita Mountains in southwest Arkansas to a muddy, turgid, intermingled flood where it joins the Red River just before emptying into the Mississippi

River in southern Louisiana. Deep woods and substantial wetlands lie alongside most of its 605-mile length.

Washita (another spelling of the river's name) is an Indian word meaning "good hunting grounds." The Ouachita Indians, for whom the river is named, and several other tribes—including the Caddo, Chickasaw, Osage, Tensa, and Choctaw—lived along its banks. I later discovered, from potsherds and other relics I found—including a human skeleton uncovered by a spate of rain—that our land was inhabited in the distant past. A team of archeologists from Northeast Louisiana University in Monroe established that the skeleton I found was very old and that of an Indian. In the past, the promontory had been a thriving Indian encampment. Indians lived there for centuries, sallying out to hunt and fish from the small peninsula whose natural advantages gave them easy access to the teeming wildlife and fishing of the area. When their time passed, the river served as a passage into northern Louisiana and southwestern Arkansas for settlers of the area.

When I saw the site and its location for the first time, I knew instantly that it was the land I wanted. It was where I would launch my career as a commercial fisherman, and it was where I would teach my sons the survival skills I learned from my father during my youth.

Even though the property was relatively cheap, it was out of our price range. Fortunately, my parents were making plans to return to Louisiana from Arizona, and Pa had enough money for a down payment on a small place for retirement. They still owned my boyhood home in Dixie, Louisiana, which they were renting to a poor family that was often behind on the monthly payment. My parents' dilemma was that while they could make a down payment on any retirement home they wanted, they weren't sure how they would maintain it once they grew older.

When I showed them the old Indian settlement, they fell in love with it as much as I had. Granny could sense that it would be an excellent retirement home, and Pa was particularly impressed with its solitude and hunting and fishing opportunities. When we began to explore how to acquire the place, we came up with a way that would fit both families' needs. Kay and I needed a down payment, and Pa and Granny needed to eliminate their worries about monthly payments and long-term maintenance. Having two houses on the place was a godsend that led to an agreement that would solve our problems. Pa and Granny used their savings for the down payment, and Kay and I agreed to make monthly payments and maintain the property. The arrangement led to several years of happy, happy, happy living in a place we all loved.

Pa and Granny elected to live in the camp house, while my larger family took the house farther up the hill. We all settled comfortably into our new homes, and I began my career as a commercial fisherman. Pa and my sons were right alongside me as I started my fishing business. For Pa, it was a return to a way of life close to that of his childhood and my younger years at Aunt Myrtle's farm. At first he actively hunted and fished the bountiful area surrounding our property; then, as he grew older, he gravitated more to taking care of the garden he'd started. Most of our food, from spring to fall, came from Pa's garden. Our meat came from fish we caught or from ducks, squirrels, and deer we shot. We usually ate fish three times a week.

Pa's first garden on the edge of the slough flooded every year or so. The floodwaters enriched the soil but sometimes delayed planting, so he began another level plot farther up the hill, which stayed dry even in the wettest of years. As Pa grew older, however, he began to slow down, and his interests became narrower. He spent his later years close to home, tending the fire in the iron stove that heated their house and playing dominoes and other games with his family and grandchildren. He enjoyed the role of patriarch of his large extended family, which numbered more than sixty during his lifetime, and he even bragged at one point that he was the oldest Robertson of his line left.

Pa helped me with projects around the place, such as building a boat launch and dock, house repairs, and a multitude of tasks that kept the place going. Both families were bent on making our lives successful. It was Granny who suggested a drop box at the boat launch we built, where customers using it could deposit payment of a small fee. The honor system is still in place—the suggested fee is two dollars—and the boat launch is used daily by those launching their boats onto Cypress Creek and the Ouachita River.

Once I began fishing full-time, it didn't take long for the business to become successful. Before too long, I was making more money than I did as a teacher. The fishing was profitable from the beginning and grew as I made enough money to buy more nets and trotlines. I caught about sixty thousand pounds of fish—thirty tons—the first year, and that's about what we averaged annually.

Before too long, I was making more money fishing than I did as a teacher.

We caught a cascade of catfish, buffalo, gaspergou (freshwater drum), alligator gar, and a number of white perch. The catfish were worth about seventy cents a pound, the buffalo thirty cents, and the market always determined the gar's price. More gar are caught and sold in Louisiana than any other freshwater fish. Fish brings a higher price during cold weather; in warm weather almost everybody in Louisiana fishes, and the surplus catch goes into the commercial market, driving prices down.

The white perch, or crappie, are game fish and cannot be sold. They are lagniappe and usually ended up on our dinner table. The man we sold our fish to at the market ate only the poorer parts of the fish, the parts he couldn't sell. But that wasn't my style. I fed my family the best of my catch and sent the rest to market. My selectivity continues today, as I carefully pick the best of the ducks killed on a hunt, usually teal or wood ducks. If I'm doing all the work, why should someone else enjoy the pick of the litter?

I decided early on that if my boys were going to eat the fish, they were going to help catch them, too. Setting out the nets wasn't too much of a task for me, but getting the fish from my boat, up the hill, and into my truck took some serious work. When it rained, it was even more arduous because the hillside was slick and muddy. After one catch, I was slipping and sliding all over the hill, struggling to carry a heavy tub to my truck.

When I got to the house, the boys were all there. Kay was getting ready to take the fish to town and sell them. We did this about two or three times a week; it was the only money we made. The boys usually went with her and always looked forward to it. I went in the house and said to them, "Y'all come over here and sit down for a few minutes. I want to explain something to you.

"Y'all are fixing to go to the store," I told them. "There will be bubble gum and shopping—y'all are going to have a big ol' time. I want you to realize that all that money you're going to spend is coming off those fish out there. You understand that?"

"Yes, sir," they answered quietly. They knew this talk was serious.

"What I can't figure out is, if you're getting all that money from the fish, why doesn't someone come down there when that boat pulls up and grab the other side of that tub to help me up the hill? That's what I can't figure out."

They all sat there staring at me, like I was speaking Spanish.

"Hey, just a thought," I said. "I can get 'em up the hill. But it would be a lot easier with y'all helping me."

From that day forward, whenever I pulled in with the boat, I'd see the whole little group coming down the hill. They'd have their tubs and be ready to help. It was a lesson that stayed with them. All four of my boys came to realize that the work was a family enterprise, and they needed to pitch in. In fact, the lesson took so well that each of them still works for Duck Commander, as do several other relatives and extended family. If you want a job with our outfit, it helps if you're blood kin.

I also assigned my boys one of the worst jobs that came with commercial fishing: assembling the bait. I would buy a fifty-five-gallon drum of rotten cheese and let it sit until it was covered in maggots. It needed to smell really bad and be as smelly and nasty as possible to draw the catfish to my nets. When the rotten cheese was ready, I'd get my boys up at daylight. They'd reach down into the drum and grab a handful of the mess and stuff it into socks. I know they were gagging the entire time—and I'm sure they lost their breakfast more than a few times—but it was a job that had to be done.

Later, when the boys were in high school, I decided I wanted to get into crawfishing. The problem with crawfish is you can never have enough bait. And crawfish are attracted to bait that's even nastier than what a catfish likes to eat. A crawfish will literally eat anything—as long as it's dead and smells really bad. So when Kay took the boys to town to sell the fish, I always told Alan, Jase, Willie, and Jep to be on the lookout for roadkill. If they spotted a dead possum or raccoon in the road, they'd pick it up and throw it into the back of the truck. They'd bring the dead animals home, chop them up, and then throw them into the crawfish nets.

Of course, I never wanted to waste anything. We had an old deep-freezer in my shop and they threw the excess roadkill in there. By the end of every summer, the freezer was filled with dead cats, dogs, deer, coons, opossums, ducks, and anything else they could find in the road. The freezer smelled so bad it would have been quarantined if health officials ever caught wind of it! My boys also hunted for snakes and put them in the freezer. They baited snake traps in the water with little perch and then pulled the traps in at night. They'd blast the snakes with shotguns, which I'm sure was a lot of fun for them.

The biggest single catch I ever made was on an early morning one June. It came after we decided to launch Duck Commander as a business, so I had recently given up commercial fishing. I was only fishing for fun and to put some fish on the family table. I was using a six-foot hoop net about twenty feet long, with two-inch mesh. My son Jase was fishing with me and I told him, "I'm going to put this old big net out and catch us some Ops."

By the end of every summer, the freezer was filled with dead cats, dogs, deer, coons, opossums, ducks, and anything else they could find in the road.

"Ops" is short for Opelousas, which are flathead catfish. I think they're the best eating species of all the freshwater commercial fish in Louisiana. Also called the motley, yellow cat, or shovelhead, the flathead catfish is aggressively predacious and known for eating everything in sight. Some of them weigh as much as 120 pounds.

I set the net out on the other side of the river and up from the boat a little bit. I dropped it in about eighteen feet of water with a little current, but not much, just enough to hold the net open. I came back after about three days. I reached and grabbed the rope and started up with the net. I thought, "That thing must be hung!" But it kept coming; it was heavy, heavy!

I kept coming with that heavy net. When I had about three hoops gathered up, I could feel something moving the whole net ever so slightly. When I got the net up high enough to where I could see down into it a little bit, all I could see were blue cats! One look, and I realized there was way more fish than I could get into my boat! It was just too much weight! There were too many fish to even move them!

So I wound up with about two-thirds of my net in the boat and a third of it in the water—literally crammed with blue catfish. After tying off the hoops that I had pulled out of the water, the rest of the net formed a bag that hung straight down from the boat. It was some weight! But the fish were quietly swimming inside the net—I had 'em!

Now I was free floating. I cranked up my motor and let it idle, but I was moving forward—those swimming fish were moving my boat. I came across the river at an angle, going real slow. I made it to the mouth of Cypress Creek and almost home with a catch of biblical proportions. I headed for the bank, where the water depth begins to decrease rapidly. The net started dragging the bottom. When I got close to the bank, I jumped out of the boat and into the water, which was about four or five feet deep. I pulled the boat closer to the bank. The fish came alive in the shallow water and were making a rumble!

I went to my truck, locked its hubs to get it into four-wheel drive, and backed into the water as close as I could get to the boat and the fish. I climbed into the boat and, with a large dip net, started scooping up the thrashing fish and putting them into my washtubs. After throwing about fifty to sixty pounds into a tub, I transferred the fish to my truck. The blue cats weighed from three to twenty pounds each. From the time I started pulling up the net, I toiled with the rascals for more than two hours.

I mean, it was work! I was sweatin'! I filled the truck bed until it was mounded up with fish. Then I drove the truck out of the water onto solid ground. Both Jase and Kay, when they came out and saw those fish, were stunned. Jase said he had never seen so many fish in one pile. When they took them to town to sell, they tipped the scales at one thousand pounds! Kay and Jase came back with three hundred dollars, and they sold them cheap—thirty cents a pound.

That's the most fish I ever caught in one net. Another time I caught eighteen Opelousas cats in one net weighing from about fifteen to fifty pounds apiece. They were big, but it wasn't nearly as many fish as I'd caught the time before.

The fishing business became somewhat lucrative—we were at least making enough money to pay the mortgage and utilities and take care of the rest of our needs—but I still didn't believe it was my, ahem, calling in life. I kept going back to a memorable hunting trip I'd made with Al Bolen a few years earlier outside of Junction City, Arkansas. A large flock of mallard ducks had flown high above us, and I hit them with a long, hailing call when they were on their way out of sight. I turned the flock, and it began to circle, dipping lower as the ducks approached our decoys and blind. When the ducks began to sail wide, I hit them again with a short *chop-chop* that turned them back toward our blind, where we waited. The flock dropped into the water directly in front of us, in perfect gun range.

When the shooting was over, Big Al told me, "Man, you weren't calling those ducks, you were *commanding* them!"

> **Big Al told me, "Man, you weren't calling those ducks, you were *commanding* them!"**

Al, who knew of my tinkering with his and other hunters' duck calls, urged me to make my own and sell them.

"And I've got the name for it: Duck Commander," Big Al told me.

I was struck by the phrase and it never left my mind: Duck Commander. It sort of has a ring to it, doesn't it?

Duck Commander was always in the back of my mind, its implementation only awaiting a trigger. When Kay and I were discussing our future one night, I told her that I wanted to build and sell duck calls but would continue to fish until I got the duck-call business off the ground.

"I don't know how I'm going to build the duck-call sales yet, but I'll figure that out. When they get to where we don't need to fish anymore, we'll be on our way," I told her.

The move to Sportsman's Paradise and my commercial fishing had turned out well. Our family was together again, and I was thriving both spiritually and emotionally. Would another life-changing gamble work again? With the good Lord behind the steering wheel, we were about to find out.

DUCK COMMANDER

Rule No. 8 for Living Happy, Happy, Happy
Never Sell Yourself Short
(You Never Know, You Might Become a Millionaire)

Some of the most successful businesses in American history started as mom-and-pop operations, on nothing more than a family's dream, hard work, and a shoestring budget. Ben & Jerry's Ice Cream opened its first store in a run-down gas station in Burlington, Vermont, in 1978. It was sold for $326 million to a competitor in 2000. Walmart started as a five-and-dime store in Bentonville, Arkansas, in 1950 before Sam Walton and his family created the world's biggest retailer. In 1946, S. Truett Cathy opened a single restaurant, a twenty-four-hour diner outside of Atlanta, which was so small it had only ten stools and four tables. He and his brother named it the Dwarf Grill. Today, Chick-fil-A sells more than $4 billion in chicken sandwiches and other food annually across the country.

Like those businesses, Duck Commander was nothing more

than a dream when I decided to launch the company. Obviously, I had no idea the business would become what it is today, but I had the courage and determination to believe we could compete with the more established companies in the duck-call industry, some of which had been manufacturing calls since the early twentieth century. My idea of starting Duck Commander began when Al Bolen made his comments about my ability to command ducks on the water. But it was during another hunting trip that my business finally started to come to fruition.

Baxter Brasher, a fellow member of White's Ferry Road Church and an executive of Howard Brothers Discount Stores, where Kay worked, asked me to take him duck-hunting. Brasher had noticed a lot of men and boys asking me questions about hunting, fishing, and duck calls before and after church, and he was curious to find out what all the fuss was about. After I showed him how it was done, Brasher was even more impressed. He told me, "You really, really ought to build a duck call."

I told him I had a design and a plan to do it but didn't have the money to make it happen.

"Well, how much money would you need?" Brasher asked.

So I asked around and checked on the price of equipment and everything else I would need. I went back to Brasher and told him it would cost about $25,000 for me to get into the duck-call business.

"Twenty-five thousand?" Brasher asked me as he shuffled some papers on his desk. "Let me see. Here's what you do: You take this piece of paper—it's my financial statement—and you take it down to the bank. Walk in there and tell them you want twenty-five thousand dollars. They're going to say, 'Do you have any collateral?' You hand them this piece of paper and say, 'There is my collateral right there. He's backing me.'"

I told him I had a design and a plan to do it but didn't have the money to make it happen.

I asked Brasher, "How much do you want?"

"I don't want anything," he told me. "The reason I don't want anything is I know it'll work. You'll do well. I don't want a dime. I want to know I helped someone get started. You just go down there and tell them what you need."

So I went down to the bank and walked in, and a clerk asked if she could help me.

"I need to see Mr. George Campbell, the man who loans the money," I told her.

She walked me back to Campbell's office and he asked, "How can I help you?"

"I need twenty-five thousand dollars," I told him. "I'm going into the duck-call business."

"Mr. Robertson, what do you have for collateral?" he asked me.

I laid that piece of paper down on Campbell's desk just like Brasher told me to do and answered, "There's my collateral."

I never will forget what happened next. Campbell looked at the paper and looked at the name. Then he said, "Brenda, will you get us some coffee?"

Now we're getting somewhere, I thought to myself. He went from "who are you," "what do you want," and "where's your collateral" to "let's have coffee."

Duck Commander—and my dream of building my own duck calls—was about to take flight.

After I had the bank loan, I went into high gear looking for the machinery I would need. By chance, I ran across a classified in the back of a magazine that was advertising a lathe, which is a woodworking machine I needed to build the barrels for my duck calls. I called the seller to inquire about the lathe he was trying to get rid of.

"How much money do you have to spend on this, Mr. Robertson?" the guy asked me.

"Well, I only have about twenty-five thousand," I told him.

"You're in luck, Mr. Robertson," the man replied. "The equipment is only $24,985."

The sucker fleeced me! The lathe was worth maybe five thousand dollars, but he took everything I had for it. It's one of the reasons we were so poor during the first ten years of operating

Duck Commander. Everything we made was going back to the bank to pay for the lathe! I later learned the lathe was built in the 1920s. It was originally used in Chicago and was in Memphis, Tennessee, when I bought it. The equipment was out-of-date. It was an old-fashioned, flat-knife lathe, but thankfully it actually worked pretty well once I got it hooked up and running.

While I waited for the lathe to arrive, I finalized my model for a duck call. I was able to call ducks from the time I was very young. I learned as a teenager using a P. S. Olt D-2 duck call, which was designed by Philip Stanford Olt of Pekin, Illinois, in the early 1900s. It was an Arkansas-style call, which is a one-piece insert with a straight reed and curved tone board. I always had a knack for making a call sound right or better. My hunting buddies were always asking me to tune, adjust, or repair their calls, and they always seemed to sound more like a duck when I finished tinkering with them.

When I decided to make my own duck calls, I enlisted the help of Tommy Powell, who went to our church. Tommy's father, John Spurgeon Powell, made duck calls, and I went to him with my concept of how one should be built. John Spurgeon Powell looked at my specifications and concluded that my call wouldn't work; he told me it was too small. But he promised me if I could get the hole drilled properly, he would turn it on his lathe and make me a call.

A lot of new ideas were going into what I was asking him to build: mine would be a smaller caller and would have a double reed, which I thought were significant improvements. The call's barrel size, thickness, and a few other specifications were to come later as I refined it. One other big improvement was actually Pa's idea, and I'm not sure I would have ever come up with it. The double reeds had a tendency to stick together, so Pa suggested we put a dimple in the bottom reed to eliminate the problem.

So we took a nail, rounded off the point, and with a hammer tapped a little dimple in the reed. When assembled with the protruded dimple of the bottom reed against the top reed, it worked perfectly. We later made a small tool from a sewing kit and just pressed the dimple into the reeds we were making. To this day, with all the automation that has come into the making of Duck Commander calls, Si, who has worked for the company since retiring from the army, still puts the dimples in the reeds by hand, one at a time.

Si, who has worked for the company since retiring from the army, still puts the dimples in the reeds by hand, one at a time.

After my meeting with John Spurgeon Powell, I cut a little six-inch-long, three-inch-square block of wood but still needed someone to drill a hole in it. To get it done, I took the block to nearby West Monroe High School's woodworking shop. The shop teacher told me he didn't have time to fool with it.

I told him, "Four dressed mallard ducks for that hole."

"Good night! Now we're talking!" he replied.

I gave him four dressed mallard ducks to drill a hole that took him just a matter of seconds. That was the beginning of my first duck call. John Spurgeon Powell turned it on his lathe and finished it off for me. I had a prototype to build what I guessed would be millions more one day.

After a few weeks, a train brought the lathe to West Monroe, and I drove my pickup to the depot yard and backed it up to the loading dock. As I got out of the truck, I told a man on the dock to load up my shipment.

"You the one here after that equipment—that machine for the duck deal?" he asked me.

"Yeah," I told him.

"Son, have you seen it?" he asked.

"Nah. I don't have any idea what it looks like," I said.

"Well, have you ever run any machinery like that?" he asked again.

"Nah, I'm going to figure that out when I see it," I said.

"Well, first of all, you ain't going to haul it in no pickup truck," he informed me. "Son, you need a flatbed—a big truck."

"Really?" I asked.

I walked back into the warehouse and looked at it. Good night! It was *iron*! I thought it was going to be little stuff, you know—for duck calls. But the machinery was huge—and heavy. It looked to me like it covered an acre back there. I never found out what it was built to turn, but it must have been something big!

I immediately borrowed a ragged dump truck I saw among several at the depot. It belonged to one of the members at church who happened to work there. I backed the truck up to the dock. I remember the depot crew standing there looking at me like I was deranged, but they loaded the lathe onto the truck for me. Away went the Duck Commander.

But further problems lay ahead of me at home. I had planned to put the lathe in a small building on my property that I was using for a shop. It measured about twelve feet by twelve feet. When I arrived with the men I'd gotten to drive the truck home and help unload, one man looked at the building dubiously and said, "It's not going in there—not through that door."

I said, "Oh yeah, it'll go in there." I got out my chain saw and stuck the snout of it into the north wall and went to cutting. *Whannnnnnnn!* I was cutting through nails and everything. They were all just standing back, looking at me like they were witnessing the Texas Chain Saw Massacre. I kept at it. *Whannnnnnnn!*

When I finished cutting my way to the top of both sides, *ka-whooom!* The whole wall fell out!

I backed the truck up to the shed, dropped the dump gate, and hooked one end of a come-along to the lathe and the other end to a tree. I dragged the heavy iron machine inside the shop. It filled the available space from end to end, leaving just enough room in front of it for an operator. We set the wall back in place and nailed it up. All in all, it was a successful operation. It's amazing what a little redneck engineering can do!

I anchored the lathe down, leaving it on the original shipping skids. It operated that way as long as it was in use. The equipment was so heavy that, within a couple of years, its weight caused the shop to sink a foot into the ground. But the lathe remained relatively level as it sank, so its operation wasn't affected. Nothing was ever done about releveling the shop.

By now it was dark outside. It had been a long day. Despite all the setbacks, I had overcome my obstacles and was exultant. The factory to make the duck calls wasn't operating yet, but everything was in place.

I was so excited about our future that I went down the hill to see Pa and Granny. They were seated at the table, playing dominoes with Alan and Jase—they played dominoes together nearly every night. Pa believed in playing dominoes with children because it taught them to add rapidly and develop strategy, thinking several moves ahead. Whether the dominoes did that or not, all the boys did well in mathematics and the rest of their school subjects.

Now, I told y'all I talk pretty dramatically when the situation warrants it, and this was maybe the biggest day of my life. I walked into my parents' house and announced to everyone, "Y'all see this duck call right here?"

I was holding the call John Spurgeon Powell built for me. Of course, they all stopped and were looking at me.

"I'm in the process of getting these duplicated on that equipment out there," I told them. "Read my lips: we're going to sell a million dollars' worth of these things before it's over."

Pa was sitting there—and they're all still looking at me. When I said we were going to sell a million dollars' worth, they all looked back down at their dominoes. Pa picked one up, smacked it on the table, and said, "Ten!" He didn't even acknowledge what I'd said!

None of them said "Good night," "That sounds great," or anything! They just kept playing. I walked out, thinking to myself, *Well, I didn't get any of them fired up*. And I thought, *Well, maybe not a million dollars' worth.*

Sometimes I still think about telling Pa I was going to make a million dollars—and that his only response was to take a ten-count. Since that time, as it turned out, we have sold way more than that. Who would have believed me at the time?

Undaunted, I set to work the next day trying to get the lathe running. It was a harder task than I envisioned. Coupled with my and Pa's lack of knowledge about running a lathe (Pa did show interest in the project once it got under way) was the fact that it came with no instruction manual on how to operate it.

I had never run a lathe, but I saw a button that said Start. It's like Jase says: when you don't know what you're doing, it's best to do it quickly! So I pressed the button, and that thing fired up. Good grief! There were big old belts spinning with no protection on them, and the whole thing was humming! I saw a big handle, and I wondered what would happen if I pulled it up. *Whiiizzzzzz!* All these blades and metal parts started moving. I said, "Whoa, whoa, now!" and shut her down. Remember what I said about on and off buttons? Fortunately, the lathe was old enough to still have them!

It's like Jase says: when you don't know what you're doing, it's best to do it quickly!

I had never seen such a thing before. I didn't have a book. Nobody was there. I didn't know how to set anything. So I just went a little bit at a time. The first thing I did was call some cat from the company that built it. When I started telling him what I was trying to do, he said, "Aw, naw, naw, man! You've got to have templates."

"What?" I asked him.

"You've got to have some templates," he repeated.

And then he started explaining what they were and how that thing worked. After that, it was trial and error to get everything working right. I hadn't been sent any templates, or jigs as some call them, which are thin metal plates used as guides to cut wood accurately into the shape you want. So I acquired what we needed.

Let me tell you: we tore up some wood out there. You wouldn't believe the pile of shavings and waste. But Pa and I were determined to make it work.

While we were getting the lathe lined up and figuring out how it worked, I came up with another idea. I decided that maybe I could get someone to build my duck calls for me so I could start selling them. At least there would still be some money coming in, while we figured out how to build our own.

I was already testing the market and had traveled to quite a few areas, including my old hometown of Vivian, as well as places in eastern Texas, southern Arkansas, western Mississippi, and as far away as the bayou parts of southern Louisiana. It was in Lake Charles, Louisiana, that I encountered Alan J. Earhart, who had been making the Cajun Game Call. It was an old duck call, and he had been building it for years. Earhart was sympathetic to my quest, so we made a deal from which both of us benefited.

Earhart agreed to build two thousand Duck Commanders at a price of two dollars each, while I was getting my equipment lined up. Earhart had his own lathe, and he switched it over to build my calls. Earhart said that of all the people he had met starting out in the duck-call business, he thought I had enough energy and drive to pull it off.

"But man," he told me. "You've got a long way to go."

I had no idea exactly how long it would take me to get Duck Commander to where it is today.

FAMILY BUSINESS

Rule No. 9 for Living Happy, Happy, Happy
It's Cheaper to Hire Your Relatives
(Unless You Don't Like 'Em)

People ask me all the time about the early days of Duck Commander, when it was just Pa, Kay, the boys, and me trying to learn how to operate a heavy lathe and build duck calls in a small woodshop outside our home. I'm sure that at various times Kay and everyone else assumed I was crazy, and they were probably right.

Like my childhood, our company started from humble, humble beginnings. When we first started fishing the Ouachita River, it was so slow you might see two buzzards fighting over an inner tube! When we ran out of roadkill to bait our nets, the buzzards fought over anything else they could find! After we launched Duck Commander, our first year of sales totaled only eight thousand dollars. I told Kay, "I know I have a master's degree, but I'm gonna stay the course on this one. I think this will work. If the Almighty is with us, it will work." It was just like when I persuaded her to move out next to the river, so I could give up my teaching job to become a commercial fisherman. I told her then, "If you get me a place on the river, I'll fish the river. I'll be the smartest commercial fisherman out there."

Of course, everybody laughed at us in the early days. People would come by our house and say, "Let me get this right: you have a master's degree from Louisiana Tech University, you could've played professional football, but you turned that down so you could do *what*?"

I always told them that I was fishing the river and following my dream. I got seventy cents a pound on the catfish and thirty cents a pound on the buffalo, which wasn't a bad living. I was determined to see it through until the duck call business was big enough to support us, and then I would hang my fishing nets up for good. A lot of my friends tell me they thought I was a complete idiot.

Now I ask them, "Well, it's forty years since you thought I was an idiot; what about now?" Now they're calling me a genius! Boy, it took forty years for them to turn, but now they finally say, "That old guy ain't as dumb as he looks."

I remember making a speech somewhere and a man walking up to me after I was finished. He said, "Mr. Robertson, I'll tell you what I got out of that speech: You're kind of like one of them old Airedale terrier dogs. You ain't as dumb as you look!"

I told the guy, "Man, I appreciate those words of wisdom." I laughed at that one; that was a good one.

I might not be the most intelligent guy on Earth, but I always had the wherewithal, determination, and work ethic to turn my business into a success, or at least to make it profitable enough to feed and care for my family, which is really all I ever wanted.

"Well, it's forty years since you thought I was an idiot; what about now?" Now they're calling me a genius!

When the serious work started at Duck Commander, I installed a shed roof on the south side of our workshop to shelter a heavy-duty table saw my brother Tommy loaned me to help get the business going. Shavings and sawdust always covered the floor in untidy piles. In one area were cedar shavings, which were cut while we made the end-piece blanks of the duck calls. In another pile was the walnut residue sheared off the call barrels, which I turned on the lathe inside my shop. Several cedar and walnut logs, the woods from which the original Duck Commander calls were made, were piled up in front.

But the most noticeable addition, and the first thing visitors saw when they came to our house, was the roughly lettered sign that proclaimed DUCK COMMANDER WORLDWIDE. I took an old board, painted it white, and lettered it with black. Then I nailed it up at an angle, which I did for a little bit of show (remember what I said about being dramatic?). People would come out to our house, see the sign above the shop door, and walk around wondering, "What have you got out there?" More than four decades later the sign still hangs in front of our property.

Obviously, there was a lot of learning on the job, including enough errors and corrections to drive me nearly mad. But it didn't take us long to get a production line going, and Alan, Jase, Willie, Kay, and Pa were my crew. Our assembly line was out on the porch of our house, which was screened in at the time. Pa was always helping me. Willie was the youngest, so his job was to sweep up the sawdust in the shop. My oldest son, Alan, was given a little more responsibility—he used a band saw to cut the ends of the calls. Then I ran a drill press to set up and calibrate the end pieces.

Jase and Willie also dipped the calls in polyurethane and dried them on nails, which wasn't a very fun job. They hung the calls on a piece of plywood, eight feet by four feet, which leaned against one of the big pine trees in our yard. Neat rows of four-inch finishing nails were driven into the plywood, about two inches apart, from top to bottom. They'd open a five-gallon bucket of polyurethane, insert their fingers into the ends of duck-call barrels until they had four on each hand, then dip them into the thick liquid—submerging a little of their fingers to make sure the resin coated the barrels completely. With a light touch so as not to mar the finish, they worked each one off their fingers as they placed them carefully and separately on protruding nails. Then they repeated the operation until the entire board was filled with shiny, coated duck-call barrels drying in the open air.

It was a very tedious job, and a big one for boys who were so young, but it was all part of our quest to build the best duck calls in the industry. The dipping ensured a smooth, clear, permanent coat of resin that protected the wood. Sometimes, there would be one little rough spot at the mouthpiece end where the barrel touched a nail. When that happened, it had to be sanded smooth before the call could be sold. Once the calls were dry, the boys sanded them down to a fine finish. I think my boys were a little embarrassed going to school with their fingers stained brown from tung oil, but it was one of the hazards of the job. There were always rows of hard tung-oil drippings in our yard, and the trunks of the trees were covered in tung oil. The especially bad part for them was when I figured out that the more you sanded and dipped the calls, the shinier they were. That meant even more dipping!

Last, and most important, I blew every single call to make sure it sounded like a duck. From day one, I was convinced my duck call sounded more like a live duck than anything else on the market, and I wanted to make sure my products were always perfect. A small flaw in appearance wasn't critical, but not so in sound. It had to sound like a mallard hen, which was the standard I established for my calls. Duck Commander still follows that same principle today. A faulty call was either fixed or rejected. We used the rejects as fire starters in our wood heater for years.

Another early problem we had to overcome was packaging. We didn't have any! In fact, I didn't even have my name on the calls. I went up to the paper mill in West Monroe, and they built me sheets of flat boxes we could cut out and then fold it into shape, in which a duck call would fit neatly. The boxes were plain white with no writing on them.

Armed with my first boxed duck calls, I left home to flood the market. The first sale of Duck Commander calls was to Gene Lutz of Gene's Sporting Goods in Monroe, and the next was to Harold Katz in Alexandria, Louisiana. Then I drove over to Lorant's Sporting Goods in Shreveport, Louisiana, a reputable old hunting store that had been in business for years. I walked in and was able to see Mr. Lorant, the owner. I put my boxed duck calls on the counter and asked him, "How many of these duck calls do you want?"

Lorant picked up a couple and looked them over. Then he

looked up at me dubiously and asked, "You want me to buy these?"

"Yeah, put them on the market," I told him. "They're Duck Commanders, and I'm going into the business."

He looked at them again and said, "Where's the name on them? You don't have any printing on your box?"

"Nah, they'll find out who I am," I replied.

Lorant paused a minute, then said to me in all seriousness, "Son, let me give you some advice: get some printing on your boxes. You have to have some printing on your box. You are not going to do any good with that."

Then Lorant told me he'd buy six of them. It was the beginning of a good relationship. Once we started building them, Lorant went on to sell thousands—tens of thousands of dollars' worth.

"Son, let me give you some advice: get some printing on your boxes."

I took Lorant's advice to heart, and our packaging became a priority. We had an attractive box printed, which was covered with a transparent plastic top that showcased the duck call. Visible through the top of the box when it was placed properly on a shelf was the duck call and its now-famous logo: a mallard drake with wings cupped and legs lowered, looking down to the land. There was even an attractive sticker affixed to the barrel of the duck call. The first logo drawings were printed in gold on a green background. "Duck Commander," "Phil Robertson," and my Luna, Louisiana, address were easily visible.

Over the next few years, many evenings were spent inside our house, with me blowing Duck Commanders and the rest of the family cutting boxes, folding them, and filling them with the approved calls. No one was exempt from folding boxes. If you came to our house, you were probably going to participate in packaging—after eating one of Kay's delicious home-cooked meals, of course. It was a sociable time, and everyone talked and enjoyed it as they worked, while tuning out my duck-call blowing. Eventually, I also pressed my brothers into service, and each took his turn on the lathe at one time or another, using the templates to turn out barrels and end pieces.

Even in the early days of the operation, I was planning for our future. As the early Duck Commanders were being built, I carefully measured the calls that sounded just like I wanted with micrometers and calipers, recording and saving the dimensions for the time when we would build molded plastic calls. My database was eventually used to design a uniform product that eliminated the flaws inherent in wood.

But even today, many waterfowl hunters still prefer the wooden calls, and sometimes their sound is superior. At one point, we were doing well enough that I wanted to recall the first calls we made because they were so crude looking. They weren't nearly as well done as the newer ones—either wood or plastic. I just wanted to get them out of sight. Some of them looked pretty ragged, and I figured they would hurt future sales. Using a list Kay kept of our customers, we sent out a letter offering them a new Duck Commander if they would send their old one back to us.

I was amazed. The offer was met with suspicion as to what we were up to. Hunters from all over were calling or writing to say they wouldn't part with their calls for anything. They told us they were the "originals," and they weren't going to give them up. We were surprised how quickly we'd established brand loyalty among our customers.

The early marketing of Duck Commander depended strictly on me, although I enlisted my brother Tommy to call on some stores in the East Texas area where he lived. I traveled in a four-state area, driving through Arkansas, Louisiana, Mississippi, and Texas. I stopped in each town I passed through, calling on small sporting goods stores, hardware stores, five-and-dime stores—any business that looked like it might have an interest in selling duck calls. I did it from an old blue and white Ford Fairlane 500 that Kay inherited from Nannie. While Alan was driving it one time, a delivery truck sideswiped it, and the whole left side—fender, door, and back panel—was gone. Neither vehicle stopped, and I chose to ignore the accident. But the Ford still ran well and was carrying the first Duck Commanders to market.

I had one big selling tool—besides my loveable personality and redneck charm, that is. I made a recording of live mallard ducks calling and then added the sound of me blowing on a Duck Commander as a comparison. I tried to sell the idea that I was closer to sounding like a duck than anyone in the world.

My approach was successful. After we sold $8,000 worth of Duck Commanders the first year, we sold $13,500 the second year. The next year, we sold $22,000. I told Kay, "We are now rolling." The next year we sold about $35,000. We didn't hit six figures until about ten years after we started, but the business grew bigger every year.

Out of that first year's sales, I made about a dollar on each duck call. We were selling them to the stores for $4.27 wholesale. I figured they cost me about $3.20 total, after paying Mr. Earhart to build them, travel, paperwork, and all. We did a lot better when we began to build them ourselves.

About the third year after I started, I decided I was going about the selling all wrong. I felt I needed to go to Stuttgart, Arkansas, the duck capital of the world. I had been driving around trying to interest these little old sporting goods stores. I needed to raise my sights and become a little more ambitious. So I took my tape and cassette player, climbed in the old Ford, and headed for Stuttgart, 185 miles away. I pulled up in front of the only sporting goods store in town, a little bitty place.

I got out with my tape recorder, the live ducks comparison, and some duck calls strung around my neck.

I needed to raise my sights and become a little more ambitious.

I walked into the store and there were two guys sitting at a table. I was about to learn they were world-champion duck callers, who just happened to be sitting in the store. The fellow behind the counter asked me if he could help me.

"Is this the duck capital of the world?" I asked him.

"You're here," he said with a proud smile on his face.

"Well, I figure this is where I need to start," I told him. "Now, here's the deal. I have a duck call here—hanging around my neck. It's closer to a duck than any duck call that has ever been made. Do y'all want to hear it?"

They all looked at each other and kind of grinned.

"Let me guess," the guy behind the counter said. "You're out of Louisiana?"

"That's where I'm from," I said.

"Blow that thing," the guy told me.

I blew one of the calls around my neck, concentrating on the plain, simple sound of the mallard hen with no frills. I understood I was blowing for an audience conditioned by duck-calling contests, which often featured forty-note high calls that not only taxed a caller's lung power but also made the rafters ring. The "lonesome hen" call blown by contestants would make you weep. They could make a duck call talk. But I was making the outlandish claim that they didn't sound like a duck.

They listened. Then they chuckled, kind of laughed. They were still chuckling when the guy behind the counter picked up my duck call, blew on it, and said, "I see your problem with this duck call right off the bat."

"What's the problem?" I asked him.

"Air leaks a little bit around here," he told me. "You've got an air leak."

"That's the way it's designed," I responded. "Air leaks and all, it's still closer to a duck than anybody's."

I turned to the men at the table and asked if they duck-hunted.

"Yeah, we do a little duck-hunting," one of them told me.

"These guys are world-champion duck callers," explained the man behind the counter, with the proper amount of respect in his voice.

"Well, good night!" I exclaimed. "Boys, let's have us a contest right here. Get your duck calls and get up here. We'll tape your duck calls beside that of these live ducks. I've already got mine on it. We'll listen to the ducks, then all the calls. Then we'll just vote on it. Whoever is closest to a duck wins!"

The guy behind the counter looked and me and said, "You see that door there? Hit it!"

He ran me out of there! But as I was driving out of town, frustrated and still fuming over my reception in a little nondescript sporting goods store, I saw a beer joint with about fifteen cars parked around it. On an impulse, I wheeled my car into the parking lot, squealing to a stop.

I walked in the door and hollered, "Hey!"

The customers were all sitting around drinking beer. They turned and looked at me.

"Is there a duck caller in the house?" I asked loudly.

They all looked at me like they were deaf.

"Is there anybody in here who can blow a duck call?" I asked again.

Several of the customers pointed to a man sitting and quietly having a beer. He looked around at me.

"Come out here, I want to show you a duck call that I built," I told him. "I want you to tell me how I can sell these things up here. They just ran me out of the sporting goods store down there."

"They did?" the man asked with bewilderment in his voice. "Yeah, let me listen to it."

He went outside with me. I blew my call for him.

"Son, let me tell you something," the man told me. "I've been blowing duck calls for a long time. My hunting call is a Yentzen—until now. How much you want for one of them things?"

"Ten dollars," I told him.

"I want one right now," he said.

"No, I'm going to give it to you," I told him.

The man invited me to his house. I introduced myself to him and followed him back through town.

"Robertson, let me tell you something," he told me later. "These guys up here are making big money selling these world-championship duck calls. They don't want any ten-dollar duck calls up here in their way. To them, they're so far above you. What they are going to tell you is that unless you win the world championship blowing like they did, you're never going to sell any duck calls."

"But their calls don't sound like ducks," I told him.

"I know they don't," he replied. "But they have a deal going here, a clique, and they're making big money."

"So what do you think I should do?" I asked him.

"Aw, you'll sell duck calls," he replied. "You'll end up selling way more than they will. I've heard a lot of duck calls. But I've never heard one that sounded closer to a duck than that. That thing is a duck! These guides up here, the ones that hunt, they'll buy them. So will all serious duck hunters. You're just going to have to stay the course."

You know what? I don't remember the man's name; I only recall that he was a rice farmer. But his advice and encouragement carried me a long way over the next few years. About ten years later, when I developed a mallard drake call, a few of them were ordered by that little sporting goods store in Stuttgart. I guess they finally realized my call sounded like a duck.

The guy behind the counter in that store wasn't the only one who had doubts about the Duck Commanders. It probably took me twenty-five years to convince the duck-calling world that there is a difference between meat calling and contest calling.

It probably took me twenty-five years to convince the duck-calling world that there is a difference between meat calling and contest calling.

The Duck Commander has come a long way. But it hasn't been easy.

Somehow, we stayed the course and it turned out. There is a God, and He blessed us because we did what was right—we loved Him, we loved our neighbor, and we hunted ducks. He is real and what He said He would do is what happened. He said, you love Me and do what's right, and I'll bless you—so much so that your barns will be full, packed full, tapped down, and running over. I only know that either our success came from Him or

I was one of the luckiest souls that ever came along with a little idea. All I can say is it's one or the other, but I'm leaning toward the Almighty doing exactly what He said He would do.

The Almighty blessed us, and Duck Commander did work, just like He said it would. Yes, it took a long, long time for us to get to where we are today. But even before our success, and long before *Duck Dynasty* came along, everybody was happy, happy, happy. In other words, it wasn't like my love for the Almighty was contingent upon whether the blessings came or not. My prayer was always: "Lord, if You bless me, I'll thank You; but if You don't, I'll be thankful for what I have. I have plenty. I'm in good shape." Even before our success came along, we had air-conditioning, color TV, hot water, and a bathtub. We had everything we needed. When I was a boy, we didn't even have bathtubs or commodes, but I was still as happy and content as I am today. As long as I was doing what God said was right and living my life for Him, I knew everything would work out in the end—one way or another.

IF IT SOUNDS LIKE A DUCK . . .

Rule No. 10 for Living Happy, Happy, Happy
If You're Going to Do Something, Do It Right
(Instead of Doing It Again)

When I was a bit of a wild child during the 1960s, one of my favorite musicians was Jimi Hendrix. A masterful showman, Hendrix was a brilliant experimentalist and one of the most influential musicians in history. Hendrix had an incredible ability to manipulate a six-string guitar and distort it to make sounds no one would have believed possible. You know what was most amazing about Hendrix? That sucker never learned to read music! He learned to play guitar by ear but did more with it than anyone before him or anyone since.

Now imagine trying to replicate a duck's sound by ear—without a duck's bill! When we're building duck calls, we try to use the same methods as people trying to learn to play music by ear. They can't read musical notes or charts, but when they hear notes, they memorize them, and then they sit down at a piano and play exactly what they heard. They duplicate the sounds in their heads and play them from memory. We do the same thing with duck calls. We hear 'em while we're out hunting, and then we build a device that sounds exactly like what we heard. Just like on a piano, we have to make sure we have the right pitch, note, inflection, and volume to ensure that our duck calls sound exactly like a mallard, green-winged teal, wood duck, American wigeon, or whatever duck species we're trying to imitate.

It isn't easy, and it requires a lot of trial and error to get a duck call to sound exactly right. After all, it's not like we were trying to replicate Daffy Duck—*thufferin' thuccotash!* Each duck species has a very unique and distinct sound; you can't call a wood duck with a green-winged teal call or vice versa. And this probably won't surprise you, but female ducks always sound different from males, even if they're of the same species.

Despite all the variations in sounds, what we've discovered over the years is that if a duck whistles, then you use a whistle to duplicate the sound. If a duck quacks, you use a call with a reed in it. One species of duck—the gadwall—requires both a whistle and a reed.

We build calls for all kinds of ducks. There is a certain percentage of waterfowl hunters who are mallard purists, but we appreciate all ducks. Of course, there are a few species that we'll draw the line on and won't eat. We don't eat the common merganser, and I understand there are particular sea ducks that are nearly inedible. For us, it's just as much fun to hunt wood ducks as mallards or green-winged teals. I think the most elegant, graceful duck is the pintail. For good table fare, our favorite ducks are the green-winged teals and close behind them are the wood ducks. If we really want a good duck gumbo or duck with dressing, we almost always go for the green-winged teal. They go fast around our table, especially if Willie has pulled up a chair!

The green-winged teals go fast around our table, especially if Willie has pulled up a chair!

Of course, the species I dislike the most is the Steven Seagal ducks—the ones that are hard to kill!

The very first duck call I made in 1972 was the Original Commander Call, which was designed for the mallard hen. The mallard is probably the most recognizable of all ducks and is the ancestor of many of the breeds we see in the United States. The mallard hen is covered in feathers of uneven hues from buff to very dark brown and usually has a brown or orange bill. The male mallard has a white neck ring, which separates its distinctive green head from its chestnut-brown chest. The rest of its body is mottled in lighter brown to gray to black, and its speculum feathers are a distinct purple-blue with black and white edging. The male mallard's bill is yellow, and its legs and feet are bright coral red. The male mallard is really a beautiful bird. Of course, that doesn't stop me from dropping them from the sky whenever I'm given the chance!

I made the mallard-hen call first because most ducks will respond to that kind of sound. We still make the Original Commander Call today, and each one tends to sounds different because every one is still made by hand from wood. Of course we still blow on every call to make sure it sounds exactly right. The Original Commander Call is the quintessential duck "quack," and the mallard hen typically gives the call in a series of two to ten quacks that start loud and get softer as she goes (sounds a lot like a woman I know at home). Now, not all mallard hens sound exactly the same. When you're blowing on an Original Commander Call to attract a mallard hen, you can quicken and sharpen the cadence to replicate a young mallard hen, or slow down and draw out the cadence to get an old, raspy mallard hen. There are three distinctive sounds for a mallard hen: quack, feed call, and hail call. The mallard hen call is very versatile and effective.

The Mallard Drake Call came along next. We were the first company to build one, so we patented it so our competitors couldn't copy our design. The male mallard doesn't quack; it's more of a quiet, raspy sound. When I set out to build the Mallard Drake, I superglued various sizes of PVC pipe together and finally mastered it. When I finally built a call that sounded exactly like a male mallard, I went tearing into our house and told Miss Kay, "I have it! We're going to revolutionize duck calls as we know them!"

I blew on the Mallard Drake Call for her.

"What is that?" she asked me. "Is it a frog?"

If you blow too high on a Mallard Drake Call, you really do sound like a tree frog—and there's no meat on those suckers! You have to catch the plump bullfrogs if you want a meal. The Mallard Drake Call is different from any other duck call. With most calls, you say, "Ten, ten, ten," while you're blowing into it. But with the Mallard Drake, you're basically saying, "Aaaaah," on a very low bass note as you raise your fingers off the call. It's an easy thing to do, unless you're a tenor. The Mallard Drake Call is controlled by your vocal cords and is really a whistle with a stem on it. You have to remember that when you're on an amplifier, whether it's with a guitar or any other musical instrument, you get maximum vibration when you hit a bass note. So you have to go really, really low when you're calling mallard drakes.

Conversely, there are three types of ducks that are whistlers: teal, wigeon, and pintail. Believe it or not, I built our first whistle from a children's musical toy set. None of the flutes and horns in the toy set sounded like a duck, but after I spent an hour with a band saw and used plenty of superglue, I built a whistle that sounded like six birds! For pintails, you put your finger in the opening while you're blowing; for wigeons and teals, you blow straight into the whistle. You can even use our whistle to call mallard drakes, doves, or quails if you want. That's why we call our whistle a six-in-one call.

The green-winged teal is the smallest of the North American dabbling ducks. It has a short neck and small bill, and its chestnut head has a green eye patch that extends to the nape of its neck. It's another pretty bird. Male green-winged teals have a high-pitched, single-note *peep* sound, while females are relatively quiet. But the females will let out a sharp, high-pitched quack when they're flushed. Like most women, you'll know when they've been bothered! When you're calling a green-winged teal, you don't do it very loud, and you use fine, little short notes while you're blowing air directly into the whistle. It's almost like a miniature mallard hen call, but when you get four or five people *peep*ing at the same time, it's exactly what teals sound like on the water.

There are also blue-winged teals and cinnamon teals, and they're identifiable by the colors their names suggest. The blue-winged teals, which have blue-gray upper wings, are common in the northern prairies and parklands of the central United States. We see a few blue-winged teals every once in a while, but they tend to winter farther to the south. The male has a high-whistled *tsee, tsee* sound, while the female lets out loud, evenly spaced quacks. The blue-winged teals are a lot of fun to hunt because they fly very fast and make erratic twists and turns as they fly low over your decoy spreads. The cinnamon teal, which has a cinnamon-red head, neck, breast, and belly, are common around the Great Salt Lake in Utah and the central valleys of California. They winter in Mexico and other parts of Central America, so we don't see them in Louisiana. The male cinnamon teal makes a series of *chuk* notes, while the female gives off more of a quack.

We see a lot of American wigeons, which are also known as baldpates and have a bluish gray-tipped bill. The males have a white crown on their heads and a green face patch. The wigeon drake gives out three high, squeaky whistles, like *whee, whee, whee.* To call a male wigeon, you stick the whistle in the corner of your mouth and clench your teeth. You blow three times and make sure you accent the second sound. The female wigeon, which has a gray head with a brownish-black crown, gives out a quack sound. We usually end up seeing a lot of American wigeon ducks; they nest in parts of Canada and are usually the first to migrate south for the winter.

The northern pintail is a long, slim duck with long, narrow wings, a slender neck, and a long tail. You can't mistake a pintail for any other kind of duck. Some people call them the "greyhounds of the air," and the males have chocolate-brown heads with a white stripe on each side of their necks. The male lets out growling, guttural notes, and they're not easy to duplicate. If you look in the mirror, you'll see a round piece of meat hanging in the back of your throat. God gave us that piece of meat to call a pintail duck. If we didn't have it and couldn't flutter it as we blew air into a whistle, we'd sound like a backhoe backing up: *beep, beep, beep!* But because God gave us that piece of meat, we can sound exactly like a pintail duck. The female pintail quacks and sounds nothing like a male.

Now, I can't take credit for all the duck calls that Duck Commander has developed over the years. One time when my son Jase was hunting with me, he had a mallard hen call in one corner of his mouth and a whistle in the other and was blowing them at the same time. As Jase was blowing on both of them, a flight of gadwalls turned and came right down to our decoys. After we shot 'em, I asked Jase, "What were you doing down there? It sounded like a gadwall."

Jase had a mallard hen call in one corner of his mouth and a whistle in the other and was blowing them at the same time.

"Why do you think they came down here?" Jase asked me. "They thought I *was* a gadwall."

As with the Mallard Drake Call, we were the first company to introduce a gadwall drake call. Gadwalls are about the same size as mallards, but there's really nothing very distinctive about them. The male gadwall is gray-brown with a black patch at its tail, while the females are patterned with brown and buff. The male gadwall makes short, deep, reedy calls that sound like a burp; the females quack like mallards, but with a higher pitch. To call a gadwall, you give the call one *tat* every four seconds or so.

Unlike the gadwalls, wood ducks are very distinctive. They're the only ducks that perch and nest in trees—they have sharp claws—and they're comfortable flying through woods, hence their name. They also have a unique shape: they're boxy with crested heads, thin necks, and long, broad tails. The males have glossy green heads with white stripes, burgundy breasts, and buff sides. The female wood ducks are gray-brown with white-speckled breasts. The male wood duck has a thin, rising and falling whistle that sounds like *jeeeeee*; the female makes a loud *oo-eek, oo-eek* sound when flushed and screams *cr-r-eek, cr-r-eek* to sound an alarm.

Keith Powell, who was one of my first employees at Duck Commander, built our first wood duck call out of wood. It has a short little reed in it, and you use your tongue to manipulate the sound. The key to calling wood ducks is you never want to use a flying call when the real ducks are flying. There's a different call for sitting, and that's the one you want to use when the ducks are in the air. If you're flying and the real ducks are flying, then everyone is flying and no one knows where to land. If you call them to sit, they'll swim right up to your blind so you can shoot 'em!

During the evolution of Duck Commander, we've built duck calls from wood, plastic, polycarbonate, and acrylic. We now have single-reeded calls, double-reeded calls, triple-reeded calls, and even reedless calls. We even have some calls today that are injection molded! Our calls come in a variety of colors and styles, but each call is still assembled by hand and custom tuned to make sure it sounds like a duck. If it doesn't sound like a duck, it's fixed or thrown into a pile of rejects. Jase, Jep, Si, John Godwin, Justin Martin, or one of a slew of other folks tests every duck call in the assembly room in our warehouse. I think our quality control is what separated our products from our competitors' a long time ago.

In the beginning, I was quality control. Even though we had the best product on the market, it took a while for sales to really pick up. In the late 1970s, I began to notice that Walmart stores were popping up in a lot of the small towns where I was doing business. Before too long, I noticed the hunting and fishing, sporting goods, and hardware stores that had previously bought my duck calls were closing their doors. I knew if I didn't find a way to get my products into Walmart, I wasn't going to be in business for very long either.

So one day, I pulled my old truck in front of the first Walmart I saw, walked in, and said, "Hey, how many of these duck calls do you want here?"

"Duck calls? You mean, off the street?" the lady behind the counter asked me.

"Yeah, yeah," I answered mildly, noting her resistance.

The clerk laughed and told me, "We don't buy any duck calls. Son, you need to go to Bentonville."

"Bentonville?" I asked her, knowing Walmart's corporate headquarters was several hours away in Arkansas. "Nah, I've just got some duck calls right here."

The clerk firmly told me no thanks and brusquely sent me away. So I drove on down the road and pulled up to the next few Walmart stores I saw. I changed my pitch a little bit to try to get someone interested, playing my tape and blowing my calls to show how they worked. Finally, one of the store managers told me, "I'll tell you what. You got an order form?"

"Nah, I don't have an order form," I told him. "I just figured you could pay me out of petty cash back there in the back of the store somewhere."

"Well, I've got a three-part order form I need to fill out," he said. "I'll tell you what; I'll try six of them."

When the store manager filled out a three-part form with WALMART at the top of it and wrote down "six duck calls," I walked outside looking at my copy and thought, *I've got me something here.* Well, when I got to the next Walmart thirty miles down the road, I showed the store manager the form and told him, "Walmart's stocking these duck calls. This last store ordered six."

He said, "Give me what you've got."

That was the beginning of our Walmart business. Using the same technique, I amassed a stack of order forms to show and prove to managers of Walmart stores across four states that other stores were buying our duck calls. I eventually built the business, as our sales loop grew wider, to where we were selling $25,000 worth of calls to Walmart each year.

Then one day our phone rang, and the voice on the other end said, "I need to talk to Mr. Robertson."

"Yeah, that's me," I answered.

"Are you the one who's getting duck calls into Walmart stores?" the man asked me.

"Yes, that's me," I told him.

"Son, let me ask you a question," he said. "How did you get duck calls into the Walmart chain without going through me?"

"Well, just who are you?" I asked.

"I'm the buyer for Walmart!" he screamed.

"How did you get duck calls into the Walmart chain without going through me?"

There was a pause.

"One store at a time," I told him.

There was a long pause.

"Let me get this right," he said. "You

mean to tell me you've been driving around in your pickup truck and convincing our sporting goods departments to buy duck calls without even conferring with me, who's supposed to be doing the buying for the whole Walmart chain?"

"Sir, I didn't mean to slight you or anything," I said. "Look, I didn't even know who you were. Bentonville's a long way. I'm just trying to survive down here!"

He thought about that for a minute, then said, "I'll tell you what I'm going to do. Anybody who can pull a stunt like that, I'm going to write you a letter authorizing you to do what you've been doing."

"Man, I appreciate that," I told him.

"I'm going to authorize you to go into our stores," he said. "You'll have that letter from me, and that makes it all aboveboard."

"Hey, I'd appreciate any help you can give me," I said.

So the buyer in Bentonville wrote me a letter and sent it to me. I got the letter and showed it to every store manager I met. They all told me, "Come on in, Mr. Robertson."

Our business with Walmart really started growing then. About a year or two later, with sales steadily accelerating, I called the buyer. "Look," I said, "it's a computerized world. We can probably speed this thing up if you buy a certain amount of my calls per store." The buyer told me to come to Bentonville and meet with him. He agreed to buy our calls and distribute them to

Walmart stores, an action that eliminated a lot of our workload and expanded the sale of duck calls into new areas of the United States. Together, we eventually built the account to sales of more than $500,000 per year—big numbers for Duck Commander, but relatively small for Walmart. Our profit from the sales put us on solid ground financially and provided the base for our future growth.

Things went on that way for about twenty years, but then Walmart began to scale down its waterfowl hunting business. Only about one million people in the United States hunt ducks. There wasn't enough money in it for a company that measures its customer base in multiple millions. We were making what we considered to be pretty good money, but it wasn't enough for Walmart, which deals in billions of dollars. The duck calls had always been more of a customer service for the company. So, basically, they got out of the duck-call business.

Fortunately, we had expanded our business into other stores, like Cabela's, Bass Pro Shops, Academy Sports + Outdoors, and Gander Mountain, so we were no longer as dependent on one big contract like Walmart. The specialty hunting stores were not only buying our duck calls, but they were also stocking our hunting DVDs, T-shirts, hats, and other hunting gear. The independent hunting stores have long been some of our most loyal clients and are still a big part of our business today. Without them, we never would have gotten off the ground. Although we reestablished our business relationship with Walmart a few years later, Duck Commander was able to survive and prosper during the years in which we didn't do business with the world's biggest retailer.

Duck Commander has been making hunting DVDs for more than two decades, although the first ones were actually filmed on VHS tapes. I watched a lot of deer-hunting and big-game-hunting TV shows, and I was convinced there was a market for waterfowl-hunting videos when perhaps no one else was. No one had really tried it with ducks, and I was certain we could do it better than anyone else. I rented camera equipment from a company in Dallas and hired Gary Stephenson, a science teacher at Ouachita Christian School, to film our first video. As with our duck calls, not a lot of other people believed my videos would be a success. In fact, Jase told me he was absolutely certain no one would watch them! *Duckmen 1: Duckmen of Louisiana* was released in 1988 and sold about one hundred copies. I set out to film *Duckmen 2: Point Blank,* which took us the next five seasons to produce. We didn't know anything about making movies, and I had no idea it would take us so long to make a second hunting video.

Jase told me he was absolutely certain no one would watch my videos!

But I knew it was only a matter of time until people started noticing our videos. They were fun to watch! *Duckmen* hunting tapes were unlike what anyone else was doing at the time. We were blowing ducks' heads off in slow motion and flipping deer in the swamp. The videos lasted about an hour each and were among the first to include rock music over hunting scenes. I have always been a big fan of classic rock. I loved Lynyrd Skynyrd, Led Zeppelin, Creedence Clearwater Revival, Pink Floyd, and Bob Seger. Lynyrd Skynyrd is definitely my favorite. If there's one rule at my house, it's that you never wake me while I'm napping. If you wake me before I'm ready, there's going to be heck to pay. One day, one of the members of Lynyrd Skynyrd called the Duck Commander office, wanting to talk to me. I was taking a nap at home, and the receptionist at the office was under strict orders not to wake me, so she took a message. I was so mad when I found out. I told everyone, "From this day forward, wake me up if the president of the United States or Lynyrd Skynyrd calls!"

I told everyone, "From this day forward, wake me up if the president of the United States or Lynyrd Skynyrd calls!"

More than anything else, the *Duckmen* videos put a face to our company. I had a long beard and so did most of the other original Duckmen—Mac Owen, Dane Jennings, and W. E. "Red Dawg" Phillips. Red Dawg was the first one to paint his face in the blind so the ducks wouldn't see him. He couldn't grow a long beard like the rest of us, so he figured he'd paint his face to look different. After a while, I figured out paint was the best way to camouflage our white faces from the ducks. Nothing stands out like a white surrender flag in a duck blind more than a white man's face! Now everyone in my blind is required to wear face paint. People grew to love our DVDs; I think there was a shock factor involved, and people wanted to see what the crazy Cajuns in Louisiana would do next! In 2012, we released *Resurrection: Duckmen 16*.

The hunting DVDs ended up being a lot like our duck calls—we didn't hit a home run in our first at bat, but we kept going back up to the plate. Eventually, the hunting DVDs caught on and became popular enough to help Willie land us a show on Outdoor Channel, which led to even bigger things with *Duck Dynasty* on A&E. Even though Duck Commander faced difficult times and what seemed liked insurmountable obstacles, we stayed the course and never gave up. I've always believed that if we did what was morally and ethically right, while continuing to steadfastly believe in what we were doing, we'd end up okay in the end. As long as we gave our best, continued to build products we believed in, and never strayed from God's purpose for us, I knew Duck Commander would find a way to persevere. It's what the Robertson family has always seemed to do.

REDNECK CAVIAR

Rule No. 11 for Living Happy, Happy, Happy
Suck the Head of a Crawfish
(You'll Want to Do It Again and Again)

After living more than six decades on Earth, I have reached the conclusion that ducks are the most protected species on the planet. In the United States of America, ducks are the most protected and overly regulated entity in history. It's amazing how many rules and regulations our government puts on duck hunters. (If you don't believe me, check with the U.S. Fish and Wildlife Service's website for all the up-to-date information.)

To even hunt ducks, I have to begin on a precise day at an exact minute, which is pretty difficult for a man who has never even owned a watch! I can't fire a shot until thirty minutes before the sun comes up, so I have to constantly look to see when the sun is going to rise and then deduct thirty minutes to determine when I can fire my first shot. Of course, the sunrise and sunset are constantly changing, depending on the rotation of Earth. But I always have to be aware of when the sun is going to come up because there might be a game warden sitting out there with a watch, waiting to write me an expensive ticket.

The U.S. government also dictates that I can have only three shells in my shotgun at once, not four or five, which would be a lot more efficient. I also have to have a precise kind of metal shot in my shells. It can't be lead; it has to be steel so it's not harmful to the ducks or the environment.

Where I live in eastern Louisiana, we are allowed to hunt ducks for sixty days each year. This past season, the first split of duck season started on November 17, 2012, and lasted sixteen days. After a two-week hiatus, duck hunting commenced again on December 15, 2012, and lasted forty-four days, until January 27. The government also tells me how many ducks I can kill—no more than six per day. But I also have to know what species of ducks I kill—I can't shoot more than four mallards, two pintails, three wood ducks, etc.—and I have to know the sex of the ducks whose lives I've ended. If I wing a duck—shoot it down and cripple it, but don't kill it—I have to make a reasonable attempt to find it or I'm in violation of federal law. I'm telling you: it's the rule book of all rule books when it comes to duck hunting. Unborn babies don't have as much protection in this country!

Here's the government's most silly rule: if I have a good day in the blind and want to give my buddy or a neighbor a few ducks to eat for dinner, I can't do it without documenting what I gave them. I have to write down my hunting license number, date of birth, legal name, physical address, and telephone number, and then specify how many ducks I'm giving them, what kind of ducks I'm giving them, and what sex of ducks I'm giving away. It's just one thing after the other when it comes to duck hunting.

Here's another dilemma: the law says I can kill six ducks per day for sixty days in the Mississippi Flyway. I was never very good in math, but I believe that comes out to three hundred and sixty ducks per season. But another federal law says I can only have a maximum of twelve ducks in my possession at once. Okay, let's see now, one law says if I start on opening day and kill six every day, I can shoot down three hundred and sixty ducks in a season. But the other law says I can't have more than twelve in my deep freezer, so the government apparently wants me to eat 'em as soon as I shoot 'em. Now, we like to eat duck more than most people, but the average duck weighs about one pound when it's dressed. The government expects me to eat three hundred sixty pounds of duck in sixty days? What am I supposed to do with the ducks that I can't eat? Feed them to my dogs?

If I'm ever elected president of the United States—and you never know—the first thing I'm going to do is downsize the Department of the Interior. I don't know of any politician who has ever said he would do that. I'd also make sure we have plenty of nesting ground for ducks, so I'd work with our friends in Canada, where most of the ducks are born. I'd take all the money we're sending to the Middle East, where we're trying to pay people to be our friends, and divert it to Canada and earmark it to help raise ducks. We don't need to be sending money to the Middle East; too many of those people are mean. The Canadians are already our friends, and Canada would be number one on my list for foreign aid. So when I'm elected president, we're going to lower taxes and make sure we give the Canadians truckloads of cash to raise mallard ducks. The American people are tired of pork-barrel spending; let's spend some money on ducks!

If I'm ever elected president of the United States—and you never know—the first thing I'm going to do is downsize the Department of the Interior.

The bottom line is the U.S. government doesn't have to be so strict about duck hunting. In my opinion, it only needs to educate people about what you can shoot and what you can't shoot. It's a great sport, but it would be even greater if there weren't so many rules and regulations.

Of course, I've always been of the opinion that I've been given permission from headquarters to shoot and kill whatever animals I want. According to Genesis, God instructed Noah to build an ark to save himself, his family, and a remnant of all the world's animals after God decided to destroy the world because of mankind's evil deeds. God instructed Noah to build the "ark of cypress wood; make rooms in it and coat it with pitch inside and out." God told Noah to "bring into the ark two of all living creatures, male and female, to keep them alive with you. Two of every kind of bird, of every kind of animal and of every kind of creature that moves along the ground will come to you to be kept alive."

After Noah did what God told him to do, the floodgates of the heavens opened on the seventeenth day of the second month, and rain fell for forty days and forty nights. The earth was flooded for one hundred and fifty days. As Genesis 7:23 tells us, "Every living thing on the face of the earth was wiped out; people and animals and the creatures that move along the ground and the birds were wiped from the earth. Only Noah was left, and those with him in the ark."

When the floodwaters finally receded, Noah and his family left the ark. According to Genesis 9:1–3: "Then God blessed Noah and his sons, saying to them, 'Be fruitful and increase in number and fill the earth. The fear and dread of you will fall on all the beasts of the earth, and on all the birds in the sky, on every creature that moves along the ground, and on all the fish in the sea; they are given into your hands. Everything that lives and moves about will be food for you. Just as I gave you the green plants, I now give you everything."

Now, I'm not a man of great intellectual depth, but it sounds to me like God Almighty has said we can pretty much rack and stack anything that swims, flies, or walks, which I consider orders from headquarters. I have permission from the Almighty to shoot whatever I want! Of course, I'll follow whatever rule or regulation the government puts in place. My days as an outlaw have long been over.

I really wonder if the U.S. government has any idea of the cost and work it takes to get ducks to fly to my land in the first place. At last count, we had fifty-four duck blinds on about eight hundred acres of our land. As Duck Commander grew and became more profitable through the years, Kay and I had a little bit of money to invest, and we decided to buy land. What I wanted was something I could feel, touch, and stand on—something tangible. When the stock market collapsed a few years ago, a lot of the young bucks came to me crying about all the money they lost on Wall Street. I never could figure it out. They said their money was in a brokerage account they could see on a computer, but then it was gone. Where did the money go? It didn't disappear. Someone had to take it. Where is it? That's why I invest in something tangible like land—no one can take it from me.

Our first purchase was a plot of forty acres in the wetlands near our house. We bought it, then added more land through the years, until we accumulated what we have now. Mac Owen, a longtime hunting companion of mine, who appears in many of the *Duckmen* videos, also wanted to get in on the investments. Together Mac and I bought surrounding land as it came up for sale—usually forty acres at a time.

Our investment has paid for itself many times over, primarily because the land we purchased was the most feasible and economical place for oil and gas companies to cross the Ouachita River with their pipelines. The fees we collected from the utility companies were more than triple what we paid for the land. I also bargained with the companies to ensure that the duck habitat would not be damaged. In the end, the pipelines were laid in a natural-looking curve. I think the plan may even have enhanced the area's appeal to ducks because I mow the pipeline right-of-way regularly, eliminating brush and encouraging more grass to grow.

We have planted, cultivated, and protected the grasses on our land primarily for ducks. Our wetlands are covered with native millets, sedges, and nut grass, as well as planted stands of Pennsylvania smartweed, American smartweed, and sprangletop, creating a mosaic of wild and cultivated plants. They are all prime foods for wildlife. The grasses are heavy producers of the seeds on which ducks thrive. Millet is one of the best foods available for ducks. In a good year, smartweed can produce more than five million seeds per acre. Ducks love them, and their craws are often found stuffed with the small black seeds. Sprangletop is another heavy seed producer; some of its seeds will remain edible for as long as seven years.

That the grasses also sustain crawfish is a bonus. Everything eats crawfish at every stage of a crawfish's life: fish, birds, raccoons, bullfrogs, snakes, turtles, large water beetles, and humans. Crawfish are a Louisiana delicacy, and we've harvested them to eat and sell. Crawfish are also an important ingredient in the swamp ecosystem, so I do everything I can to propagate them.

Crawfish are an important ingredient in the swamp ecosystem, so I do everything I can to propagate them.

Shortly after we bought the land in the wetlands, I observed all of the water leaving through one low drainage area on the edge of our land. The water dumped into a creek before emptying into the Ouachita River. To control the water depth on our land, I built a low levee across the area. I marked the highest level the water reached on trees, which allowed me to determine how high and long to make the levee. As I was building it, I installed a forty-eight-inch culvert through it at the lowest spot, and then put a weir, or gate, across it to control the water depth. I can adjust the water depth of the wetlands six inches at a time simply by adding or taking out a top board from the weir.

I regulate the flooding of my land in accordance with what crawfish require—which, coincidentally, meets the needs of migrating ducks as well. The crawfish normally hatch in October, when the rains return. They grow through the winter, reaching adulthood in March. Hopefully, enough rain will fall to refill the area. If the area isn't filled naturally, I use a big pump to draw water from the river. Normally, I have to do some pumping to ensure that most of my land is covered with water to a depth of twelve to eighteen inches—ideal for both the crawfish and duck populations. The depth is determined by how far a duck can stretch its neck to feed when it bobs underwater. After duck season is over, I drain the land to promote the growth of grasses and trees.

After we purchased the wetlands, a Louisiana Fish and Wildlife Department survey showed that 65 percent of the timber in the area was bitter pecan trees, which can grow as tall as one hundred feet. The wood is not as desirable as hickory or regular pecan, but it is resilient and is used to make such things as axe and hammer handles. The worst thing about bitter pecan trees is that they drop pignuts, which taste so bad that most wildlife won't eat them. I set out to eliminate the bitter pecan trees and replace them with oak trees that would produce more palatable fare for a wider variety of wildlife—including both squirrels and deer, which love acorns.

It turned out to be a formidable task. After the bitter pecan trees were cut and sold, the following year suckers began to sprout from all the stumps. Left alone, multiple tree trunks would grow from the stumps, and the area would be reforested with bitter pecan trees, thicker than before. So I got a lawn trimmer, the kind with a blade, and went from stump to stump, one at a time, and mangled off all the sprouts. Then I treated the stumps with poison to finish killing them off. It took me three years to clear them all.

Then I was thinking about how to get the area seeded with oaks. I had planted and seeded many oaks and cypress trees but was still working on it when the Almighty stepped in and flooded everything in the area in 1991. The water picked up acorns and deposited them over all the area I'd cleared. When spring came, there were thousands and thousands of oaks of all kinds, sprouting every foot or so. It was a blessing from above, and while the flood destroyed the home where Pa and Granny were living and its water rose to the front steps of our house, the floodwaters provided us the now heavily wooded areas where we hunt today.

About 90 percent of your success in duck hunting is determined by the location of your duck blind, and we've made major improvements to water conditions, soil conditions, and how natural feed gets to the holes we're hunting. I've kept detailed records of every one of the hunts on our land for more than two decades, including specifics about weather, wind direction, types of ducks we saw, and the position of the sun. It's amazing to look back and see how much better the hunting has been over the last few years after the improvements were made.

For instance, on opening day of the 1995 duck season, we hunted Dog Bayou, a blind on my land, and we killed one mallard, seven teals, and one ring-necked. A few days later, we hunted the Dog Bayou and didn't even fire our guns. Good night; we stayed until two o'clock in the afternoon and didn't kill a duck! During the 1995 season, we killed 266 ducks in 60 days. Now we try to average twenty ducks per day between four or five of us in the blinds. During the first split in 2012, we killed more than two hundred ducks in the first ten days. We've gone from two hundred ducks in 1995 to more than one thousand ducks now.

I've kept detailed records of every one of the hunts on our land for more than two decades.

The crazy part is we can make as many improvements as we want to our duck blinds, but they'll never be as good as the ancestral holes. Some of the land next to mine used to be a swamp, but the owners leveled it in the 1960s and turned it into rice fields. Some guys got in a duck blind over there and noticed that ducks kept flying to one particular spot on the field. They asked the farmer why ducks were sitting there, and he told them it's where a lake used to be. The trees and the water are gone, but the ducks are still flying there because it was where the lake once was. It's in their genetic makeup to fly there.

It's one of the phenomena of Mother Nature that can't be explained through science. There are a lot of them, and the only explanation I can come up with is that God is in charge and has a blueprint for how everything works. Take, for instance, the Arctic tern, a medium-sized bird, which is famous for flying from its Arctic breeding grounds to Antarctica and back every year, covering more than 43,000 miles round-trip. The terns travel down the coast of Brazil or Africa to get to their wintering ground every year. Some evolutionists want us to believe that the reason they fly to Antarctica every year is because once upon a time one tern found its way there, told some terns about it, and then they all started going there. Makes a lot of sense, doesn't it?

I, for one, believe the terns were born knowing they had to fly to Antarctica every winter to survive. To prove the point, researchers once robbed a tern's nest and raised the little birds away from their mother. Then they banded them when they were old enough to fly. The terns had never seen Antarctica and had never been around another tern to tell them to fly there. So when it was time for the terns to fly south, the researchers flew over the Arctic Ocean and dropped them from an airplane. The terns made one circle and then flew south, arriving in Antarctica a few weeks later.

Why would they do that? Because there were about twenty different life forms that relied on the terns to survive. The Arctic fox couldn't survive without its eggs, and certain plants and worms couldn't live without its droppings. Hawks couldn't survive without feeding on the birds. The terns were part of the food cycle in both the Arctic Ocean and Antarctica.

The ducks that fly south from Canada each year and winter throughout Florida, Louisiana, Texas, parts of Central America, and beyond are the same way. Everything from alligators to snapping turtles to skunks rob ducks' nests and eat their eggs. Foxes, coyotes, and birds of prey eat their babies when they're young. Humans hunt ducks, too, and they put meat on our tables. It's the Almighty sending literally millions and millions of pounds of protein from one end of a continent to the other end, feeding all of these things along the way.

The Almighty sends literally millions and millions of pounds of protein from one end of a continent to the other end, feeding all of these things along the way.

It's like the mayfly on the river. A mayfly starts out as a larva in the water and looks like nothing more than a little maggot. When the water level rises, the larvae crawl up the trees on the riverbank. They build cocoons that look like spiderwebs and then emerge as flying creatures. You see mayflies flying all over the river and they live only long enough to drop their eggs into the water. Why? Because when they die and fall into the water, fish come up and eat them. Mayflies are fish food! It's a cycle: mayflies drop their eggs and then they die, fish eat them, the larvae climb up the trees, and then it starts all over again. Who's feeding the fish? The Almighty is feeding the fish.

God is feeding everything, including you and me, and a lot of us in His ecosystem eat us some crawfish.

PRODIGAL SONS

Rule No. 12 for Living Happy, Happy, Happy
Learn to Forgive (Life's a Lot Easier That Way)

The good Lord blessed Kay and me with four healthy, obedient sons, each of whom grew up to become a godly man who loves his wife and children and shares God's Word through his work with Duck Commander and in our church. But I'm not sure I needed to see how they came into this world! A few weeks before our youngest son, Jeptha, was born in 1978, Kay informed me she wanted me at the hospital to witness his birth.

Now, I didn't want to be in the delivery room when Jep was born. When our oldest son, Alan, was born, I wasn't there and he turned out fine. I wasn't there when Jase came, but everything still turned out okay. When Willie came next, I didn't want to press our luck, so I didn't go to the hospital again (in fact, I was fishing when he was born). But when Kay became pregnant with

Jep, she told me it was the last baby we were going to have, so she wanted me beside her to witness God's greatest miracle. Women being the strange creatures they are, Kay decided she needed a coach for the birth of her last child, and she insisted that I was the one to do it.

When the day arrived for Jep's birth, Kay decided she was going to deliver him without an epidural or any kind of medication. I knew then that I had a tough woman! Over the next several hours, I watched my wife thrashing around and gritting her teeth, and then I saw Jep's head emerge from my wife's loins. Let me tell you something: I salute womanhood worldwide, because women are exceptionally tough for enduring the misery of childbirth. I've cleaned hogs and gutted deer, but in my experience on Earth I've never witnessed such a brutal event.

I knew right then that my sex life was over—although I somehow managed to get over my concerns thirty days later! Let me put it to you this way: after going through it once, I'd never go back and do it again. It was rough to watch, so I can't imagine having to experience the pain. If men were in charge of carrying and birthing our babies, we'd have a lot fewer people on Earth, because we'd only do it once—I can promise you that!

Each of our boys was a blessing, and after I repented and had my life in order again, I set out to give them the same sort of childhood I had as a boy, learning to hunt and fish and live off the land. Alan, Jase, and Willie were very close when they were growing up, and then they kind of took Jep under their wings after he was born because there was such an age gap between them. My philosophy on discipline was very simple. Since rules are made to be broken, I kept the rules few and far between. However, there was a code in the Robertson house: three licks was the standard punishment. It wasn't ten licks or twenty licks for doing something wrong; it was always three: thump, thump, thump! It was a principle, and my boys always knew what their punishment would be if they stepped out of line.

They received three licks if they disrespected their mother. As it says in Ephesians 6:1–3, "Children, obey your parents in the Lord, for this is right. 'Honor your father and mother'—which is the first commandment with a promise—'so that it may go well with you and that you may enjoy long life on the earth.' " I never had to tell my boys not to disrespect me; that rule was understood and it never crossed their minds to break it. None of my sons ever disrespected me, not even once. Nobody ever bowed up and told me I wasn't going to tell them what to do.

There was literally flawless obedience when they were living under my roof—at least when I was home. If I told them to go to bed, they jumped up and went to bed. If I told them to rake the leaves, they raked the leaves. If I told them to clean the fish, they cleaned the fish. People would come over to visit us and were amazed at how obedient our sons were. Their teachers always told us our boys were among the most well-behaved students in school. I believe it's because my boys were always aware of the consequences of not doing what they were told to do. They always respected me, and they respected their mother because I didn't want them taking advantage of the woman who put them on Earth.

I also didn't allow my sons to fight with each other. They could argue and disagree all they wanted—and Jase and Willie managed to do it regularly. I didn't have a problem with them raising their voices at each other to make a point. I wanted to encourage them to argue and make a case for their beliefs. But if it came to blows and there was meat popping, they were getting three licks each. I didn't care who threw the first punch. If it ever came to physical blows, I'd step in and everybody involved got three licks.

Another thing I didn't allow was tearing up good hunting and fishing equipment. I wanted them to respect someone else's property and to be thankful for what we had, even if it wasn't much. If one of the boys borrowed one of my guns or fishing poles and tore it up while they were using it, they received three licks. I always wanted my boys to have access to my guns to hunt, just like I had access to Pa's guns when I was growing up. When I was young, I knew if I broke a gun, we probably weren't going to eat that night because we were so dependent on wild game for food. But since my boys knew there was going to be a meal on the table every night, they weren't always as respectful of my equipment. When Alan was about fourteen, he and a few of his buddies borrowed all of my Browning shotguns to go bird-hunting. They were hunting on a muddy track and because they were careless and immature, mud got into a few of the shotgun barrels. They were very fortunate the guns still fired and didn't blow up in their faces! When Alan returned home, he was so scared to tell me what happened to my Browning shotguns—my Holy Grails—that he enlisted Kay's help to break the news. I'm sure Alan thought I was going to beat him on the spot, but I simply told him to go outside. I was afraid to whip him right then because I was so angry. After cooling off, I pulled Alan and his buddies together and gave them a stern lecture about gun safety and respecting other people's property. I also told Alan—after I gave him three licks—that he was on probation from using my guns for a long time.

There was another time when I discovered that one of my boat paddles was broken. None of my boys would fess up to doing it, so I gave each of them three licks. It was kind of a military-style group punishment. It turned out that one of their buddies actually broke it, but he didn't confess to the crime until several years later. I'm sure he realized that if he'd confessed when the boys were younger, they all would have whipped him!

As hard as Kay and I worked to instill morals, principles, and a belief in what's right and wrong in each of our sons, it wasn't always easy. People might watch *Duck Dynasty* and sometimes think we're the perfect family. They see how much we love and respect each other. But the reality is that it wasn't always easy. We had our trials and tribulations like every other family out there, and there were actually times when Kay and I believed we would lose more than one of our sons. They were the scariest times of our lives.

As hard as Kay and I worked to instill morals, principles, and a belief in what's right and wrong in each of our sons, it wasn't always easy.

Alan, our oldest son, probably had the roughest childhood because he was the oldest boy when I was having all of my problems. Kay was essentially a single mother for a long time, so Alan was given a lot of responsibility when he was only a young boy. When Kay started working at Howard Brothers Discount Stores, Alan was only seven but was left at home to care for Jase and Willie. Alan had to grow up really fast and didn't get to enjoy his childhood or play baseball and other sports like his brothers did, at least not until I turned my life around. Alan also attended four or five different schools because we moved around so much, which I'm sure wasn't very easy for him either.

Alan was a very popular kid in high school, and before long he was hanging out with the wrong crowd. I can remember one time when he and some buddies were camping at a spot down the road from our house. They were drinking beer and did some foolish things, like knocking down mailboxes along the road. Some neighbors came to our house the next morning to complain about it, and I jumped in my truck to find them. I brought Alan and his buddies back to our house and lined them up against my truck. I gave each of them three licks. There was one boy I didn't even recognize, but I told him if he ever wanted to come back to the Robertson house, he was getting three licks like the rest of them!

After Alan graduated from high school, his behavior was so wild and out of control that Kay and I didn't want him around his younger brothers anymore. He was the oldest boy and his brothers looked up to him, but he wasn't setting much of an example for them. So we threw Alan out of our house, which certainly wasn't an easy thing to do. My sister Judy was living in New Orleans at the time, and Alan moved there to live with her. You want to talk about going from the frying pan to the fire!

Alan lived in New Orleans for about two years, and he started dating a woman. She told Alan she was divorced, but she was really only separated from her husband. The husband followed Alan home from work one day and beat him really bad with an iron tire tool. When a policeman showed up at the scene and talked to Alan, he could sense there was something different about him.

"Son, where are you from?" the policeman asked Alan.

"West Monroe, Louisiana," Alan told him.

"I don't know what went wrong in your life and how you ended up here, but go back to wherever you're living. Pack up everything you've got, and go back to your mom and dad. I can tell you're a good boy and just got off track."

Alan told me he looked up at the police officer, as the sun was shining behind him, and he looked like an angel. Alan believed the police officer was sent by God to help him turn his life around.

Alan came home and we greeted him with open arms. We cooked a big meal and celebrated his homecoming. It was like the Parable of the Lost Son in the Bible. In Luke 15:11–24, Jesus tells us that there was a wealthy man with two sons. When the younger son asked for his share of the estate, the man divided his property between his two sons. Before too long, the younger son left for a foreign country and squandered his wealth through unrighteous living. Then a severe famine wiped out everything, leaving the younger son homeless and hungry. After briefly working as a swine herder, the boy repented and returned home to his father:

> *While he was still a long way off, his father saw him and was filled with compassion for him; he ran to his son, threw his arms around him and kissed him. The son said to him, "Father, I have sinned against heaven and against you. I am no longer worthy to be called your son." But the father said to his servants, "Quick! Bring the best robe and put it on him. Put a ring on his finger and sandals on his feet. Bring the fattened calf and kill it. Let's have a feast and celebrate. For this son of mine was dead and is alive again; he was lost and is found."*

The incident in New Orleans helped Alan turn his life around. He worked for Duck Commander for a few years, then attended seminary and worked as a pastor at White's Ferry Road Church in 1988, eventually becoming a senior pastor there. While Alan is still heavily involved in the church and often preaches on Sunday, he rejoined the family business in 2012. He helps maintain our schedules and travels with me to speaking engagements and other appearances around the country. Alan has a calming effect on everyone around him, and he's really good at defusing situations. He's the one who rides herd around his brothers and is the voice of reason and wisdom among them. Alan and his wife, Lisa, have two daughters. His oldest daughter, Anna, has been working with Duck Commander since high school. Her husband, Jay, who was a teacher and coach at a high school, started working with us building duck calls during the summer, but now he's with us full-time.

Unfortunately, we also had to go through some of the same struggles with Jep as he grew older. When Jep was in high school, he was the only boy living at home because his brothers were married and living on their own. The older boys like to say Jep had it a lot easier than they did growing up. I was still pretty strict on the boy, but our business was doing a lot better, so he probably had a few more luxuries than the older boys did.

I'll never forget one night Jep was coming home late and got his truck stuck in a muddy road close to where we live. It was in the late 1990s, so Jep had one of the early cell phones in a bag in his truck. It was after midnight, and he called home and Kay woke me up to get Jep out of the mud. I had a Jeep that I bought brand-new in 1974, but it was pretty old by then, and the lights didn't work anymore. I usually only drove the Jeep to my duck hole and back. So I had Kay follow me in her car to provide lights for me to see. It was still raining pretty heavily when we got to the field where Jep's truck was stuck. I jumped out of my Jeep to winch his truck out, but then Kay pulled up right next to me, not realizing she'd driven into the soft mud! Now Jep was stuck in front of me, and Kay was stuck behind me. "I am surrounded by idiots!" I screamed.

Jep went all the way through middle school without having any problems, and then we sent him to Ouachita Christian School, which was pretty expensive. We figured if he went to high school there, he wouldn't get into any wild stuff. But with only four or five months of high school left, Jep broke up with his girlfriend. And then he started sailing backward. I couldn't believe it and didn't want to believe it, to be honest. He moved into an apartment in West Monroe with his cousin, who was attending college at the University of Louisiana–Monroe. Just like Alan, Jep started drinking, cutting up, and using drugs. We knew Jep was drinking because we could smell alcohol on his breath at church on Sunday if he'd been out drinking the night before. Kay would always ask me, "What's that smell?" I'd tell her, "That's whiskey on Jep's breath."

Just like Alan, Jep started drinking, cutting up, and using drugs.

Willie was actually the one who brought the seriousness of Jep's problems to our attention. Willie was working with the high school youth group at White's Ferry Road Church, and he found out Jep had asked one of the kids to go to a bar with him. Willie came to our house and said, "I'm done. We've got to do something right now. I'm just tired of it." We called Alan and decided to have a family intervention. Alan lined everything up, and we were all waiting for Jep when he came to the house one night. Kay was terrified because she was certain I was going to throw Jep out of the house, like I'd done with Alan.

I told Jep, "Give me the keys to your truck—the one I'm

paying for." He pulled the keys out of his pocket and handed them to me. I told Jep what his brothers had told me about his behavior.

"Son, you know what we stand for," I told him. "We're all trying to live for God. We're not going to let you visit our home while you're carrying on like this. We're paying for your apartment. We're paying for your truck. You've got a decision to make. You're either going to come home and basically live under house arrest because we don't trust you, or you can hit the road—with no vehicle, of course. Somebody can drop you off at the highway and then you'll be on your own. You can go live your life; we'll pray for you and hope that you come back one day. Those are your two choices."

Jep looked at me, lowered his head, and started pouring out his sins to me. He said he'd been taking pills, smoking marijuana, getting drunk, and on and on. He was crying the whole time, as he confessed his sins to us and God.

I'll never forget what Jep said next. He looked up at me and asked, "Dad, all I want to ask you is what took you so long to rescue me?"

After Jep said that to me, everyone in the room was crying.

"You still have a choice," I told him.

"Well, my choice is I want to come home," he said.

Jase has always been our most straitlaced son, so he was the hardest on Jep when he strayed.

"Son, you can't hang out with those people," Jase told him.

"Daddy won't let 'em get to me," Jep said.

"Daddy won't and we won't, either," Jase promised him. "But you have to come to all the good things to help you. You've got to find better friends. You can't be running around. You have to break it off with the bad influences."

Thankfully, our second prodigal son was coming home. It was a heart-wrenching episode for all of us. Alan was so distressed by his little brother's struggles that he left our house, drove down the road, and then stopped and dropped to his knees and wept in a field.

Alan was so distressed by his little brother's struggles that he left our house, drove down the road, and then stopped and dropped to his knees and wept in a field.

Like Alan, Jep turned his life around after overcoming the struggles of alcohol and drugs. He came to work for Duck Commander and found his niche as a videographer. He films the footage for our Duckmen videos and works with Willie on the Buck Commander videos. Jep is with us on nearly every hunt, filming the action from a distance. He knows exactly what we're looking for in the videos and films it, downloads it, edits it, and sends it to the duplicator, who produces and distributes our DVDs.

Having worked with the crew of *Duck Dynasty* over the last few years, I've noticed that most people who work in the film industry are a little bit weird. And Jep, my youngest son, is a little strange. It's his personality—he's easygoing, likable, and a lot more reserved than his brothers. But he's the only one who will come up to me and give me a bear hug. He'll just walk up and say, "Daddy, I need a hug." The good news for Jep is that as far as the Duck Commander crowd goes, one thing is for sure: weirdos are in! We covet weirdos; they can do things we can't because they're so strange. You have to have two or three weirdos in your company to make it work. It's truly been a blessing to watch Jep grow and mature and become a loving husband and father. He and his wife, Jessica, have four beautiful children.

Like I said earlier, Jase was the only one of our four sons who stayed the course and never deviated to the right or left. He always looked straight ahead; he never drank, never cursed, and always lived his life the way God wanted him to live. I think one of the reasons Jase and Willie never strayed too far is because they were so involved in the youth group at White's Ferry Road Church. Willie's only problem was that he believed he was a ladies' man until he met Korie. He was always jumping from one girl to the next until he settled down. It really made an impact on both of them. Jase was always looking out for his brothers. Even though Jase and Willie were very competitive growing up, Jase always had Willie's best interests at heart. One time, Willie and Jase were at a friend's house in high school. Jase walked into the basement and found Willie playing strip poker with some other kids.

"What are you doing?" Jase asked him.

"Playing strip poker," Willie replied.

"You've stripped enough," Jase told him. "Let's go."

The thing I really like about Jase is that he's as obsessed with ducks as I am. I rarely took my boys hunting with me when they were very young. In fact, I never took them when I was still an outlaw. "Not this time, boys, we might be running from the game warden," I'd tell them. But after I repented and came to Jesus Christ, I started taking my sons hunting with me, beginning with Alan. Before we moved to where we live now, it was a pretty long haul from town to the Ouachita River bottoms. Alan got carsick nearly every time I took him hunting, but he didn't think I knew. We stopped at the same gas station every time, and he'd walk around back and lose his breakfast before he climbed back into the truck. I was proud of him for never complaining.

I took Jase hunting for the first time when he was five. He was shooting Pa's heavy Belgium-made Browning twelve-gauge shotgun, which he could barely even hold up. It kicked like a mule! The first time Jase shot the gun, it kicked him to the back of the blind and flipped him over a bench.

"Did I get him?" Jase asked.

I knew right then that I had another hunter in the family, and Jase is still the most skilled hunter of all my boys. I trained Jase to take over the company by teaching him the nuances of duck calls and fowl hunting, and he is still the person in charge of making sure every duck call sounds like a duck. Not only did Jase design the first gadwall drake call to hit the market, he also invented the first triple-reed duck caller. Jase and I live to hunt ducks. We track ducks during the season through a nationwide network of hunters, asking how many ducks are in their areas and what movements are expected. Then we check conditions of wind and weather fronts that might influence duck movement. We talk it all over during the day and again each morning, before the day's hunt, as we prepare to leave for the blind.

When Kay and I began to ponder becoming less active in the Duck Commander business, we offered its management to Jase, who had been most deeply involved in the company. But he had no desire to get into management. Jase likes building duck calls and doesn't really enjoy the business aspects of the company, like making sales calls or dealing with clients and sponsors. Like me, Jase is most comfortable when he's in a duck blind and doesn't care for the details that come with running a company. Jase only wants to build duck calls, shoot ducks, and spend time with his family (he and his wife, Missy, have three kids).

So then we offered the company's management to Willie, who seemed to have the most business sense among our sons. I knew from the time Willie was only a little boy that he could sell beachfront property in Iowa if he put his mind to it. When I was a commercial fisherman, Willie sold fish on the side of the road with Kay or me. Willie can still quote some of the sales pitches: "Yes, sir, these are golden buffalo, the pride of the Ouachita River." Willie was even selling carp, a worthless fish you couldn't sell at the fish market, but he was able to unload quite a few of them with his salesmanship and charm. Willie always said if you can sell fish, you can sell anything. He sold candy from his locker while he was in elementary school and sold worms from an old wooden boat on our river dock. The boy always knew how to make a dollar.

Willie attended college at Harding University in Searcy, Arkansas, and then finished up at Louisiana-Monroe. He gained some management experience from working at Camp Ch-Yo-Ca, a Christian youth summer camp, where he met his wife, Korie, whose family owned the camp. They were married shortly after Korie left for college and now have four children.

Willie, at age thirty, agreed to take over Duck Commander.

For the first few months, he cleaned the yard around my house and did other odd jobs while he learned the business. Before too long, Willie convinced me he was capable of doing a lot more. He became involved in the business side of the company, expanding our Internet operations (Korie's dad, Johnny Howard, was selling our merchandise through a catalog and online before she and Willie bought the operation) while also landing us new sponsors and endorsement deals. Willie also landed the company its TV deals with Outdoor Channel and then A&E, which really put Duck Commander in the fast lane.

In 2005, Kay and I sold majority interest of Duck Commander to Korie and Willie, and Willie became the company's CEO. I have to admit he took Duck Commander way past anything I could have done with it. They purchased a thirty-thousand-square-foot warehouse in West Monroe, which was previously the storage space of Howard Books, which Korie's family also owned. They moved Duck Commander's operations from my house to the warehouse. They also simplified and computerized the company's bookkeeping and accounting, which Kay had handled for years, and made it more efficient.

Willie also gets credit for making flowing, untrimmed beards the standard appearance for Duck Commander employees. In a lot of ways, he became the new face of the company. I couldn't be prouder of him. He's taken the company where I never thought it could go. He's a great businessman, and he's a heck of a hard worker. He's a visionary, and he had a vision for what Duck Commander could be. I call him Donald Trump II because he's a deal-maker and knows how to network in the hunting industry.

With Willie in charge, it was easy for me to walk away from Duck Commander. When Willie and Korie took over the company, I told them, "Y'all take care of the company and send me my check every month. As long as the checks keep coming, I'll know y'all are doing well. I'll stay in the woods, and as long as a check comes in the mailbox every month, you won't hear anything from me." I don't go to the Duck Commander warehouse very much anymore. I'm not often up there sticking my nose into their business. A lot of old guys who start businesses and then turn them over to their children want to hang around and can't let them go. Not me. When I told them to take it over and run with it, I meant it and have left them alone.

Willie also gets credit for making flowing, untrimmed beards the standard appearance for Duck Commander employees.

The thing that has probably pleased me the most about Duck Commander since Willie took over is that it's still a family business, just like when I started the company. Heck, you basically have to have Robertson blood in your veins to get a job there! Jase, Jep, Willie, and Si are still very involved in the day-to-day operations of Duck Commander, and now Alan is back in the fold, too. Now all of my boys have come home to where it started.

Through all of our trials and tribulations, Kay and I have realized that raising a family is about love and forgiveness. Our boys weren't perfect growing up, but they always had an anchor—our faith in Jesus Christ—and that helped us get through our struggles. As it says in Proverbs 22:6 (KJV): "Train up a child in the way he should go: and when he is old he will not depart from it." My boys might have strayed from God's path for them at times, but they always had their faith to fall back on. If you don't have faith, there's nowhere to turn. My boys always knew where to go when they ran into trouble.

RIVER RATS

Rule No. 13 for Living Happy, Happy, Happy
Share God's Word (It's What He Asks of You)

For the first twenty-eight years of my life, I didn't know the gospel and I didn't know Jesus Christ. Now I'm trying to make up for lost time. Jesus said all the authority was given to Him, and He told us to go preach the gospel and make disciples of all the people we baptize. Basically, Jesus is telling me to go forward and share with people what I didn't know until I was saved. So I've been sharing everything I've learned since I was converted. Nowadays, I get asked to speak to churches, colleges, hunting clubs, and other groups around the country. The Almighty has put me on the road, but some of my best work still occurs on the Ouachita River right in front of our house.

When I was still a commercial fisherman, I sometimes had over one hundred hoop nets and trotlines stretching all the way across the Ouachita River. But these pirates on the river kept stealing my fish. Now, people have been shot in Louisiana for taking fish out of someone else's nets or off their trotlines—which might make sense when you realize someone's livelihood is being stolen.

When I saw people stealing my fish, I'd run them down with my shotgun and scare the daylights out of them. It didn't do much good, though, and they kept stealing from me. But I kept scaring them, and I was making enemies up and down the river. People were probably saying, "That ol' sucker down there is about as mean as a junkyard dog."

I kept reading and studying my Bible, while the stealing continued unabated. I read Romans 12:17–21, where it says:

> *Do not repay anyone evil for evil. Be careful to do what is right in the eyes of everyone. If it is possible, as far as it depends on you, live at peace with everyone. Do not take revenge, my dear friends, but leave room for God's wrath, for it is written: "It is mine to avenge; I will repay," says the Lord. On the contrary:*
>
> *"If your enemy is hungry; feed him;*
> *if he is thirsty, give him something to drink.*
> *In doing this, you will heap burning coals on his head."*
>
> *Do not be overcome with evil, but overcome evil with good.*

I read the verse and sat there thinking, *There ain't no way that's going to work. No way! Be good to them. But, Lord, they're stealing from me!* But then I had a revelation: *Hey, wait a minute! I've never tried that. I keep running them off with a shotgun.*

It honestly made no sense to me, but I was going to try the Lord's way. So I decided the next time I saw someone lifting one of my nets, I would initiate the biblical way of dealing with them. I was going to be good to them. Sure enough, I walked out one day and heard a motor running. I looked and saw some guys pulling up one of my nets. I stood there and watched them for a few minutes. My boat was parked right on the riverbank, and I took off running and jumped in it. I had my shotgun with me. I was going to try God's way, but my faith was still a little weak, so I had my shotgun as insurance! I was going to try to be good to them, but if they wanted to get mean, I was going to have to survive.

It honestly made no sense to me, but I was going to try the Lord's way.

So I ran out on the river, and these guys were still coming up with my nets. I cruised right up on 'em. They saw me coming, dropped the net, and threw the float back into the water—and started fishing.

"Hey! What are y'all doing?" I shouted.

"We're just trying to catch a few fish," one of them told me.

"What were you doing with that net in your hand?" I asked him.

"Well, you know," he said as he started to stutter and mumble. "What is that? Is that what that is?"

"Is that what that is?" I repeated. "Y'all know what's on the other end of that float!"

Then I changed my tactics. In a cheerful and exuberant voice, I shouted, "Good times have come your way!"

They looked at me, wondering exactly what I was up to. I still had my hand on my Browning A5 shotgun.

"What?" one of them asked.

"Good times have come your way," I said again. "I'm going to give 'em to you. You were going to steal my fish. Evidently, you've planned a fish fry, but y'all aren't catching any. But you want a fish fry. Since you didn't catch 'em, you're going to steal 'em. Well, here's the good news: I'm going to give you what you were trying to steal—free of charge."

"Nah, we were just going to—" one of them started to say, but I cut him off.

"Nope, you want a fish fry," I said. "We're going to have us a fish fry. How many people you got coming?"

I reached over and grabbed the rope on the net and told them to keep their boat right there. "Let's see what y'all were fixing to catch," I said.

I raised my net up and looked in it.

"Whoo! Y'all would have done pretty good," I said.

By then I'm sure they figured I was certifiably nuts.

"I've got a lot of fish in here," I said. "Get your boat over here."

They started paddling and were watching me, probably to make sure I wasn't going to shoot them. I dumped the fish from my net into my boat and told them to bring their boat closer. I began throwing even more fish into their boat.

"What about this big white perch here?" I asked them. "I'm probably supposed to throw him back. What do y'all think?"

"Nah, we'll keep 'im," one of them said.

The fish kept hitting the bottom of the men's boat, and they kept watching me throw them over. Finally one of them protested mildly, saying, "I think that's probably enough."

"Look, you start frying fish, and kinfolk will start showing up who haven't been around in months," I told them. "Let's make sure you have enough."

So I threw all of my fish into their boat.

"Now! Y'all got plenty," I said.

"Yes, sir, that's plenty," one of them replied.

"Now, here's the deal," I told them. "Why steal something if you can get it for free?"

"Man, look, we're sorry," one of them said.

"I understand," I said. "Look, I live right over there. From now on, just come up there if you aren't catching anything. I'll give y'all the fish. That way, you won't have to steal. You'll get your fish. You're happy. Everybody's happy, happy, happy."

I let the net back down into the river and said, "Good to see y'all."

The men pulled away in their boat and started motoring down the river. They had plenty of fish. They were looking back at me, probably thinking, *Is this guy for real?* Maybe they remembered I had a shotgun and were about half-scared, but I never saw them again.

After that episode, everyone quit stealing from me. Every time I saw someone eyeing my nets, I'd offer 'em free fish. I was giving away less fish than what was previously being stolen from me.

I reread the texts from Romans 12 and thought, *You know what? I get it.* What the Almighty is saying is that no matter how sorry and low-down somebody might be, everybody's worth something. But you're never going to turn them if you're as evil as they are. If you're good to them, you might appeal to their conscience—if they have any conscience. Now, there are some people who might be so mean you probably can't be good to them. But most people are perplexed after someone is good to them when he should have been mean. Most of the time, they end up giving up their evil ways.

The Almighty was right—as He always is. The incident on

the river had a profound impact on me. From that point forward, I wanted to help others, whether it was by sharing the gospel and baptizing them, giving them fish, or assisting them in any way possible. Over the past twenty years, my sons and I have literally led thousands of people to Jesus Christ. Alan, Jase, and Willie are ordained ministers and attended seminary at White's Ferry Road Church. Often, after one of us speaks at a church or somewhere else, as many as one hundred people will come forward, expressing their desires to become Christians. Many visitors to my house walk down the hill with us to be baptized at the boat launch—sometimes even at night, with car headlights illuminating the scene.

> **What the Almighty is saying is that no matter how sorry and low-down somebody might be, everybody's worth something.**

One of the first opportunities I had to speak to a large crowd was at the Louisiana Superdome in New Orleans in the early 1990s. I was invited to speak and demonstrate duck calls during a hunting and fishing show. I had a crowd of about one thousand people listening to me, and I blew my calls and gave them some hunting tips. Then I reached into my bag and pulled out a Bible. I told them, "Folks, while I'm here, I think I'm gonna preach you a little sermon." I thought I owed it to them to share the gospel.

"I'm standing under a sign that says, 'Budweiser is the king of beers,' and everybody's got their beers here today," I told them. "But I'm here to talk about the King of Kings. I know I might look like a preacher, but I'm not. Here's how you can tell whether someone's a preacher or not: if he gets up and says some words and passes a hat for you to put money in, that's a preacher. This is free. This is free of charge, which proves I'm not a preacher."

I preached for about forty-five minutes, and afterward several men came up and thanked me for sharing my story. A few of them even invited me to preach at their churches, so that's kind of how my road show started. I like to think of myself as a guerilla fighter for Jesus. Because of the success of *Duck Dynasty,* I'm getting more opportunities to speak to larger audiences now. But I don't care if I'm talking to one person or one thousand; if I can help save one lost soul and bring him back to Jesus, it's well worth it to me.

The good Lord leads us to lost souls in many different ways. We meet some of them at our speaking engagements, others at church, and some simply stop by the house. I'll never forget the time when someone called my house to order duck calls, back when Duck Commander was still being run out of our living room. The man kept using the Lord's name in vain during his conversation with me.

"Let me ask you something," I told him. "Why would you keep cursing the only one who can save you from death?"

There was silence on the other end.

"You got my order?" the man asked.

"Yeah, I got your order," I told him.

Click. He hung up the phone. A few minutes later, the phone rang again.

"Mr. Robertson, I've never thought about what you said," the guy told me.

"Well, you ought to," I told him. "Let me ask you something: Where are you from?"

"Alabama," he said.

"You're about ten hours away," I said. "You ought to load up and head this way. I'll tell you a story about the one you've been cursing."

About a week later, there was a knock on the front door. This young buck stepped in the house and asked, "You know who I am?"

"I don't reckon I do," I told him.

"I'm that fella from Alabama who was cursing God," he said.

The man had a buddy with him, and I told them the story of Jesus Christ. By the time I was finished, they were on the floor crying like babies. I took them down to the river and baptized both of them that night.

I remember another time when I gave a duck-call demonstration at a sporting goods store. True to my homage to the Almighty, I blew on some duck calls and then preached from the Bible. When I was finished, I concluded with what I always tell my audience: "Where else can you go on a Friday evening in America and get first-rate duck-call instruction and a gospel sermon at the same time?"

Well, about five years later, a guy who was there wrote me a four-page letter. He said he went to the sporting goods store to listen to a duck-call guru because he wanted to become a better duck hunter. However, he wasn't prepared to listen to what I had to say about the Bible, about how we're all sinners and we're all going to die. He thought I'd taken advantage of him. When the man went home, he burned every one of my duck calls and for the next several years told anyone who would listen to him that I was the sorriest, most low-down man he'd ever met.

He shared that story on the first two pages of the letter he sent me, but I didn't hold it against him and kept on reading. On the third page, he told me he woke up one morning and realized he couldn't get what he'd heard out of his mind. He couldn't forget me telling him that God loved him, his sins had been paid for, and that he could be raised from the dead. After a couple of years of romping on me so badly, he asked himself why he was so mad at someone who loved him enough to tell him that story. So he picked up a Bible and started reading it himself. It confirmed everything I'd told him. He told me his wife was thrilled, his kids were happy, and they were a much closer family now. He felt guilty because he thought I knew he'd been poor-mouthing me, which, of course, I didn't, and wanted to apologize for being an idiot.

Here's the point of his letter: if you really love someone and want to tell them about what God's done for us, there's no way to escape without being persecuted. I usually tell anyone I talk to that I'm going to share the gospel because I love them. I tell them it's not contingent on how they feel about me. If they hate me, I'm not going to hold it against them. If they don't like me, they can walk away. But I have to love my enemies. If anyone has a better explanation as to how I can be resurrected, I'm open to listening to new ideas. I'm all ears when it comes to an alternative, but I've never found another way in which I'm going to make it out of here alive. I don't know any other way, so I'm sticking with what I know to be the gospel.

> **I'm all ears when it comes to an alternative, but I've never found another way in which I'm going to make it out of here alive.**

The man who wrote me the letter was baptized and saved, but he went down kicking and screaming. Most of the other people we've converted over the years have accepted Jesus Christ as their savior more willingly. For about twenty years, we had Bible study at our house on a weekday night and house church on Sunday nights. One time, Jep and his best friend, Trey Fisher, brought eighteen teenagers to the house, and we baptized every one of them that night in the river.

We were never really sure what we'd find on the riverbank when we walked down for a baptism. One night, we took about twenty people down to the river to take their confessions and baptize them. About the time we were ready to walk into the water, a couple of rednecks pulled up in their boat. It was obvious they'd had a couple of beers to drink.

"What the hell is going on around here?" one of them yelled.

"I'll tell you what," I said. "We just preached the gospel to these people, and we're gonna baptize 'em right here. You all want in on the action?"

I ain't never seen a motor crank up that fast and leave!

Our dogs always seemed to follow the crowd to the river for baptisms. I was baptizing a young man one time, and just as soon as I pulled him out of the water, the dogs started fighting for some reason. Without skipping a beat, I told the young man he must have had an evil spirit in him, which God had miraculously transferred to the dogs! There were about ten dogs squealing and barking, and I told him the dogs were going to fight the demon out of them! The funny part is everyone on the riverbank thought I was telling the truth!

We conducted another baptism at our house one night

when the river was really high, which brings water up close to our house, along with the snakes, alligators, and other dangerous debris. My boys went out with flashlights and shotguns to clear our path; they were always on sentinel duty when we baptized someone at night. In fact, during a baptism one very dark night, I accidentally stepped off the normal path and led us into an alligator or turtle bed, and we both disappeared into the water. I like to think that baptism was a twofer!

A lot of the people we've converted over the years have become our very close friends and some of them were even married in our front yard. We've probably conducted a dozen weddings at our house, with Alan officiating most of them. Paul Lewis was Willie's best friend growing up. Paul received a full scholarship to play basketball at Southeastern Louisiana University in Hammond. He even played against Shaquille O'Neal one time and seemed to have a very bright future. But in 1995, Paul was arrested for transporting drugs in Texas and was sentenced to fourteen years in federal prison. He ended up serving twelve and a half years, which was a hard lesson to learn, and Willie was at the prison to pick him up the day he was released.

Willie gave Paul a job at Duck Commander, where he met his future wife, Crystle, a former Texas police officer. They both rededicated their lives to Jesus Christ and were married in our front yard. Paul is African-American; Crystle's mother is Hispanic and her father is black. So the wedding crowd consisted of African-Americans and Hispanics but mostly white, bearded rednecks. About the time the wedding proceedings were starting, a friend of mine was putting his boat into the river at our boat dock. My friend later told me he realized then that there must be a God, because every other time he had seen so many ethnicities together, there was usually fighting involved! But there, under the towering pines and oaks next to Cypress Creek in our front yard, he saw a lot of people from different backgrounds who seemed to genuinely love each other and were enjoying being around each other. It was a perfect picture of what Christ's body should look like on Earth. My family and I are proud to create scenes like that one as a witness to what we believe.

Whenever I think of all the people we've baptized over the years, I always recall a conversation Jep had with one of his buddies in the backseat of our car when he was really young. Jep's friend Harvey asked him what it meant to be a Christian.

"Well, when you get to be about thirteen or fourteen years old, my daddy will sit you down and study the Bible with you," Jep told him. "He'll make sure you know what he's talking about. And then he'll tell you that Jesus is going to be your Lord and when that happens, you can't act bad anymore. My daddy will ask you if you want Jesus to be your Lord. If you say yes, we're all going down to the river. We'll be so excited that we'll be skipping down there. My daddy will put you under the water, but he won't drown you. He'll bring you back up and everybody will be clapping and smiling. That's what he'll do."

Nowadays, you don't see many families—the husband, wife, and children—that are so evangelistic. I think it's pretty rare in today's world. The thing that pleases me most about my sons is that no one ever told them to do it. They just decided to be that way. Maybe it was handed down when they heard me telling Bible stories and saw me baptizing people in the river. I didn't have Jesus in my life until I was twenty-eight. But during the last thirty-eight years of my life, I've been telling everyone I meet about him. It was a big change for me. I was converting people to Christianity even before I started making duck calls. Then came the business, the blessing, and the fame, but I've stayed the same throughout. Everywhere my sons and I go, we're telling people the good news about Jesus, blowing duck calls, and making people happy, happy, happy—then down the road we go.

"My daddy will put you under the water, but he won't drown you."

FOUNDING FATHERS

Rule No. 14 for Living Happy, Happy, Happy
Read the Bible (We Can Still Save This
Once-Great Country—It's Not Too Late)

After I became a Christian, one of the first changes I made in my life was to take a more active interest in politics and how our government works. I'd never voted until I was twenty-nine, but I decided I ought to do so in order to help put godly men and women in positions of authority—instead of a bunch of heathens—since God works through people.

After studying several political parties to find out what they believe and stand for, I decided my political ideology was more in line with the Republicans. I definitely was no Democrat—that's for sure—but I don't really consider myself one or the other. I'm more of a Christocrat, someone who honors our founding fathers and pays them homage for being godly men at a time when wickedness was all over the world. Our founding fathers started this country and built it on God and His Word, and this country sure would be a better place to live and raise our children if we still followed their ideals and beliefs.

I'm worried about the United States of America, there's no question about it. There's wickedness all over our country. America is a country without morals and principles, and it's a far cry from the great nation our founding fathers created in 1776. Great men like George Washington, Thomas Jefferson, and Benjamin Franklin, who signed the Declaration of Independence and whom you see on our money today, agreed that God and the Bible would be their moral compasses for constructing the greatest nation on Earth. But now we've taken the Bible out of schools, we've taken the Ten Commandments out of courtrooms, and stores like Walmart aren't even allowed to publicize Christmas anymore! What kind of country are we living in nowadays?

It really seems pretty simple to me. We're in the year A.D. 2013 We've been counting time by Jesus for more than two thousand years. He must have done something right! In his Thanksgiving Proclamation in New York on October 3, 1789, Washington, the very first president of the United States, said, "Whereas it is the duty of all nations to acknowledge the providence of Almighty God, to obey his will, to be grateful for his benefits, and humbly to implore his protection and experience." I'm with George Washington. It was Jefferson, our third president, who said, "All men are created equal." Man didn't crawl out of the ocean like some of these evolutionists would like us to believe; Jefferson believed men were *created* equal. He also said, "We hold these truths to be self-evident, that all men are created equal, that they are endowed by their Creator with certain unalienable Rights, that among these are Life, Liberty and the pursuit of Happiness." Those are God-given rights, folks. I'm with Thomas Jefferson.

Sure, our founding fathers weren't perfect, and they made mistakes along the way. They allowed slavery to take place in our country for close to a hundred years and didn't allow women to vote in the beginning, but we as a people atoned for our mistakes and corrected them. The difference between our founding fathers and the cats that are ruining our country today is that men like Washington and Jefferson created the greatest country on Earth and these modern-day politicians didn't!

In a letter to several governors of the first states, Washington wrote, "I now make it my earnest prayer, that God would have you, and the State over which you preside, in his holy protection." There it is; is that the last time you heard one of our politicians offer a meaningful prayer to God Almighty? The only thing today's politicians want to talk about is separation of church and state, but our founding fathers wholly embraced their Creator.

Jefferson, the principal author of the Declaration of Independence, could speak ten languages and was studying French,

Latin, and Greek when he was nine. When John F. Kennedy, our thirty-fifth president, brought together the Nobel Prize winners at the White House in 1962, he told them, "Ladies and gentlemen, I think this is the most extraordinary collection of talent, of human knowledge, that has ever been gathered together at the White House, with the possible exception of when Thomas Jefferson dined alone." That's how much respect and admiration JFK had for Jefferson. And why wouldn't he? Jefferson authorized the Louisiana Purchase from the French and it turned out to be a pretty good deal!

Jefferson was a smart cat, and his fears about America's future are sadly coming to fruition. Jefferson once famously said, "To take from one, because it is thought that his own industry and that of his father's has acquired too much, in order to spare to others, who, or whose fathers have not exercised equal industry and skill, is to violate arbitrarily the first principle of association—the guarantee to every one of a free exercise of his industry and the fruits acquired by it." Jefferson warned us that socialism would ruin the American democracy, and look what's happening in our country now. Today, our government is saying the democracy will thrive if you take from those who are willing to work and give to those who aren't. I have to pay more taxes so that everything can be free for those people who don't want to work? It's nonsense. Our government is doing exactly what Jefferson warned us against. So the question is, who is right? I think Jefferson was on the right side.

Jefferson also said, "It is incumbent on every generation to pay its own debts as it goes. A principle which if acted on would save one half the wars of the world." What is our national debt now? More than $16 trillion, and it's climbing every minute with no debt ceiling in sight. We made a grave mistake and didn't pay our debts as a country as we moved forward. Once you don't pay, you dig a never-ending hole like the one we have now. Look at the financial disaster we're leaving our future generations. Our children and grandchildren are going to be saddled with debt up to their eyeballs! My reading of history has convinced me that most bad government comes from too much government. Ronald Reagan, our fortieth president, once famously said, "As government expands, liberty contracts." Right again!

You know what Jefferson had to say about the health care programs our government is trying to force down our throats? He said, "To compel a man to furnish contributions of money for the propagation of opinions which he disbelieves and abhors, is sinful and tyrannical." We shouldn't have to pay for stuff we hate, and I don't want to pay for a health care program that endorses legalized abortions. No one has the right to make us pay if we don't want it. Now, the government is saying we have to pay for programs like health care, whether we like it or not. It's sinful and tyrannical, according to Jefferson.

Jefferson also warned us to make sure we maintain our right to bear arms. He said, "No free man shall ever be debarred the use of arms." Jefferson was telling us, "Boys, make sure you keep your guns." In a democracy, the strongest reason for the people to retain their right to keep and bear arms is as a last resort to protect themselves against tyranny.

Jefferson was one of our first presidents, so you'd think the first thing he'd want to do is confiscate everyone's guns. But he actually said the opposite and believed that if things ever went south, the people were going to need their guns. That's pretty serious talk, but that's what Jefferson said. Washington agreed with him and basically said firearms are America's liberty teeth. In his first message to Congress on the State of the Union on January 8, 1790, Washington said, "A free people ought not only to be armed, but disciplined." Do you see their point? It's by the people, for the people, Jack!

John Adams, our second president, said, "Statesmen . . . may plan and speculate for Liberty, but it is Religion and Morality alone, which can establish the Principles upon which Freedom can securely stand." Adams told us that if we don't have God in our lives and aren't morally righteous, we're going to lose it all. That's where we are now, and I fear that's what's fixing to happen.

Now we can't figure out what's wrong with America's youth. Our children are plagued by violence, alcohol, drug abuse, teenage pregnancies out of wedlock, and high dropout rates. Well, Noah Webster, who is considered the father of American education, basically believed that the Bible was America's basic textbook in all fields. In his *History of the United States,* Webster wrote, "The most perfect maxims and examples of regulating your social conduct and domestic economy, as well as the best rules of morality and religion, are to be found in the Bible." Webster must have been a pretty intelligent guy, because I'm still using a *Webster's Dictionary*! But we're not even allowed to start the school day with a prayer or have a Bible in a classroom. Webster believed you had to vet everything through the Bible. We got away from it and now we're paying the price. We should have listened to Webster.

Webster must have been a pretty intelligent guy, because I'm still using a *Webster's Dictionary*!

What are we going to do with our youth? How are we going to reduce crime? How are we going to prevent our children from having babies? What are we going to do? The only solution our government can come up with nowadays is to pour more money into our problems and research solutions. Webster said what we need to do is put the Bible back where it ought to be. I'm right there with him!

Without the Bible as a blueprint for living our lives, I'm not surprised to see our country struggling so mightily. Romans 1:28–32 says:

> *Furthermore, just as they did not think it worthwhile to retain the knowledge of God, so God gave them over to a depraved mind, so that they do what ought not to be done. They have become filled with every kind of wickedness, evil, greed and depravity. They are full of envy, murder, strife, deceit and malice. They are gossips, slanderers, God-haters, insolent, arrogant and boastful; they invent ways of doing evil; they disobey their parents, they have no understanding, no fidelity, no love, no mercy. Although they know God's righteous decree that those who do such things deserve death, they not only continue to do these very things but also approve of those who practice them.*

The apostle Paul was writing about the Roman Empire, but he might as well have been talking about present-day America. We fought Operation Desert Shield and Operation Desert Storm in the early 1990s, and then we continued to fight in Afghanistan and Iraq for more than a decade to weed out terrorists. According to the U.S. Department of Defense, we lost nearly seven thousand brave soldiers during those wars. But there's a bigger war going on in America. According to the Centers for Disease Control and Prevention, over sixteen thousand people were murdered in the United States in 2010. While a good chunk of our firepower was in the Middle East trying to get a handle on terrorism, we were losing an even bigger war right here in the good ol' USA. Sadly, our children are the ones doing a lot of the killing.

I'm extremely worried about our country's youth. Remember the scene from *Duck Dynasty* when I joined my grandson on a date with his girlfriend in my boat? I told him, "Son, no hands below the neck." What was I trying to tell him? My greatest fear is for one of my grandchildren to come up and tell me they have herpes. Don't you think it a little ironic that what follows sexual immorality is herpes, chlamydia, AIDS, syphilis, and gonorrhea? How could something as much fun as sex all of the sudden bring these horrible diseases upon us? Doctors have been researching these diseases for centuries, but they can't cure most of them. They can't get rid of most of them. What do you call that? You call that the consequences of disobeying the Almighty.

Look, you're married to a woman and she doesn't have AIDS, chlamydia, syphilis, gonorrhea, or any of the rest of them. Here's the good news: you don't have it and she doesn't have it. Guess who is never going to get it if you keep your sex right there? The only way it can be transmitted to you or your spouse is if you go out and disobey what the Almighty says. When it's one woman and one man, you won't catch this stuff. But if you disobey God, His wrath will be poured out upon you. It's not a coincidence that horrible diseases follow immoral conduct—it's the consequences that follow when you break God's laws.

During the 1960s, I was involved in a lot of the sins I'm talking about. Remember, before I was converted when I was twenty-eight, I was running with the depraved crowd. I've been there and done that. I'm sorry to say it, but my generation gave itself over to sinful desires and sexual impurities. Thankfully, it's not too late to save our next generation.

What in the world ever happened to the United States of America, folks? Our country is so different from the nation that was founded more than two hundred years ago. I'm absolutely convinced that the reason America went so far and so fast is that our founders were God-fearing men. It was godly from the start. Our founding fathers fled the wickedness of Europe and came to America to build a nation built on principles, morals, and their beliefs in Jesus Christ. They drew upon their faith and biblical ideals to actually construct the framing documents of our great country.

The irony of it all is that we're right back to what they ran from 237 years ago. We're right back to old King George. Our forefathers' greatest fear was that the very thing they revolted against would come full circle and we'd be right back to where they started. When Webster was asked what the greatest thing that ever passed through his mind was, he said it was his accountability to God. I agree with him wholeheartedly. I'm not going askew from the principles on which the United States was built;

I'm right there with our founding fathers. I'm a patriot and a Christian, and I'm moving forth with what they started. But now it's gotten to where I'm some kind of nut or Bible beater.

I say, so be it. I'll still go across the country spreading God's Word, like I've done since I was twenty-eight. I may be only one man reading Scripture and quotes, carrying his Bible, and blowing duck calls to crowds, but, hey, it has to start somewhere. It's what makes me happy, happy, happy.

LETTERS FROM THE FAMILY

A NOTE FROM ALAN

Out of the many memorable lines and quotes I have heard from my dad through the years, the one that always seems to stand out the most is "Son, don't ever tell people how good or great you are at something; let them tell you." For a man who has achieved his own level of greatness in the eyes of so many, those words were both prophetic and wise. To be the best at anything, one has to have a lot of confidence and a certain amount of ego and drive. But one must also have humility to make a life-changing impact on people. I realize now that that is what Dad was teaching me all those years ago. Of course, to become a legend, one that other people admire and want to emulate, you also have to add faith and dedication to what you love. A good woman doesn't hurt either.

My mom has always been Dad's biggest cheerleader, from

when he was a high school quarterback to when he became a Christian to when he faithfully plunged into this dream that is now known as Duck Commander. Her humility and dedication held them together when he was not the man he needed to be, and now she keeps him humble as his right hand and soul mate. Believe me, there would be no Duck Commander legend without Miss Kay!

What I respect most about my dad is that he allowed and continues to allow God to guide him. He offered himself to the Creator and humbly accepted a path that has now led to fame, recognition, and greatness, but has led mostly to glory to God and a life change for thousands of people. What I respect most about my mom is that she never gave up on him. Through her love for God and us boys, she led Dad to his relationship with God and changed all of our destinies. Their motive for Duck Commander has always been Kingdom first.

From my perch as the oldest son, I have had the opportunity to see the longest and greatest impact Dad's life change and legacy have had on our earthly family, our forever family, and the world we live in. I have also personally experienced his love and support throughout my days here on Earth, even when some of those days were dark and I didn't want to listen to him or Mom. I have grown and flourished as a man and as a man of God because of the influence of my parents, and I am forever grateful for them.

I thank my mom for her tenacity, long suffering, and close friendship. She taught me how to forgive and see potential goodness in people that others cannot see. She taught me that hope is one of God's greatest virtues when things seem dark and difficult. I thank my dad for his guidance, commitment to God, and visionary faith. He saw what we couldn't, and he has taught me to appreciate what can be done when others say it cannot be done. He taught me how to work hard and achieve your dreams. He taught me to appreciate God's creation through a love of the outdoors and the simple beauty in the smallest things. From a smartweed stalk to a crawfish hill to a buttonwillow thicket, Dad has always seen the hand of God in the nature that surrounds us. He also taught me that people are worth loving because God made us to be loved and to share a message of love and redemption.

My dad would follow his own advice and never tell you how great he is, but I don't mind telling you at all.

A NOTE FROM JASE

I'm the second son of Phil and Kay Robertson. Si (Phil's youngest brother) named me on the riverbank. Si went to the river to tell Phil that Kay was having a baby. I've always heard that Phil's response was something to the effect of, "What do you want me to do about it?" Si asked him, "What do you want to name him?" Phil replied, "Name him after you." So I was given the name

Jason Silas Robertson. Maybe that's why Si and I love to argue so much. My dad called me "Jase" about half the time, and somewhere through the years the name stuck.

I was five or six when I noticed a change in my dad's life. I was probably eight when I realized this change was going to be permanent and for the better. Up until that time, my life was filled with a lot of fear. I remember seeing scary-looking people and a lot of fistfights, usually ending with the flashing lights of police cars. I just tried to stay out of the way and survive. This all seemed to culminate one night with my most vivid memory as a child. I remember being awakened in the middle of the night and having to move out with my mom and brothers at the direction of my dad.

We moved to West Monroe, Louisiana, and it seemed like an eternity before I saw my dad again. It was a few months, and I remember my dad pulling up in a cool-looking Jeep. I could tell something had happened—he was a new creation.

It was not until I was fourteen that I figured out what happened. I had gone to a Bible study and had gotten "stirred up" about this one called Jesus. I asked my dad about it, and he told me that's the same message he'd heard. Not long after that conversation, Phil and I waded into the Ouachita River and he baptized me. I then realized why he was a new creation.

The years we spent on the river were some of my fondest

memories. We commercial-fished together, hunted everything, and spent a lot of time around the table, eating what we caught and playing dominoes. I think what made it so special was that we were a reconciled family and brothers in our faith. Through this we became really good friends. He taught me how to blow a duck call and how to skin a catfish. Most importantly, he taught me how to be a godly man.

I remember countless gospel studies with all kinds of people and lots of river baptisms. I learned how to be hospitable and to value people no matter what their skin color or whether they were rich or poor. Most important for me, I learned that as a follower of Christ you could have a lot of fun. It was not so much what we were doing around the riverbank but whom we were with on the riverbank. Thanks, Dad!

A NOTE FROM WILLIE

I'm happy I get to write about my dad when I'm older in life. The older I get, the more I'm starting to realize how great he really is. Not great because of all of his many accomplishments, but because of who he is and how he has lived his life. I know he has not always been what he wanted to be in life, but all of us have made mistakes; it's how we deal with them that makes us great or not. Dad spent much of his younger years searching for something. When he found it, he sold out for what it gave him—peace and hope. He lived his early life with neither, and I would have to say I would have done the same if I didn't know Jesus. He lived his life without peace, and he in turn gave no peace. He lived his life without hope, so he gave none as well. He lived only by what he saw. But after he accepted Jesus Christ as his savior, he learned to live by what he couldn't see. And that is what he taught me after he found it.

I find myself living more and more like my dad as I get older. It's probably because we were somewhat in the same birth order. I am the third in four children and he was the fifth in seven. We shared the same type of childhood. We both had nothing when we were young but never wanted any help and were self-made men. We had to really stand out to "stand out." Neither of us ever feared failure, and if we did, we surely wouldn't admit it. Each of us decided we would never live our lives in the trap of some man-made structure or like caged birds doing what we are supposed to do. Both of us knew at early ages that we needed a great partner to help us in life. We both put our spouses through trying times to make them prove to us that they really loved us for who we really were. And both women saw something in us that we did not see in ourselves, something that could be great with a little help and patience.

I would love to give all the credit to our gals, but without the Lord, it would have been impossible. We will bow to no man, but we bow to something bigger than us. God is the only thing that can tame the wild horse in both of us. It is as simple as that. It just makes sense to have hope beyond our lives on Earth. If the only thing we can rest on is how good life is here on Earth, then it may be comprehensible to think life ain't so bad. But I have to wonder, what if I were born somewhere else on the planet? Somewhere that wasn't so good? What if we couldn't hunt, prosper, be happy, and have such a good family? It wouldn't seem fair, would it? That is why we put our hope in something else. God's way is better.

My father went through all the bad to teach me not to do it, and I didn't. I don't have to testify about how bad I used to be. Yes, I made and continue to make bad decisions, and I am in no way perfect. I also have done many things the right way and have been a positive influence on many people. I have brought many people to the Lord and counseled teens, college kids, and married people. I have worked for the church, gone to seminary, and completed mission work. And I did most of it when I was still only a teen. I don't deserve any glory. I simply followed the examples my parents showed me and did what my heavenly Father told me to do. The byproduct was I knew my dad would be pleased with what I was doing with my life.

My dad taught me to be a salesman, hard worker, good man, visionary, entrepreneur, problem solver, good husband, good father, and great hunter. He taught me to be independent, confident, and fearless, but most of all godly. I never remember him talking about his accomplishments on the ball field, and he never was big on homework, ball practice, or how we looked. He did, however, do what my wife said many years ago, which was to "hot-wire us to God." Not so we would make him happy, but so we would make Him happy. I always tried to do what was right not only because it would make my dad happy, but because it would make the Lord happy.

As I sit here in my recliner, watching *The Good, the Bad and the Ugly,* literally turning into my dad, my hope is that I really do turn out to be somewhat like him. I am totally confident that we will live forever and continue to be together in the after-realm. That is the hope we share. That is why we live together without fighting and arguing, and that is why we continue to work together as friends. We are happy as a family—we share in joys, work through our problems, deal with sorrows, care for each other, and always look to the bigger picture. Yes, my dad has taught me a lot. I can only try to make him happy by putting all the things he has taught me into practice. I see no bad in him, only the good. I see no mistakes, only the achievements.

My biggest achievement was to bring him some of the glory he deserved in this life. He did so much for hunting, so much for his family, and so much for so many people. My biggest fear was that people would not know how much he accomplished. I have worked hard to make the right business moves so my father would receive the recognition he deserves. I am so glad to show America that there are still families that do the right things and care for people but can still succeed in this mean ol' world. My mom tells me all the time that I am just like my dad, and she usually says it after some of my lesser moments. But I still smile and think that those are the things that were passed to me by him. My dad has passed on to his boys the essence of what he is. And it will take all four of us to show it. None of us alone can embody who he is. He is remarkable and noble. My father is a truly great man.

A NOTE FROM JEP

I guess growing up in the Robertson household was like growing up in a lot of American households. Since I was really young, we were skinning fish, cleaning squirrels, and picking dewberries. They were everyday events. Okay, so maybe my upbringing was a little atypical. I do think I had it a little easier than my older brothers, since Dad had repented by the time I was born. I remember getting up early in the summers and going with Dad to run the nets. He would even let me drive the boat every now and again. We would take our catch back to Mom, and then she and I would take off to the fish market to sell our catch. Something about the smell of those fish markets has always stayed with me. Those places had a stench that is beyond words. I would usually find something outside to do the rest of the day, whether it was fishing, shooting bows and arrows, or building forts.

On many nights, I remember folding boxes for the duck calls we were selling. To be honest, I don't think I did nearly as many as my brothers. But I guess I chipped in here and there. My grandmother Granny would get me to go searching for night crawlers, so I could take her out perch fishing. Those were some great times, and she taught me a lot about being patient and about life in general.

As I grew to become a man, at some point I lost sight of all those life lessons my dad and grandmother taught me. At around nineteen years old, I went on a six-month drug-induced rampage that nearly cost me my life. My brother Willie knew what I was up to and got the family together to give an intervention. I'll never forget how scared I was that day when I walked in Mom and Dad's house with all my brothers sitting around. I still remember hearing my dad say, "I know you've been up to no good; how bad is it?" I broke down and told them everything. There were a lot of tears and hugs, and I've never felt the love of a family like I did that day. My dad put me on house arrest for three months, and it was probably the best time of my life. I learned how to reconnect with God and my family and get back with some true friends, who are my closest friends to this day.

I have since married the most beautiful, spiritual, wonderful woman on this planet, and we have four amazing kids. My dad has shown me through his life how to work hard to support your family, love God, and even fit in a little hunting. My dad has always been there for me in good times and bad, and I hope I can do the same for my children. I love you, Dad!

A NOTE FROM KAY

When people dream something as a child, it doesn't always come true. But my childhood dream of what kind of man I would marry and spend the rest of my life with did come true.

I always knew my husband would be tall, dark, and handsome, but he also had to have a rugged look, as if he'd just walked out of the wilderness. He had to love the outdoors and be able to survive there if needed. I also wanted him to be able to take command of any situation when needed.

I wanted him to be a leader but with a sense of humor, too. I wanted him to work and make a living. I wanted him to be a man's man, but with gentleness and love for me and his children, and be ready to defend us at all times. More than anything else, I wanted to feel loved and protected.

What I didn't know when I found the man who filled my dreams was that I had found a diamond in the rough. It would take a lifetime to perfect that diamond on the long journey of life.

Phil and I have had many good years, some hard years, a few sad years, and a lot of struggling years to get where we are now. God put us in each other's paths. It has always been a wonderful ride for me.

I have a husband who is my best buddy and friend, my lover, my Christian brother, my champion, and the person who will always be there through thick and thin.

There is no greater love than your love for God, but right under that is your love for your husband, your partner for life. One of the great tragedies I see is people not putting every effort into the foundation of their marriage. My grandmother told me that it's one man and one woman for life and that your marriage is worth fighting for. We had a few hard and bumpy years, but prayer, patience, and some suffering and hope—plus remembering an old lady's words—were what got me through the difficult times. We have given it our all for our marriage and family, and my dreams did come true. Phil is and will always be my hero!

Acknowledgments

Thanks to my oldest brother, Jimmy Frank, for his historical excellence, vivid memory, and storytelling. Thanks to Mark Schlabach for his insight, skill, and help with writing this book. Thanks to our old friend Philis Boultinghouse for her help in editing and mostly for not being anything like Denny. Thanks to John Howard for his help in making this project come together. I thank all of those who worked hard for little or no pay helping us get started almost forty years ago. I thank Gary Stephenson for his early work in bringing our hunting exploits to the screen and many others who have helped that process all of these years. I thank all of our Duck Commander employees for their hard work and dedication and all of our great customers and fans who have given rise to this ducky phenomenon. Thanks to the Outdoor Channel and A&E for bringing our family to the airwaves of this great country. Finally, a special thanks to all of the Robertson family, all of whom live the legacy set forward in this book. To Granny and Pa, who await the great resurrection, and to my brothers and sisters and their families and especially to my best friend and travel buddy, Miss Kay, and to my four sons and their families. Most of all I thank my Lord and Savior, Jesus Christ, son of the Almighty God, for washing away my sins, teaching me a better way to live, and guaranteeing my eternal inheritance.

How Faith, Family, and Ducks Created a Dynasty

Willie and Korie Robertson

Howard Books
A Division of Simon & Schuster, Inc.
1230 Avenue of the Americas
New York, NY 10020

First Howard Books hardcover edition October 2012

For information about special discounts for bulk purchases, please contact Simon & Schuster Special Sales at 1-866-506-1949 or business@simonandschuster.com.

The Simon & Schuster Speakers Bureau can bring authors to your live event. For more information or to book an event, contact the Simon & Schuster Speakers Bureau at 1-866-248-3049 or visit our website at www.simonspeakers.com.

Designed by Stephanie Walker

Manufactured in the United States of America

50 49 48 47 46 45 44 43 42 41

Library of Congress Cataloging-in-Publication Data

Robertson, Willie, 1972–
The Duck Commander family : how faith, family, and ducks built a dynasty / Willie and Korie Robertson.
p. cm.
1. Robertson, Willie, 1972– 2. Robertson, Willie, 1972—Family. 3. Television personalities—United States—Biography. 4. Businessmen—United States—Biography. 5. Duck dynasty (Television program). I. Robertson, Korie, 1973– II. Title.
PN1992.4.R54A3 2012
791.4502'8092—dc23 2012030712
[B]

ISBN 978-1-4767-0354-1
ISBN 978-1-4767-0362-6 (ebook)

For our parents,

Phil and Kay Robertson and John and Chrys Howard,

and

for our children,

John Luke, Sadie, Will, Bella, and Rebecca

Contents

THE DUCK COMMANDER Family

PROLOGUE

BORN AND "CORN" BRED

THESE COMMANDMENTS THAT I GIVE YOU TODAY ARE TO BE ON YOUR HEARTS. IMPRESS THEM ON YOUR CHILDREN. TALK ABOUT THEM WHEN YOU SIT AT HOME AND WHEN YOU WALK ALONG THE ROAD, WHEN YOU LIE DOWN AND WHEN YOU GET UP. TIE THEM AS SYMBOLS ON YOUR HANDS AND BIND THEM ON YOUR FOREHEADS. WRITE THEM ON THE DOORFRAMES OF YOUR HOUSES AND ON YOUR GATES.
—**DEUTERONOMY 6:6–9**

For as long as I can remember, my life has centered around three building blocks: faith, family, and food. The dinner table is where the Robertson family shares wisdom, confessions, laughter, faith, and dreams. This is family time, and I am thankful to have learned a good many important life lessons around that table.

Even before we started filming our family dinners for our TV show *Duck Dynasty,* I always thought of the Robertson dinner table as a stage in a Broadway play. Whoever was talking at the time had the spotlight and everyone else was the supporting cast. As kids, we learned about how to keep everyone's attention with a good story and about comedic timing.

This is also where we perfected the art of exaggeration. I think Kay's the best at it, or the worst, depending on which way you look at it. She can turn a simple story about her dog going missing for thirty minutes into a long gut-wrenching tale of love, loss, and everything in between. Along with the comedic moments, we've never lacked drama, either!

At the family table, I learned how to defend an argument and stand up for what I believe. The Robertson dinner table is like a weekly debate session. If you offer an opinion about something, you'd better be able to defend it. This is where we learned to argue passionately about our convictions, and the Robertson family, of course, has never been short on opinions. We have arguments about everything from crawfish pie to religion to shotguns. The debates can sometimes get loud, but they're never ugly or disrespectful. It's just that each of us feels very strongly about our beliefs, and we're not going to change our minds about something unless someone else offers a very good case to the contrary.

The dinner table is where I learned to follow my dreams. This is where Dad told us he was going to start Duck Commander, and where I told my family I was getting married and heading off to college. Our hopes and aspirations were never shot down, never debated, only encouraged. We might have been eating fried bologna at the time because that was all we could afford, but there was hope that one day we would be feasting on a big fat rib-eye steak. I remember one time around the dinner table Alan told my parents he wanted a Chevy Blazer. My dad said, "There will come a day where we'll all have Chevy Blazers!" He didn't actually tell Alan no; Phil was only telling all of us, "Have patience and believe." And we did, no matter how difficult things were.

At the dinner table we learned to respect our elders. In a lot of homes, the kids make their plates first, but it was never that way in the Robertson house. At our house, the kids always ate last. We would get what was left after the adults made their plates, which was usually a fried chicken neck and rarely a breast or thigh. But we learned to be thankful and content with what we had and that the world didn't revolve around us.

We learned to be hospitable. There were always extra faces around our family's table. No matter how little we had, we always had room to set out one more plate. If we had unexpected guests, Mom pulled out more meat from the freezer and added it to gumbo, or made another batch of her delicious biscuits. In the Robertson house, it's almost an unpardonable sin to not have enough food. Kay likes to say you never run out of three things: toilet paper, butter, or ketchup. But she stocks up on more than that. If the world is ever coming to an end, we're definitely going to Kay and Phil's house. That woman's got enough food in the freezer to live for months, and if we did run out, we could count on Phil to go catch something to fill our bellies.

We also learned that a good meal goes a long way. After Phil started Duck Commander, it didn't take him long to figure out food was a great way to get people to help. All of his workers loved to eat his ducks, crawfish dishes, fried fish, or whatever he or Kay was cooking that day. If a big order needed to be packed up to go out to a buyer, we'd have a fish fry and invite fifty people over. Mom and Dad would feed them and they'd be more than happy to pitch in. Phil and Kay never had to pay a dime; they just cooked for the crew, which always left our house full and happy, and left everyone hoping to be invited the next time we needed some extra help.

Back when Duck Commander was all being run out of Kay and Phil's house, my mom cooked lunch every day for our family and employees. Yes, times have changed. Now we couldn't even fit all of our employees in Mom and Dad's house! We've grown, but all of these lessons still remain. As Robertsons, we value the time around the table with our family; we are still trying to one-up each other with the best story, still defending the last stupid decision we made, and still laughing with one another and loving each other along the way.

1

RICE 'N' BEANS

CONSIDER IT PURE JOY, MY BROTHERS, WHENEVER YOU FACE TRIALS OF MANY KINDS, BECAUSE YOU KNOW THAT THE TESTING OF YOUR FAITH DEVELOPS PERSEVERANCE.
—JAMES 1:2–3

I know this might be hard to believe, but Phil was actually fishing when I was born. I was born on April 22, 1972, which was two days before Phil's birthday. I guess he was out celebrating a couple of days early because when I came into the world at Tri-Ward General Hospital in Bernice, Louisiana, Phil was sitting in a boat fishing for catfish at Bayou D'Arbonne Lake. I was the third of Phil and Kay's four sons, and Phil was only at the hospital to witness the birth of my youngest brother, Jeptha. Phil claims watching Jep's birth traumatized him so much that he wasn't sure he could ever have sex again. Of course, he says, it only took him about six weeks to get over it. I guess I'm just glad Phil was there nine months before I was born or I wouldn't be here today.

Phil likes to joke that he named me after one of his former students, who was a good football player but had failed the eighth grade three times. The truth is that I was named after Willie Ezell, my maternal grandfather, who passed away from a heart attack when Kay was only fourteen. I was born with very long, curly hair, and Kay joked that I looked a lot like the boxing promoter Don King. When Kay was getting ready to leave the hospital, they put me out in the hall with the other newborn babies. Sounds like a good chance for babies to get switched at birth to me, but apparently that's how they did it back then. Anyway, there was no chance of mistaking me for one of the other babies. People who walked by would stop, look at me, and then ask, "Who is that kid with all the hair?" They're still asking that same question about me today.

Phil was born and raised in Caddo Parish in Northwest Louisiana, near where the state converges with Arkansas and Texas. His father, James Robertson, was the son of Judge Euan Robertson, the longtime justice of the peace in Vivian, Louisiana. James Robertson married Merritt Hale; we always called them Pa and Granny.

Phil Alexander Robertson was born on the family's farm outside Vivian on April 24, 1946. Phil had four brothers and two sisters, and they spent much of their childhood living in an old log house located on land owned by Pa's aunt Myrtle Gauss. The cabin was pretty rustic and didn't even have indoor plumbing. But the log house came with more than four hundred acres, which is where Phil and his brothers learned to hunt and fish. The woods surrounding the farm were filled with squirrels, quail, and doves, and the Robertson boys could hunt for duck and fish for white perch and bream at nearby Black Bayou and Caddo Lake.

Pa started working in the oil industry when he was young, after black gold was discovered in East Texas and at the Caddo Pine Island Oil Field in Caddo Parish in the early twentieth century.

When Phil was in high school, his family was forced to move because Aunt Myrtle sold her farm. They relocated to Dixie, Louisiana, which is about fifteen miles north of Shreveport. Granny had suffered a nervous breakdown and was diagnosed with manic depression. Pa hoped the move would stabilize Granny's condition. She was twice confined to the Louisiana mental institute at Pineville, where she received electric shock treatment. Her condition didn't improve until years later, when doctors discovered that lithium could control her mental imbalance.

A short time after Phil's family moved to Dixie, Pa fell eighteen feet from the floor of a drilling rig and landed on his head. He broke two vertebrae in his back and ruptured his stomach. The accident nearly killed him. Doctors fused the vertebrae in his back with bone from his hip and repaired his stomach. But Pa was forced to wear a heavy plaster of Paris cast from neck to hip for nearly two years and obviously couldn't work. Making matters worse, Granny was confined to the mental hospital at the same time, so Pa was left to care for five of his children while he was immobilized.

Phil's older brothers, Jimmy Frank and Harold, were

enrolled in classes at Louisiana State University in Baton Rouge. Both of them volunteered to come home and work to help the family make ends meet. But Pa insisted they stay in school and finish their education. The family somehow survived on Pa's disability checks of thirty-five dollars a week. Phil's older sister, Judy, did most of the cooking and cared for her younger siblings, Silas and Jan. Phil's other older brother Tommy and Phil gathered pecans and sold them to local markets. The family subsisted on rice and beans, cornbread, and whatever fish and game the boys could catch. Rice and beans was a staple dish at the Robertson dinner table. A hundred-pound bag of rice and several cans of beans would last for weeks. There are dozens of ways to prepare rice and beans, and the recipes could be altered by adding a simple gravy or squirrel, quail, or fish, so it was a perfect meal for the struggling Robertson family.

About the only thing Phil cared about other than hunting and fishing was playing football. The Robertson boys learned to play football in the backyard of their log home. They constructed a goalpost with oak-tree uprights and a gum-tree crossbar. Four of the Robertson boys played football at Vivian High School and later North Caddo High School (after the parish consolidated several schools). Jimmy Frank played center and guard but always wanted to be a quarterback. He taught his younger brothers how to play the position. Tommy was a track star and was the first Robertson

ABOUT THE ONLY THING PHIL CARED ABOUT OTHER THAN HUNTING AND FISHING WAS PLAYING FOOTBALL.

to play quarterback, but moved to halfback when Phil made the varsity team at North Caddo High. Harold broke his elbow while playing on the freshman team and never played football again. Silas was a hard-hitting defensive back, but Phil ended up being the best athlete in the family. He was a first-team, all-state quarterback and all-district outfielder in baseball.

Phil and Kay started dating when she was in the ninth grade and he was in the tenth. She assisted the Robertson family at times by giving them food from the general store her family owned in Ida, Louisiana. Phil and Kay broke up during the Christmas holidays the year they started dating because Phil didn't want a girlfriend interfering with hunting season. But then Kay's father passed away the next May, and Phil attended his funeral. They started dating again soon thereafter.

After finishing high school, Phil received a football scholarship from Louisiana Tech University in Ruston, where his brother Tommy was already playing for the Bulldogs. Kay moved there with Phil and completed her senior year at Ruston High School. She was pregnant at the age of sixteen with my oldest brother, Alan. Phil and Kay moved into the same apartment complex where Tommy and his wife, the former Nancy Dennig, lived, which made the transition to college a lot easier. Phil was redshirted his freshman year at Louisiana Tech but then won the starting quarterback job the next season. He was ahead of Terry Bradshaw on the depth chart.

In his book *It's Only a Game,* Bradshaw remembered Phil: "He'd come out to practice directly from the woods, squirrel tails hanging out of his pockets, duck feathers on his clothes. Clearly he was a fine shot, so no one complained too much."

During one practice before his senior season, Phil saw a flock of geese fly over the practice field. Phil looked up at the geese and thought, "Man, what am I doing here?" He quit the football team a few days later, handing the starting job to Bradshaw. Bradshaw later led the NFL's Pittsburgh Steelers to four Super Bowl championships and was inducted into the Pro Football Hall of Fame in 1989. Phil stayed at Louisiana Tech and earned a bachelor's degree in health and physical education in 1969 and a master's in 1974. He spent the rest of his fall days in the bayou, hunting ducks and squirrels, instead of throwing touchdowns.

To be honest, I came along at a difficult time in Phil's life. After he earned his bachelor's degree at Louisiana Tech, he was hired to teach English and physical education at a school in Junction City, Arkansas. Phil spent most of his time fishing, hunting, and drinking with the guy who hired him. They were doing some pretty wild and crazy things, and Phil was reprimanded a few times by the school board for his boorish behavior. He quit his teaching job before they could fire him and signed an eighteen-month lease to run a honky-tonk at the bottom of the Ouachita River near El Dorado, Arkansas. Phil was drinking a lot and spending very little time with us. Kay was so worried about Phil that she began working as a barmaid at the honky-tonk to keep an eye on him.

TO BE HONEST, I CAME ALONG AT A DIFFICULT TIME IN PHIL'S LIFE.

When Phil and Kay were at the bar, they'd leave Alan, Jase, and me with Aunt Rose, who was my favorite babysitter. She wasn't actually our aunt, but in the South, when you're a kid you've got to put something in front of the name of any adult you talk to. It's a sign of respect, and having good manners is a big thing for us Southerners. Aunt Rose made clothes for us and took good care of us. I loved that woman.

There was another babysitter that I didn't have such warm feelings for. The only thing I remember about her is that she would always try to feed us Raisin Bran. Not that there is anything wrong with Raisin Bran, but I just happened to hate it. I would refuse to eat it, and she would lock me in the closet! Unfortunately for me, I spent a lot of time in the closet that summer. I'm not sure if Jase actually liked Raisin Bran or if seeing me locked in a closet was enough of a deterrent to make him eat it, but he seemed to be her favorite and immune to the closet torture. I'd complain to Kay and she would always say, "Why don't you just eat the Raisin Bran?" I guess I was stubborn even as a little kid.

There wasn't much Kay could do about it anyway; she was just trying to keep our family's head above the water. Phil's bar was nothing more than a low wooden building attached to a mobile home. He was the bartender and cook. He served fried chicken, pickled pig's feet, and boiled eggs. Occasionally, he'd cook venison or wild boar. But more than anything else, Phil just drank a lot. Phil's sister Jan was so concerned about his drinking that she brought a preacher, William "Bill" Smith, from White's Ferry Road Church in West Monroe, Louisiana, to his bar to try to save him. Phil took one look at the man and said, "Are you some kind of preacher?"

Smith said he was a preacher, and Phil asked him if he'd ever been drunk. Smith admitted he used to drink a few beers.

"Well, what's the difference between you and me?" Phil asked him. "You've been drunk and I'm getting drunk right now. You ain't putting the Bible on me."

Smith left the bar, and Phil went back to drinking.

One night, Phil was arguing with the bar's owner and his wife. He was drunk and threw the woman across the bar and beat both of them up pretty badly. When the police arrived to break up the melee, Phil slipped out the back door. Before he left, Phil told Kay she wouldn't see him for a while. Then he stayed in the woods for several weeks while the authorities were looking for him.

Phil left Kay behind to clean up the mess. The bar owners eventually agreed not to press charges against Phil, but Kay had to give them all the money they had earned while operating the bar. She was broke and unemployed. She moved our trailer to a spot close to D'Arbonne Lake near Farmerville, Louisiana. Kay got a job working in the corporate offices of Howard Brothers Discount Stores in Monroe, Louisiana, which, ironically, was owned by Korie's family. Our lives were beginning to intersect when we were just babies. God had a plan.

Kay was handling payroll and employee benefits. Phil finally came home and got a job working in the offshore oil fields in the Gulf of Mexico. Kay was happy our family was back together again.

During the time that Phil was working at the offshore drilling sites, Kay had to put us in a day-care facility while she worked. I was only three years old, but even then I was always trying to impress my friends. One day I decided to do something that had never been done before—climb up the slide backward. I shimmied my way up the slide while the other children oohed and ahhed. Once I got to the top, I turned to raise my hands in victory and to prove once and for all that I was king of the playground. I made a minor tactical error, however. That slide was slippery, and I fell eight feet to the ground right on top of a tree root. The teacher called my mom, who rushed me to St. Francis Medical Center, where they found I had shattered both of the bones in my thighs. One of the bones was splintered all the way from my knee to my hip.

I WAS ONLY THREE YEARS OLD, BUT EVEN THEN I WAS ALWAYS TRYING TO IMPRESS MY FRIENDS.

Being in the hospital was kind of fun because I got lots of attention and sympathy. What was not so exciting was the nearly full-body cast they had to put me in to keep me immobilized until the bones could fuse back together. They had to put me to sleep to insert a pin in my leg to hold the bone together. The cast completely covered my broken leg and went halfway down the other leg. It came all the way up to my chest, so I could not move at all from my waist down.

Word somehow got to Phil. I'm not sure how it happened since cell phones weren't invented then, and even if they were, Phil certainly would not have had one. At any rate, he found out and rushed home from his offshore job. He came to the hospital and started yelling at Kay for letting me break my leg, as if there was anything she could have done about it. At that point in my life, it didn't seem like Phil was really interested in us kids, but when I got hurt his concern was evident. He even spent the night in the hospital with me until I was allowed to go home. I don't know how he, Kay, and I all slept in that little hospital bed, but we did, and I felt loved and cared for, despite our somewhat nomadic existence up until this point in my life.

One of Phil's friends, Jerry Allen, owned a car dealership. Jerry brought me one of the roller seats that mechanics use to work on cars. I rolled around our trailer on the seat for three or four months, bumping into everything in the house. My aunts and uncles tell me they still remember me rolling around the seat in the yard, trying to keep up with my brothers and cousins. I must have looked like an ape trying to navigate the creeper with nothing but my arms! I remember that part being pretty fun, but my brothers just remember the smell. They say that cast stunk like crazy! You can imagine the smell after a summer in the Louisiana heat in a full-body cast. The doctors cut a hole out of the back, and Alan remembers having to carry me to the bathroom every time I had to go. It was rough. I probably should apologize to him for that one.

Also, I learned a difficult life lesson: sometimes in trying to be king of the playground, you could end up off the playground for about six months if you're not careful. In other words, as it says in the Bible: "Don't think of yourself [or climb] more highly than you ought, but rather think of yourself with sober judgment in accordance with the measure of faith God has given you" (Romans 12:3).

Things were okay for a while, but Phil was still drinking a lot, and one rainy night during a drinking binge, Phil told Kay he wanted her to take her sons and leave. He said he was sick and tired of all of us and wanted to live his own life. We spent the night at my uncle Harold's house, and then the church helped us get a low-rent apartment.

I was really too young to remember many of the details, but I know Kay was very worried that she was about to lose her husband and her sons were about to lose their father.

Willie's Beans and Rice

You can be creative with this. Don't worry about doing it exactly the way it is written. If you don't have an ingredient, make it anyway. I make beans every time we make or buy a ham—the ham bone is the key. You will find hunks of that ham when it cooks off the bone that you never knew existed, and they are delicious. Never *throw a ham bone away!*

1 pound dry kidney or pinto beans
1 ham bone with as much ham left on it as you want (I buy one that is honey glazed, take the ham off for sandwiches, then use what's left for beans)
10 cups water, divided
⅓ cup olive oil, plus 1 teaspoon for frying
a couple of slices of bacon, cut up
1 large onion, diced
2 tablespoons minced garlic
1 green bell pepper, diced
2 stalks celery, diced
2 bay leaves (if you don't have any in your cabinet, don't worry about it)
½ teaspoon cayenne pepper (less if you are feeding kids)
1 tablespoon parsley flakes (again, don't sweat it if you don't have them)
1 teaspoon Phil Robertson's Cajun Style Seasoning
1 pound andouille sausage, sliced (add more if you like sausage, or a different kind if this is too spicy)
a pinch of brown sugar
2 cups long-grain white rice
Louisiana Hot Sauce

1. Rinse beans and transfer to a large pot with ham bone and 6 cups water. Make sure the water covers all the beans.
2. In a skillet, heat olive oil and cut-up bacon over medium heat. Sauté onion, garlic, bell pepper, and celery for 3 to 4 minutes.

3. Stir cooked vegetables into beans.
4. Season with bay leaves, cayenne pepper, parsley, and Cajun Style Seasoning.
5. Bring mixture to a boil and then reduce heat to medium and cook 4 to 6 hours, or until beans are tender. Check every 2 hours and add more water if needed.
6. Cut sausage into slices and brown in skillet on medium heat with a teaspoon of olive oil.
7. Stir sausage into beans toward the end of cooking time and continue to simmer for thirty minutes.
8. Add brown sugar to taste.
9. In a saucepan, bring 4 cups water and rice to a boil. Reduce heat, cover, and simmer for 20 minutes. Serve beans over steamed white rice and add plenty of Louisiana Hot Sauce.

2

FRIED BOLOGNA

THEREFORE, AS GOD'S CHOSEN PEOPLE, HOLY AND DEARLY LOVED, CLOTHE YOURSELVES WITH COMPASSION, KINDNESS, HUMILITY, GENTLENESS AND PATIENCE. BEAR WITH EACH OTHER AND FORGIVE ONE ANOTHER IF ANY OF YOU HAS A GRIEVANCE AGAINST SOMEONE. FORGIVE AS THE LORD FORGAVE YOU.
—COLOSSIANS 3:12–13

About three months after Phil kicked us out of the house, Kay was working at Howard Brothers' corporate offices when one of her coworkers told her Phil was sitting in his truck in the parking lot. Kay looked out the window and saw Phil hunched over the steering wheel. She figured he was probably drunk again. But when Kay got to his truck, she found Phil crying. It was something she had never seen before and probably has never seen since.

"I want my family back," Phil told her. "I'm so sorry."

Fortunately for all of us, Kay was strong enough to forgive Phil and take him back. But she took him back with the following conditions: Phil had to quit drinking and walk away from his rowdy friends. Kay enlisted the help of William "Bill" Smith, the preacher at White's Ferry Road Church in

West Monroe, Louisiana, who Phil had run out of his bar several months earlier. In one of their early conversations, Smith asked Phil if he trusted him. Phil told him no, he didn't, so Smith held up a Bible.

"You don't have to trust me," Smith told him. "Trust what's written in here."

From that day forward, Phil started his study of God's Word. He attended church several times a week and started going to Bible study nearly every night. He was baptized at the age of twenty-eight and gave up drinking and partying altogether. We moved into an apartment on Pine Terrace in West Monroe in 1976. Kay rented the apartment under an assumed name and didn't give our address or phone number to any of Phil's friends. We shared the apartment with Granny and Pa, so seven of us (my youngest brother, Jep, wasn't born yet) were living in a two-bedroom apartment. It was pretty cramped, but we didn't care. The only thing that mattered was our family was back together again.

Alan, Jase, and I slept on the floor of the living room in army sleeping bags that my uncle Si had given us. Si had brought them back from Vietnam and they were stuffed with real goose feathers. I was only about four years old at the time and had a habit of wetting the bed nearly every night. Phil used to get onto me for peeing in the bed and would threaten to spank me every morning that my sleeping bag was wet. Like I could help it! I eventually figured out that I could hold my sleeping bag up to an old butane heater and dry it. I would pee in the bed and then wake up early so it would be dry before anybody else woke up. I can only imagine how bad that sleeping bag must have smelled! I doubt that I was fooling anyone. One of our kids was a bed wetter and I never disciplined that child for it. Bed-wetting was something I totally understood.

Phil took a job teaching at Ouachita Christian School, a new school in Ouachita Parish. He thought he needed to be around Christians as much as possible as he continued his spiritual healing. Phil still says the kids he taught at Ouachita Christian School influenced his Christian walk more than anyone else. They really left an impression on him at a time when he needed it most.

Kay kept working at the department store office, so my brothers and I spent a lot of time together. Alan was the oldest and was left in charge. He assumed the responsibility of caring for his younger brothers. He was a free babysitter for Phil and Kay more than anything else, as we still didn't have much money. Kay remembers some really rough times when Alan would feed Jase and me our bottles and put us to bed—he was only seven or eight years old himself.

KAY REMEMBERS SOME REALLY ROUGH TIMES WHEN ALAN WOULD FEED JASE AND ME OUR BOTTLES AND PUT US TO BED—HE WAS ONLY SEVEN OR EIGHT YEARS OLD HIMSELF.

My brothers and I really had a good time living in the apartment. I've always been a people person, and there were a lot of kids who lived in the complex. We would go out in the parking lot and do choreographed dances. This was the 1970s, so I guess we were being influenced by the movies of that time, which involved a lot of singing and dancing. *Saturday Night Fever, The Rocky Horror Picture Show,* and *Grease* were always some of our favorites.

Alan was in charge of feeding us lunch when Kay and Phil were at work. When it was just the kids, our standard meal was fried bologna sandwiches—they were cheap and easy to make. And for that reason, Mom always had a loaf of bologna in our icebox. We became bologna connoisseurs. Even though we were kids, we were still Robertsons, which meant we took our food very seriously. No ordinary bologna sandwiches with mayonnaise slapped between two slices of bread for us. I think we tried every way you could make bologna better. Our favorite way, which I still make from time to time today, involved cutting three slits in the bologna, creating three triangles that were held together by the middle. We did that so the bologna wouldn't bubble up too much while we were frying it. We would almost burn one side, then flip it and put a slice of cheese on the top while the other side was cooking. In the meantime, we would warm the bread in the pan so that it had a little flavor from the grease and was slightly toasted. Yum, I'm getting hungry thinking about it! A little cheese or butter on anything makes it better. All of our meals at that time involved at least one of those two items. Granny lived to ninety-six years old and Pa till eighty-seven, so I guess it wasn't all that bad.

WHEN IT WAS JUST THE KIDS, OUR STANDARD MEAL WAS FRIED BOLOGNA SANDWICHES.

The apartment got a little less cramped when Granny

and Pa moved to Arizona to work on the oil fields for a few months, but we didn't live there for long because soon Phil decided he could make more money as a commercial fisherman than a teacher and wanted to start working toward that goal. Being out in the woods or on the water was still what brought him the most joy. He told Kay to search for some land with access to water that eventually flowed into the Gulf of Mexico.

Kay searched the real estate listings in the newspapers and found an advertisement for a piece of property titled "Sportsman's Paradise." There were two houses on the land—which were really nothing more than fishing camps—and it came with six and a half acres. It was located just off the Ouachita River at the mouth of Cypress Creek. It was at the end of a dirt road in one of the most remote locations in the parish. When Kay took Phil to see the land, he knew instantly that it was where he wanted to live. Phil was convinced he could make a living fishing, and he wanted his sons to learn to hunt and fish and survive off the land like he had as a child. He believed our family could subsist on the fish and game we killed, along with fruits and vegetables we could grow in a garden. Phil wanted us to learn to become a man just like he had as a child growing up in the outdoors.

One of the houses was a white, two-bedroom frame house and the other was a smaller camp house that had green wooden siding. About the same time Kay and Phil were trying to buy the land, Pa and Granny were returning home from Arizona. Kay and Phil reached an agreement with my grandparents. Pa and Granny would provide the down payment for the property, and Phil and Kay would assume the monthly mortgage payments as my grandparents eased into retirement. Our family would live in the white house, and Pa and Granny would live in the green one.

I still remember the day Phil and Kay took us to see our new home for the first time. It is one of the happiest memories from my childhood. We pulled to the end of the dirt road and all the kids jumped out of the car and ran to the house. It was like heaven to us. Woods surrounded the house, which sat on stilts at the top of a hill to avoid flooding from the river. You could see the Ouachita River from the front porch. Phil and Kay still live in the same house today. I don't think there's anything that could convince them to leave that house. It is home.

I STILL REMEMBER THE DAY PHIL AND KAY TOOK US TO SEE OUR NEW HOME FOR THE FIRST TIME.

After we moved into the house, Alan and Jase started school again. I was still too young to attend, so I spent most of my time with my granny and pa. Phil worked at the school for that first year while he got his commercial fishing business going and Kay continued to work at Howard Brothers Discount Stores.

This was a fun time in my life, with great memories of spending time with Granny and Pa. I had them all to myself while Jase and Alan were in school. I would sit at the table with them and play cards and dominoes, and we watched a lot of TV even though we only had three channels. We watched *The Price Is Right* in the morning and soap operas like *All My Children* and *As the World Turns* in the afternoon. When Granny was eighty, she actually appeared on *The Price Is Right* and won the game! It was "Spring Break Week," and she competed against a bunch of college-aged kids. Granny was really good with numbers. Bob Barker would ask her the price of an item and she'd immediately yell out, "Six dollars, Bob!" Most of the college kids on the show didn't know anything and were looking to the crowd for help, but Granny knew the price of everything almost immediately. She won two cars and a trip to Fort Lauderdale, Florida, on the Showcase Showdown.

Granny was very opinionated and fun to be around. She would take me places, like the county fair or into town. She even let me burn things—which I loved. This was not a weird pyromaniac thing. When you live in the country, burning things is a way of life. There is no trash man who comes to pick up your trash. You just make a pile and burn it. I was barely five years old, at the time, but I made a deal with Granny that I would clean up her yard if she would let me burn the pile. Every day, I'd go out in the yard and rake up piles of leaves and sticks and set them on fire. I burned everything. I just loved building fires, and—you can ask Korie—I still do. We've had the fire department visit us a few times when they have had reports that a fire I started

I MADE A DEAL WITH GRANNY THAT I WOULD CLEAN UP HER YARD IF SHE WOULD LET ME BURN THE PILE.

was out of control, but I'm proud to say that they've never had to actually put one out. I always had the fire under control by the time they arrived.

I'd help Granny in the garden, too. One time I pulled the stem out of a cantaloupe because I thought that's what I was supposed to do. Pa thumped me upside the head for doing it, and then Granny slapped him upside the head for hitting me. All of my cousins believed I was Granny's favorite because I spent so much time with her.

Granny was still having mental problems at the time, but I was too young to understand what was going on. She would do some really odd things. We had a chicken coop, and sometimes she would sit out there and crow with the chickens. Sometimes she would have her clothes on and sometimes she wouldn't. One day I was walking on the concrete sidewalk between our houses, and Granny kicked open the screen door on the front of her house. She had a rifle and shot out a string of lights hanging between the trees. I guess that's where my dad got his shooting skills. She was a heck of a shot.

One time Granny had a bunch of bananas and started peeling them and cleaning her windows with them. Before she went to the hospital for an extended stay, she went through her house and painted everything that was a rectangle with red paint. She even painted her Bible red! When Granny came back from the hospital, she couldn't figure out who painted everything in her house red. She didn't even know she had done it.

Being young, I didn't know anything was wrong with her. I just thought all the eccentric things she did were normal. That was just how she was. I was a bit of an entrepreneur, though, and took advantage of her generosity. She owned a small boat dock at the mouth of Cypress Creek and people would leave a dollar every time they used the dock. Because of that dock, Granny always had a pocket full of money. I'd take her garbage out and she'd pay me like $120 without even realizing it. She even paid me to throw away Pa's stuff one time when she was mad at him. I threw a bunch of his tools in the river. I still feel kind of bad about that one, but I was just a little kid. I didn't know any better, plus she had a pocket full of green bills calling my name.

Pa was the quietest man I've ever known. He would sit at the table playing solitaire with a cigarette hanging out of his mouth. They both smoked like freight trains. I can't believe I don't have lung cancer from spending so much time with them. I was definitely exposed to some serious secondhand smoke. Pa would be playing cards, and Granny would want to get his attention, so she would walk by the table and grab a handful of his cards and throw them in the fireplace. Pa would look at her and just say, "Aw, crap," and then start watching TV as if nothing had happened.

Like Phil and Kay, our granny and pa taught us how to be independent, confident, and self-sufficient. They raised seven great kids, my dad and aunts and uncles, and made it through some really tough times together. I loved both of them dearly and am thankful for the time I got to spend with them. I think there is something really special about spending time with people from their generation. It's called the Greatest Generation for a reason. They knew how to make the best of what they had—even if it was just fried bologna.

Fried Bologna Sandwiches

If you are worried about grease or butter, then you probably should not eat this. I have to admit, I don't eat them much anymore, but when I do, it takes me back in time.

1 tablespoon butter
2 slices thick-cut bologna
bacon grease if you have it (Granny always saved her bacon grease to cook with)
2 slices bread
2 slices of any type of cheese

1. Melt butter in frying pan.
2. Cut three slits in each slice of bologna and fry in butter. Add cheese. Remove from pan when done.
3. Warm bacon grease in frying pan.
4. Toast slices of bread in hot bacon grease.
5. Place bologna and cheese between slices of bread.

3

FRIED CATFISH

BUT AS FOR ME AND MY HOUSEHOLD, WE WILL SERVE THE LORD.
—JOSHUA 24:15

K*orie:* "More fish, Papaw! More fish!"

My papaw Howard loved to hear me say those words. We would catch fish together almost every day, then would go straight inside and fry them up. I loved eating fish; I even ate the tails. Most important, I loved spending time with Papaw. My brother, Ryan, was always shooting squirrels with his BB gun, and I remember Papaw teaching me how to skin one of the squirrels that Ryan killed.

Other than that, I guess Phil would call my family yuppies. Living in West Monroe, Louisiana, you can't be too much of a city girl, though. It's a pretty small town, where most people enjoy hunting and fishing to some extent. But I did live in a subdivision and attended a private school, and the only time I remember my dad going hunting was on a business trip with some of his big clients. So I guess that qualifies us as yuppies.

Alton Howard, my papaw, was semiretired at fifty-three

years old. So while he lived in a big, beautiful house in a subdivision, he had time to teach us a thing or two about country living. Papaw grew up in Rocky Branch, Louisiana, in an environment much like the one Phil grew up in. Papaw always told us stories of feeding the hogs and getting oranges in his stocking for Christmas. His family worked hard to survive, and he learned how to live off the land. Papaw served four years in the Army Air Forces during World War II. Then Papaw came home, where he met my beautiful mamaw, Mamie Jean, in a bowling alley in West Monroe. They married and set out to make their fortune. Partnering with one of his brothers, Papaw opened a jewelry store, where I remember "working" as a young girl. I enjoyed going to the store and helping clean the glass counters and wrap the gifts at Christmastime. They had a machine that made bows, and I especially loved making them. The jewelry store was just the beginning, though. Papaw and my father, Johnny, were involved in more than twenty business ventures together, including a chain of stores called Howard Brothers Discount Stores (this is the company Kay worked for when she and the boys first came to West Monroe).

The discount stores opened their doors in 1959 as a Gibson's franchise. This was a few years before Wal-Mart opened. The company went public in 1969 and changed its name from Gibson's to Howard Brothers Discount Stores, which became a very successful chain, with seventy-eight stores all over the Southeast. My dad finished college and went straight to work for the family businesses. So Duck

Commander's being a family business was nothing unusual for me. I was very familiar with the unique benefits and challenges that come with a family-run operation. My mamaw Howard loved to cook for her family, and we lived just across the pond from them so we ate at their house quite a bit. Mamaw was and still is a great woman of God. She's always reading Bible verses to us and is living proof that the prayers of the righteous are powerful and effective. My papaw loved her dearly and called her "Queenie." She would set the table, and my dad and papaw would sit down to eat and talk over their latest business deals. I loved to listen in.

The discount stores were sold in 1978, but my father continued to work for the company for five years and then went on to other business adventures. He visited a Price Club store, the forerunner of Costco, on a trip to California and came back and told my papaw, "Here's something Sam Walton will never do!" The Wal-Mart stores had grown exponentially during those years, and the last thing they wanted to do was be in competition with Sam Walton. And so my papaw and father started SuperSaver Wholesale Warehouse Club in 1984. They didn't realize that about that same time Sam Walton was opening new stores called Sam's Club. SuperSaver grew fast, with twenty-four stores opening in only eighteen months! Papaw and Daddy were about to take the company public when Sam Walton called with an offer. Sam bought SuperSaver from my family in 1987 and those twenty-four stores became Sam's Clubs. So needless to say, I came from a very business-minded family! It's what they loved to do. For the Robertsons, the motto has always been faith, family, and ducks. But for my side of the family it's more like Faith, Family, and Business!

I had a great upbringing. I came from strong Christian families on both sides and was blessed to always have the security of a mom and dad who loved God, loved each other, and took care of our needs. My mamaw and papaw on my mom's side, Jo and Luther Shackelford, met in San Diego, California, where my papaw served in the marines during the Korean War. He was recruited to play basketball for the marines, and my mamaw was a cheerleader. Papaw Shack was six feet four inches, and a strong legacy of basketball players continues to this day in our family because of him. He went to college on the GI Bill and earned a master's degree in engineering from Oklahoma State University. He and my mamaw lived in Shreveport, Louisiana, for most of my childhood, which is only about an hour and a half from West Monroe, where I grew up, and I loved going to visit them. When I was young, I called them Mamaw and Papaw Shreveport!

When I went to visit, Mamaw would have the fridge stocked with all of my favorite things, and Papaw always had a joke to tell and a hug and a kiss for me. He was the kindest man I have ever known, with a word of encouragement always on his lips. My papaw was a salesman for most of his life. Mamaw always said he could "sell a refrigerator to an Eskimo." Mamaw was a busy stay-at-home mom with six kids. She could do absolutely anything and still can. She doesn't look like your typical grandma. And at eighty, if she doesn't yet, I don't think she ever will! She's always stylish and up for the next adventure. She is truly a product of the Greatest Generation, with the ability to sew all her kids' clothes and cook fantastic meals, and even, as my mom tells us, once enclosed their garage to make a game room and laid the brick all by herself! She started working with my Papaw in real estate after her kids were grown and is still working today. She's running their real estate office and serving on the board of the Northeast Louisiana Association of Realtors, along with keeping up with her grandkids and great-grandkids.

My parents, John and Chrys Howard, met at Camp Ch-Yo-Ca (the same camp where Willie and I met) and were married a few years later when my mom was eighteen years old. They headed off to Harding University, and I was born two years later on October 24, 1973. When we go back to Searcy, Arkansas, where the Harding campus is, my dad loves to point out where I was conceived, in a trailer between a meatpacking plant and a graveyard. Awkward!

Now back to my parents' meeting at camp. Camp Ch-Yo-Ca, which stands for CHristian YOuth CAmp, was started in 1967 by my mamaw and papaw Howard, along with several other men and women. They had a dream of having a place for kids and teens to get out of their normal environment, spend time in the woods, have fun with friends, and, most important, grow closer to God. Growing up, my mom, along with my brother, Ryan, and sister, Ashley, and I, lived out there every summer in an RV parked in front of the craft shed. The camp was only about ten minutes from our house, but it is set in the middle of one hundred acres, and when we were there, we felt like we were in the middle of nowhere. My dad would come in and out because he still had to work, of course. He was busy growing the family business.

Some of my favorite memories are of being at camp. We spent the entire summer outdoors. There were no televisions, just Ping-Pong tables, swings, a lake for fishing and canoeing, and a giant swimming pool. Since we were the "camp kids," we were there for every session, and we loved it. We roamed free and played all day. We would sneak into the kitchen and go into the walk-in refrigerator to cool off. It's hot in Louisiana in the summertime! I was kind of shy as a child, so one summer when I was about nine, everybody's favorite camp director, Howard Karbo, decided I was not getting near enough attention. He started the "Korie Howard Fan Club." This fan club didn't exactly do anything, and I think there were only about two members. While I was a little embarrassed by the attention, what girl wouldn't be flattered to have her own fan club?

My mom taught the crafts and later went on to be a director at the camp, and still is today. My mom has more energy than any woman I know. She works so hard for those kids. She has a servant spirit like none other. She has worked most of her life as a volunteer in some capacity, whether at the camp or at the Christian school that we attended. She started a program at our school for kids with learning difficulties and worked there every day for twelve years, never taking a paycheck.

By that time, my family had launched a publishing company called Howard Publishing, which was later sold to Simon & Schuster, and she was needed there. She eventually went on to work as a senior editor and creative director for the company. Mom was the kind of mother who loved to make things fun for everybody. She was the one who planned the class parties, and the youth group at our church always hung out at my family's house. They still do to this day. Mom brought all of that fun to the publishing company, having monthly lunches to honor the employees and a month of activities at Christmastime, including Pancake and Pajama Day. (I've thought of doing that at Duck Commander, but I'm not sure if I could talk the guys into coming to work in their PJs. Actually, the thought of that is a little scary!) Her work in this area helped the company win the "Best Christian Workplace in America" award for five years in a row!

Mom continues to make life fun for her grandkids. They call her Two-Mama and call my dad Two-Papa, and we couldn't live without them! We built a house next door to my parents about five years ago, and our kids just go back and forth. It's been an extra blessing while we're filming the show. Life's busy, and I never feel guilty about leaving my kids with Two-Mama while I film or work. Two-Mama is always there, and I know they're in great hands!

Some of my other favorite memories of growing up are of us traveling as a family. I think traveling is a great gift to be able to give your kids in order to expose them to different cultures and people around the world. My dad always took time off to take us on awesome vacations. We went snow skiing every winter and to the beach every summer. We were blessed to be able to go incredible places like China, Austria, and Germany, and we even went to two Olympic Games. Not all of the places we traveled were that exotic though. Every year, we went with Mamaw and Papaw Howard on what we called "Grandkids' Vacation." My papaw Howard had an RV, so this was usually a road trip to Branson, Missouri. One year the RV broke down right in front of a mall. Papaw said that was his most expensive breakdown ever. We shopped the whole time we waited for the RV to get fixed!

Like I said, Dad was a hard worker. He didn't golf, hunt, or have any other hobbies besides work and family. He never missed any of our sporting events, and nowadays, he never misses one of the grandkids' activities. He may be in the stands reading over a contract, but he is there. He's a great Two-Papa. One time our daughter, Bella, was telling me how Two-Papa's favorite thing to do is to take them anywhere they want to go. All the grandkids know that if they want something, ask Two-Papa. Every time they ask him to take them on a snow cone run, he stops whatever he's doing and says, "I was waiting for you to ask me that!" And they hop in his T-Bird and go get snow cones. The best thing about it is that he not only takes them, but he makes them feel like that's exactly what he wanted to do.

After Dad sold Howard Publishing to Simon & Schuster, he continued as the president of the company for three years. Then after he and Mom took some time off to travel,

Daddy came to work for us at Duck Commander, working with budgets and contracts. You know we like to keep it all in the family! He is an invaluable asset with all of his business knowledge and experience. Plus, Dad's a detail person, while Willie is more of a big-picture guy. Like everything else at Duck Commander, it seems that when Dad came on board, God provided us with what we needed most, and He continues to do it over and over again.

Yep, there are a lot of differences between our two families. Unlike Kay, Mom is not a cook. She actually doesn't even care about food. Never has. I would say Mom pretty much just eats to live rather than lives to eat like the Robertson family. Dad had colon cancer in 2000, and my parents became pescetarians after that, which means they eat only fruit, veggies, and things that swim. They actually went to a "camp" to learn how to eat vegetarian. We've made fun of them for years for going to "veggie camp," but I have actually tried to get Willie to go there with me sometime. I don't want to give up meat, but it wouldn't hurt to get more veggies in our diet. I doubt I'll ever get him to set foot there, but he did actually get into juicing recently. We are using my parents' juicer until we make sure it sticks. He's loving it; he says it's fun creating new juicing "recipes," and they actually don't taste that bad! So while my mom is no Miss Kay in the kitchen, there are things we can learn from both sides of the family in regards to food.

It's pretty plain to see the differences in our families, but what you may not realize is that they are alike in the most critical way—our faith. Some of the most important lessons my parents taught me were those of generosity and service. I really can't remember a time when we didn't have someone living in our home who needed a place to stay—from struggling single moms with kids to entire families that needed somewhere to live while they got back on their feet. I saw this same trait in the Robertson family, and I loved it. They may not have had as much as we did growing up, but the generosity of spirit and hospitality was there just the same. Their home was always open, and there was always an extra spot at the dinner table for whoever needed a helping hand or just someone to talk to. As it says in Psalm 41:1–2: "Blessed are those who have regard for the weak; the Lord delivers them in times of trouble. The Lord protects and preserves them—they are counted among the blessed in the land—He does not give them over to the desire of their foes."

My family has been very successful in business, but none of that would have mattered without our faith in God. While we were growing up, my parents would often tell us that all the blessings we had were nice, but if we lost it all tomorrow, we would still be just fine. And I always believed it. I think that is one of the reasons Willie and I were willing to take the risks we needed to with Duck Commander. We always had the faith that if we failed, if we lost it all, we would just shake ourselves off and get right back up. As long as we had our faith and our family, nothing could really hurt us. God has blessed us, life is good, but if the fame and fortune that we've enjoyed through Duck Commander were all gone tomorrow, I would still say the same thing: that God is good.

FRIED CATFISH

Go catch 'em! It's hard to mess up this recipe. Be patient and wait on the grease; make sure it is hot. When the catfish come out, you only have a few seconds to "hit" them with seasoning. Cut the dark parts out of the fish; they taste terrible.

peanut oil (enough to fill pot to about 4 inches deep)
8 catfish fillets, skin removed
1 tablespoon salt
2 tablespoons pepper
Phil Robertson's Cajun Style Seasoning, to taste
3 cups cornmeal

1. Heat a fryer or a deep pot halfway filled with oil to 350 degrees.
2. Sprinkle both sides of each catfish fillet with salt, pepper, and Cajun Style Seasoning.
3. Coat fish with cornmeal.
4. Place fillets in fryer and deep-fry for approximately 7 to 8 minutes until well-done.
5. Set catfish on paper towels and add one more sprinkle of Cajun Style Seasoning.

4

FREE LUNCH

I AM NOT SAYING THIS BECAUSE I AM IN NEED, FOR I HAVE LEARNED TO BE CONTENT WHATEVER THE CIRCUMSTANCES. I KNOW WHAT IT IS TO BE IN NEED, AND I KNOW WHAT IT IS TO HAVE PLENTY. I HAVE LEARNED THE SECRET OF BEING CONTENT IN ANY AND EVERY SITUATION, WHETHER WELL FED OR HUNGRY, WHETHER LIVING IN PLENTY OR IN WANT. I CAN DO ALL THIS THROUGH HIM WHO GIVES ME STRENGTH.

—**PHILIPPIANS 4:11–13**

I still remember my first day of school. Kay put me on the school bus and waved good-bye.

Korie: Willie rode the school bus on his very first day of kindergarten! And he wasn't even scarred for life! I'm kidding, of course, but this did shock me when I first heard it. It was so different from my experience. At our house, the first day of school was a big deal every year, not just kindergarten. Mom would take pictures of us in our "first day" outfits, drive us there, go in and meet the teacher, and make sure we had all of our supplies.

Today, we make a big deal out of the first day of school in

our home as well. We got together with my mom on the first day for a prayer before the kids start the new school year, asking God to bless them and to allow them to be a light for Him to their friends throughout the school year. We've been doing that ever since John Luke started his first day of kindergarten. He doesn't let me take his picture with his teachers anymore, but I still take whatever pictures I can. I, at least, make him take one picture with his brother and sisters on the first day of school and he appeases me, because I'm his mom, and he loves me!

I can just imagine little Willie getting on that school bus for his first day all by himself, full of confidence and certain that if he just flashed those dimples, the world would be his. And it usually was.

Somehow I made it to Pinecrest Elementary School and jumped off the bus with my little book satchel. The principal was standing there when I got off the bus.

"Hey, I'm Willie Jess Robertson and I'm looking for the kindergarten room," I told him in the most professional way I could.

The principal pointed down a hall and said, "It's right down there."

I got to my teacher's room and one of my best friends, Mel Hamilton, was crying because I wasn't there yet. I consoled him and was proud that someone needed me. School was going to be fun.

When I started kindergarten, we received free lunches

because our family didn't have any money. I thought everybody was on free lunch; I didn't even realize we were poor. But there were actually only about three kids in my class receiving free lunches, and I was one of them. There was a little boy who sat in front of me in kindergarten, and I thought he was really poor. He would come to school covered in dirt and didn't smell very good. One day, I took a bar of soap to school and put it on his desk. I wasn't trying to be mean or anything; I just didn't think he had any soap at home. Later in life, once I realized that we were getting the free lunches because we were poor just like that little kid, I remember thinking, "Man, were we that poor?"

I THOUGHT EVERYBODY WAS ON FREE LUNCH; I DIDN'T EVEN REALIZE WE WERE POOR.

Over the next few years, I noticed that our family was beginning to make more money. When we went from receiving free lunches to getting reduced lunches, I thought that was a sign that Duck Commander was taking off. When we started paying for our own lunches, I thought, "Man, we must be rich now!"

The Robertson boys had a good reputation at school. Phil and Kay made sure that we treated our classmates and teachers with respect. They always insisted we behave at school and listen to our teachers. Even if we weren't the best-dressed students and didn't even have enough money to pay for our lunches, we were all voted class favorite at one time or another. Actually, I was voted "class favorite" several years in elementary school and was class president in ninth grade, with the campaign slogan "Don't be silly, vote for Willie!"

I learned how to make extra money at an early age. I thought I was the cutest kid in school, so I was surely going to use it to my advantage. In elementary school, the concession stand never sold the candy I liked to eat, so I decided I was going to bring my own candy to school and sell it to my classmates. It started with a box of chewing gum someone had given us. I took the gum to school and sold it for thirty cents apiece. Then I had Kay take me to the store, and I bought Lemon Heads, Red Hots, Mike and Ikes, and all sorts of other candy. I stored the candy in my locker, and my classmates started calling me the "Little Tycoon." I was making like three hundred dollars a week, minus the 10 percent I paid Kay for driving me to the store for supplies.

Now, there were some occupational hazards associated with the job. Darla Leonard, who rode my school bus, was older than me. She would strong-arm me every morning and make me give her free candy.

"No, it's thirty cents," I would tell her.

"How about nothing?" Darla would say before grabbing a fistful of my hair.

It made me so mad, but she was bigger than me, so there wasn't much I could do about it. She goes to our church now, and I could definitely take her these days. She's a tiny little woman, so it's funny to think that I was once scared of her.

After a few months of selling the candy, the principal called me to his office.

"I'm hearing you're selling candy to other students," Mr. McCall told me. "Are you?"

There was no denying it.

"The concession stand's sales are way down and they're complaining about it," the principal said. "I'm going to have to shut you down."

I quit selling the candy, but I still found other ways to make money. I sold everything from pencils and erasers to orange juice tops (which I claimed once sat on Abraham Lincoln's eyes!). The kids were just used to giving me their money, so I found creative ways to take it. I would eat June bugs for fifty cents and sing on the school bus for a quarter. One of my favorite moneymaking schemes involved my turning into a human jukebox. Kids would put quarters under my arms, and I would start singing. The only songs I knew were the ones my older brother Alan had on eight-tracks. Foreigner's "Juke Box Hero" was always the number one request, but I also sang songs by the Beach Boys, the Gap Band, Molly Hatchet, and Michael Jackson. I was the school bus entertainment. We went to a small country school so everyone lived far apart. I think we were on the bus about two hours each way, so this was a great way to pass the time.

I WOULD EAT JUNE BUGS FOR FIFTY CENTS AND SING ON THE SCHOOL BUS FOR A QUARTER.

Phil's philosophy about education was a lot like his philosophies about everything else in life. If my brothers or I told Phil we wanted to quit high school, he would look at us and say, "You wanna drop out of school? Knock yourself out, but don't come running to me." Then Phil would tell us that he wouldn't recommend quitting school. He would always tell us to make the best grades we could make, get our homework done, earn our diplomas, and get out of there. I've heard people talk about "helicopter parenting," where the parents hover over their kids, watching their every move. There was no danger of that in our house. We were pretty much on our own and were expected to do the best we could do with it.

Phil never told us we had to go to college or anything like that. If we woke up in the morning and decided we wanted to blow off school, we would just blow it off. Phil would never say anything about it. I never asked for Phil's permission to stay home; if I didn't want to go to school, I just didn't go. But Phil always told me if I missed too many days and got kicked out of school, I would have to deal with the consequences. We missed the maximum amount of days you could possibly miss every year, mainly during hunting season. We took full advantage of sick days to spend time in the woods.

Korie: This was not the case in my house. If you stayed home from school, you were going to the doctor, so you had to weigh the pros and cons. We took school seriously. We were never punished for making bad grades or anything like that; it was just expected that we'd work hard in school and do the best we could. And we did. Mom would say that school and the after-school activities we were involved in were our "job," and we were expected to give it our all. If we started something, we couldn't just quit it because we didn't want to do it anymore. We had to finish what we started. If it was a sport, we were part of a team and had a responsibility to our teammates to give it our best.

Mom was big on our learning new skills, so I took everything from tennis to baton lessons, diving to piano lessons, and played every sport at least one year. I think it gave me confidence that I could do anything if I worked at it. I still impress my kids with my backflips off the diving board and gymnastic tricks on the trampoline, but the piano lessons never stuck. The best I can do today is "Chopsticks," and I took piano for three years! I just wasn't good at it. My brother, on the other hand, plays piano beautifully.

MOM WOULD SAY THAT SCHOOL AND THE AFTER-SCHOOL ACTIVITIES WE WERE INVOLVED IN WERE OUR "JOB," AND WE WERE EXPECTED TO GIVE IT OUR ALL.

With our children, I try to find the happy middle ground between how I was raised and Willie's upbringing. We expect our kids to do well in school and they all do, but there are times when we just decide to stay home. I figure the school gives us fifteen days a year for a reason. We might as well take them. Also, I want our kids to learn several different skills so they can find the thing they are good at and that they love, but I don't sign them up for quite as much as we did when I was a kid. I remember feeling like we were always on the go and just wanted to be home more at times. So I make sure our kids are involved in at least one sport, but the other lessons we try to space out so we don't spend our afternoons in the car rushing from one event to the next. I like for them to have the time to just be home and to explore and sometimes even to be bored and learn to create their own adventures.

When I was growing up in West Monroe, you technically didn't start high school until you were in the tenth grade. The ninth grade was still considered a part of middle school back then. We attended a middle school out in the country, but then everybody moved up to West Monroe High School in the tenth grade. When I was getting ready to go to the tenth grade in 1987, though, they were in the process of building a new high school. All of the kids from my part of the parish were allowed to choose whether they wanted to start the school year at West Monroe or go to the new school that was called West Ouachita.

Well, I decided to try out the new school since it was closer to home, and it seemed like the best choice. I went to the first day of school and checked in. I went to PE class on the first day, but we couldn't play basketball because they still hadn't put up the lights in the gymnasium. We had to sit there for an hour doing nothing. After about three days of sitting there, I said, "Screw this. I'm going to West Monroe High." I realized I wanted to be in town anyway, so I just transferred schools during the first week of school.

After about a month, the principal from West Ouachita called our house.

"Willie hasn't been to school for twenty-seven days," the principal told Phil.

"Well, he leaves for school every morning," Phil told him. "I don't know where he's going. I thought he was going to school."

"WILLIE HASN'T BEEN TO SCHOOL FOR TWENTY-SEVEN DAYS," THE PRINCIPAL TOLD PHIL.

When I got home that day, Phil asked me where I had been.

"School," I told him.

"Uh-uh," Phil said. "The school called and said you haven't been there in a month."

"Oh, yeah," I told him. "I transferred to West Monroe. I don't go to that school anymore."

"Okay," Phil said. "I figured something was up."

Korie: Can you imagine a tenth-grader transferring schools without even notifying his parents? Willie just showed up at West Monroe High School and said, "Hey, I'm here." He didn't even think about telling Kay and Phil about transferring.

When I got to high school, like most teens, I was becoming more and more social, so my entire objective was to get to town and stay there. Phil and Kay lived way out on the Ouachita River (they still live there today), and it's about a twenty-minute drive into town. Once I went to town, I knew I wasn't going home for a few days, because Phil and Kay never made a special trip to pick us up.

We lived so far out of town that I rarely spent the night at home during the week during my high school years. I spent a lot of nights with my best friend, Paul Lewis, who is African-

American, and his dad would cook all this weird stuff. I ate possum for the first time at Paul's house. I started eating the meat on my plate, and I was like, "Oh, my goodness." It had these tiny little legs. Paul's daddy had shot a possum and just threw it on the grill. It was nasty. Paul's daddy would also cook turtles and raccoons. You could bring him just about anything you killed, and he would cook it.

I was running around town with Paul all the time. I think it's safe to say I was the only white kid in his neighborhood. We were shooting basketball on the square one day, and a cop drove by and called me over to his police car. The cop asked me, "What are you doing over here? You don't need to be in this neighborhood."

"I know everybody in this neighborhood," I told him. "I practically live here."

Korie: By the time Willie was in high school, his parents pretty much just let him do his own thing. Willie slept wherever he could find a bed and meal. He even stayed at our house sometimes, which was fun. We were just friends at the time, so my parents didn't have a problem with it. He'd stay with Paul and with Mike Kellett, our youth minister, quite a bit too. Because Willie's parents' house was so far out of town, he and his brothers fended for themselves and were really, really independent. Willie didn't get his driver's license till he was seventeen years old just because nobody took him. He never told us he didn't have his license, though, and would drive my mom's van sometimes when he stayed at our house.

She didn't find out till we were married that he didn't have his license when he was driving her car. My dad about died!

Even though Kay and Phil let us run around town in middle school and high school, I don't think it was neglect or anything like that. Phil just never let anyone tell him what to do or how to do it, so I guess he figured we'd be the same way. He doesn't believe in going by what the world says you "should" do to have a good life or to be successful. Phil's philosophy was pretty simple: just follow what the Bible says and you'll be all right. And for the most part, we did.

PHIL'S PHILOSOPHY WAS PRETTY SIMPLE: JUST FOLLOW WHAT THE BIBLE SAYS AND YOU'LL BE ALL RIGHT. AND FOR THE MOST PART, WE DID.

I think my life was also shaped in a big way by what Kay and Phil and Pa and Granny taught each of us at an early age: be content with what you have and don't worry about what you don't have. Even in the lean times, there was a lot of love and laughter in the house. Some of my best memories are from when we had nothing. Who says you can't live on love? I think we did. We were thankful for what we had, comfortable with who we were, and always confident. We were Robertsons, for goodness' sake! And that meant something. When I was younger, I never believed I was different from anyone else—even if we were receiving free lunches.

WILLIE'S MEATLOAF

Be creative on this one. I got my foundation for this out of The Joy of Cooking *(which I go to all the time), then I started making stuff up. My only note on this: If the meat is full of grease, drain it. Check the meat while it is cooking. It's tricky to drain but do it if you have to. Growing up I hated meatloaf, but this one I like.*

2 pounds ground beef
1 pound andouille sausage
2 cups white onion, diced
1 clove garlic, minced
1½ cups bread crumbs, divided
⅔ cup parsley flakes
1 teaspoon oregano
1 teaspoon thyme
2 cups ketchup, divided
1 15-ounce can tomato sauce
4 eggs, beaten
2 cups mozzarella cheese
1 cup Parmesan cheese
1 tablespoon Phil Robertson's Cajun Style Seasoning
1 teaspoon salt
1 teaspoon pepper
5 or 6 slices bacon

1. Preheat oven to 350 degrees.
2. In a large cast-iron pot, combine ground beef, sausage, onion, garlic, 1 to 1¼ cups bread crumbs, parsley, oregano, thyme, 1 cup ketchup, tomato sauce, eggs, and mozzarella cheese. Use hands to thoroughly mix together.
3. Smooth meat mix in bottom of pot.
4. Cover meatloaf with Parmesan cheese, remaining bread crumbs, Cajun Style Seasoning, salt, and pepper.
5. Top meatloaf with remaining cup of ketchup and bacon.
6. Cook for 1½ hours, until middle of meatloaf is no longer pink.

5

TOAST 'N' PIZZA

A FRIEND LOVES AT ALL TIMES, AND A BROTHER
IS BORN FOR A TIME OF ADVERSITY.
—PROVERBS 17:17

When you watch *Duck Dynasty,* it might be pretty easy to see that Jase and I are very competitive. When we were younger, whether it was fishing, hunting, playing sports, or just about anything else, Jase and I loved a good competition. It wasn't just against each other. We would challenge anybody, but since we were the closest in age and lived all the way down at the mouth of the river, a long drive from civilization, for the most part we were all we had. So competing against each other and, more important, beating each other (and then reminding the loser about the details of our victory afterward) became our favorite pastime. It was that way when we were kids, and it's still that way today—whether it's in business, duck hunting, fishing, or golf.

When we were younger, we would spend every weekend and summer day competing against each other in something. Every day was about who could catch the most fish, throw the football the farthest, or shoot the most squirrels. When we wanted to go fishing, Phil and Kay would never buy bait for us, so we would have to go out and find our own bait. I was really good at it. We'd catch crickets or grasshoppers or dig for earthworms. Our neighbors had some catalpa trees and they were always covered with black worms that had two lines on their backs. We would take those worms and just go wear fish out with them. I used those worms in one of my earliest business ventures. I set up an old boat and literally filled it with cow manure. Our neighbors had cows, so I spent days picking it up to get an entire boatful. I would just pick it up with my hands. Worms thrive in cow manure, so I created a worm farm in it, and these worms were huge! Remember the boat dock that Granny charged people to use? Well, it was an easy marketplace. My customers were coming to me. I would set up my little stand and sell worms for five cents apiece all day long. Nowadays, Korie's always asking me to go buy bait for the kids when they want to go fishing. Now, I can afford it, but something seems wrong about buying something you can find for yourself if you'll just go outside and turn over a few logs.

I carried my fishing pole with me everywhere. We would fish on Cypress Creek, which ran next to our house, as well as sneak on other people's ponds to fish. As Jase and I got older, we started expanding our fishing territory. Judge John Harrison, the state district judge in Monroe, had a fishing camp up the road from our house. The judge was only there on the weekends, so we'd sneak under his gate and fish his pond all week when he wasn't around. The judge had built a bridge across his pond, and the first time I saw it, I was like, "You've got to be kidding me!" I was so excited my arms were actually shaking while I held my fishing pole off the bridge. I threw my line into the pond and a fish immediately hit the hook. My cork flew under the water, and I immediately dropped my pole. I ran back to our house as fast as I could to get Jase.

THE JUDGE WAS ONLY THERE ON THE WEEKENDS, SO WE'D SNEAK UNDER HIS GATE AND FISH HIS POND ALL WEEK WHEN HE WASN'T AROUND.

"I've found the mother lode!" I told Jase. "You will not believe how many fish are in this pond!"

Jase and I ran back to the judge's pond, and we stayed there the entire summer. We probably caught every bream in the pond and then we put out trout lines. We even carried our boat up the river and into the pond and fished from it all summer. When we were done fishing for the day, we would leave our poles behind and hide the boat. One time when we came back, the judge had taken our fishing poles, so we knew he was onto us, but that didn't stop us. By the end of the summer, we had cut a ditch under the gate from sliding under it. When we were finished with that pond, you couldn't even get a bite anymore. We literally caught every fish in the pond!

Whenever Jase and I were fishing, we always had our own fishing spots. Jase would always try to creep over to my spot if the fish were biting, and we would end up getting in a fight right there on the bank. One day Jase and I were fighting, and

I looked at him and said, "You're a whore." I'd heard the word somewhere and didn't really know what it meant, but I knew it was bad. Jase turned around and looked at me.

"What did you call me?" Jase asked.

"I said you're a whore," I told him.

Jase didn't know what the word meant either, but he still ran as fast as he could back to the house to tell Phil what I had called him. Of course, Phil knew what it meant and I got a whippin' for it.

When we were old enough, I think we got a whippin' nearly every day for fighting and misbehaving. Jase would usually get three licks from Phil, but I would only get one because I would already be screaming and twisting before the first lick ever hit me. Jase always tried not to cry because he thought it made him tougher than me, but I didn't care. It was self-preservation. Hebrews 12:11 says, "No discipline seems pleasant at the time, but painful. Later on, however, it produces a harvest of righteousness and peace for those who have been trained by it." This is so true!

Since I was the baby of the family at the time, my older brothers and their friends could hit harder than me, so I had to come up with a different tactic if I was ever going to get a lick in. I figured the only way to get them good was to throw something at them, then count on my running skills to get away. I had a pretty good throwing arm; must've gotten that from my old man. One day Jase pushed me out of the recliner and stole my seat in the living room.

"I'm the king of the house," Jase yelled proudly.

I was so mad I went to my room and got a twelve-gauge shotgun shell. I was leaning out the door and said, "You're the king of the house, huh?"

"Yep, king of the house," Jase said.

I reared back and hit Jase right in the forehead with the shotgun shell. He caught me at the top of the hill behind our house and shoved dirt in my mouth. I knew if I told Phil and Kay about it, I would be in trouble, too, so I kept my mouth shut and planned my next attack.

Alan was the oldest boy in the family. He was really too big and too much older than us to be fighting with Jase and me, but he always liked to get our fights started and then just sit back and watch. It was like entertainment for him to see how our fights would play out. Al always brought his buddies over to the house to play basketball, and they would start picking on me because I was the youngest. One day I'd had enough of their teasing and grabbed a basketball and hit one of Al's buddies right upside the head with it. I took off running. I knew I couldn't outrun Al, but I was faster than all of his buddies. I ran into the woods and they never caught me.

Al and his friends loved to play tricks on me. Sometimes after I had gone to sleep they would shake me, hollering, "Willie, wake up; it's time for school." I was a pretty heavy sleeper, but I'd wake up, get dressed, brush my teeth, and then go sit on the couch. They would all look at me and just start laughing because it would be like one o'clock in the morning.

WHILE WE ALWAYS SEEMED TO BE IN TROUBLE AT HOME, WE WERE NEVER IN TROUBLE AT SCHOOL OR CHURCH.

Our fights usually ended with a good whipping. We probably deserved even more than we got. We were rough boys who all had a strong, stubborn streak, and while we always seemed to be in trouble at home, we were never in trouble at school or church. We were well-mannered, respectful kids. Kay and Phil say that our teachers always bragged on how good we were. But at home, it seemed like we were always either about to get a whippin' or just coming off one.

Korie: Hearing all these stories about the whippings and fighting always shocks me. It is just so different from the way I grew up. First of all, we didn't call them whippings, we called them spankings, and we did get them, but they were few and far between. I had one brother and one sister and we just were not allowed to fight. I remember pinching my brother when we were little, but that was as bad as it got. I honestly do not remember one time when one of us hit the other because we were mad.

Calling someone stupid or saying "shut up" were absolutely forbidden, as well. One of my mom's favorite sayings was "If you can't say something nice, don't say anything at all." So when my sister and I were mad at our brother, we would give him what we called the "silent treatment." We wouldn't talk to him and basically ignored him for as long as we deemed necessary. It drove him crazy, but we were following Mom's advice. That's pretty much the end of our family's fighting stories!

An example of our getting away without the whipping we deserved, or at least Jase deserved, happened when Kay was over at Granny's house watching *Dallas*. For some reason, Jase thought it would be really funny to lock me out of the house, and I was furious. I kept banging on the door, but Jase had turned the music up loud so he wouldn't hear me. He kicked his feet up on a table and kept yelling, "I can't hear you. I can't hear you." I went to Granny's house and told Kay what Jase had done. Kay went marching back to our house and was hotter than a catfish fry in July. She started banging on the door, but Jase thought it was still me and just kept blaring the music and enjoying having the house to himself. Kay got so angry that she banged on the glass pane and her fist went right through the window, cutting up her hand pretty badly.

This caught Jase's attention. When he saw her hand, he knew he was in big trouble. "When your dad gets home, he's going to whip y'all's butts," Kay told us.

I hadn't even done anything, but Phil didn't usually conduct an investigation to find out who was at fault. He just whipped whoever was in the vicinity of the crime. Jase and I ran back to our room and padded up with anything we could find—socks, underwear, and pillowcases. We sat on our bed with our butts padded, waiting for Phil to get home, certain we were in big trouble. Phil came into the house and saw the bandage on Kay's hand.

"What in the world did you do?" Phil asked her.

"Look at what these boys did," Kay told him. "Jase locked Willie out of the house, and I was banging on the door for him to let us in. My hand went right through the window."

"Kay, that's the dumbest thing I've ever heard. Why would you bang on a glass window?" Phil said.

Phil walked right by her and took a shower. Jase and I were standing there with padded behinds, our mouths wide open with relief.

Phil was always in charge of disciplining us, but sometimes Kay tried to take matters into her own hands. Unfortunately for Kay, she was really an uncoordinated disciplinarian. One day when Phil was out fishing, Kay announced that she was going to whip us. She grabbed a belt that had a buckle on one end and told us to line up for a whipping. Now, Kay never liked whipping us and always closed her eyes when she swung because she didn't want to watch. This time, she reared back and swung and missed, and the buckle flew back and hit her right in the forehead. Jase and I just looked at her, started laughing, and took off running into the backyard. I really don't know how she survived raising us four boys.

Korie: Poor Kay! All that testosterone in one house! Maybe that's why she is so great to us daughters-in-law. She is thankful we took them off her hands. She has definitely enjoyed all of her granddaughters. She has set up a cute little library and a place for tea parties. They have coloring contests and dress-up parties. She didn't get to do any of that with her four boys so our daughters have gotten the full "girly" grandma treatment.

One time, I was painting something outside and came into the house with green paint on my hand. Kay looked at me and said, "I'm going to whip you for bringing paint in the house."

I ran out of the room and put my painted hand on the bed to maneuver my way around her. The bedspread had a green handprint on it for like ten years. I ran through the kitchen and tried to kick open the back screen door, but it wouldn't open, so I ran face-first into it. Before I could get into the backyard, Kay grabbed a fistful of my hair. Kay would always pull your hair; that was the only way she could really control us. We all had little bald spots on our heads from where Kay pulled out our hair. I don't think Jep's hair ever grew back fully. He still has some bald spots back there.

Kay also liked to turn her wedding ring around and knock you upside the head. She would just turn it around and give you a whack if you were out of line. One time, she hit Jase in the forehead with a steel Stanley broom. Jase was messing with me about something, and Kay said she was tired of listening to it. Phil looked at her and said, "Well, do something about it then." So when Jase came around the door, Kay hit him right in the forehead with a broom! Jase was so mad he ran away. No one knew where Jase was after he left; he sat on top of the house like a big rooster for two days.

I was usually the one running away when I was in trouble or mad about something. This generally just involved going to the top of the hill behind our house and staying there until I was cold, hungry, or bored. I would get in trouble for something and then announce angrily, "I'm running away." It would take me thirty minutes to get all my stuff packed to leave, and Kay would be right there helping me pack. I would ask her, "Mom, where's the Beanee Weenees? Where's my sleeping bag?" She'd run into my room with a can of Beanee Weenees and my sleeping bag, making sure I had everything I needed. Of course, I would always come home as soon as I smelled dinner. I spent more time packing up than I spent away.

JASE WAS SO MAD HE RAN AWAY. HE SAT ON TOP OF THE HOUSE LIKE A BIG ROOSTER FOR TWO DAYS.

For whatever reason, Kay always bought our clothes in pairs. If she bought Jase a blue shirt, I'd get an identical blue shirt. If she bought Jase yellow shorts, I'd get the same pair of yellow shorts. When we were riding the same school bus, Jase would usually get to the school bus stop before me. I always liked to wear the same clothes Jase was wearing because I knew it drove him crazy. Once I saw what Jase was wearing for the day, I would wait until he went outside, then I'd run back in the house and put on the same shirt he had on. Jase would always hit me when I showed up wearing the same clothes as him. Not sure why I did it, because it was a guaranteed lick, but somehow seeing Jase's face was worth it. And although I hate to admit it, maybe there was a little part of me that wanted to be like my older brother.

Phil was good at finding other ways of disciplining us, too.

Every Sunday, our family would load up in Pa's Lincoln Town Car to make the drive to church. There were two bench seats in the car, and eight of us would be packed in there like sardines. It was really too cramped and a fight would undoubtedly break out every Sunday. There was just way too much touching. One time, Phil stopped the car about four miles from our house and told Jase and me to get out. He made us walk those four miles home. We missed Sunday lunch and still got a whipping when we got home. That cut down on the fighting for a while. Somehow after that we figured out how to get along, at least when Dad was in the car.

Kay used to drive an old, beat-up Volkswagen Beetle to work. There was a hole in the back floorboard, which was probably about two feet by three feet wide. She could have been arrested for having kids in the backseat of her car with a hole that big! Every time we went for a drive, Phil would put a board over the hole. Of course, Jase and I would move the board as soon as we pulled out of the driveway, so we could see the road while we were driving. You could have literally stuck your hand down and touched the road. Our favorite thing to do was throw trash out the hole. And that was another thing that usually ended in a whipping when we got home.

Some of my most fun childhood memories are of when my cousins came over. My dad had six siblings, so when the cousins all got together, we were quite the crew. It's safe to say that our cousins didn't grow up the way we did. I'm pretty sure most of them actually lived in subdivisions! I'm sure they thought we were a little backwoods. But they all say they loved it when they got to come visit us. I think they were surprised by how rough we all were, though. We would get in a big circle and two people would wrestle in the middle. It didn't matter if you were a boy or a girl; if you were brave enough to join the fight, you were fair game. I would always end up wrestling my cousin Amy, who was older and bigger than me. But my killer move was putting the leg scissors around her head. If I ever got my legs wrapped around her head, it was lights out. I would wrap my legs around her head and squeeze as hard as I could. One time I was wrestling Amy and she was screaming and crying, and her little brother, Jon, came running up and yelled, "Leave my sister alone!" He was wrapped around my neck and before too long, both of them were just whaling on me. Alan was always the referee, so he had to pull John off my head and send everyone back to their corners.

When we weren't wrestling, we'd take my cousins into our room for a pillow fight. This wasn't just your normal pillow fight. We always had to take it up a notch. There would be one person in the middle of the room with a pillowcase over their head. The other people were holding pillows, whose pillowcases we'd stuffed with blue jeans and anything else we could find. When the lights went out, we would pummel the person sitting in the middle. I don't know how we didn't end up killing each other. I liked to grab my smaller cousins and throw them in a headlock and make them smell

WHEN WE WEREN'T WRESTLING, WE'D TAKE MY COUSINS INTO OUR ROOM FOR A PILLOW FIGHT.

my armpits, too. Those were the good ole days. I was just awful.

Jase and I fought like crazy when we were younger, but as we got older we were really close. We never played organized sports when we were kids because Kay and Phil were so busy trying to get Duck Commander off the ground and make enough money to feed our family that there was no time to chauffeur us kids to baseball or basketball practice. But once we got old enough to drive ourselves, we played every sport we could. We went to a big public high school, so there wasn't much chance of our getting a lot of playing time on the basketball court or in the baseball field. So we played church- and city-league basketball and softball all that we could, and we always played on the same team. Those were some really fun times.

Every year I would play on West Monroe High School's basketball team until church league started. This worked out pretty well. I got out of having to go to PE. I got to practice with the team, so I got really good; then I would quit and play in a league where we could dominate. I was always in charge of assembling our church-league team, which was pretty easy because we only had six players. The team consisted of Jase, Paul, his two brothers, our youth minister, and myself. None of us liked having to sit out of the games, so we didn't carry much of a bench.

We had a really good team. I bet we averaged more than a hundred points per game. In a lot of games, we would run over the scoreboard, so the final score would read forty-two points to twenty-seven, when we'd actually scored one hundred and forty-two points. The scoreboard couldn't even keep up with us! Jase was a set three-point shooter, but he couldn't make layups to save his life. He would run back and always shoot a three-pointer; it was the only shot he ever took or made. In one game, Jase scored thirty-four points—thirty-three came on three-pointers, and he made one foul shot. He always took a high, arching shot and made most of them. I was the point guard of the team, but I liked to shoot the ball, too. When I went to college, I continued to play in recreation leagues, and I played for my fraternity, too—but more about that later.

At any rate, Jase and I had finally figured out a way to turn our competitive natures to sports, and it was serving us well. That is why our last fight—I was sixteen and he was eighteen—came as a surprise to both of us. Our last fight was a bad one. And it was over toast and pizza! I was at home one night and our friend "Curly" Don Foster was sitting on the couch. Curly Don was living with us at the time; one of our friends always seemed to be living with us because Phil and Kay were always willing to help out anyone who needed it. Curly Don and I were watching TV and cooking a frozen pizza in the oven. Jase walked into the house and started making himself some toast, which he then wanted to put in the oven, but my pizza was already in there. We had a small toaster oven, but Jase didn't want to use it because he was making like twelve pieces of toast and he wanted to cook it all at one time.

"I'm going to take your pizza out for a minute and cook my toast really fast," Jase told me.

"Uh-uh, son," I told him. "When my pizza is done, you can have the oven."

"No, I can just change the oven to broil and put my toast right on top," Jase said. "It will cook really quick."

I wasn't having any of it. Both of us grabbed the oven door and started arguing about who was going to cook their meal first. I looked at Jase and shouldered him right into the refrigerator, making a big dent in the door. We were both into watching wrestling, and Jake "the Snake" Roberts was one of our favorite wrestlers. Jase picked me up and put me into Roberts's signature move, the "DDT," picking me up by my pants and lifting me so my legs were straight up in the air. All of a sudden, Jase dropped my head right into a barrel of flour Kay kept in the kitchen. Flour went everywhere. The entire kitchen was covered in a cloud of white!

I put my shoulder into Jase again—I don't know why I kept trying to use that move—and we went flying across the kitchen table. Fortunately, the table didn't break. But the flour barrel splintered and lay flat on the kitchen floor. Jase and I were both covered in flour, and the kitchen was an absolute mess.

THE FLOUR BARREL SPLINTERED AND LAY FLAT ON THE KITCHEN FLOOR.

Curly Don was sitting on the couch watching us fight.

"Don't y'all look like two fine Christians?" he told us, once we settled down enough to hear what he was saying.

I ran out of the house and jumped into Uncle Si's Nissan

truck and drove around for a while. I knew I had to go home and clean up the mess before Phil and Kay got home, or we'd both be in big trouble, but I needed to calm down first. I walked back into the house and apologized to Jase. He did his best to apologize to me (he told me to shut up or something). We've never had a physical fight since. We both realized we were too old and too big to be fighting like that. We could hurt each other or break something else. And to be honest, Curly's comment about our being fine Christians really made an impact on us. Jase and I are brothers, and we realized that wasn't the way God wanted us to be treating each other. Kay was always quoting 1 John 4:20: "For whoever does not love their brother and sister, whom they have seen, cannot love God, whom they have not seen." This was a time in our life when our spiritual walk was growing, and this was a lesson that has stuck with me.

All of our Robertson confidence and stubbornness could serve us well in life, but if we were selfish and didn't use it for the good, it could be to our detriment. We had to figure out how to get along with each other and with others, and we were learning those lessons. Most important, we had to learn how to love as God defines it. As 1 Corinthians 13:4–5 says, "Love is patient, love is kind. It does not envy, it does not boast, it is not proud. It does not dishonor others, it is not self-seeking, it is not easily angered, it keeps no record of wrongs." These were tough lessons for a couple of

WE HAD TO FIGURE OUT HOW TO GET ALONG WITH EACH OTHER AND WITH OTHERS.

country boys, but I'm glad Phil and Kay kept "beating" it into us and Curly Don was there at the right time to remind us.

We shook hands and cleaned up the kitchen. The worst part was that during all the commotion, I burned my frozen pizza.

Duck Sausage Pizza

Looking for something weird? Well, here it is! We love pizza at the Robertson household. I have tried all sorts of weird toppings on pizza, and am actually building a pizza oven so I can explore even more. Cooking is all about the exploration. Pizza is the most fun food you can experiment with. Put on whatever you like.

1 tablespoon extra-virgin olive oil
2 garlic cloves, minced
⅛ cup crushed red pepper
1 thin pizza crust, fully baked
1½ cups grated mozzarella cheese
½ cup tomatoes, diced
½ teaspoon dried oregano
⅓ cup green onions, diced
2 smoked duck sausages, sliced
½ cup grated Parmesan cheese

1. Preheat oven to 450 degrees.
2. Mix olive oil, garlic, and red pepper in small bowl.
3. Place pizza crust on baking sheet.
4. Sprinkle pizza crust with mozzarella cheese.
5. Top pizza with tomatoes, oregano, green onions, sliced sausage, and Parmesan cheese.
6. Drizzle olive oil mixture over pizza.
7. Bake pizza about fifteen minutes, or until cheese is melted and crust is brown.

6

ROADKILL

GOD BLESSED THEM AND SAID TO THEM, "BE FRUITFUL AND INCREASE IN NUMBER; FILL THE EARTH AND SUBDUE IT. RULE OVER THE FISH IN THE SEA AND THE BIRDS IN THE SKY AND OVER EVERY LIVING CREATURE THAT MOVES ON THE GROUND."

—GENESIS 1:28

Growing up Robertson meant we were all involved in the family business, whatever it was at the time. As we got older that meant helping with duck calls, but in the early days, Phil had other ways to support his family while Duck Commander was getting off the ground. Some of these jobs we enjoyed; others, not so much.

For several years, Dad was in the commercial fishing business, and of course, we all helped out. I started fishing with Phil when I was about six years old. Jase was older than me, so he would go out on the boat and be his motorman, while Phil pulled up the nets.

One of the worst jobs was baiting the nets, which involved filling socks with rotten cheese. I can still recall the horrible smell! Phil would buy a fifty-five-gallon drum of rotten cheese, which was always covered in maggots. We had to reach our hands down into the drum to scoop the cheese and then shove it into an old sock, gagging the entire time. We filled the socks with the rotten cheese at daybreak, and then Phil would go out and set out the traps. At daylight, Phil and Jase would leave and run the fishing nets until about ten o'clock in the morning. Kay and I would be waiting on the dock for them when they returned, and then Jase and I unloaded the fish and carried them back to the house.

After we put the fish in the back of the truck, Kay and I would then drive to town to go to the markets and sell the fresh fish. One store would take maybe half of the fish, and then we'd head to another store to sell the rest. If we had any fish left after hitting the markets, we'd sit on the side of the road and sell them to the public. I learned pretty quickly that the faster you sold the fish, the faster you got to go home. I learned how to be a good salesman by selling those fish on the side of the road when I was a kid. When it's hot, fish spoil quickly, so there was no time to waste. Once I saw that Mom was more likely to spend some of that cash we made on something I wanted at the store if I did a good job that day, that was just the motivation I needed to work on my craft.

As I got older and wanted to buy more things, I realized selling stuff was my ticket. I mostly wanted an awesome boom box, tapes, and parachute pants. Mom wouldn't buy me the really cool parachute pants with all the zippers; she got me crappy ones that just looked like a windbreaker and didn't have zippers all over them. One summer I sold enough worms on the boat dock to finally get those pants, which looked exactly like Michael Jackson's. They were awesome.

When I was in high school, Phil decided he wanted to get into crawfishing. Like most other things, I'm sure we were doing it unlike anyone else. The problem with crawfish is you can never have enough bait. A crawfish will literally eat anything—as long as it's dead and smells really bad. So if Jase and I spotted a dead possum lying in the road, we'd pick it up and throw it in the back of the truck. We were always looking for roadkill! We took the dead animals home, chopped them up, and threw them into the crawfish nets. Getting the bait became just as fun as the crawfishing.

We had an old deep-freezer in the shop and started throwing roadkill in it. By the end of the summer, the freezer was filled with dead cats, dogs, deer, coons, possums, ducks, and anything else we could find in the road. It smelled awful! We also put tons of snakes in there. We baited snake traps in the water with little perch. We'd pull up the traps at night and then blast the snakes with shotguns. We'd get maybe eight snakes a night; most of them were water snakes but there were always a couple of water moccasins. You never knew what you were going to find in a snake trap.

One night I caught a huge water snake and shot it in the head. I carried it up to the freezer and came back about ten minutes later with my cleaver to chop it up. I reached down in the freezer and grabbed the snake. That snake coiled up and reared its head back with its mouth wide open, ready to strike.

It apparently wasn't dead yet, but it nearly scared me half to death! I threw it down and hit it with the cleaver as hard and as fast as I could. Water snakes aren't poisonous, but that was a big snake. Its bite certainly would have hurt. My heart was racing!

Whenever one of our friends or cousins came to the house, we made them look in the freezer. It looked like a pet cemetery in there! Our family's staple foods were the fish and the crawfish we caught, and you had to have food for the crawfish and bait for the fish as well. The stuff we found on the road worked great for both of these duties, and it was free. We were making lemonade out of lemons, son!

We hunted snakes a lot when I was a kid. In the summer of 1991, the Ouachita River flooded Phil's property pretty badly. Granny and Pa's house was lower to the ground than Phil's, so there was almost six feet of water in their house. Once the snakes got into their house, they couldn't get out. I remember floating around the property on a big Styrofoam block, shooting snakes in the water. We would just sit on the front porch and shoot water moccasins.

Korie: Willie and I were dating by this time, and this was just crazy to me! Because everything was flooded, we had to park up the hill and take a boat to get to their house. They would always have a gun in the boat and would shoot snakes as we rode up. I remember one day when I was down there, Granny needed something from the kitchen in her house, which was literally halfway underwater. Willie got on a block of Styrofoam and paddled into the dark, snake-infested house to retrieve the pot his granny wanted to salvage from her upper kitchen cabinets. It seemed like he stayed in there way longer than he should have. I was scared to death for him, but he came out triumphant and I was proud of my man!

Our crawfish business ended up being pretty lucrative. We sold crawfish commercially to the markets in Monroe. We actually put a boat up on sawhorses and sold live crawfish out of it in the Super 1 grocery store. It was hard keeping the boat filled with crawfish all the time. Like with a snake trap, you never know what you're going to find when you pull up a crawfish trap. You can pick up a trap and find poisonous snakes and about everything else. I picked up a trap one time and there was a big, green river eel in it. This was a good find for crawfish bait. When Phil shoots a duck, he bites its head to make sure it's dead. That eel was still alive, and I didn't have anything with me to kill it, so what's the logical thing to do? I bit the eel's head as hard as I could, and let me tell you something, you can't bite through an eel's head! It's hard and slimy, and just nasty. It took me a week to get the slime out of my teeth! I never tried that again.

When we were growing up with nothing more than an idea in Dad's head for a duck call that sounded exactly like a duck, folks would sometimes look at us with pity and wonder why Dad didn't shave his beard and get a regular job. Some would even poke fun at us. We made it through some really tough times. We were a lot like that roadkill. Most people just saw a dead, stinky animal that had the bad luck to run out in front of the wrong vehicle. But when we saw roadkill, we saw something that could catch a sackful of crawfish. We saw potential in the most unlikely places!

Crawfish Balls

Phil's the king of the crawfish balls. These are his go-to appetizers. When he cooks them, I usually fill up on them before we get to the main dish.

1 stick butter
2 white onions, diced
¼ cup green onions, diced
1 bell pepper, diced
2 stalks celery, diced
8 cloves garlic, diced
¼ cup parsley flakes
1 teaspoon thyme
1 teaspoon basil
2 or 3 dashes of Louisiana hot sauce
salt and pepper to taste
1 pound lump crabmeat (cleaned)
1 pound crawfish tails, cooked
2 eggs
1½ cups Italian bread crumbs
⅔ cup all-purpose flour
peanut oil

1. On medium-high heat in a medium-size pan, sauté butter, white onions, green onions, bell pepper, and celery until vegetables are soft, about eight to ten minutes.
2. Add garlic, parsley, thyme, basil, and hot sauce.
3. Place mixture in a large bowl and season with salt and pepper.
4. Add crabmeat and crawfish tails. Mix well.
5. Beat eggs, add to mixture, and mix well.
6. Add enough bread crumbs to hold mixture together.
7. Make small patties and roll in flour.
8. Deep-fry in peanut oil on medium heat for 3 to 5 minutes or until golden brown.

7

OMELETS

THAT IS WHY A MAN LEAVES HIS FATHER AND MOTHER AND IS UNITED TO HIS WIFE, AND THEY BECOME ONE FLESH.
GENESIS 2:24

Growing up in the Robertson house, you never had much space or time for yourself. Our house had only two bedrooms, so I shared a room with Alan and Jase for most of my childhood. And then Jep came along, and it was just too crowded. I started looking for other places to sleep, where I wouldn't feel like I was packed in like a sardine.

When I was in middle school, I moved into the cook shack in front of our house, which was screened in at the time. It was during the summer so it wasn't cold, and it had a sink, which was really cool. I had a hot plate out there and cooked my own meals. I even moved into the building where we made the reeds for the duck calls. Neither of these places was very big and they didn't have any insulation, heat, or air-conditioning. They weren't exactly the lap of luxury, but for me, they were mine. And for some reason I always felt like I needed my own space.

Korie: I always thought it was cool that Willie was trying to make his own little place in the world. He liked to fix up his space and paint it. He was a big baseball fan and loved the Los Angeles Dodgers. When he moved into the cook shack, he painted it Dodger blue. Even though it wasn't much, Willie always tried to make it as nice as he could. He put pictures on the walls and would add his own little touches. He tried to have a nice little place to live. I've always been impressed by his ingenuity.

After a while, I figured out I needed to live in a place that was actually attached to the house, so I moved into a small back room that was our laundry room. Korie showed me the laundry room when I visited her house for the first time. I asked her, "Who lives in here? Man, you could fit a double bed in here!"

Korie: I met Willie for the first time when we were in the third grade at Camp Ch-Yo-Ca, the camp I grew up at. Willie and Jase went to my session of the camp, and Alan came for high school week. Kay was cooking in the kitchen that summer, so her boys could attend the camp for free. I remember thinking Willie was the cutest thing I had ever seen and was so funny. We called him by his middle name, Jess, at the time. He had these big dimples and the cutest sideways smile. I had a diary that I never really wrote in, but that summer, I wrote: "I met a boy at summer camp and he was so cute. He asked me on the moonlight hike and I said 'yes'!" I even wrote "Korie Loves Jess" on the bunk of the cabin I was staying in that summer.

Yes, Willie asked me to go on the moonlight hike with him. It was always a big deal every summer figuring out which boy was going to ask you to accompany him on the moonlight hike, and I was thrilled when he asked me! Willie was definitely my first crush. After camp that summer, I didn't see Willie for a couple of years. We went to different schools and his family went to a small church out in the country. Our family attended one of the bigger churches in town, White's Ferry Road Church.

Willie was definitely my first crush.

When I was in the fifth grade, Ray Melton, the preacher at our church, tried to recruit Phil to start coming to White's Ferry Road. Ray's daughter, Rachel, and I were best friends, and they were going to Phil's house for dinner one night. They invited me to go along. I still remembered Willie from camp, so needless to say, I was just dying to go. I begged my parents to let me go with them. They said yes! I even remember what I wore to Willie's house—a black top with fluorescent green earrings. Don't judge . . . it was the eighties.

When Rachel and I got to the Robertsons' house, the first thing Phil said to us was: "Have you met my boys, Jason Silas and Willie Jess? They'll make good husbands someday. They're good hunters and fishermen." I was so nervous. I could not believe this was happening. The other thing I remember about walking in their home was that Phil and Kay had a sign on their door that said, "Honeymoon in progress." Phil and Kay have never been shy about their honeymooning . . . another thing that shocked me about their family.

Once we had eaten, Willie took us back to his room, which was actually the laundry room. He made us laugh the whole time. He would stick his thumb in his mouth and pretend that he was blowing up his muscles. He did acupressure tricks and showed us our pressure points. This was all very impressive to a couple of fifth-grade girls.

After a while, I decided I was going to try to really impress Korie. I started punching the tiles on the ceiling of the laundry room, which was a trick one of my buddies taught me. I'd rear back and just punch my fist through the ceiling and busted tile would fall over onto the floor. I'm sure she was really impressed.

Korie: After leaving Willie's house, I didn't see him for another two years. In the seventh grade, Phil and Kay finally decided to move the family to our church. Willie called me on the telephone while I was babysitting some of my cousins. We didn't have cell phones at the time, but he had called my house and my mom gave him the number to my aunt's house. He told me they were going to start coming to our church. I was so excited. Willie asked me where I was going to go to college, and I told him I was going to Harding University. Willie thought I said Harvard and told Phil I was going to an Ivy League school. Phil told him: "That's big-time, son."

When the Robertson boys came to our church, everyone was excited because Jase and Willie were definitely the cool new guys. They ended up having a huge influence in our youth group, baptizing nearly a hundred teenagers over the next couple of years. It was incredible. There was tremendous growth in our youth group after they joined our church. Of course, all the girls liked Willie and thought he was cute. I think he dated about every girl in the youth group at one time or another.

OF COURSE, ALL THE GIRLS LIKED WILLIE AND THOUGHT HE WAS CUTE.

One time Willie was dating one of my friends and we were riding on the bus during one of our youth trips, and Willie's girlfriend gave him money to buy her a drink at a gas station. He came back on the bus with a pack of baseball cards and didn't even buy his girlfriend a drink. I remember it made me so mad. I told my friend, "You should break up with him right now." We all thought he was the worst boyfriend ever for doing that!

I'll never forget the first time Willie asked me out. We liked each other off and on through middle school and high school, but we didn't attend the same schools so we never really dated. He was attending West Monroe High School, and I was going to Ouachita Christian School, which is where Phil used to teach. When I was in the eleventh grade (Willie was a year older), he sent one of his friends, Jimmy Jenkins, to ask me out for him. Willie was pretty cocky and all the girls in the youth group were dying to go out with him. But I remembered how he treated my friend, so I told him no. It was a big blow for him, but he needed to be knocked down a few notches. We both continued dating other people over the next year but then were both single around Christmastime during my senior year in 1990.

Willie and I saw each other at the mall a few weeks after Christmas, and it was just one of those moments. Willie was attending seminary school at White's Ferry Road Church and was living with six guys in a small house in town. A couple of days after we saw each other in the mall, Willie walked into his house and there was a chair turned around facing the front door. It had a yellow piece of paper taped to it. It was a message for him, telling him that I had called. I knew that since I had rejected him the last time he asked me out, I would have to be the one to break the ice again. He called me the next day and we went to lunch at Bonanza. It didn't take long before we started dating each other pretty seriously, in January 1991.

Like I said, Willie was living with six other guys in town, but even then, he wasn't exactly living in the house. There was a small storage building out back, which he turned into his own room. He painted all the furniture black and white, and Granny made him a quilt to put on his bed. He had a TV and a window unit for air-conditioning, which he bought with his own money. It was like his little bachelor pad and the first place he could really call his own. Willie was working for my uncle Mac, who owned a cabinet-building shop. Willie worked for Mac throughout high school, cleaning up the shop and doing some woodwork. Mac helped Willie buy his first car, which was a 1980 Ford Mustang. It was bright orange and had white leather seats, which were all torn up, but it got him where he was going.

I used to love going to Willie's little house before school. He would cook me these elaborate omelets and even put a garnish on the top of them. Up till that time, I was never one for waking up early, and I'm still not, for that matter. But during our dating days, I didn't mind getting up early if it meant I got to spend a little more time with Willie. Plus, his cooking really impressed me. Willie's actually very romantic, which a lot of people might not realize. He's written me a ton of love notes and even poems, and he likes to cook for me. Thankfully after twenty years of marriage those things haven't changed.

> WILLIE'S ACTUALLY VERY ROMANTIC. HE'S WRITTEN ME A TON OF LOVE NOTES AND EVEN POEMS.

Willie and I dated for about eight months, and then I was getting ready to leave for school at Harding University. Willie was still attending seminary school, and I wanted him to go to Harding University with me. But Willie said he wasn't leaving West Monroe. He wanted me to stay in West Monroe with him. We broke up before I left for school in August, and I'm sure he thought I'd find someone else at college, because that's what typically happens when you leave home. Willie called me one night in September 1991 after I had been gone a few weeks and said, "Let's get back together." I knew I loved him, but I told him I wasn't sure about it. He was trying to change my life, and it was really his way or no way. I just didn't know what to do.

"Let me think about it," I said. "I'll call you back tomorrow."

I *was* convinced she'd found someone else. I was telling all my buddies that it was over between us, and I was gathering other girls' phone numbers to prepare myself to move on. I just knew it was over, and I wasn't waiting to hear it from her the next day. I was convinced she wanted to end our relationship but couldn't muster the courage to tell me. Korie called me the next day, and I was ready to tell her that I didn't want to get back together anymore and that our relationship was over. I was certainly going to end it before she ended it. I just knew she already had a new boyfriend at Harding.

"I've got something I want to tell you," Korie told me.

"What do you want to say?" I asked her, deciding I'd better hear her out first.

"Let's get back together," she said.

My ears started buzzing. I threw all the girls' phone numbers in the trash can. About a month later, Korie and I decided we were going to get married.

Korie: I had turned eighteen in October 1991, so legally I was allowed to do whatever I wanted. But I knew I had to call my parents, Johnny and Chrys, to get their permission. We had had some discussions about my getting married that summer that had not gone so well, so I knew they were not going to be excited about it. I mustered up the courage to make the phone call.

"Look, I'm legal, so I'm just going to say it," I told them. "I'm getting married, and you're going to have to be behind me or not."

Of course, my parents told me it was the worst idea ever, and they were naturally worried that I was going to leave school and come home. They asked me to at least wait until I'd finished college. I hung up the phone and called Willie immediately.

"I just told them and it didn't go so well," I blurted out.

"They've already called me and they're on their way over here," he said.

I was trying to save money, so I was living with my brother Alan and Alan's wife Lisa. Korie's parents came to the house to see me, and I sat on the couch with Johnny and Chrys. It was not pretty. The argument was so loud that Alan came out of his room. He looked at us and asked, "What in the world is going on?" Johnny was making all of his arguments, and I was acting like a little punk, twisting his words to put them in my favor, which only made him madder and madder.

Johnny told me that according to studies he'd read, 50 percent of all marriages between young people ended in divorce. He had the articles with him to support his arguments.

"So you're calling that right now?" I asked him. "In all your wisdom, you know we're going to get divorced?"

"I'm not saying that," Johnny told me.

"You just said it," I responded. "You just said half end in divorce. Well, what if we're the good half?"

Then Johnny went on to say that if we got married, he didn't want me coming to him for advice. But then later on in the conversation, he told me I could ask him about anything.

He was completely irrational, and I, of course, had to point that out to him.

"You just said I couldn't ask you for advice," I told him.

He was so mad, I thought he was going to leap off the couch and hit me. Before they left, Johnny looked at me and asked me one last question.

"What's your plan?" he asked.

"What's my plan?" I said to him.

HE WAS SO MAD, I THOUGHT HE WAS GOING TO LEAP OFF THE COUCH AND HIT ME.

"What exactly is your plan?" he said. "Where are you going to work? Where are you going to live?"

"Well, I reckon I'll just buy a trailer and put it on the back property at Phil's house," I told him.

That threw Johnny over the top. He and Chrys stormed out of Alan and Lisa's house, and I was convinced there was no way they were going to give us their blessing to get married. I called Korie to tell her how the meeting went.

"It went terrible," I told her. "We were yelling at each other. It was pretty ugly."

Then Korie had to hang up because her parents were calling her phone. She called me back a few minutes later.

Much to my surprise, her parents told her, "Okay, if you're determined to do this, we're going to support you."

Johnny didn't say much to me for the next few months, during the planning of the wedding, and I knew Korie's parents still didn't like the idea of her getting married so young.

I told Phil that Korie's parents didn't want us getting married and asked him what I should do.

"Here's what I'd do," Phil said, while sitting back in his recliner. "I'd call them up and say, 'Y'all missed that. The wedding was last week when we went to the justice of the peace and got married. Y'all missed the whole thing.' "

Korie: I had never heard my dad yell like he did that night at Willie before that time, nor have I heard it since, but you know daddies and their daughters. I think Willie understands this a little more after having daughters of his own. Thinking back, it makes me laugh to imagine Willie and my dad in that room squaring off. My daddy has since said he didn't have a problem with Willie's marrying me, it just scared him for me to do it at only eighteen. Which was the same age my mom was when they got married, as I kindly pointed out. I had a scholarship to Harding University, which is where both my parents went to school, and that was kind of the plan for my life—to graduate from Harding University and then get married and raise a family. My parents were worried I was going to get married, quit school, and start having babies. But as soon as they decided to support us, that was it. They were completely behind us and wanted to make sure Willie and I would be happy. They

AS SOON AS MY PARENTS DECIDED TO SUPPORT US, THAT WAS IT. THEY WERE COMPLETELY BEHIND US AND WANTED TO MAKE SURE WILLIE AND I WOULD BE HAPPY.

never said another word about not wanting me to get married so young. Willie and my father rode together to the church before our wedding, and Daddy told him he would never say another word about it, and he hasn't.

We had the biggest, most beautiful wedding on January 11, 1992. It was like a winter wonderland, complete with ice sculptures and white trees. There were probably about eight hundred people at our wedding, and it was a big mix of both of our families. Phil wore corduroy pants and a button-down shirt—he refused to wear a suit or tuxedo—but I didn't care. It was a wonderful wedding. My parents took us to Hawaii the next summer, which was kind of like our honeymoon because we didn't have a chance to take one after we got married.

The day after Willie and I were married, we took another big step in our lives—we moved to Searcy, Arkansas, where Willie started classes with me at Harding University.

Crawfish Omelets

I love crawfish! I have cooked them every way you can. If you don't live someplace where you can catch crawfish in the wild, you can usually get them in the freezer section of the grocery store. If you can't find them there, consider buying them online and having them shipped to you. Crawfish are so delicious, I promise, it will be worth it!

4 large egg whites
2 large eggs
¼ teaspoon Louisiana hot sauce
1 tablespoon water
1 tablespoon fresh chives, chopped
¼ cup cooked crawfish tail meat, chopped
1 tablespoon Phil Robertson's Cajun Style Seasoning
1 teaspoon sour cream
2 tablespoons butter
¼ cup ham, chopped
⅓ cup mushrooms, sliced
2 tablespoons shredded cheddar cheese

1. Combine egg whites, eggs, hot sauce, water, and chives in a small bowl and whisk for 2 minutes.
2. Combine crawfish, Cajun Style Seasoning, and sour cream in a small bowl.
3. In a small skillet melt butter; add ham and mushrooms. Sauté for 3 minutes.
4. Pour egg mixture into skillet. Let it set slightly and cook for 3 minutes.
5. Flip omelet and add crawfish mix onto half of the omelet and cook for 2 minutes.
6. Top with cheddar and cook long enough to melt cheese.

8

CHICKEN STRIPS

BY WISDOM A HOUSE IS BUILT, AND THROUGH UNDERSTANDING IT IS ESTABLISHED; THROUGH KNOWLEDGE ITS ROOMS ARE FILLED WITH RARE AND BEAUTIFUL TREASURES.
—PROVERBS 24:3–4

K*orie:* Willie and I lived in an apartment at Harding University right after we were married. It was just a little one-bedroom apartment, but we loved it. We had the best time decorating it with all of our wedding gifts. After living in the apartment for a semester, we decided that we were wasting money by paying rent every month. We really thought we should buy a house, so we started to look around. Of course, Willie and I were both still taking classes, so we didn't have the money to buy a house by ourselves. Fortunately, my father agreed to help us with the down payment and cosigned the loan for a house. He helped us get our first house, which really meant a lot to us.

We ended up finding a little starter home in Searcy that was still being built, so we were able to pick out the flooring, carpet, and paint color for the walls. The house was only about nine hundred square feet, but we were thrilled to own our first home. We paid about $47,500 for the house and sold it for $60,000 when we moved back to Monroe, so it ended up being a pretty good investment. We had a few other married friends in college, and they would come to our house on the weekends because we were the only ones who owned a house. Willie would cook for everybody, and it was a lot of fun.

I was a year ahead of Willie in college, and I was able to concentrate on school while he worked and took classes. Willie had lots of jobs while we were in college, including working at a bowling alley for a while. If you know Willie, whenever he gets into something, he doesn't ever just do it halfway. He immediately thinks he's going to become a professional at it. So for a while, he wanted to be a professional bowler. Then, after college, he took up golf and was convinced for a while he was going to be a professional golfer.

After I started playing golf pretty regularly, I paid for a lesson from an instructor. The guy had been a professional golfer and even won the Arkansas Open.

"I'm thinking about being a pro golfer," I told him.

He just looked at me and said, "No."

The guy hadn't even seen me swing yet and he was already telling me no.

"You haven't even seen me swing," I told him.

"You ain't got it," he said.

Eventually, I was able to get my handicap down to four, but that was about as close as I ever got to the PGA Tour.

Korie: Willie and I worked together for a little while as telemarketers, and it was the worst job ever. We were in this crowded room with a lot of other people on phones, making cold calls to raise money for leukemia research. At the end of every night, they would show you how much money you had raised. Willie would always raise a ton of money, but I could never get anyone to donate. I was stuck with calling people in New York, while Willie was calling people in Alabama. Nothing against Northerners, but I don't think they are as nice to telemarketers as people in the South. Either that or Willie was just better at it than I was! I think we had that job for about two weeks. It was so horrible.

WILLIE WOULD ALWAYS RAISE A TON OF MONEY, BUT I COULD NEVER GET ANYONE TO DONATE.

Willie also worked as a janitor—he likes to say he was a maintenance supervisor—for a real estate agency, and he went around fixing broken windows, trash disposals, and things like that at the company's rental properties. Willie also worked at an ice cream plant and had to spend most of the day in the freezer. He hated it. He never has liked to be cold.

When I was working at the ice cream plant, Phil came through Arkansas on his way to a speaking engagement. It was the first time Phil had been to Harding University, so he hadn't even seen our new house. I was really pumped that my dad was coming to town because I had a club basketball game that night, and Phil had never seen me play while I was in high school. I went and asked my supervisor at the ice cream plant if I could have the night off since Phil was coming to town. He told me no. I was like, "Screw it. I quit." I hated that job anyway.

It was the only time Phil ever saw me play basketball, and I scored thirty points in the game. It was worth losing the job over. I had a lot of fun playing in the intramural leagues at Harding University. I was the athletic director of my fraternity, so I was allowed to play on every one of our teams if we didn't have enough players. I always played on the A team, but I could play on the lower teams, too. Once I scored seventy-four points on the D team because no one else on the team could really play, so I took just about every shot in the game. I kept begging the coach at Harding University to put me on the school's basketball team. The coach was in his first season, and he was also my badminton teacher. I made a deal with him: If I beat him in a badminton match, he had to put me on the basketball team. I beat him like a drum, but he still didn't put me on the team. I'm still mad at the guy for not holding up his end of the bargain.

Korie: Of course, Willie and I never had any money as married college students. At one point we had to borrow some friends of ours' washer and dryer to do our laundry. To thank them for letting us use their washer and dryer, we took them out to Shoney's one night for dinner. Willie and I cooked in every night; we rarely went out to dinner because we were on such a tight budget. The waiter brought us our bill that night and it was like forty dollars. I didn't even know you could spend forty dollars at Shoney's! Daddy had worked with Willie and me on keeping a budget. He taught us to write down all of our expenses so we could see how we were spending our money. If we ever had to borrow any money from Dad, he always wanted to see a plan for how we were going to pay him back. Daddy really taught us some valuable lessons about money. We budgeted about sixty dollars a week for food. After paying the bill at Shoney's, we had about twenty dollars left for the entire week!

Whenever Willie and I went to the grocery store to buy food for the week, there was always a big argument at the check-out lane. If we had any money left in our budget, Willie would want to buy baseball cards or a *Star Trek* book. He has always been a big collector. I wanted to buy a magazine like *People* or *Entertainment Weekly,* and we never had enough money to buy both. We'd fight over who was going to get to spend our disposable income, which ended up being about three or four dollars a week. These are some of the things you fight over when you get married at eighteen and nineteen!

When we were newlyweds, our favorite meal was chicken strips and macaroni and cheese. We would buy a big bag of frozen Tyson chicken strips and fry them in a Fry Daddy. When they came out we would season them, then dip them in butter. Willie would make these special sauces for the chicken strips and we'd always have a box of Kraft macaroni and cheese with them. We rotated the chicken strips with chili dogs and, of course, fried bologna sandwiches, and that would be our meals for the week. Sometimes we would even splurge on thick-cut bologna. Willie tried to get me to eat fish sticks, but I'd never eaten them in my life. I just couldn't stomach eating frozen fish out of a box.

WHEN WE WERE NEWLYWEDS, OUR FAVORITE MEAL WAS CHICKEN STRIPS AND MACARONI AND CHEESE.

When we were taking classes, we'd come home between classes and eat lunch together every day. We would cook lunch and then watch *Matlock* together and see who could guess the killer. Willie bought a little white truck from one of our professors for seven hundred dollars. The best part about the truck was it still had a faculty parking sticker on the windshield. We were so excited we could park the truck in the faculty lots when we went to class. Because we were married, we could even write excuses for each other when we were sick. Willie always seemed to catch a cold during March Madness and on the opening day of baseball season.

During our last year at Harding University, we spent the summer in a study-abroad program in Florence, Italy. It was an unbelievable experience and was our first time really being away together. We traveled all over Europe on a Eurail pass. We didn't have any money for hotel rooms, so we would just sleep on trains and wake up the next morning in a new country. It was so exciting. As part of our studies, we had to visit certain museums and write essays on the art we saw. I was an art education major, so I loved every bit of this part of our trip, but it was a totally new experience for Willie. By the end of the trip, he said he had more culture than the yogurt section of the grocery store!

Willie and I are both pretty directionally challenged, so we spent most of our time lost. We would jump in a bus that seemed to be going in the right direction and end up having to walk for miles to get back to town. We were both super skinny from all the walking when we got back, despite the good Italian food we ate while we were there.

We had the best time, but there were a few scary moments, as well. One night we were sleeping on the train heading to Barcelona, Spain. We were traveling through the south of France and a group of thieves were on the train. Willie was sleeping with his feet on the door, so every time they would try to open the door he would wake up and they would run off. One time, he didn't feel the door open and the thieves grabbed the backpack of one of the girls who was traveling with us. Willie jumped up and started chasing them through the train! They dropped the backpack, but Willie kept chasing them through a couple of cars. I was standing there thinking, "What's going to happen if he catches them!" Luckily, Willie had that same thought, gave up the chase, and came back to our car. He didn't sleep the rest of the night; he just sat up and protected us. What a man!

Another exciting but scary adventure happened in Salzburg, Austria, where we were staying at a youth hostel named Stadtalm Naturfreundehaus. It was at the top of a mountain that surrounded the city and had the most beautiful view. It had bunk beds in the rooms and only had one bathroom that everyone shared. You had to put coins in the shower for the water to come out. It only gave you like two minutes of water. I remember calling down the hall to Willie to bring more coins. Two minutes wasn't quite long enough.

The way you got to the hostel was on an elevator through the middle of the mountain. One night, we got back to the elevator about eleven thirty P.M., after exploring the city, only to find that the elevator closed at eleven P.M. We had no idea what to do. We certainly didn't have enough money to get another hotel room for the night, so we went back into the town and asked around to see if there was any other way to get up there. We found out there was a staircase that would get you there eventually, but it was a long walk up the mountain. We didn't have any other choice. We walked what seemed like forever. At one point, we passed a guy in a trench coat, just sitting by himself on a bench on the trail. We were totally freaked out. Well, I was, at least. We finally got to the top about two A.M. We ended up sitting outside under the stars and talking once we got there, and we thanked God for keeping us safe. It ended up being really fun and romantic, but I was scared to death walking in a foreign city up a creepy trail in the middle of the night.

When I finished school at Harding University in 1995, we moved back to West Monroe. Willie still had a year left of school, so he enrolled at Northeast Louisiana University (which is now the University of Louisiana at Monroe) and he took a job working at Camp Ch-Yo-Ca. Willie probably could have gone to work part-time for Duck Commander, but he'd helped Phil make duck calls when he was a child, so at this point he really wasn't interested in doing it again. Duck Commander was still pretty small, and Jase and their friend Bill "Red Dawg" Phillips were already working there. Duck Commander couldn't afford to take on another full-time employee, but Willie still helped out at Duck Commander from time to time, especially during hunting season, and we would always go to SHOT Show—the big hunting-industry trade show—with the whole family every January. Willie would drive a seventeen-passenger van to SHOT Show and would work as their driver.

Willie really did some unbelievable things with Camp Ch-Yo-Ca, which was a nonprofit and seemed to lose a lot of money every year. Willie was determined to make sure the camp at least broke even financially every year. He studied kinesiology at Harding University and then went into the health and human performance program at Northeast Louisiana. The program required him to take some business courses. Willie took the camp's deficit from about $150,000 to $5,000 in a couple of years. The kids would come to camp for about six weeks during the summer, but Willie started renting the camp's facilities to churches and youth groups during the off-season. He started a program for schools to bring their classes to the camp for nature hikes, and he even added tennis courts, hiking trails,

WILLIE WAS DETERMINED TO MAKE SURE THE CAMP AT LEAST BROKE EVEN FINANCIALLY EVERY YEAR.

and other amenities. He was very creative in finding ways to create new revenue for the camp. Willie learned how to operate a business on a budget and the camp proved to be a good training ground for him.

Another man helped out at the camp who made a big impact on Willie during this time. His name was Dewie Kirby. He was the dad of my uncle on my mom's side. He was retired and moved across the street from us at the camp to help do maintenance and help Willie take care of the camp. Willie and Dewie worked together on many projects, and Willie grew to love Dewie as another father figure who taught him about work and family.

I was pregnant with our first child when we moved back to Monroe. Our oldest son, John Luke, was born in October 1995, and then Sadie came along not long after in June 1997. To help make ends meet, Willie started working as a youth minister at our church in addition to keeping his job at Camp Ch-Yo-Ca. He was great with teenagers and college-aged students and always had a few teens working with him at camp. He remembered how important it was that Mac gave him a job as a teenager and took the time to teach him how to work. He tried to do the same for others.

During this time, the pull to get more involved in the family business of Duck Commander was coming over us. Since the camp business was seasonal and everything pretty much shut down in the wintertime—which was the busy time for Duck Commander—we were able to help out some and do several things from our home. We were fortunate to be able to do this as a family and spent quite a bit of time together with our babies.

I tried to find ways to help us financially during this time. After John Luke was born, I was a stay-at-home mom but still found ways to utilize my art degree. I started making hand-painted duck calls. I numbered them and had Phil autograph cards saying they were limited editions of five hundred each. I painted sitting mallard, flying drake, and wood duck editions. They ended up selling in stores like Bass Pro Shops and Cabela's. While the babies were sleeping, I would paint the duck calls, put them in a package with moss and a card, and ship them out the door.

I really think the first few years of our marriage were Willie's formative years. He still wasn't sure what he wanted to do with his life, whether he wanted to preach, work for the family business, or do something entirely on his own. I knew that whatever he decided he would do it with all his heart and be successful at it. This was a time for him to test out and find what he really wanted to do. We were eating frozen chicken strips, but we were eating them together and finding ways to make them delicious.

Chicken Strips

I can't hunt chicken. Well, I guess I could, but I don't think it would be much fun, but I do like to eat it from time to time. This is one of those popular dishes that kids love. Can't go wrong here.

2 pounds chicken tenderloins
1 egg
½ cup buttermilk
1 cup all-purpose flour
1½ teaspoons garlic powder
½ teaspoon paprika
1 tablespoon Phil Robertson's Cajun Style Seasoning
1 teaspoon salt
1 teaspoon pepper
Peanut oil (about 3 inches in pan)
1 cup butter, melted

1. Whisk egg and buttermilk in a small bowl.
2. Combine flour, garlic powder, paprika, Cajun Style Seasoning, salt, and pepper in separate bowl.
3. Dip chicken tenderloins in egg mixture and then flour mixture.
4. Heat oil in skillet to 375 degrees.
5. Cook tenderloins for three minutes on each side or until no longer pink.
6. Drain chicken strips on paper towels.

9

DUCK GUMBO

"FOR I KNOW THE PLANS I HAVE FOR YOU," DECLARES THE LORD, "PLANS TO PROSPER YOU AND NOT TO HARM YOU, PLANS TO GIVE YOU HOPE AND A FUTURE."
—**JEREMIAH 29:11**

Phil's duck gumbo takes a long time to make. It starts at four A.M. on a wet, cold Louisiana morning during duck season. Well, it actually starts a long time before that day, sometime in the heat of summer, when he's out on the land pumping water into the hole in front of the blind or repairing a torn-down blind. But let's take all of that for granted for a moment and start with the day he actually kills the ducks for the gumbo.

Phil wakes up in the early-morning hours of a cold December day and pulls on his hunting gear. He walks out of his bedroom to find Jase, Uncle Si, Godwin, Martin, and me walking through the door to drink black coffee and discuss our plan for the day. Phil guzzles his coffee and then loads up the truck with decoys, shotgun shells, and his favorite gun. He puts his duck calls around his neck and his black Lab, Trace, happily jumps into the truck. Phil then drives to the land, loads up on the boat, and climbs into a blind to sit and to wait. He waits until the sun comes up for the legal shooting time to begin, and then waits some more for ducks to fly by. And when they do, Phil blows his calls, with Jase calling along beside him, helping to replicate the exact sound of the ducks for the decoys in the spread. Phil watches and listens for the familiar sound of the ducks turning, locking their wings, and changing their patterns to check out what is below. His heart starts pumping when he realizes the ducks have heard them and are coming his way, then he waits some more. He waits until the ducks are right in front of the blind and then calls out, "Cut 'em!" Phil and the rest of the hunters in the blind raise their shotguns and shoot. Trace takes off through the water, excited for the opportunity to do his job, bringing the bounty back to the blind. Now Phil has his ducks for the gumbo.

Next, Phil brings the ducks back to the house and picks their feathers clean. Then he carefully cuts them into pieces for the gumbo, cautious not to lose any of the precious meat. Now Phil can finally begin to make the roux. Building a successful family business is a lot like making a great gumbo.

Phil started duck hunting when he was a kid. He used a P. S. Olt duck call, which was very popular among duck hunters at the time. In the late 1880s, Philip Olt converted a chicken coop on his family's farm into a wood shop and started making duck calls. Olt's D-2 Duck Call and A-50 Goose Call were some of the first manufactured duck calls in the world, which is why he is often called the "father" of the manufactured call.

Phil had a gift for making his calls sound better, and his hunting buddies always insisted that he tune their calls, too. When Phil was hunting with his friend Al Bolen in1972, Big Al watched him make a long-hailing call as he was trying to turn a flock of mallard ducks within shooting range.

"Man, you weren't calling those ducks," Big Al told him. "You were *commanding* them!"

And so . . . Duck Commander was born.

On the day Phil officially announced he was starting Duck Commander, he told Kay, Granny, and Pa that he was going to sell one million dollars' worth of duck calls. Of course, they all thought he was crazy and went back to eating dinner. It took many years for Duck Commander to get off the ground. Phil always likes to say he's a low-tech man living in a high-tech world, and he didn't know very much about woodworking, marketing, or manufacturing when he started. But Phil had a dream, and his veins were filled with determination and patience, which is probably more valuable than anything else.

> "MAN, YOU WEREN'T CALLING THOSE DUCKS. YOU WERE *COMMANDING* THEM!"

When Phil was getting started with his company, he enlisted the help of Tommy Powell, who went to church with us at White's Ferry Road Church. Tommy's father, John Spurgeon Powell, made duck calls in a small wood shop, and Phil took him his drawings for the world's first double-reed duck call. John Powell looked at Phil's specifications and told him it wouldn't work.

"It's too small," Powell told him.

But Powell told Phil if he could get a block of wood properly bored, he was willing to give his duck call a try on his lathe. Phil took a block of wood that was about three inches thick and six inches long to West Monroe High School's woodworking shop, where he worked out a swap with the shop teacher. In exchange for four dressed mallard ducks, the shop teacher drilled a hole in Phil's block of wood. Phil took the wood block to Powell, who turned on his lathe and produced the first Duck Commander duck call.

With a working prototype, Phil set out to make his dream come true. He borrowed $25,000 from the bank with the help of Baxter Brasher, an executive at Howard Brothers Discount Stores, and purchased a lathe for $24,985. Later, Phil learned the lathe was only worth about $5,000 and had been built in the 1920s! The lathe was transported from Memphis to Monroe, and Phil picked up the heavy machinery at the train station with a borrowed dump truck. Phil drove the lathe to our house and cut out the wall of an outbuilding with a chain saw. Somehow, he was able to drag the lathe into his shop by tying a come-along to a tree. Once everything was in place, Phil put a sign outside the shop that read DUCK COMMANDER WORLDWIDE.

PHIL PUT A SIGN OUTSIDE THE SHOP THAT READ DUCK COMMANDER WORLDWIDE.

Phil didn't even have an instruction manual for the lathe or templates to cut the wood for his calls. Obviously, there was a lot of on-the-job learning. But it didn't take Phil long to get a production line going, and Alan, Jase, Kay, Pa, and I were his crew. When I was young, we spent most of our days helping him manufacture and package the duck calls. In the beginning, Phil cut end pieces out of cedar and barrels out of walnut. He tried all kinds of wood; he even brought back cypress logs from his fishing runs and cut them into blocks.

Our assembly line was out on the porch of our house, which was screened in at the time. Pa was always there helping Phil. One of the earliest problems with Phil's duck call was that the two reeds had a tendency to stick together. Pa told Phil that he should put a dimple in the reeds to keep them separated. Phil took a nail and put a dimple in the reeds with a hammer. Uncle Si still uses the same technique in our reeds today.

The great thing about Duck Commander is that it was a family business from the start and remains that way today. When I was younger, I helped by sweeping up the sawdust in the shop. My oldest brother, Alan, used a band saw to cut the ends of the calls, and Phil ran a drill press to set up and calibrate the end pieces. Jase and I also dipped the calls in polyurethane and then dried them on nails. Once the calls were dry, we sanded them down to a fine finish. I was embarrassed going to school because my fingers were always stained brown from tung oil. There were always rows of hard tung oil drippings in our yard.

The especially bad part for Jase and me was when Phil figured out that the more you sanded and dipped the calls, the shinier they were. That meant more dipping for us! Phil would tell us, “Hey, go dip the duck calls. There’s about twenty of them.” But when he said there were twenty or twenty-five, it always meant there were seventy-five to one hundred, and “thirty or thirty-five” meant there were probably one hundred and fifty. Phil was a notorious foreman on the duck-call assembly line.

Last, and most important, Phil blew every single call to make sure it sounded like a duck. From day one, Phil was convinced his duck call sounded more like a live duck than anything else on the market, and he wanted to make sure his products were always perfect. Duck Commander still follows that same principle today.

PHIL BLEW EVERY SINGLE CALL TO MAKE SURE IT SOUNDED LIKE A DUCK.

In the early days, the work never seemed to stop. My brothers and I cut boxes and folded them to package the duck calls. I don’t think child labor laws applied to us down on the mouth of Cypress Creek. When it was dark and you went inside to eat dinner and watch TV, you started folding boxes. We sat in the living room folding boxes, and they’d be scattered across the room. There was a plastic sleeve with a logo that we slipped over the boxes. The Duck Commander logo—which is now famous—is a mallard drake with wings cupped and legs lowered, looking down at the land. The logo was printed in gold on a green background and was placed on each of the calls. Phil’s name was also on the package, along with our home address.

Duck Commander is a lot like Phil’s duck gumbo. The

gumbo is perfect only when it has the right blend of ingredients—garlic, bell peppers, onions, shallots, sausage, spices, and, of course, duck. When my brothers and I were growing up, everyone in our family played an important role in the evolution of Duck Commander, and we still do today. If you take the onions or sausage out of Phil's gumbo, it's not going to taste nearly as good. And if you were to take Alan, Jase, Jep, or Uncle Si out of Duck Commander, the company wouldn't be as good as it is today.

Korie: The entire business was run out of the Robertsons' house. When Willie and I were dating, every time I went to their house, I was folding boxes. Phil is very charismatic and people love to be around him, and he learned pretty early that if you were willing to feed people, they were usually willing to work. Kay and Phil often had big fish fries at their house, and they would usually turn into packaging parties. People would call their house from stores to place orders. People from Wisconsin would call to buy one or two duck calls. When Willie was a little kid, he was answering the phone, taking orders. Customers called at all hours of the day. Willie answered the phone and always said: "Duck Commander, can I help you?" It was usually somebody in Texas or California wanting a duck call. Willie grabbed a napkin or paper plate and wrote down the order. There was always a big stack of paper plates or napkins sitting on the counter with orders written on them. The next day, Kay got the orders together and shipped them out at the post office.

I get asked this question a lot: why do Willie and Jase call their parents by their first names? I've asked Willie and he doesn't even know the answer, but we think it is because growing up when the business was being run out of their home, they would have to take these business calls for stores and orders on their home phone. The boys began referring to them as Phil and Kay in the business conversations and it just stuck. Jep, the youngest, didn't work as much in the family business as a kid, because he was born so much later and by that time they had more employees to take the phone calls, and he still calls them Mom and Dad. So that's our theory as to why Jase and Willie call them Phil and Kay. I can assure you it is not a sign of disrespect.

With a finished product, Phil hit the road in a blue and white Ford Fairlane 500 that once belonged to Kay's grandmother—Nanny. Phil liked to call the trips his "loop," and he was usually gone for about a week. With his calls stacked in the backseat and the trunk, Phil made a big circle around southern Arkansas, East Texas, West Mississippi, and into all parts of Louisiana, selling his duck calls at any sporting goods store or hunting shop he could find. He sold his first duck calls to Gene Lutz of Gene's Sporting Goods Store in Monroe.

In Lake Charles, Louisiana, Phil met Alan Earhart, who had been making the Cajun Game Call for years. Earhart liked Phil and agreed to make two thousand Duck Commander calls for him at the price of two dollars each. Phil would still cut the reeds and put the calls together, blowing each one before it went out the door, but Earhart cut the barrels. Phil figured if Earhart could handle a part of the manufacturing for a while, he would have more time to concentrate on sales calls and spreading the Duck Commander name.

Phil sold about $8,000 worth of Duck Commander calls in the first year. By the second year, his sales increased to $13,000; they rose to $22,000 in the third. By the fourth year, Duck Commander grossed about $35,000.

About five years into running Duck Commander, Phil realized many of his longtime customers were going out of business. There was a new superstore chain called Wal-Mart (as it was spelled then) moving into a lot of towns in Arkansas and Louisiana. As soon as a Wal-Mart store went up, a sporting goods or hardware store closed its doors a few months later. Phil realized that if Duck Commander was going to survive, he had to figure out a way to get his duck calls into this new chain. After initially being told that he had to go through Wal-Mart's corporate office, Phil persuaded a local store manager to buy six of his duck calls. He took the Wal-Mart sales order to the next Wal-Mart down the road and showed the manager what the other store had bought, and there he sold a dozen more. Eventually, Phil was selling $25,000 worth of duck calls to Wal-Mart alone, selling to them one store at a time, and his business was starting to expand.

One day, Phil got a call from one of Wal-Mart's executives.

"How did you get your product in our stores?" the man asked.

"Store to store," Phil told him.

"Well, you have to go through me," the man said. "I'm the buyer."

Somehow, Phil won over the buyer and the man sent him an authorization letter, which allowed him to sell his duck calls to any Wal-Mart store that wanted them. The next year, Phil even persuaded the buyer to purchase bulk orders of Duck Commander calls to distribute to stores across the country. Eventually, Duck Commander was selling $500,000 worth of duck calls to Wal-Mart each year. Phil's dream was beginning to come true.

Phil was a pioneer because he wasn't afraid to take risks. I don't think anyone ever quite understood what he was doing. But Phil was very self-confident and believed in his dream. He was a real showman and when he took his calls on the road, he was a great salesman. When he started the business, Phil actually carried an audio recording of live mallard ducks. He played the tape and then blew his call, which convinced customers that his calls truly sounded exactly like a duck, thus were the best on the market.

PHIL WAS A PIONEER BECAUSE HE WASN'T AFRAID TO TAKE RISKS.

Phil was always a dreamer and a visionary and was focused on the big picture. He knew he could make his dream come true by pulling his family together.

When I think of the journey it took for Duck Commander to get to where it is today, I think of it as a lot like Phil's duck gumbo. You can't go to the grocery store and buy all the ingredients. Well, I guess you could, but it wouldn't taste the same. There are no shortcuts for the kind of duck gumbo my family makes. It takes hard work, patience, and perseverance on the days when you sit in the blind and wait and the skies are clear. And you need strength of character on the days when it's cold and rainy and you wish you had stayed in bed. It takes camaraderie and a willingness to work with the other hunters in your blind to set up the decoys and call in unison. And, most important, it takes a passion and a love for what you are doing to see it to the end. All of these traits were present in making Duck Commander what it is today and are still present in the way we work.

THERE ARE NO SHORTCUTS FOR THE KIND OF DUCK GUMBO MY FAMILY MAKES.

There have been tough times in the life of Duck Commander. Times when we've lost big accounts, years when the duck numbers were down because of the weather in Canada, and even times when we didn't know where we would get the money to make it through another season. There have been times when we had to bring in extra help to get an order out on time and times when we had to let someone go because there was not enough work or money to pay them. There have been times when the money came at just the right moment to pay the light bill.

Phil tells about one such time in the early days of Duck Commander. The bank note was due and Kay informed him that they simply did not have the money to pay it. They were broke. Phil says that he tried everything he could think of to get the money to pay the debt. He and Kay were at the end of their rope. Kay was in tears with worry over what was going to happen to all they had worked for. Phil remembers telling Kay, "Let's go check the mailbox, maybe there will be a check in there." Kay told him, "There is no reason to look because no one owes us anything."

Phil knew it wasn't likely, but for some reason, he felt like they needed to look. They walked to the mailbox together and pulled out an envelope postmarked from Japan. It was an order for duck calls with a check for eight hundred dollars to prepay for them. It was exactly the amount they needed to pay the bank note! Duck Commander had never sold a duck call to Japan before then and as far as I know has never sold one since. But somehow, at a time when Phil and Kay needed it, the Lord provided. That's the only way to explain it.

Phil remembers another time that same eight-hundred-dollar bank note was due and once again there was no money to pay it. This time Phil went out to run the nets, hoping to catch enough fish to sell to at least take care of part of the payment. He took his boat out and began setting lines. The fish started biting before he even put any bait on the hooks! He says he pulled fish in hand over fist. He filled up his boat in no time and had more than enough to pay the bill with the sale of the fish he caught that day. Again, Phil says he never saw anything like what happened that day before or since.

The truth is, the Lord has always provided. Like He cares

Days before Willie came into this world. Alan, Jase, Kay, and Phil, 1972.

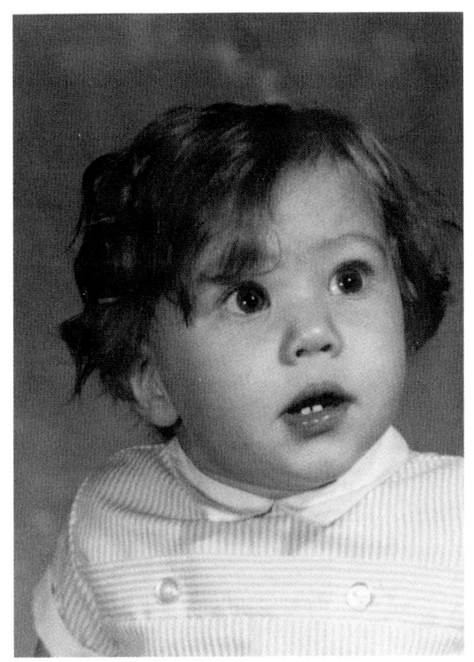

Willie's baby picture, 1972. Check out that hair!

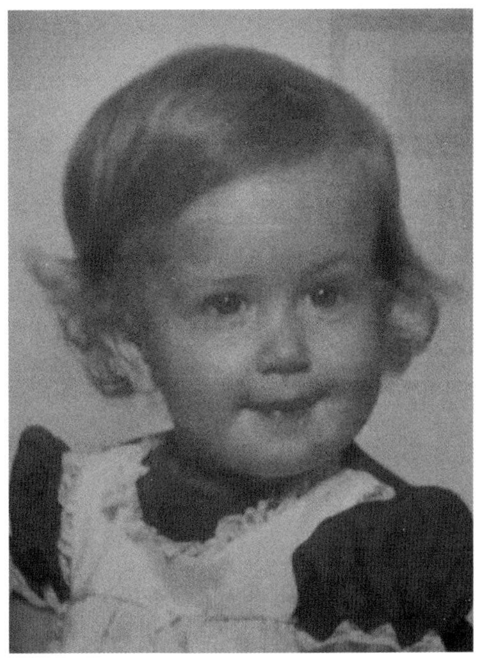

Korie's baby picture, 1973.

Willie with his granny, 1975.

Korie with her brother and Papaw Howard, who taught her how to fish and skin a squirrel (and push a wheelbarrow). Alton, Korie, and Ryan Howard.

Robertson family photo taken for the church directory, 1988. Clockwise from top: Phil, Alan, Jase, Kay, and Willie. (*Photograph © Olan Mills Photography*)

Uncle Si hanging out on the steps with Willie and Jase, 1974.

Korie's family's annual ski trip, Colorado, 1990. Left to right: John, Chrys, Ashley, Korie, and Ryan Howard.

The Robertson men BTB (before the beards) playing golf on the family beach vacation in 2001. Willie, Jase, Alan, and Jep.

Willie and Korie. Young love! Camp Ch-Yo-Ca, 1991.

Willie and Korie on their wedding day, January 11, 1992. So happy! (*Photograph © Lamar Photography*)

Korie and Willie on their honeymoon trip to Hawaii, 1992.

Korie's 1995 college graduation from Harding University, with proud grandparents Luther and Jo Shackelford.

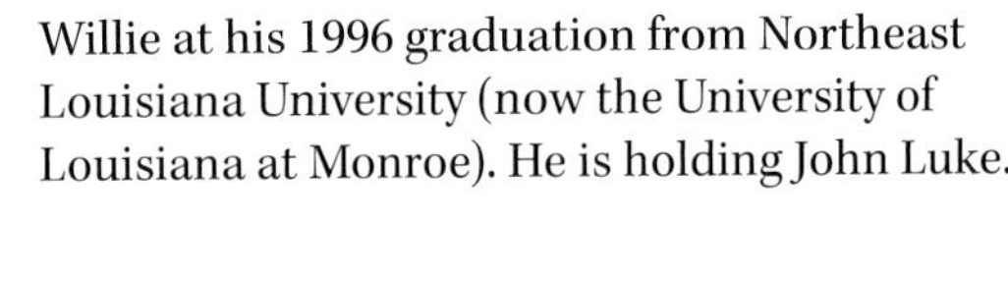

Willie at his 1996 graduation from Northeast Louisiana University (now the University of Louisiana at Monroe). He is holding John Luke.

December 15, 2001, the first time Willie and Korie held Little Will. They were in awe of this sweet little boy!

Willie with Sadie and John Luke on the steps of the house at Camp Ch-Yo-Ca, 1998.

Willie before the beard, rocking blond tips. Left to right, Sadie, Korie, Willie, and John Luke at Gulf Shores, Alabama, in 2000.

John Luke and Sadie in 2002 at their school's Grandparents' Day, getting hugs from their two grandmas, Kay Robertson and Chrys Howard.

Korie with the kids, 2003: (clockwise) John Luke, Sadie, Bella, and Will.

The first year Rebecca was with Korie and Willie for their annual beach vacation at Gulf Shores, Alabama, 2006. First row: Rebecca, Korie, Bella, Will, and Willie. Back row: Sadie and John Luke.

Family beach trip to Gulf Shores, Alabama, 2012. Front row: Rebecca, Bella, Korie, and Sadie. Back row: Will, Willie, and John Luke.

Sadie and Will in 2012. So proud of how the kids love each other.

Sadie and John Luke celebrating the Fourth of July, 2012.

Papaw Phil in 2012 teaching Bella about building duck blinds.

Papaw Phil with the grandkids, 2005. Back row: John Luke and Reed (Jase's son). Front row: Bella, Will, Phil, Sadie, and Cole (Jase's son).

Family trip to California, 2012. Left to right: Rebecca, John Luke, Bella, Sadie, and Will.

All the grandkids and great-grandkids with their awesome Mamaw Kay. Back row: Cole, John Luke, Reed, Kay, Sadie, Bailey, and Will. Front row: Bella, Lily, Merritt, River, Carly, Priscilla, and Mia.

Willie and Phil in 2006, posing for the label for our seasoning bottles.

Phil and Willie in the "Boss Hog mobile" for a Benelli commercial, 2010.

The women of Duck Dynasty, 2012. Left to right: Missy, Korie, Jessica, and Kay.

Si with his now-famous glass of tea at Willie and Korie's house, July 4, 2012.

Korie's first deer! Willie was proud. Olla, Louisiana, 2010.

The Duckmen had a good day in the blind on Robertson land, 2011. Jase, Phil, and Willie.

Willie doing a photo shoot for Buck Commander Weaver Scopes. (*Photograph © Lee Kjos Photography 2011*)

John Luke and Willie in 2011, getting ready to pick the ducks.

Willie singing "Take Me Out to the Ball Game" at an Atlanta Braves game in 2010. He is on top of the dugout during the seventh-inning stretch.

Willie and Korie in 2012 accepting the Golden Moose Award for Duck Commander.

Willie and Phil's first late-night appearance. (*Photograph © Conan O'Brien, 2012*)

Phil, Korie, and Willie in 2012 on Sunset Boulevard with the Duck Dynasty billboard.

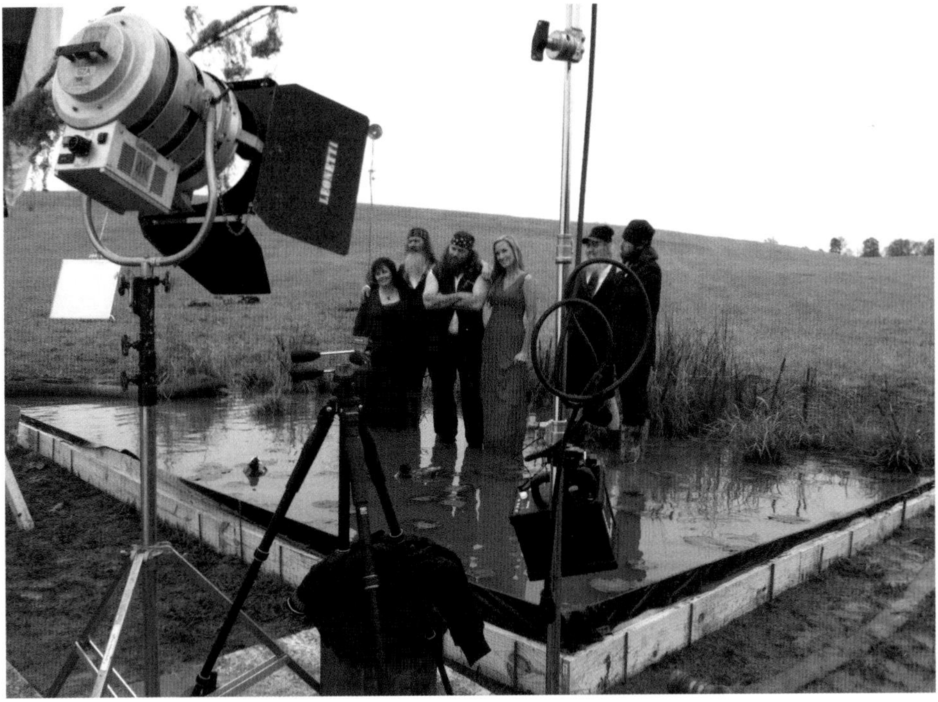

The Duck Dynasty photo shoot. It was freezing that day! Kay, Phil, Willie, Korie, Si, and Jase.

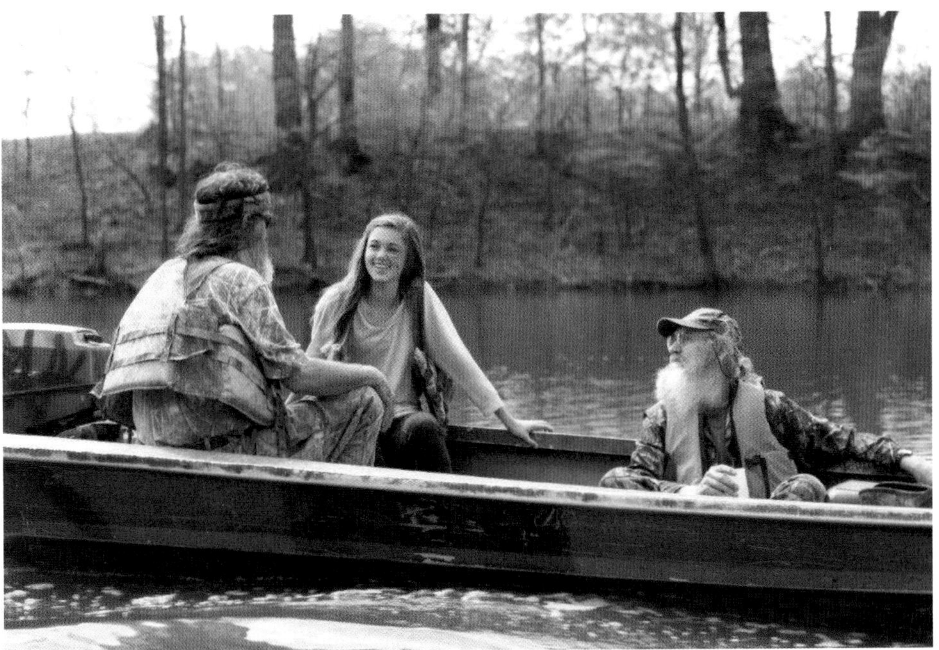

Phil and Si taking Sadie out to run the nets and teach her a few life lessons.
(*Photograph © A&E, 2011*)

First time on the red carpet for A&E's Upfront, 2012. Willie, Korie, Phil, Kay, and Si.

Korie in 2012 with two women who are great examples of godly wives and mothers—Korie's mother and grandmother, Chrys Howard and Jo Shackelford.

Phil and Kay with all their boys at the 2012 Duck Commander 40th Anniversary Party. Jep, Alan, Phil, Kay, Jase, and Willie.

for the birds in the air and clothes the lilies in the field, He has cared for us. We haven't done everything right. We didn't have all the right business plans, goals, or budgets. Sometimes, we didn't know how a bill was getting paid until the very last minute, but we always had faith that He would provide. Miracles like the two described above didn't happen every time. Sometimes, we had to hold our checks, and there were times when Kay had to borrow at high interest rates or make deals with one store to get money at a time she needed it. But there was always that faith that the Lord would provide.

THE TRUTH IS, THE LORD HAS ALWAYS PROVIDED.

I think that's the only way you can ever be truly successful in this world. You have to acknowledge that it is from above. And you have to have the confidence that even if you lose it all, things will be okay. You have to be willing to fail, and all the while work your tail off to succeed. You have to continue doing the work, believing in what you are doing, and most important, keeping your faith in who you are. The faith of our family is not in the things we have. Our confidence is not in the monetary success we have gained. It is in the One who made us and who is there for us in good times and bad.

Phil's duck gumbo is never finished until he knows it's absolutely perfect. In many ways, Duck Commander is a lot like his gumbo. It took forty years to build Duck Commander into what it is today. Phil has always had a lot of perseverance and patience, which are valuable attributes to have in everything from business to cooking to hunting. Let's face it: most people today wouldn't take a few days to make duck gumbo. They go out and buy a mix and throw it together. But if you wait and you're truly patient, the end result is going to be something that is unbelievably spectacular and special.

Duck Gumbo

This is Phil's duck gumbo recipe. Making gumbo is an art and Phil's is a masterpiece. It takes time and patience to make it just right.

8 ducks
salt and pepper to taste
1 bay leaf
3 cups flour
3 cups peanut oil
3 white onions
3 green onions
handful of fresh parsley
1 clove garlic, chopped
cayenne pepper to taste
Phil Robertson's Cajun Style Seasoning to taste
sausage

1. Place fully cleaned ducks into a large pot filled with water.
2. Add salt, black pepper, and bay leaf to pot.
3. Boil ducks for 2½ hours.
4. While ducks are boiling, prepare roux in another large pot: For 8 ducks, mix 3 cups of flour and 3 cups of peanut oil.
5. After stirring flour and oil to a consistent paste, heat on medium low.
6. Stir thoroughly until color is a dark chocolate brown. (Should take 35 to 40 minutes.)
7. Dice up white onions, green onions, and parsley.
8. Once roux is dark brown, mix in onions and parsley. (Watch out for the steam!)
9. Add garlic.
10. After ducks have boiled for 2½ hours, take them out of pot (saving broth) and separate meat from bone.
11. Take broth and fill roux pot just over half full.
12. Turn heat up to boiling again.
13. When the peanut oil rises to top of pot, remove it with spoon.

14. Sprinkle a small amount of cayenne pepper and Cajun Style Seasoning into pot.
15. Dice up sausage into nickel-size pieces.
16. Dump duck meat and sausage into gumbo.
17. Let it simmer for 3 to 4 hours.
18. Serve gumbo over rice and enjoy!

10

FROG LEGS

LET PERSEVERANCE FINISH ITS WORK SO THAT YOU MAY BE MATURE AND COMPLETE, NOT LACKING ANYTHING.
—JAMES 1:4

Many things in life—whether it's food, business, or even someone's personality—slowly evolve over time. They don't necessarily get better overnight, but if you keep working at them and stay focused, chances are they're going to end up being better than when you started. Take for instance my recipe for frog legs. When I was growing up, Kay's frog legs were one of my favorite meals. But as I got older, I started experimenting with ways to cook frog legs and added my own personal touch to her recipe. Kay has probably never heard of garlic-infused grape-seed oil (she's never used anything but butter or Crisco), but that's what I like to use to fry my frog legs. And for the record there are many infused olive oils I like using nowadays. Kay still doesn't understand how they "infuse" oil, but I tell her, "Don't question, just enjoy." It took me about three days to figure out the perfect recipe for garlic frog legs, and I made a lot of mistakes along the way.

Believe it or not, after I'd mastered the recipe, I pulled the meat off the legs and turned it into frog soup. I was just thinking, "I have those frog legs left over, they have a great flavor, what could I do now?" Pull all the meat off, make a great roux, and just throw them in. Plus, I never like any meat to go to waste. That's the really crazy thing about life: you often start out intending to do one thing but end up doing something entirely different.

When Korie and I moved back to West Monroe, Louisiana, and I finished college at Northeast Louisiana University, I had no intention of going to work for Duck Commander. I liked to duck-hunt but wasn't into it as much as Phil, Jase, or Uncle Si, and I wanted to go out and make a name for myself doing something on my own. I enjoyed working at Camp Ch-Yo-Ca and really liked being around kids, and I was also working at White's Ferry Road Church as a youth minister. I loved the freedom working at the camp gave me to create and grow. And watching kids' lives change for the better was pretty satisfying. But before too long, Korie and I had a house full of our own kids. After our oldest son, John Luke, was born in October 1995, our oldest daughter, Sadie, came along in June 1997. Then we adopted little Will in December 2001, and Bella, our baby girl, was born in September 2002.

Working at Camp Ch-Yo-Ca was a lot of fun, but it was a nonprofit, so there wasn't much room for financial growth. And with four kids to feed, I realized I probably needed to find another job where I could eventually bring home a little more bacon. I never really thought about making a lot of money—

didn't really care, to be honest. I guess I always thought we should do it in reverse. Rather than go out and try to kill myself on a career while I was young and my kids were little, I wanted to be home with them more during that critical time. Then later, when they got older, I'd go out and try to do a little better for us. Korie and I didn't have a ton of money, but we were happy, and we never let the balance of our bank account dictate our happiness. I learned a lot running Camp Ch-Yo-Ca and felt like I made a sizable contribution, but I came to a point in my life when I knew it was time to make a change. Duck Commander was starting to get bigger, so I went to Phil and asked him about working there.

Rather than go out and try to kill myself on a career while I was young and my kids were little, I wanted to be home with them more during that critical time.

"Oh yeah, come on board," Phil told me.

"What am I going to do?" I asked him.

"We'll figure something out," Phil said.

He never even asked how much I made or needed to make. You gotta love Phil.

I ended up cleaning the yard at Phil and Kay's house for about six months. I was just trying to learn as much as I could about the business, and Phil and Kay would give me little projects like constructing outbuildings and things like that. I poured concrete pathways between the buildings and tried to improve the work environment in the little ways I could. Kay was stoked to have someone do her "pet" projects that she had been wanting since we were kids. And the fact that she had one of her sons doing it was even better. But I had a college degree, so I wanted to put it to use and be more involved in the business side of Duck Commander. At the time, we were making hunting DVDs, selling about ten thousand of them a year. More and more people were catching on to Duck Commander, and I thought we should start trying to take advantage of the exposure and popularity.

"Dad, I need to talk to people," I told Phil. "I need to talk to our customers. I need to know what they're thinking, what they're buying, why they're buying this, and why they're buying that." We didn't have much money, so there was no marketing budget to speak of, which meant I needed to do it cheaply. We only talked to our customers when we went to shows around the country.

About that time, websites were getting more and more commonplace. I remember watching TV and every advertisement seemed to include a website address, where customers could go to learn more about the company and its products. I went to Phil and told him we needed a website, even though I really didn't know how to get to one. By that time, Duck Commander was using the Internet for some of its business dealings, but down at Phil and Kay's house, where the business was being run, the Internet access was spotty at best. It was, and still is, only accessible through satellite, and if it rained hard, you could forget it.

"If a man wants a duck call, he can pick up the phone and call me," Phil told me.

Korie: Phil told Willie he needed to go talk to my dad, Johnny, because he owned the website URL for Duck Commander, DuckCommander.com. Daddy had a background in publishing and realized pretty early that the Internet was eventually going to become the way in which companies sold their products to consumers. So he asked Phil if he ever intended to build a website, and Phil, of course, told him no. Over the years, Dad had helped Phil and Kay with the legal aspects of Duck Commander, like helping them file for patents and trademarks and borrowing money from the bank. Because Duck Commander was so seasonal—the company did really well during hunting season but sold very little during the summer—Phil and Kay sometimes borrowed money from my dad to get them through the slow times. Daddy always believed in Phil's company and his products and felt they had a good thing going.

So Dad worked out a deal with Phil and Kay. They agreed to let him launch DuckCommander.com and would give him products like duck calls and DVDs to sell on the site as payment for the money they owed. Daddy sold them until he'd made enough money for Phil and Kay to pay him back, and then he started buying the products directly from them to sell on the website. Dad rented mailing lists, printed catalogs, and mailed them all over the country. He even launched the first

Duck Commander TV commercial in an area of California that was really big into duck hunting. The first commercial showed Phil, Jase, and Si shooting ducks in slow motion at pretty close range, and Dad received a bunch of angry e-mails from animal rights activists. It didn't take them long to get over it, though. And he sold even more DVDs.

When Willie decided he wanted to get more involved with Duck Commander, he went to Dad to ask him to sell Duck Commander's website and mail-order business to us. We paid Daddy a down payment on it and then paid him a percentage of the sales until we paid him back what it was worth when we bought it. Willie and I ran the website out of our house. At the time, I'd been working as the children's minister at our church, so I left that job and ran the website from home while raising our children. Every night, I would wake up to feed Will or Bella a bottle and sit at the computer answering e-mails and filling orders. Every customer received a personalized e-mail from Willie or me.

I WOULD WAKE UP TO FEED WILL OR BELLA A BOTTLE AND SIT AT THE COMPUTER ANSWERING E-MAILS AND FILLING ORDERS.

I was taking full advantage of being Phil Robertson's son. People would always e-mail me back and ask, "Are you really his son?" Phil had started this club called Duckaholics Anonymous, and it was like a twelve-step program for serious duck hunters. It was a great idea, but Phil kind of let it fizzle out.

We relaunched Duckaholics Anonymous and sold memberships to the club through the website. We'd send them newsletters, giveaways, and things to get them even more involved in Duck Commander. I would always answer the Duckaholics Anonymous members' e-mails first, and we'd talk to them through the website. We tried to make the membership super exclusive. This was before Facebook, but we decided we really needed to be more interactive, so we'd publish a quote of the day or something fun like that, kind of like we do on Facebook now. This was also the time when Phil began doing a lot of speaking. He had spoken at a few church men's events and the word was spreading. He got invited to speak all over the country. So we began posting those dates on our website so people could go hear him.

Korie: We paid a company about $25,000 to completely overhaul the website. The new site included message boards, forums, and a complete online retail store. People would call the phone number on the site and thought they were calling a warehouse, but they were actually calling our house! We'd get phone calls at two o'clock in the morning from someone in California who wanted a duck call or T-shirt. We'd just wake up and take their orders. Daddy had put together an extensive mailing list of customers who had bought from him in the past, so Willie and I made up some postcards and sent them to about thirty thousand people around the country telling them to come visit our new site. Willie and I had some money that we'd saved, but we were going into quite a bit of debt to make all of this happen. It was a risk, but one we knew we had to take.

I got a phone call from the post office one day, telling me I needed to come and pick up several thousand postcards that had been returned because of bad addresses. I didn't even know how that worked. I found out that you have to pay for the ones coming back to you, but it was the only way at the time to clean up your list and know which ones were good and which ones weren't. I went to the post office to pick them up and there were boxes and boxes of them. I loaded up my old Chevy Suburban and headed back to the house. Wouldn't you know it? I pulled out in front of a car and it T-boned me just as I left the post office. I had a sick cut on my head, and the postcards went flying everywhere. There were pictures of Phil with the web address DuckCommander.com all over Highway 34 in Ouachita Parish. Some of them were even stuck to my head! Fortunately, I wasn't seriously hurt, and the other people in the car were fine. We did end up getting sued by four people—which was odd, because there were only three passengers in the car that hit me! I could have easily died that day. I let the accident inspire me and realized the Lord let me live for a purpose. It was a reminder of sorts—"Life is short, son; make it count." The wreck was my fault, no

I LET THE ACCIDENT INSPIRE ME AND REALIZED THE LORD LET ME LIVE FOR A PURPOSE.

doubt, but I survived, and not everyone walks out of a vehicle after getting hit by another car at seventy miles per hour.

Korie: When the hunting DVDs came out every June, it was always a busy time. We would take preorders for the DVDs, and Willie and I would go to Office Depot and buy bubble envelopes and write every address by hand. While we were waiting for the DVDs to be finished, the envelopes would be scattered around our house, and we were trying to keep the kids out of them the entire time. Alan's oldest daughter, Anna, had graduated from high school by this time and started working for us, helping package orders. She would get to our house in the morning and I would hand her a stack of orders I had printed out late the night before. I don't know what I would have done without her. About this same time, Willie had started making a lot of trips with Phil to his speaking engagements. Willie would set up a booth wherever Phil was speaking, selling DVDs, hats, T-shirts, and other Duck Commander memorabilia. This further confirmed to Willie just how popular Duck Commander was becoming, and he began to realize that the company was capable of doing so much more.

At the bigger hunting shows I attended with Phil, I started talking to other companies about sponsoring our hunting DVDs. We already had some corporate sponsors, like Browning and Mossy Oak, but they weren't paying us a lot of money. Realtree, which produces the world's most popular camouflage, decided it wanted to get more involved in the waterfowl industry. In one of their planning meetings, Michael Waddell (who worked for them at the time) suggested they do that by partnering with Duck Commander. Most of the folks in the meeting seemed to shrug it off and thought there was no way to get the Duck Commander guys. We had been with Mossy Oak for a long time, and they thought even trying to get us would be fruitless. But one of the guys there that day thought he would give it a shot and contact Duck Commander. He went to—what else!—the website to get the phone number to call us. That was Brad Schorr. Brad had just started working for Realtree and had been a fan of Duck Commander for a long time. To him, it seemed like a natural fit and was certainly worth a try. Brad was trying to make a name in the company and knew this could be just the thing to do that.

Brad called the house one day and left a message with Korie for me to call him. Korie didn't give me the message.

Korie: Oops, I obviously didn't realize the importance of this call. With four babies to feed and everything else we were juggling at the time, I'm sure this wasn't the only thing I forgot. Thankfully, Romans 8:28 assures us, "And we know that in all things God works for the good of those who love Him, who have been called according to His purpose." Even in those times that we drop the ball.

Fortunately, Brad called back a week later and this time Korie gave me the message. Realtree was interested in sponsoring us. I was excited. I called Brad and we talked for like three hours. I was like a sponge soaking up all of the knowledge I could. I knew we were going to have to make some big moves to take our company to the next level and this was just the kind of change that I was ready to make.

I headed down to Phil's to talk it over. Phil was open to the idea but was worried about what our fans would think. Realtree was tied in with Benelli Shotguns, so a move to Realtree was going to also mean a move to Benelli. Phil had grown up shooting Browning shotguns and Browning had been good to us. Browning had produced a line of limited-edition Duck Commander gear and used Phil's image for their marketing campaign at one point, but that relationship had started to decline. All of the people that we had relationships with at Browning had recently lost their jobs or moved on for one reason or another, and we found ourselves without the connection that might have compelled us to stay. We knew that Benelli made an excellent gun, and Phil was intrigued and eager to try it out. After much discussion, it was decided that the time was right and it was the correct move to make. Jase was not so sure but in the end agreed to go along. So, we made the big switch to Realtree and Benelli Shotguns in 2005. It was right in the middle of hunting season, and I was making my first big move in the hunting industry. The decision served as a statement that Willie Robertson was here and Duck Commander was gonna do things differently.

It wasn't long before several other big sponsors came along. Federal Premium Ammunition was next. Federal became a huge partner for us, eventually putting Phil's face on their boxes of Black Cloud shells. That deal was made over a drink one night in Las Vegas. Federal had a new technology called flight stopper and was about to launch some new pellets that had never been used in shells at the time. They mixed the new pellets with standard pellets in a shell, which produced a tighter pattern that increased a gun's range. I knew putting us with this new technology would be a great fit. I told Kyle Tengwall, Federal's director of marketing at the time (he is now the vice president of marketing), "You should put Phil's picture on the box." I didn't know at the time that the only other man who has had his face on a box of shotgun shells was John Wayne. I was just throwing it out there, and fortunately Kyle agreed. He and I have become good friends over the years doing a lot of good business together. This was just the beginning. We picked up several other sponsors as well. Soon, our business was growing, not just in sales, but also with a great deal more sponsorship dollars than we had ever had before.

THE DECISION SERVED AS A STATEMENT THAT WILLIE ROBERTSON WAS HERE AND DUCK COMMANDER WAS GONNA DO THINGS DIFFERENTLY.

It was an exciting time. Phil was pretty pumped. "You're the man! That's what I'm talking about!" he said, telling everyone at Duck Commander, "Will was right about making the switch." Even though Phil started Duck Commander and is considered a legend by duck hunters everywhere, he was really never comfortable in the role of CEO. Phil was always kind of an enigma in the hunting industry. When he went to SHOT Show and the other big hunting conventions, he kind of kept to himself, and let's face it, he doesn't exactly look like the kind of guy people are comfortable just walking up to and striking up a conversation with. For Phil, the hunting shows were an opportunity to walk in, sell the products, and leave. All of the other hunting companies knew Duck Commander had a cult following from the hunting DVDs, but they wondered if Phil was a little too dangerous to touch. He was kind of rogue and did things that everyone else was afraid to try. In fact, none of us were stereotypical duck hunters; we're not the white-collar guys who dress up in camo on the weekends and go hunting.

The other hunting companies knew Duck Commander had a cult following from the hunting DVDs, but they wondered if Phil was a little too dangerous.

Korie: Duck Commander was well-known in the hunting industry and had a strong group of loyal fans, but no man is an island, and neither is any good company. Phil wasn't the kind of guy to network at the industry shows and events. But Willie has enough of Kay's social gene in him to get the job done. He enjoys meeting new people. Willie feels like there is something he can learn from everyone he meets, and you never really know when a new relationship will be an important one in business or a good friend down the road. When Willie started meeting with these other companies, they realized the

Duckmen were not as scary as they had once believed. One of the executives said Willie "looked like them, but thinks like us." Willie had the beard and camo like Phil and Jase, but he had a mind that could connect the dots with the business end of things. Willie always told the executives he met with, "You know what? We are what we are, but we have a really good reputation. We're a family-owned operation, and we've always done things the right way. We don't make excuses for who we are." And lots of companies got it and were excited to jump on board.

By the time I came back to work at Duck Commander, Al had gone to seminary and become a preacher and Jase had become a really big part of the operation, making the duck calls and appearing on the DVDs with Phil. We know that if something ever happens to Phil, Jase will be right there to continue his legacy. Jase is second in command in the duck blind and, like Phil, knows how to make a duck call sound just like a duck. Jase and Phil love to hunt and they love being in the blind more than anywhere else. It's almost like Phil's personality is split right down the middle between Jase and me. Jase got Phil's passion for duck hunting and I got his entrepreneurial spirit. So even though Jase and I don't agree all the time, when it comes to Duck Commander, we make the perfect team. Each of us brings his own unique set of skills to the table without stepping on the other's toes in the process. We each do what we were born to do and what we truly love. I don't think it gets any better than that.

Even though things were starting to pick up for Duck Commander, the company was still a mess financially. In the early days of Duck Commander, Phil made the duck calls and DVDs, and Kay ran the business. It got to be too much for only Phil and Kay to handle, so Jase, and eventually his wife, Missy, began taking on more and more, but he never enjoyed the business side of the company. Jase somewhat reluctantly began making sales calls to Walmart and some other big customers, but even he'll tell you he never really had a passion for it. Kay was overwhelmed with the bookkeeping, accounting, and payroll. She was doing the best she could, but it was really just too big a job for her. She was feeling stretched physically and mentally and was even having stomach ulcers because she was so stressed out. Even though sales were picking up, Duck Commander was still only a seasonal business. We did really well during hunting season, but after hunting season ended, it was a struggle to keep our doors open. Kay was out of her league when the business started actually growing. It is hard to keep up with inventory, payroll, employees, and everything else. She was about ready to cash it in.

To help make ends meet during the summer, Kay gave some of our local customers huge discounts. If a retailer called and ordered products for the next hunting season, Kay would offer them a big discount if they paid for their products in advance. That's how badly Duck Commander needed cash flow during the summer. In the end, we would end up losing money on those products, but it was the only way Kay could keep the business going during the slow times.

Finally, after working at the company for several months, I went to Kay and Phil and told them I wanted to take over the business operations of Duck Commander. Kay was more than happy to turn them over to me because she was completely overwhelmed. But I told them I had to have complete authority to do what I needed to do. Korie and I talked about it for a long time and decided to buy half of Duck Commander from my parents. We took out a second mortgage on our house to buy half of the company. Duck Commander really needed a cash investment at the time, and Kay and Phil had stretched their borrowing power to its limit. I told them, "If I'm going to do it, then I'm going to do it."

Korie: When Willie and I bought half of Duck Commander, we knew we were taking a leap of faith. There were definitely some obstacles we were going to have to overcome, but we believed in what Phil and Kay started and wanted more than anything to see it reach its full potential. Phil and Kay were super supportive. In a lot of companies, when control is passed from one generation to the next, the older generation has a hard time letting go and is somewhat resistant to any kind of change. Phil and Kay weren't that way at all. In fact, they were completely the opposite. They gave Willie all the respect and room he needed to learn and grow. Willie gave them just

WE BELIEVED IN WHAT PHIL AND KAY STARTED AND WANTED MORE THAN ANYTHING TO SEE IT REACH ITS FULL POTENTIAL.

as much respect in return, asking Phil and Kay for advice and suggestions when needed. The transition ended up being seamless.

After I took over the business operations of Duck Commander, one of the first big decisions I made was to get us more involved in retail stores like Gander Mountain, Cabela's, Academy Sports and Outdoors, Dick's Sporting Goods, and Bass Pro Shops, as well as the huge independent stores like Mack's Prairie Wings and Simmons Sporting Goods. We had been doing business with them for a while by that time, but I knew it needed to be more of our focus. Those stores were in the hunting business three hundred and sixty-five days a year. For several years, Walmart was about 80 percent of our business. It was great having our products in Walmart, but it was always a tricky situation. Walmart stocked hunting products during hunting season and then replaced them with something else when hunting season was over. You'd go meet one of Walmart's buyers and expect to get eight dollars for a duck call. But then the buyer would tell you he wasn't paying more than four dollars. Now, nobody wanted to come home and tell everyone that he'd lost the Walmart account, especially when it was such a huge percentage of our business. It was always a big day around the Robertson house when Walmart wired its money to our account to pay for its products. But by the time you shipped the products the way Walmart wanted them shipped, you really weren't making much money. Those big checks that came in always seemed to get spent before we knew it, because there wasn't much profit in them, which created a big cycle of debt for several years.

I wanted to make sure Duck Commander would be okay if anything ever happened to the Walmart account. So we invested in our relationships with the year-round hunting stores, which became a big part of our business. Wouldn't you know it? Within two years, Walmart decided it was getting out of the waterfowl market altogether. Typically, a setback like that will kill a company. Fortunately, we had a contingency plan and were able to survive without Walmart for a few years. I'm happy to say, though, that in the last two years, Walmart began stocking our duck calls and other products again, and it has become a mutually beneficial relationship once again.

After Walmart stopped buying from us that year, I went three months without being able to cash my own paycheck. Korie and I had to rein in our spending. I told her, "Don't buy anything unless it's absolutely necessary." We were living on a tight budget. I knew I needed to get Duck Commander on an even tighter budget till I could find another source of revenue to keep the company afloat. Duck Commander was like a batch of frog legs sitting in the fridge waiting for you to figure out how you were going to cook them. The hard-

DUCK COMMANDER WAS LIKE A BATCH OF FROG LEGS SITTING IN THE FRIDGE WAITING FOR YOU TO FIGURE OUT HOW YOU WERE GOING TO COOK THEM.

est part of having frog legs for dinner is catching the wild frogs and bringing them home. Then you have to clean them and get the meat ready to eat. Phil had done the hard part with Duck Commander. It was primed and ready to take off. All that was needed was a guy who could imagine what else it could be.

Garlic Frog Legs

I had some frogs and garlic and dreamed this up one night. It is so good. For the few hundred who will actually go get frogs, try it. The rest, well . . . use chicken instead. Good luck.

8–10 pounds of frog legs
1 can of beer
Phil Robertson's Zesty Cajun Style Seasoning
2 cups flour
1 stick butter
¼ cup garlic-infused grape-seed oil
2 cups white wine
bulb of garlic, cloves peeled
1 cup fresh mushrooms

1. Soak frog legs in beer for an hour or so. Drain.
2. Season frog legs with Zesty Cajun Style Seasoning.
3. Roll frog legs in flour and set aside.
4. In a large black skillet bring butter and grape-seed oil up to high (don't burn the butter; it will brown when burning). It doesn't take much oil and butter, just about a half inch or so.
5. When oil and butter starts sizzling, put frog legs in and brown on each side. The oil-and-butter mixture should be about halfway up the legs, just enough to brown them.
6. If butter gets low, throw another half stick in. Set browned frog legs aside.
7. With what's left in the pan, add white wine, garlic, and mushrooms, and cook for 3 to 4 minutes.
8. Add frog legs to white wine mix. Cover and simmer for 30 minutes until meat is falling off bone. (You will know it's done, believe me!)

11

CHICKEN FEET

PRAISE BE TO THE GOD AND FATHER OF OUR LORD JESUS CHRIST, WHO HAS BLESSED US IN THE HEAVENLY REALMS WITH EVERY SPIRITUAL BLESSING IN CHRIST. FOR HE CHOSE US IN HIM BEFORE THE CREATION OF THE WORLD TO BE HOLY AND BLAMELESS IN HIS SIGHT. IN LOVE HE PREDESTINED US FOR ADOPTION TO SONSHIP THROUGH JESUS CHRIST, IN ACCORDANCE WITH HIS PLEASURE AND WILL.

—EPHESIANS 1:3–5

Korie: When I was a student at Ouachita Christian School, my senior-year Bible teacher, David Matthews, adopted a little five-year-old boy. In class that year, we talked a lot about how important it was for Christians families to adopt and that children should never be left without a home and loving parents. The idea always stuck with me. James 1:27 says: "Religion that God our Father accepts as pure and faultless is this: to look after orphans and widows in their distress and to keep oneself from being polluted by the world."

When we were dating, like most couples, Willie and I talked about how many kids we wanted to have. I told Willie about my desire to adopt and he was all for it. We both grew up with big families so we decided we wanted to have four kids, with at least one of them through adoption. We never knew how that would happen. We didn't know if we would adopt a boy or a girl or a newborn baby or older child. We decided we would remain open, and if God wanted it to happen, it would happen.

There were several families at White's Ferry Road Church that adopted children, including one couple that had adopted biracial twins. Their lawyer came to them and asked if they were interested in adopting another biracial child who was about to be born. They told her they couldn't do it at the time, but they remembered that we had expressed an interest in adopting a child. Their lawyer called Willie and me and told us how difficult it was to place biracial children in homes in the South. We were shocked. It was the twenty-first century. We committed to being a part of changing that in our society. Skin color should not make a difference.

We told the lawyer we were definitely interested, and we started to go through the process of adopting the baby in 2000. We began paying for the mother's living expenses and medical bills, and Willie and I were really getting excited about bringing another child into our home. Our oldest son, John Luke, was almost five, and Sadie, our daughter, was three. We thought it was the perfect time to bring another baby into our home. But then we found out the mother had promised the baby to a few other families, who were also paying her expenses. The woman had nine children, some of which she had kept and others she had given up for adoption. The lawyer told us we needed to step away from the situation. We were absolutely devastated and heartbroken. It was such a roller-coaster ride and so emotional and traumatic. Willie and I decided we still wanted to adopt a child, but we weren't going to force the issue. Maybe it just wasn't in God's plan for us right then.

WE STARTED TO GO THROUGH THE PROCESS OF ADOPTING THE BABY IN 2000.

After we lost the child, Willie and I decided we would have another baby naturally and then maybe adopt a fourth child a few years later. I had gotten pregnant very easily with John Luke and Sadie. Well, nine months went by and I still wasn't pregnant. I wasn't really worried about it, but it seemed a little strange since I'd gotten pregnant so easily the first two times.

We had a friend who was teaching birthing classes at a children's home. The class was for pregnant teenagers, some of whom were putting their babies up for adoption. She knew we were still interested in adoption, so she asked us if we were ready. We filled out the paperwork and only a couple of weeks later, the adoption agency called us and told us it had a couple of babies available. There was a boy who was already born and a girl who was about to be born. The director showed us a picture of the boy and we fell in love instantly! He was beautiful, a perfectly healthy eight-pound, two-ounce bundle of joy. We felt like he was ours from the moment we saw him and couldn't wait to get him in our hands. We rushed through the adoption process. The adoption agency came out and did three days of home studies with us, and then we went and picked him up the very next week. It was that fast. Willie and I felt extremely blessed and thankful for this precious baby boy who was now ours and were confident that this was God's plan for our life and for this little boy's life all along.

We made a nursery in our house and set up a crib, and our son Willie Alexander Robertson came to our home when he was five weeks old in mid-December 2001. We named him after Willie, of course, and his middle name came from his papaw Phil, whose middle name is Alexander. Little Will didn't even weigh nine pounds when we got him and was just so happy and sweet. He had been living with a foster family who took excellent care of him. We went down to Baton Rouge, Louisiana, and picked him up. Then we returned home to a house full of friends and family, who had made a huge WELCOME HOME WILL sign and showered us with gifts and love. Will was just perfect and precious, and I have enjoyed every minute of mothering him. We are forever grateful to Will's birth mother, who loved him enough to give him the life she knew he deserved.

WILLIE ALEXANDER ROBERTSON CAME TO OUR HOME WHEN HE WAS FIVE WEEKS OLD IN MID-DECEMBER 2001.

In the meantime, I still wasn't taking birth control. It all happened so fast, and I was too busy making bottles and changing diapers to think about it. For our tenth wedding anniversary in January 2002, Willie surprised me with a trip to Cancún, Mexico. We drove to Dallas, and I thought we were just going to spend a few days there. Always the romantic, Willie didn't tell me we were going to Mexico until he handed me a note at the airport! It was an awesome surprise, but I was a little reluctant leaving our two-month-old baby at home. Thankfully, my mom was in on the surprise and was fully prepared for and capable of caring for the three little ones we had left with her and my dad. Willie and I had an awesome time in Cancún—it was the first real trip we had had since having kids—and we enjoyed it to its fullest. We came home refreshed and renewed and thankful for our life together.

Needless to say, I was a little shocked about a month later when I found out I was pregnant, but with that news we were even more certain of God's plan for our life. God had closed my womb until Will was in our home, and then opened it to give us our fourth child. Our baby girl, Bella Chrysanne, was born in September 2002. So that's how we came to have two babies just ten months apart.

I'd be lying if I didn't admit that things were nuts there for a while. And I can promise you, while I helped in the discipline department, it's Korie who gets all the credit for doing the hard work. She is an incredible mom and has always taken the role of motherhood very seriously. I don't know how she did it all, but she did, usually with a baby on each hip. This was also my motivation to start being good at business, so I could provide enough money for all these younguns. Let me tell you something: KIDS AIN'T CHEAP. Doctor bills, food, Pampers, and all that other stuff cost money, and I committed to go and push myself further to bring home more bacon, and a lot more cabbage, as in cash.

I'D BE LYING IF I DIDN'T ADMIT THAT THINGS WERE NUTS THERE FOR A WHILE.

It's amazing how when you have four children, you get four different personalities. You would think that when you raise kids the same way in the same home with the same values, they should all turn out the same, right? Wrong. God made every child special, with a unique personality and temperament, fears and hopes, likes and dislikes. And aren't we glad He didn't make us all the same? Life is just so much more interesting that way. Not to mention challenging.

Korie: John Luke and Sadie had their own unique challenges. John Luke was hospitalized with RSV (respiratory syncytial virus, which causes respiratory tract infections) when he was three months old and it seemed to damage his lungs, so we spent a lot of time at the doctor's office with wheezing, bronchitis, and pneumonia, but other than that, he was an easy, fun kid to raise. He loved to read, just like I do, so we spent hours reading books, and he seemed to love to learn about everything. He was also a climber who loved the outdoors. He loved animals so much so that at one point we weren't sure if he would follow in the family hunting tradition. He had every kind of animal, from goats to rabbits, to snakes, to leopard geckos, to an iguana.

One time, when he was about six years old, he and Willie

found a bat down at the camp that for some reason they decided they were going to nurse back to health. We set up a little cage for the bat on our back porch and warned John Luke not to touch him. He begged and begged to touch the bat, and one day decided that he would not really be touching him if he put on gloves first. So he put on some of my yellow rubber kitchen gloves and without my knowing tried to pick up the bat! Of course, the bat bit him on his little finger. He came and told me what he had done and showed me. Sure enough, there were two little bite marks on his finger. I immediately Googled what you do for bat bites and found out that bats are highly likely to carry rabies! We rushed John Luke to the hospital. They gave him the first round of rabies shots just in case and said that they would have to test the bat. If the bat tested positive for rabies, then John Luke would have to go through about five rounds of shots. The doctor asked if we still had the bat and said that we had to turn it in to have it tested for rabies. That's when John Luke started crying. "He doesn't have rabies, I know he doesn't. It's not the bat's fault!" he cried. He was devastated that they had to kill the bat to test him because of something he had done. John Luke said that he would get the shots so that the bat wouldn't have to be tested. This was huge. John Luke hated shots and still does, but he was willing to get more if he could only save the bat.

THAT'S WHEN JOHN LUKE STARTED CRYING. "HE DOESN'T HAVE RABIES, I KNOW HE DOESN'T. IT'S NOT THE BAT'S FAULT!"

As John Luke got older and started hunting with Willie, he took to it naturally. I guess it's in his blood, as they say. The first time John Luke killed a deer, he was so proud to be able to feed our family. We ate on it for weeks. He was becoming a man and fully understood the circle of life. I'm so proud of the young man he has become. He is a leader at his school and at our church and an incredible big brother to his younger siblings.

Our daughter Sadie Carroway was as healthy as she could be. I had her in the summer when Camp Ch-Yo-Ca's sessions were in full swing. Her delivery was easy, and I was at the camp with her when she was only a few days old. The kids passed her around and loved on her. I was a young mom and didn't worry a bit about germs. Maybe that's why she never gets sick: she was exposed to everything with all those little hands touching her as a baby, and she developed immunities. Who knows? She was like the little camp mascot. She was a happy baby who reached for her bed when she was tired. But she seemed to have a stronger spirit than John Luke. We could tell from an early age that she was going to be a competitive little one. She loves sports and had a baseball birthday party at two years old! She's got a lot of her daddy in her. She loves to entertain and make people laugh.

When Sadie was only four years old, she was already doing impersonations of all the family members—just like her dad. She also went through a stage where she would preach. It was the cutest thing we had ever seen. We have a video of her preaching where she says, "It doesn't matter if you are a teacher or a stealer, a policeman or a jail person. God still loves you, and He wants you to be in heaven with Him. He doesn't want you to go down there with the devil. He loves you and He will forgive all your sins. All you have to do is ask Him. . . ." It goes on and on. She sings some songs, then she breaks into a cheer. "Let's give it up for God!" she shouts. She had so much wisdom for such a little one. Willie nicknamed her "the Original" from the time she could talk. It fits her perfectly.

WHEN SADIE WAS ONLY FOUR YEARS OLD, SHE WAS ALREADY DOING IMPERSONATIONS OF ALL THE FAMILY MEMBERS—JUST LIKE HER DAD.

Then came Will and Bella. These two little ones who had come into our life around the same time were quite the handful! Will was a very happy baby. He would literally wake up laughing. We loved to listen to him talking to himself in his bed for a while when he first woke up. He was a very easy baby; then he became a very busy toddler!

Bella wasn't so easy as a baby but is the most fun child one could ever have. She contracted salmonella when she was only three weeks old. It was terrifying! We never found out for sure how she got it. There were some other cases of salmonella from formula that had been reported, but we had also picked up a turtle on the side of the road coming home from church that day. Turtles can sometimes carry salmonella. She, of course, didn't touch the turtle, but one of us could have touched it and then passed it to her. We just weren't sure. Anyway, I was holding her that night when all of a sudden she felt warm. A three-week-old baby should never have a fever.

I knew immediately something was wrong. We rushed her to the hospital. They didn't know what was wrong with her, so they did a spinal tap to make sure she didn't have meningitis. It was horrible to see our little baby go through that ordeal. By the next morning she was having severe diarrhea. It took several days before they figured out exactly what was wrong with her and gave her antibiotics she needed to make her better. She was so sick and was in the hospital for about a week. She lost weight and was the tiniest little thing, but eventually made a full recovery and we were very thankful!

Poor thing, though, she had stomach trouble for about a year after this. She just couldn't hold down anything. I had to feed her every three hours, even through the night, until she was about nine months old, just to try to put some meat on her bones. She cried so much she was perpetually hoarse. But she was the most beautiful little thing and had the most confident little spirit. She started walking at nine months old. Those little toothpick legs didn't look like they could hold her up, but they did, and once she started walking, she was off.

Like I said, the babies were only ten months apart, so Will wasn't even walking when Bella was born. But once they both started walking, there was no stopping them. We called them Destructo 1 and Destructo 2. I used to tell people that one would raise the window and the other would climb out. This was our life for a while. I couldn't keep my eyes on them enough to keep them out of trouble. Bella seemed to have a perpetual knot on her head and our house was always a wreck. If Will and Bella were left alone for any length of time, I can promise you something was going to be destroyed. They would squeeze the toothpaste out of the tube and smear it all over the bathroom mirror, get into the pantry and dump all the cereal out of the boxes—and this was all before eight A.M.!

ONCE WILL AND BELLA STARTED WALKING, THERE WAS NO STOPPING THEM. WE CALLED THEM DESTRUCTO 1 AND DESTRUCTO 2.

We could not take those two anywhere. They were born with the full confidence that they knew exactly where they were going when their legs hit the floor, and they were off. I couldn't keep up with them. I never put them on a leash, but I probably should have. I carried them as much as I could, one on each hip. People would say, "How do you do that?" I told them it was better than the alternative; if I put them down, they would both go in different directions and it was all over. Keeping them on my hip was the only way I could stay in control. Once they got too big for me to carry, I would make them hold my hand. They would try so hard to squirm out of my hand, but I would just squeeze and make them hang on.

Korie says that once she could tell all the kids, "Go brush your teeth and put your PJs on," and they could actually do it by themselves, she knew we would survive! For a while there, she was so consumed with babies that I don't know how she did anything else. But she did. We would end up most nights with at least three of the four kids in our bed. Our rule was that none of the kids could start out in the bed with us, but if they woke up in the night, they could come get in our bed. This was very different than when I was growing up. We would have never climbed in bed with our parents. Phil was not the snuggling type. But it was fun waking up to all the love and laughter, even if our backs suffered for it. Our babies were growing along with the Duck Commander business and our website, and I was starting to do some traveling with Dad for his speaking engagements. It was busy, but it was fun! I loved watching the kids change and grow into their own unique little people.

Korie: We have one more daughter who came to us from a unique place. Growing up, our family traveled a lot and I always thought it was important for kids to experience different cultures and learn from people who grew up differently than them. Of course, it's tough to travel with four little ones, so I thought I would bring someone to us. We decided to take in an exchange student. I didn't know at the time she would become such an awesome big sister to our kids and we would become her American family forever and always.

Rebecca Ann Lo joined our family when she was sixteen years old. She came as an exchange student from Taiwan and must have wondered what she'd gotten herself into joining a family of bearded men who hunted for a living. She was the youngest of four in her family in Taiwan, but when she joined our home, she became the oldest. Also, she lost her father at a young age and I think having a strong father figure in Willie really helped her growth. Our kids were young when Rebecca joined us in the summer of 2004, and they were so excited to welcome her into our family. We made signs welcoming her to America, and when she stepped off the plane, the kids could barely contain their excitement. Will hid behind a chair because he just didn't know what to do. Bella went up and held her hand, and John Luke and Sadie started talking a hundred miles an hour. They had a new playmate and were eager to tell her everything there was to know about our family. We quickly realized she couldn't understand a word we said!

REBECCA ANN LO JOINED OUR FAMILY WHEN SHE WAS SIXTEEN YEARS OLD. SHE CAME AS AN EXCHANGE STUDENT FROM TAIWAN.

She had learned some English in school in Taiwan, but with our Southern accents, Rebecca just could not understand us. Somehow she and I figured out how to communicate, and we bonded. She stuck to me like glue for a while. If someone asked her a question, she would look to me to answer. I read her children's books at night and taught her English through reading the menus at restaurants! I remember the first day I took her to school; I literally had to pry her fingers off my arm. It was like having another kindergartener. She was scared to death. But by the end of the school year, she was speaking English well, with even a little bit of a Louisianan accent. And we fell in love with her and didn't want her to leave. We told her that if she wanted to come back for her senior year, she was more than welcome. Her mom said no at first. She had, of course, missed her daughter and wanted her to come home. But a few weeks before the next school year started, Rebecca called and said excitedly, "Mom said I can come!" She booked her plane ticket back to Louisiana and has been here ever since.

When Rebecca came to live with us, everybody thought I looked like Johnny Damon, an outfielder with the Boston Red Sox, who had a big ol' beard. Korie's dad, Johnny, even gave me a life-size cutout of Damon, which I kept in my office. Well, that entire first year that Rebecca lived with us, I told her I used to be a professional baseball player. She went to a party for foreign exchange students and told everyone that I was an ex–Major League Baseball player! She kept telling everyone, "Willie is very famous." She thought it was the coolest thing and even told her mother and sister I was famous. I finally broke the news to Rebecca that I wasn't really a baseball player. Fortunately, she still loved me anyway. I can only imagine her family's surprise when they went on the Internet and found out whom she was really living with!

After Duck Commander signed a licensing deal with Weaver, which makes rifle and shotgun optical scopes, I wanted to tour their manufacturing center in Taiwan. We took Rebecca as our translator and toured Taiwan. I promised Rebecca I would eat something weird while I was there. I took a small bite of fried chicken feet, but there wasn't any meat. I'm not sure how the Taiwanese eat those. It's a chicken's foot.

I couldn't stomach eating the century egg, which is another Chinese tradition. They preserve duck, chicken, or quail eggs in a mixture of clay, ash, salt, lime, and rice hulls for several months. The egg yolk turns dark green and smells like ammonia. I've eaten some pretty crazy stuff in my life, but that wasn't one of them!

Rebecca's mom and sister came to visit us for a couple of weeks one time, and her mom cooked delicious Taiwanese food for us. Rebecca has been back to Taiwan a couple of times to visit her family there. But we are her American mom and dad. We are family. She graduated from Louisiana State University with a bachelor's degree in fashion design and merchandising, and we are so proud of everything she has accomplished. More important, we are proud of the beautiful Christian lady she has become and the great big sister she has been to our kids. We love her and are thankful God saw fit to place her in our home.

Armadillo Eggs

You didn't think I was going to give you a recipe for chicken feet, did you? I don't really know why these are called armadillo eggs, but they are, and they are tasty. This is a base for many dishes I make. Anything can be added to it at any time. I have used cherries, jams, candied jalapeños, real mozzarella slivers, and many different kinds of meat. If you're not sure it's done after grilling or broiling your bacon, put it in a black pot, add a little butter or olive oil over the top, cover for ten or fifteen minutes, and let steam.

6 to 8 whole jalapeños, sliced
1 package cream cheese
2 pounds breakfast sausage, formed into 6 to 8 patties
1 pound thin-sliced bacon
1 stick of butter, melted

1. Slice jalapeños in half lengthwise.
2. Use one half of each jalapeño for each armadillo egg. Scoop out seeds and veins and then fill each half with cream cheese.
3. Mold sausage patty around jalapeño, making sure to cover the entire jalapeño pepper.
4. Wrap each armadillo egg with a slice of bacon.
5. Cook "eggs" on open grill until bacon is crispy and sausage is thoroughly cooked, about ten to fifteen minutes.
6. Remove eggs from grill and cover with melted butter.

12

FAST FOOD

CHILDREN, OBEY YOUR PARENTS IN THE LORD, FOR THIS IS RIGHT. "HONOR YOUR FATHER AND MOTHER"—WHICH IS THE FIRST COMMANDMENT WITH A PROMISE—"SO THAT IT MAY GO WELL WITH YOU AND THAT YOU MAY ENJOY LONG LIFE ON THE EARTH."

—EPHESIANS 6:1–3

K*orie:* After people watch *Duck Dynasty,* I often get comments on Twitter and from fans that I come into contact with about how well-mannered our kids are. In the South, traditionally children are expected to say "Yes, ma'am" and "No, sir" to adults. It's important for children to show respect for their elders, but I'm afraid that even in the South, that is something that is fading from our society. I'm really proud of our kids for the way they behave, the way they act toward adults, and their manners in general.

When the *Duck Dynasty* crew was here filming the scene where Phil had our kids clean up an area of his land to make a football field, I think the crew members expected our kids to be griping and complaining about having to do it. But our kids would never do that, at least not within earshot of their papaw Phil. Even if they didn't want to do it, they would never complain to their grandfather if he asked them to do something. That's not the way they were raised.

In the Robertson house, kids are expected to fit in with the family and do what the family does. Whenever I need the kids to do something, I always say, "All right, kids, it's family cleanup time," "family wash-the-car time," or "family clean-out-the-garage time." You get the idea. When I announce "family time," everyone is expected to join in. It's nonnegotiable, and you don't get paid for it. You just do it, because you are part of the family.

IN THE ROBERTSON HOUSE, KIDS ARE EXPECTED TO FIT IN WITH THE FAMILY AND DO WHAT THE FAMILY DOES.

Not that our kids don't have plenty of activities of their own. But sometimes when a family's life totally revolves around the kids, parents can start to feel like their children are a burden. We've never felt that way. Our lives didn't end when we brought children into the world. When our kids were younger, I just put them on my hip and took them with me wherever I went. If it meant they had to fall asleep on my shoulder while I was answering e-mails or filling orders, then that's just the way it would be. Kids only know what you teach them. If you let the whole world revolve around them when they are younger, when they realize that's not really the way the world works, it's not very pretty.

Having said all that, somebody told me once that they'd never seen anyone watch their children as much as we do. We'll sit around at night just watching them doing tricks and performing for us. That was something I brought from my side of the family. My family absolutely loves to watch our kids perform. It's really one of our favorite things to do. I think enjoying your children and delighting in them is a gift that you give your children. It's a way to show them that they are loved and valued. Plus, there's nothing cuter than a three-year-old showing off her latest dance moves.

Hey, wait a minute, I will never forget being in the eighth grade and one Friday night telling Phil about "break dancing." Phil said, "What's that?" I told him, "Let me show ya." I put my boom box down, put in my cassette of Midnight Star's "No Parking on the Dance Floor," and did an entire dance while Phil watched from his recliner. He seemed impressed. "That's some kinda moves, Will," he told me. "Not sure what that is, but at least it's entertaining." So even the Robertson side did a little watchin'!

Korie: Another thing we've always tried to teach our children is that people are more important than things. If one of the kids is watching TV and somebody wants to talk, you stop watching TV and listen to them. You never put more importance on a thing than you do on a person. This is hard for older siblings to learn when there are little ones in the family destroying your favorite toys. But it was a lesson we were intent on teaching. If you are going to teach these tough lessons, though,

WE'VE ALWAYS TRIED TO TEACH OUR CHILDREN THAT PEOPLE ARE ALWAYS MORE IMPORTANT THAN THINGS.

you have to model them in your own life. When your neighbor borrows your lawn mower and tears it up, you have to act with love and forgiveness. It's in the little things and the big things. Your children are always watching.

This was a hard lesson for me because I came from such a poor family. When I was a child, you really took pride in having any possessions. But Korie and her family could always go out and buy a replacement when something got lost or broke. She actually taught me a lot about this lesson in our early marriage days. I was used to protecting my stuff from my brothers like the Secret Service.

Korie: Willie and I have always thought that your home should be the happiest place for your family. If you're excited when your kids or husband walks in the front door, then you'll have a much happier family. A lot of people don't make it a habit to do that. They go to work and give their best to the outside world because they know if they're negative or griping or complaining, they might lose their job. They're not going to make a sale with a frown on their faces, so they're always putting on their best smile. It should be that way at home too. I always tell our children that the people they love the most and the people who love them the most are their family. So your family should be the people you treat the best.

When the kids come home every day, we really try to make it a point to greet them, be happy, and ask them how their days went. I do the same thing for Willie, and he does the same thing for me. When Willie comes home, I'm excited. I hug him and kiss him. We find out what happened in each other's day, and it sets the right tone for everything else. Our kids see our love for each other, and they realize that's how they should be treating one another too.

I think having happy kids and a happy marriage is all about respect. Willie and I have a mutual respect for each other, and we try to treat each other respectfully. Sadie once asked me why marriage is so hard. She realized married couples don't always make it and that there are a lot of people getting divorced. Our kids see that Willie and I are happy and think marriage looks pretty easy. Of course, they didn't see us during the early years, when times were tough. In those days we fought our way through all the things newlyweds have to figure out in order to live together peacefully. I told Sadie that sometimes it's hard because you go into a marriage with expectations, and you think the other person is going to be a certain way. You want them to be that way because that's how you always envisioned your husband or wife, or that's how your daddy or mama was when you were growing up. But until you can let those expectations go, and value your spouse for who he or she really is and be thankful for it, then a marriage is never going to work.

HAVING HAPPY KIDS AND A HAPPY MARRIAGE IS ALL ABOUT RESPECT.

I'm very different from Willie's mom, and Willie is very different from my dad. So if you go into a marriage with all these unrealistic expectations and try to change your spouse to be exactly like you want them to be, then you're always going to be fighting and miserable. But if you can let those false expectations go, you can learn to appreciate and be thankful for who that person is, and then marriage can be a great thing.

I think marriages start to go bad when selfishness creeps in. Korie and I are super laid-back, in a lot of ways like my parents were. I never liked taking orders, never liked being bossed around, and I didn't marry a parent figure. There is no sense in my giving her orders or her giving me orders; we're both adults. I married somebody to share my life with. You have to let your spouse be the person they want to be, and you have to let them do the things they want to do. If she doesn't feel like cleaning the kitchen one day, she doesn't have to. If I feel it needs to be cleaned, I can do it myself, or hire someone to do it. I don't tell her what to do. I'm not her father. She does the same for me.

Korie ended up working at Duck Commander with me, but if she wanted to do something entirely different, I would have supported her. As the kids have gotten older and as the business has grown, there have been times where I've told her, "If you want to stop, you can stop. Don't feel like you have to work." I've asked her several times if she didn't want me to go on the road, and if she hadn't wanted me to go, I wouldn't have gone. Now, she'd have had to realize that the business might have suffered from it, but if it did, then so be it. Making a little extra money is never worth it if it's at the expense of your family. If you work with your spouse, then you really have to respect each other and communicate well. Those are the keys to living and working with your spouse happily.

Korie: When Willie was growing up, he always knew what the consequences were if he misbehaved or acted out of line, and it was the same in my home. We try to never yell at our kids or even raise our voices at them. I can honestly say that I have never heard Willie yell at our children but he has always disciplined them with an immediate action. I remember one time when the kids were fighting and driving me crazy. The TV was turned up really loud, and they were yelling at each other, fighting over some toy or what movie they were going to watch next. Willie came through the door and saw that I was about at my wit's end. He just walked over and turned the TV off. The kids looked at him and thought, "Wait, what just happened?" There was complete silence in the room. Without saying a word, Willie was telling them, "If you're going to fight, then you're not going to get to watch TV." The argument was over, and there was no discussion or arguing back and forth. Willie just put an end to it.

THE ARGUMENT WAS OVER, AND THERE WAS NO DISCUSSION OR ARGUING BACK AND FORTH. WILLIE JUST PUT AN END TO IT.

That's how discipline generally works in our house. When our kids were toddlers, if one of our kids woke up from a nap and was whiny or in a bad mood, then he or she was expected to turn around and go straight back to his or her room. If one of the kids is driving everybody else crazy, then he or she is removed from the situation. They're sent to their room until they can get along with everyone else.

But Willie seems to get his point across better than me. I'm usually the one who wakes the kids up for school in the morning, and Bella takes forever to get out of bed. I have to admit, I was the same way for my mom, so maybe I have too much patience for it. But I have to roll her over and keep prodding her to get up. Then I have to go back and check to make sure she didn't go back to sleep after I left. But Willie literally just walks into a room and turns on a light. He says, "Get up," and they get up. I'm always like, "How in the world did you do that?" I guess that's just the difference between mamas and daddies, and it's important to have that balance.

When the kids are misbehaving, I don't count to three. One is enough. I try not to be the one always saying no, but when I do, it should carry some weight. I try to be the parent who disciplines our kids because I don't want Korie to be burdened with it. I think Korie and I have really defined roles in how we handle situations. Korie's tolerance line has always been a lot higher than mine. My kids will test me, but they understand that when they reach my tolerance line, that's it and it's over. The key is being consistent so you never confuse them.

I never raise my voice. Phil never yelled at us when I was growing up. When Phil said it, he said it and didn't have to scream. I see people yelling at their kids, and I always think, "I ain't going to do that." Phil let his actions speak louder than his words. I think one of the most powerful things that happened to us as kids was when my oldest brother, Alan, was seventeen. He and his buddies went camping and were drinking beer. Then they decided to knock down a bunch of mailboxes up the road in a drunken redneck night. A neighbor came down the next morning and talked to Phil. Jase and I were pretty young, and we could hear the adults whispering in the kitchen. I remember hearing Phil say, "Okay, I got you." Phil walked out the front door, climbed in his truck, and drove off.

Phil drove to Alan's camp and found beer cans all over the ground. He told Alan to get in his truck. Then he told the three other boys, "If you ever want to come to my house for the rest of your life, get in my truck, and you're getting a whippin' for tearing up those mailboxes." Two of Alan's friends came over to our house pretty regularly, so they figured they'd better get in the truck. The third guy had never even seen Phil, and Al and the other two boys told him they wouldn't hold it against him if he didn't come. I guess he figured, "How bad can it really be?" The four of them climbed in the back of the truck, and Phil drove them back to our house. Jase and I hid in the azalea bushes and watched Phil whip four seventeen-year-old men. One of them was Bill "Red Dawg" Phillips, who was one of Alan's best friends and later worked for Duck Commander and appeared in several Duckmen videos. Phil told him, "I've known you all your life. I'm so disappointed. I can't believe you pulled a stunt like this." Greg Eppinette, who would later become one of our cameramen on the Duckmen videos, was also there. Phil told him, "I know your parents. We've been to church together. You tell your daddy why you got this." Then Phil whipped him. Next was the boy Phil had never laid eyes on. "Son," Phil said, "I don't know who you are but you tell your daddy that I whipped you and why I did it, and if he has a problem with it, he can come talk to me." Last was Alan, who was wearing these short little running shorts. It was the 1980s, and he looked like Richard Simmons. You want to talk about influencing young ones. It hurt Jase and me to watch that belt hitting Alan's pasty thighs. That was pretty much all it took to keep Alan in line for the rest of high school, and Jase and me as well.

After raising four kids, I think discipline has to start when they're young. A lot of our friends will say, "Oh, he's out of control," and their son is ten years old. I'm always thinking, "He's probably going to be out of control when he's eighteen. You missed it." By the time a kid is ten years old, his parents have missed their window of opportunity to really lay down the ground rules. I'm not saying it's over, I'm just saying the sooner you start teaching your kids what is expected and being consistent with your discipline, the better. Kids respond better when the boundaries are clearly defined. All of our children are old enough now that spankings are pretty much a thing of the past. I know that they will continue to find ways

THE SOONER YOU START TEACHING YOUR KIDS WHAT IS EXPECTED AND BEING CONSISTENT WITH YOUR DISCIPLINE, THE BETTER.

to test our boundaries, but disrespect is not tolerated, and if I see even an ounce of it, I promise, I can still think of some ways to make them regret it.

Of course, John Luke and Sadie always tell Will and Bella that they have it a lot easier. But I think the two younger kids saw how the two older kids acted, and they learned that's what was expected of them. If the two older kids were terrors, then the two younger kids would have probably ended up being terrors, too.

Korie: Willie commands respect from our kids because they know there is always going to be an immediate reaction if they misbehave. You have to discipline out of love, and there are lots of ways you can do that. We discipline them because we love them and we want to help them to grow into happy, healthy adults. Now that John Luke and Sadie are teenagers, they say that we are more relaxed than their friends' parents. We don't have to do much discipline anymore because we instilled that respect when they were young. And I have to say, we have really good kids. Of course, our kids aren't perfect. We've been on trips where everything was great until the ride home. Will and Bella will start arguing over something ridiculous, and they turn into typical nine- and ten-year-old kids. They'll have their struggles and their difficult times, but they know that we love them and will always be there for them, no matter if they're "a policeman or a jail person." They're ours!

Sometimes people ask us if we're worried how the fame will affect our kids. You know what? We're all in the same boat. Everybody is trying to raise their kids to be compassionate, loving, and responsible adults. There are some famous people who have kids who have messed up, but there are people working at a mill whose kids have messed up. We're all doing the best we can to raise our children. It's not really about fame. It's about spending time with your children, disciplining them when they need it, praising them when they need it, and letting them know they're loved.

All right, enough about our awesome kids. I hope you don't think we are saying we are the perfect parents or have the perfect family. Far from it! We do try to glorify God in the way we treat one another and the way we raise our children, and then we ask God to do the rest. Many of you reading this could certainly teach us a thing or two about marriage and child rearing, but these are just some things that we've done in our home, and if they help any of you, then it was worth writing it.

I HATE TO ADMIT IT, BUT I'LL JUST GO AHEAD AND THROW IT OUT THERE: I'M NOT THE COOK THAT KAY IS. OKAY, I'M NOT EVEN HALF THE COOK KAY IS.

Korie: You may have been wondering why we named this chapter "Fast Food." Well, I hate to admit it, but I'll just go ahead and throw it out there: I'm not the cook that Kay is. Okay, I'm not even half the cook Kay is. That's why on *Duck Dynasty* you always see me chopping vegetables. It's a joke around here that in every scene I'm in with Kay, I'm always chopping vegetables. Willie says I put my apron on to toss the salad. I'm just not a good cook. I'm always rushed and have a hundred other things going on, so I burn the bread, or I'll start cooking something and realize I don't have the main ingredient!

Willie's the cook in our house. He is incredible. He can just throw a bunch of stuff together along with something he caught or brought out of the woods and it turns into a gourmet meal. Am I ever thankful that I married a man who can cook! The problem is, when he is not around, I am helpless. The kids and I have to survive on breakfast for supper. I'm good at pancakes, bacon and eggs, or something easy like tacos, but that's about the extent of it.

I promise I tried. When we got married, Kay gave me all of her recipes, along with a set of my own black skillets. I cooked for a while, but the more kids I had, the worse I seemed to get. I just couldn't do it all, and I had to admit it just wasn't my thing. Willie says he retired me from the kitchen when Will and Bella came along. It doesn't bother me. I'm good at a lot of things. Cooking just doesn't happen to be one of them. I'm good at being a mom; Willie's good at cooking. It works for us.

So, having said all that, I have to tell you that sometimes—well, more often than I care to admit—we just eat fast food. There, I said it. The end of every episode of *Duck Dynasty* shows us all around the dinner table, and that's real. It's what we do. We love to get together and enjoy a big meal together as a family. We do it often, but not every day. Sometimes we just go through the drive-through line and talk about our day in the car on the way to the next sporting event, and then we wait for Daddy to get home from his latest hunting or business trip so he can whip us up one of his gourmet meals!

HOMEMADE MAC AND CHEESE

Korie: This is an easy mac and cheese recipe that both kids and adults love. It is one of Kay's recipes that I make often. It's so easy, I can even do it!

1 package (16 ounces) large elbow macaroni
8 tablespoons butter
salt and pepper to taste
8 tablespoons flour
2½ cups milk
2 cups cheddar cheese, grated

1. Cook macaroni according to package directions.
2. While macaroni is boiling, melt butter on medium heat in a medium-sized saucepan and add salt, pepper, and flour. Stir continuously.
3. When butter is melted, add milk.
4. Stir until it thickens, then turn off heat.
5. Strain the macaroni and pour it into a pan.
6. Cover with butter sauce and mix together.
7. Add grated cheese on the top and put in oven at 350 degrees until the cheese is melted.

13

FRIED BURGERS

WHAT, THEN, SHALL WE SAY IN RESPONSE TO THESE THINGS? IF GOD IS FOR US, WHO CAN BE AGAINST US?
—ROMANS 8:31

If you've watched *Duck Dynasty,* you know all about Kay's skills in the kitchen, but don't overlook Phil when it comes to cooking. One of Phil's specialties has always been good ol' hamburgers. Of course, they're not ordinary burgers. There is a very specific way that Phil cooks a burger. Most people put a patty of meat on the grill and just mash the heck out of it with a spatula, squeezing all the juice out of it as they try to cook it as fast as possible. But Phil's philosophy is to never put a spatula on a burger. Phil's famous burgers are not cooked on a grill—although he does grill burgers, but that's a whole 'nother story. His famous burgers are cooked on a griddle or in a frying pan. They just taste better that way. While most people take about a quarter-pound of hamburger and make as big of a patty as they can, Phil prefers smaller, thinner patties. Phil never takes any shortcuts with his cooking, so he applies more pepper than needed, and the cooking surface is a lot hotter than required. When Phil throws a patty on the griddle, he sears one side and then the other, locking in all the juices that give a burger its flavor. He browns his buns on the griddle and they soak up the grease, which makes them taste even better. Phil's burgers are some of the best around.

When I got older and had my own place, I started cooking my version of Phil's burgers. I cook them kind of like Phil does, but I've changed some things to make them my own. Phil taught me a long time ago that there's no use in changing something if it works, so I still cook my burgers on a griddle or in a pan, use thin patties, and toast my buns in grease, just like he does. But to make them different, I've at times added jalapeños, bacon, onions, different seasonings, and even blue cheese to the meat. I've covered them with all kinds of different cheeses. We started calling my burgers "Willie burgers." You know your burger is good when people start calling it by name. "Willie burgers" have become kind of famous among our family and friends, and there's a big debate as to whether my burgers or Phil's taste better.

Cooking burgers is pretty easy, which is probably why they're so popular at barbecues or when you're sitting by the swimming pool on the weekends. Not everyone can cook them well, but anyone can cook them. You fire up a grill or griddle and go to work. I feel like it's kind of that way in business, too. From day one, Duck Commander wasn't anything flashy. It started with a pretty common man with a very big dream. With the exception of Phil's invention of the double-reed duck call, the things we've done with Duck Commander over the years haven't necessarily been revolutionary. We didn't bring in a consultant from Harvard Business School to create a business model or strategic plan for us. In fact, very little of what we've done has been by the book, but I think we took some chances and risks over the years in our quest to make Duck Commander a success. Some of them worked out; some of them didn't.

I like to joke that the Robertson family and bad ideas go together like biscuits and jam. Every action in life begins with a decision, and unfortunately, we don't always make the best ones. Indeed, we've made some bad decisions over the years, but we wouldn't be where we are today without having taken some risks. Even when we faced tough times and what seemed like insurmountable odds, we persevered through our mistakes and landed on our feet again. We've always thought that if we did what was morally and ethically right, while continuing to steadfastly believe in what we were doing, we'd be okay in the end. More than anything else, Duck Commander is about building solid products, fostering relationships that last, and treating our employees like family. Well, most of us are family!

I LIKE TO JOKE THAT THE ROBERTSON FAMILY AND BAD IDEAS GO TOGETHER LIKE BISCUITS AND JAM.

Even after Korie and I took over Duck Commander in 2005, Phil was still the king. I didn't immediately start making rogue decisions when I became CEO, and I wasn't interested in changing the way we'd done business for the previous thirty-something years. I never thought, "I'm going to change this, and I don't care what Phil thinks." I always went to him for advice before making a big decision, and he still has a very influential voice in how we operate today. There's a reason Duck Commander was already a solid business when I took it over, and it started with the foundation Phil built in the early days. We follow pretty simple business practices and we've stuck to them, even in turbulent times. Phil was determined to build his company with his family, and that's something that's really important to me as well. Unlike a lot of modern businessmen, Phil wasn't going to let his career get in the way of his family. That's an attribute pretty much anybody can respect and appreciate.

Korie: Phil and Willie are so much alike. We went to a marriage seminar at our church one time, and Phil and Kay and Jase and Missy were there as well. Each of the couples took a personality test to see if their personalities were compatible. We all laughed because Phil and Willie scored high in the characteristics for having a dominant personality. They were almost identical in a lot of areas, but somewhat different in that Willie was high in the social category as well. I think Willie got that part of his personality from his mother.

It's funny because people look at the Robertsons and think Jase and Phil are just alike, and they are certainly similar in their love for ducks. But when we took the personality test, we saw that Jase's personality is much more like his mother's. So I guess it makes sense that Phil and Jase get along so well in the duck blind. They make a good team, just like Phil and

Kay do at home. Kay has always said that Willie is a lot like Phil and even calls him "Phil Jr." at times. While I wouldn't go that far, I definitely see the similarities. They both have strong, charismatic personalities. They are both big-picture guys with big ideas and deep beliefs. Whatever either of them is doing in life, he does it all the way, and they are both very opinionated, which can sometimes be a challenge. Phil and Willie haven't always been as close as they are now. As they grew, they recognized the attributes they have in common and learned to value one another's differences and strengths. Willie says it couldn't have happened until after he was thirty, though. He needed to grow up and mature, and Phil has gotten more relaxed as he's gotten older. Willie loves to hunt with his dad and brothers, but there have been times when he's had a hard time sitting in Phil's blind. You can only have one leader in the duck blind, only one man who lines up the men and yells, "Cut 'em!" when it's time to shoot. Willie and Phil have both always been leaders, whether it's in the blind or in business.

YOU CAN ONLY HAVE ONE LEADER IN THE DUCK BLIND.

After I took over Duck Commander from Phil, not all of my decisions were popular. When we started *Benelli Presents Duck Commander* on the Outdoor Channel in 2009, while it was hugely successful and helped change hunting shows for the better, it was quite different for people who grew up watching our Duckmen videos. They were used to seeing Phil biting ducks' heads and watching ducks fall from the sky in slow motion. Really, our hard-core fans were used to seeing us kill a lot of ducks. But the show on Outdoor Channel revealed a lot of the business side of Duck Commander as well, which gave viewers a behind-the-scenes look at the company and our operations. Some people really liked seeing those aspects of Duck Commander, but change is hard for some people and there were some hard-core fans who only wanted to see the Duckmen shooting ducks from a blind for an hour. I can certainly appreciate both sides of the argument.

Korie: We started catching a little bit of flak from some of our longtime fans, and a lot of their criticism was aimed at Willie because he'd recently taken over the company. On the forums on our website, some people told us they liked the way the old videos were filmed and accused Willie of trying to ruin the company. They said Duck Commander was getting too corporate and too big, and it was all Willie's fault. After a while, I'd had enough. I couldn't stand it any longer. People didn't realize that Willie was trying to make Duck Commander financially solvent, and with the TV show, he was appealing to a much broader audience. In the old days, Phil made just enough money to pay the bills and feed his family.

But as Jase, Willie, and Jep got older and started working for the company, there were a lot more families to feed. Each of the Robertson boys had his own wife and children to provide for. There are a lot of other Duck Commander employees to pay as well, and most of them are our relatives and very close friends. Willie had to find ways to increase Duck Commander's revenue, or we were going to have to start laying people off, which we certainly didn't want to do. Putting a Duck Commander hunting show on the Outdoor Channel was one of the best decisions we made. We got new sponsors who were paying us money to wear and use their products, and, of course, there were contractual obligations that came with those agreements.

After I'd read enough of the complaints, I wrote a blog entry on our website entitled "Stand by Your Man." I explained to the disgruntled fans that Willie was only trying to make Duck Commander better, and that without the changes he made they wouldn't be able to see Phil, Jase, and Si shooting ducks anywhere, because there wouldn't be enough money to produce the DVDs. Willie wasn't out to change the core of what Duck Commander was. After all, he's Phil's son, so it's his heritage as well. He was just trying to expand the company and grow it into something even more people could appreciate and love. To this day, we still make the hunting DVDs for the serious duck hunters just like we did in the old days. I think people slowly started to realize that Duck Commander was really a business and it had bills to pay and expenses like any other company. And after my diatribe, the fans who were complaining on our forums apologized for criticizing Willie and we all made up!

Believe it or not, Phil has been making the hunting DVDs for more than two decades. The first ones were actually filmed on VHS tapes. Phil was convinced there was a market for waterfowl hunting videos when perhaps no one else was. There were a lot of deer- and other big-game-hunting videos on the market at the time, but no one had really tried it with ducks. Phil rented camera equipment from a company in Dallas and hired Gary Stephenson, a science teacher at Ouachita Christian School, to direct and film his first video. Much like Phil's duck calls, not a lot of other people believed the videos would be a success. *Duckmen 1: Duckmen of Louisiana* was released in 1988 and sold about one hundred copies. Undeterred, Phil set out to film *Duckmen 2: Point Blank,* which took the next five seasons to produce. Obviously, it was a very laborious venture and none of the Duckmen knew much of anything about filmmaking.

Like almost everything else Phil put his hands on, the Duckmen hunting tapes were unlike what everyone else was doing at the time. The videos lasted about an hour each and were among the first to include rock music over hunting scenes. Phil has always been a big fan of classic rock. He loves Lynyrd Skynyrd, Led Zeppelin, Creedence Clearwater Revival, Pink Floyd, and Bob Seger. I still remember when Pink Floyd's *The Wall* came out in 1979. Phil bought the eight-track and plugged it in Alan's player, and then he just lay in the bed and listened to the entire tape. Lynyrd Skynyrd is definitely one of his favorites, though.

> LYNYRD SKYNYRD IS DEFINITELY ONE OF PHIL'S FAVORITES.

If there's one rule at Phil's house, it's that you never wake him while he's napping. It was a rule when I was a kid, and it's still that way today. One day, one of the members of Lynyrd Skynyrd called the Duck Commander office, which at that time was Phil and Kay's house, wanting to talk to Phil. I can't remember who answered the phone at the time, but he or she wasn't about to wake up Phil from his nap. Phil was so mad when he found out. He told us, "From this day forward, wake me up if the president of the United States or Lynyrd Skynyrd calls!"

I grew up listening to classic rock but then started liking country music when I was in college. Phil couldn't understand why I liked listening to it. While I was home from college for a break one time, a bunch of Phil's buddies were over at his house, and Phil called me down and started making fun of me for listening to country music. He told me rock 'n' roll was the only music worth listening to. I got mad, stormed out of the house, and said I was never coming back. I told you we were both opinionated! Of course, Phil listens to country music now.

Rock music wasn't the only thing different about the Duckmen videos. Phil, Jase, Si, and I have the long beards, and so did most of the other original Duckmen, Mac Owen, Dane Jennings, and Bill "Red Dawg" Phillips. Phillips was the first Duckman to paint his face. "Red Dawg" couldn't grow a long beard. His beard was pitiful, so he figured he'd paint his face to look different than the rest of us. After a while, Phil figured out paint was the best way to camouflage our white faces from the ducks. After all, a man's face stands out like a white surrender flag in a duck blind. Before too long, everyone in Phil's blind was required to wear face paint. By the time *Duckmen 3: In Yo' Face* came out in 1997, the videos had a pretty large cult following. There were a lot of funny and uncouth antics involved, like spitting contests, shooting water moccasins (a.k.a. congos or ol' Jims, as Phil likes to call them), and picking the feathers off ducks. The hunting scenes were really kind of in your face and over the top. In *Duckmen 2,* Phil flipped a deer with a rifle shot, which the cameraman, Greg Eppinette, captured in slow motion. Phil became nearly as famous for flipping the deer as any of his duck hunting. There was definitely a shock value to the early Duckmen videos. We released our sixteenth Duckmen video in 2012, and they're still very popular.

As we began to grow and develop more relationships in the hunting industry, many people started telling us we should get our own TV show, but we really couldn't figure out how it was going to make money. I did not know anything about the business side of hunting shows. I knew I had to learn everything I could about this venture before I jumped into it. I felt I had a good grasp on entertainment but needed to know the financial side, because one thing we didn't have at that time was a lot of money. Duck Commander was still operating on a very tight budget.

Most hunting shows are paid programming, so you have to buy the airtime from a network and sell the advertisements on your own. And most hunting shows don't make money, but companies write it off as advertising. I didn't feel like I had the money to invest in something like that at the time. But we knew we would have a really good product if we could ever do it, because Duck Commander had so many unique personalities.

About this same time reality shows were really taking off. Korie liked watching reality TV, and we became convinced our family had what it took to venture into it. After seeing *American Chopper*, we were even more convinced our family could have its own show. People weren't watching *American Chopper* because they loved motorcycles. The success of that show was due to the big personalities and the relationships between the dad and his sons. We knew we had that and then some!

We caught a break when Steve Kramer, an in-house producer with Benelli Shotguns, went on a hunting trip to Arkansas with Phil, Jase, Jep, and me. Kramer watched how we interacted and listened to our stories about our antics in the duck blind. He had a background in reality TV and was producing commercials for Benelli. When we went to SHOT Show a couple of months later, Kramer called us into a meeting. He told us Benelli thought we could do a TV show and went over what he thought the show could be. It was exactly what Korie and I had been talking about! We just kept looking across the table at one another with smiles on our faces. We were very much on the same page with what Kramer was laying out creatively. But then we told him we couldn't afford to produce a show. He said he thought Benelli would be willing to back it financially, although they would need me to help get other sponsors on board as well. Benelli would be willing to put its name on the show for advertising, even if it could not recoup the money it was going to invest. It didn't happen right away, however. When we left the meeting, I said, "Let me try to talk Phil into doing it." Kramer said, "We've got to work out the details with Steve McKelvain [Benelli's vice president of marketing]." Almost a full year went by before cameras rolled.

Kramer was our executive producer, and the show swept the Golden Moose Awards the first year, which are kind of like the Oscars for outdoor TV. Kramer brought a lot to the table, and the quality was different from anything else on outdoor TV. He was passionate about making the show the best it could be creatively and stylistically. Benelli produced the first two seasons of *Duck Commander* but then decided it couldn't pay for the production costs anymore. It was a really expensive show to produce by hunting-show standards. By that time, though, we were able to take it on ourselves. We hired Warm Springs Productions, which had worked with us in season one, to produce season three.

Phil was really never convinced that the show on Outdoor Channel would work. "Who's gonna watch this?" he proclaimed. But I told Phil he had to trust me on the idea and that the move would help our business. He reluctantly agreed to do it, and from day one I worked very hard to make sure it would not be miserable for him. His reluctance gave me the motivation to make sure it was successful. Duck Commander's sales grew, and the show gave the entire company a new spirit—a spirit

I TOLD PHIL HE HAD TO TRUST ME ON THE IDEA AND THAT THE MOVE WOULD HELP OUR BUSINESS. HE RELUCTANTLY AGREED.

of confidence. It was cool seeing the fans' reactions to the episodes at hunting shows, signing autographs, and selling more products. But more than anything else, it was preparing us for something so much bigger.

Now, the Lord works in mysterious ways for sure. In September 2010, we found an e-mail in one of the generic boxes at DuckCommander.com. It was from Scott Gurney, who owned Gurney Productions, a TV production company in Los Angeles. Gurney wrote that he knew of *Duck Commander,* watched our show on Outdoor Channel, and really thought we had what it takes to go to the next level. One of our employees called me and asked if he should call Gurney back. He forwarded me the e-mail and I took it from there. I called Scott and we talked for a few hours. He was a big thinker and got me really excited about what he thought we could do. At one point, Scott said, "Man, you get a show on a major network, you will sell T-shirts in Walmart."

"We already sell T-shirts in Walmart," I told him.

"Oh, yeah, I keep forgetting you guys have a big following," Gurney told me.

As we're about to start our second season of *Duck Dynasty* on A&E, I get asked this question all the time: "How did you end up getting a show on a major network? How did they find you?" Everyone wants to know how you end up doing a reality TV show. Well, that's how we did it. Most folks don't do a show on a small network and then get discovered. But looking back, the experience we had on Outdoor Channel was invaluable. That's where we learned our craft of making great TV. It was where we got a taste for fame, became prepared, and learned to focus. We witnessed the ins and outs of making television shows, and learned how to work on TV schedules, and, perhaps most important, saw what worked and what didn't. Oh, did we learn!

We didn't know A&E would be where we would end up. We made a highlights video, or "sizzle reel," as it's called in Hollywood, and Gurney pitched it to the networks. It was well received by many of them, but Gurney called and said A&E was most interested. Our only experience with A&E up to this point had been an appearance on an episode of *Billy the Exterminator* the year before, when Billy and Ricky came to West Monroe to exterminate our duck blinds. As far as I know, that was the only time Billy and Ricky had to literally abort the mission! Our blind was full of snakes and, even worse for Ricky, wasps. Unfortunately, Ricky is allergic to wasps and got stung right on his nose. The producers called "Cut!" and rushed Ricky to the hospital! That was the end of our filming with A&E up to this point.

Gurney told us that A&E wanted to do two episodes and if they liked them, they would pick up a full season. It wasn't a guarantee. Initially, we had bigger offers from some other networks, but let's face it, this was A&E we were talking about! And Gurney said that it was where we needed to be. We were still cautious, though. If A&E didn't like the episodes, nothing would happen, so we didn't tell too many people about the opportunity at first. We just kind of quietly made the episodes and waited to see what happened.

Thankfully, A&E's executives liked what they saw. The show turned out funnier than even we expected. When we watched it for the first time as a family, we laughed the entire way through. Phil even said, "Willie, you might be right. I think this could work."

I basically bet the farm that having a TV show would do wonders for our company, and it did. When the *Duck Commander* show came out on Outdoor Channel, our sales numbers began to increase. Then when *Duck Dynasty* began airing on A&E, the growth was absolutely phenomenal. I really cannot even explain what the growth has been like. The crew at our warehouse is working their tails off to keep up. I'm so proud of the growth that we made while still staying true to our roots. I am proud to say that I proved Phil wrong on the whole TV venture. A&E is absolutely a first-class network. They have been so cool to work with. Phil had big reservations about doing the show, but I persuaded him on the idea. A&E wanted to do a dinner scene with a prayer at the end of every episode. I told Phil that it would be a chance for us to show America a family that loves each other and was, dare I say, positive in so many ways. This wasn't only a sales pitch to Phil because I really believed God had called us for something truly special.

I BASICALLY BET THE FARM THAT HAVING A TV SHOW WOULD DO WONDERS FOR OUR COMPANY.

And I guess the rest is history, 'cause we're still sharing our message on TV. *Duck Dynasty* is kind of like Phil's burgers. He took something very simple and made it into something that people have talked about for years. Phil made VHS tapes of his duck hunts, and I tried to make them better. I still remember when I told Phil we should switch from VHS tapes to DVDs and he thought I was crazy. Phil laid the groundwork with the Duckmen videos, and I just added to them. I make the same type of burger Phil does, but just added a little to them and make them for a future generation. The idea behind the burger is the same as Dad's, just with some glitz and glamour. And by the way, when I'm at Phil's house and he's making burgers, I'm the first in line to eat about three of them. They are fabulous.

Willie Burgers

I usually just make my burgers plain, just meat and salt and black pepper, especially for the family. Blue Cheese is my favorite add-on if you want to take them up a notch. I can knock out eight to ten burgers in fifteen minutes. My kids' favorite side is my fries: I peel potatoes, cut them up in slivers, fry them in peanut oil, and immediately *apply Cajun seasoning, and then I throw a pinch of sugar on (shhhhh, that's my secret). Do all this while they are still piping hot—you wait, you lose.*

1 pound ground round
salt and pepper to taste
Phil Robertson's Cajun Style Seasoning, to taste
8 ounces blue cheese
1 package bacon
hamburger buns

1. Make hamburger patties that are small and thin, mixing in the blue cheese if you wish.
2. Generously season hamburger patties with salt, pepper, and Cajun Style Seasoning.
3. Cook bacon.
4. Sear one side of hamburger for about 3 to 4 minutes, but never touch it with a spatula (and don't push out the juices!). Then flip the hamburger once and don't touch it again.
5. Top with bacon.
6. Warm hamburger buns in the grease from the patties.

14

DUMPLINGS, HOT WATER, CORNBREAD, AND FRIED SQUIRRELS

A WIFE OF NOBLE CHARACTER WHO CAN FIND? SHE IS WORTH FAR MORE THAN RUBIES. HER HUSBAND HAS FULL CONFIDENCE IN HER AND LACKS NOTHING OF VALUE . . . HER CHILDREN ARISE AND CALL HER BLESSED; HER HUSBAND ALSO, AND HE PRAISES HER.
—PROVERBS 31:10–11, 28

Before Korie and I started running Duck Commander, everything happened at Phil and Kay's house. That's where all of the duck-call manufacturing, packaging, shipping, and billing took place. Every Duck Commander employee worked at Phil and Kay's house, which is a pretty good ways out of town and not the ideal working situation. They are too far out of town to get regular cable or Internet service, so everything was on satellite. Every time it rained hard we would lose service. We'd be waiting on a big order and the lights would go out. Plus, the "offices" were only old buildings and old trailers that were pieced together as the company grew. About six years ago, Korie and I moved to a new house and relocated most of Duck Commander's business operations to our old house. We ran the website and did all of the clerical work there. The manufacturing was still taking place at Phil's house because that's where the machinery was located. But in the winter of 2008, the Ouachita River flooded its banks, and the water slowly made its way up to my parents' house.

I can still remember asking Phil how he was going to ship orders if his property flooded.

"Well, I guess we'll put them on a boat," Phil told me, with a scary sense of seriousness in his voice.

It was right in the middle of duck-hunting season, and Duck Commander was very busy. We couldn't afford to take a chance on my parents' house flooding, along with all of the duck calls that were being made down there. If there were any delays in our manufacturing or shipping, it would cost us a lot of money. So Korie and I purchased a warehouse from her father, Johnny. Duck Commander's employees were excited about working at the new warehouse because most of them lived in town and their drive wasn't going to be nearly as far. But they were also a little sad about leaving my parents' house because Kay had been cooking them lunch every workday for nearly four decades.

When Duck Commander was working out of Phil and Kay's

house, it was a very casual work atmosphere. Kay would cook a big meal for lunch every day, and they would all eat and then most of the employees would take a nap. Then they'd all sit around and talk. Eventually, they would get back to working. But if somebody got a hankering to go fishing, everybody just went fishing. I think moving to our old house was a good transition before moving it all to a warehouse in town. If we had gone straight to a big warehouse, everyone would have had a hard time adjusting. We've always strived to keep that family atmosphere that Kay and Phil started, while finding ways to become more efficient and productive. I think we've achieved that. If you ask around our offices, people will tell you that they actually like coming to work. It's a fun environment with people who love each other, have interesting personalities, and enjoy what they do. It doesn't get any better than that.

IF SOMEBODY GOT A HANKERING TO GO FISHING, EVERYBODY JUST WENT FISHING.

Kay was a little relieved to get everybody out of her kitchen and out of her house, but I think she felt a little sadness, too. She and Phil were so used to having so many people around the house all the time. They were kind of like, "Wait a minute. What are we going to do now?" Now Kay brings her grandkids down to the house and plans outings and fun things for them. And, of course, if Phil or Jase runs the nets and catches a big mess of catfish, all work stops at the warehouse while everyone heads down to Phil and Kay's for an impromptu fish fry. Kay still enjoys cooking for anyone who drops by, and the whole family joins in for dinner often. Kay's not getting off that easy!

At everyone's birthdays, Kay will cook the birthday girl or boy her or his favorite meal. Some of the meals that people always want Kay to cook are the ones she made when I was younger, like hot-water cornbread, dumplings, and fried squirrels. Those are still some of my favorites, too, and they always take me back to my childhood when I eat them. When I was little, we didn't have much money to buy groceries, so Kay made meals that were inexpensive and didn't require a lot of ingredients. She could make a meal for Phil and her four growing boys with about five bucks' worth of food, and there would usually be seconds for all of us.

Kay makes hot-water cornbread with cornmeal, salt, sugar, boiling water, and oil. Her cornbread is an old-fashioned recipe; she fries the cornbread cakes, rather than baking them, and they're delicious. Kay's dumplings involve simple ingredients as well (all-purpose flour, baking soda, baking powder, Crisco, and buttermilk), and the only things she needs to make fried squirrels are flour, seasoning, and oil. Of course, the squirrels are free and you can eat as many as you can shoot. You know what Kay says about squirrel brains—they make you smart! I guess Jase never ate enough of them when we were younger.

As you might guess, Kay takes quite a bit of pride in her cooking, and everyone brags about her food. But the Robertson men are not easy on her when she messes a meal up. Phil says the best way to ensure someone will continue to be a bad cook is to brag on bad cooking. That will never happen in the Robertson house.

PHIL SAYS THE BEST WAY TO ENSURE SOMEONE WILL CONTINUE TO BE A BAD COOK IS TO BRAG ON BAD COOKING.

A Robertson family tradition is eating seafood for Christmas dinner, and it's usually better than you could get at any five-star restaurant. But at our Christmas dinner in 1998, Kay fried the shrimp for way too long. Kay and Phil's shrimp are usually fried lightly, but not these; they were dark brown and tasted like rubber.

"Whoa, Kay, what happened, did you forget how to cook?" I asked her.

Phil was even more critical, but it was all in good fun.

"Don't you know you're only supposed to cook shrimp for three minutes?" Phil asked her. "These are terrible. I wouldn't even put them in my crawfish nets."

At every Christmas dinner since, we always ask Kay if she's going to serve overcooked shrimp and everyone has a good laugh at Kay's expense. She doesn't mind; she can dish it up as good as she can take it.

Korie: I ate those shrimp and thought they were delicious. But in the Robertson family you can't get away with anything. I think I burned the bread like once and Willie loves to joke that you know when dinner's ready at our house when you hear me scraping the bread! They're a tough crowd in the kitchen, but it's all in good fun. I tell people you have to have healthy self-esteem to be married to a Robertson.

Kay lived in a house full of Robertson boys and men, and I'm still not sure how she survived. There were Phil, me, and my three brothers, and there were usually a couple of our friends hanging around. But Kay has a lot of patience and has always been very funny—I think that's where I get my sense of humor—and she has a mechanism for turning anything into fun. I'm not sure Phil has ever really understood her humor. Jase and Phil are a lot more serious and have a much more dry sense of humor, so Kay and I are always making fun of them and have our inside jokes about them. Sometimes, Kay and I will be in the kitchen laughing together, and Phil will walk in and tell us we're being too noisy. He'll be trying to watch the late news and will say, "Hey, *Saturday Night Live* is over." Every time Phil walks out of the room, I'll make a face at him, almost behind his back. Phil says he doesn't even know how to laugh, while Kay is always jovial and constantly has a big smile on her face. You know what they say about how opposites attract.

Korie: The thing that has impressed me most about Kay is that she really rarely gets truly aggravated or mad at Phil and the boys. She knows how to not sweat the small stuff. She's been through a lot in her and Phil's marriage, and I think it taught her that most things are really not worth getting mad at. She has a really fun side to her. Willie and Jep are always putting food down her back, grabbing her from behind, or throwing something into her hair, and I'm sure it got pretty old about twenty years ago. At some point, most people would be like, "Okay, enough already." But Kay laughs every time. She doesn't take herself very seriously, which I think is one of the most important qualities for enjoying life and one I have made sure to try to pass on to our children.

One of the reasons Kay laughs so much now is because in the beginning, when Phil was drinking and they didn't have much money, there wasn't a lot of laughing going on. But now we laugh at almost everything together. On our birthdays, Kay likes to send us very random cards, like Earth Day or graduation cards. Her favorite thing to do at Christmas is to give us gag gifts. After we've exchanged gifts as a family, she'll give everybody a joke gift. Kay will often forget why she thought it was funny when she bought it. She'll give someone salt and pepper shakers and won't even remember why she gave them!

Of course, Kay's gifts always say they're from her dogs. If you get a present from her rat terriers—or some random famous person whose name is on the tag—you know it's actually one of Kay's gag gifts. Every one of Kay's rat terriers has been named Jesse James or some version of his name, because if one dies she'll still have another one with her. Somehow, that helps her cope with the trauma of losing one of her pets. She's had like twenty of those dogs and they've all been named Jesse, JJ, or Jesse James II. She calls one of her dogs Bo-Bo, but his real name is Jesse James.

EVERY ONE OF KAY'S RAT TERRIERS HAS BEEN NAMED JESSE JAMES OR SOME VERSION OF HIS NAME.

Kay loves her dogs. One time, Phil chopped a copperhead in three pieces with a shovel, and then he picked up the snake's head and threw it close to one of Kay's dogs. Even though the snake was cut in three pieces, it somehow managed to bite the dog's head and latch on to its eye. The dog's head swelled up like a basketball. Phil looked at me and said, "Don't tell your mother." I was like, "Uh-huh, she'll never notice." The dog was fine. These are country dogs; they can take a little snake venom and keep on going. Phil is always throwing dead snakes at dogs to see their reaction, but not the poisonous ones anymore. He's not going to take a chance on hurting one of Miss Kay's beloved dogs.

With Kay, everything is an exaggeration and every conversation with her centers around food. When I call their house to talk to Phil, if Kay answers the phone, I have to listen to what they ate for lunch that day or dinner the previous night. I might be calling to talk to Phil about a big business deal, but Kay only wants to talk about how she cooked green beans, ham, and fresh corn, or how she'd already cooked lunch, but then a couple more people came over so she pulled a couple packages of sausage out of the freezer. Then she'll ask you what you had for lunch and dinner, and she'll want to know exactly how you cooked it. She always wants to know the details. Every conversation with her involves food, and it's either the best thing she ever put in her mouth or it was a disaster. I'll never forget the time she cooked meatloaf for Phil and ran out of ketchup. She never runs out of ketchup and couldn't believe she'd let it happen. It was like the Japanese bombed Pearl Harbor again.

Korie: Kay is the most patient person I know. Phil, on the other hand, let's just say patience is not his virtue. When we were filming Kay's cooking video, *The Commander's Kitchen,* Phil was getting a little aggravated with me because he didn't want to wait to cook his frog legs. It was taking us a little while to set up the cameras and everything, and A&E was there to film an episode of *Duck Dynasty* so it took a lot longer than we expected. I kept telling Phil he had to wait to cook his frog legs until his scene. We were making a TV show, you know? But Phil didn't want to ruin his frog legs, so I kept catching him trying to cook them, and I kept telling him he had to wait, and he was getting more and more frustrated.

We finally got to the scene where Phil was supposed to cook the frog legs, but then the A&E producers interrupted him. Phil gave me a look that indicated he was finished. Making sure his frog legs were perfect was the most important thing to him, not whether our cooking video or *Duck Dynasty* episode turned out right. I could only laugh and let him finish. Nobody tells Phil what to do, and I certainly wasn't about to start. We made it work: he cooked the frog legs, and they tasted fantastic. This became the first episode of *Duck Dynasty* and we got a great cooking DVD out of it. It turned out to be a very good day.

NOBODY TELLS PHIL WHAT TO DO, AND I CERTAINLY WASN'T ABOUT TO START.

I'm not sure Kay ever gets enough credit for helping our family and Duck Commander survive when times were tough.

Let's face it: if Kay hadn't been strong enough to forgive Phil for the way he acted when I was young, our family and consequently Duck Commander wouldn't be here today. Thankfully, Kay's heart was big enough to look past Phil's transgressions and remember the man she married. After Phil kicked us out of the house, Kay made a thorough examination of her life and surrendered herself to Jesus Christ. She knew forgiving Phil was the right thing to do for her sons. If she wouldn't have forgiven Phil for things he'd done, or if he hadn't made changes in his life, we wouldn't be here today. As Phil began his Christian walk, he realized Kay was the best thing that ever happened to him, and they've been happily married ever since.

During the past four decades, Phil and Kay have been through some very difficult times and tackled them together. In the early days of Duck Commander, Kay was burdened with how the bills were going to be paid. We sometimes joke about Kay's not finishing high school—she gets mad at me when I tease her about it because she did receive her GED after Alan was born—but I think it's pretty remarkable that she kept Duck Commander afloat for so long without having any kind of business background. When Phil started making duck calls, he was an excellent salesman, but other than that, he wanted nothing to do with the business side of the company. He just wanted to make his calls and hunt and fish.

Before Kay and Phil turned Duck Commander over to Korie and me, the company was doing over $1 million in sales. Kay was in charge of inventory, accounting, payroll, and bookkeeping, with the help of other members of the family, but she was the one primarily in charge, and she had absolutely zero business training. She'd worked for Howard Brothers Discount Stores for a while, but Kay was in no way trained to oversee a multimillion-dollar business. She didn't even have a desk! Every night, Phil would sit in a recliner in the living room, and Kay would sit by him at the end of the couch. She kept all of Duck Commander's bills and sales orders in a little basket and that's how she would run the business. It's incredible when you think about it; we never would have made it without her.

Korie: Willie has always wanted to impress Kay and help her as much as possible. He realized a long time ago that his mother was working extremely hard but never got much of the glory because Phil was the star of Duck Commander. Kay's role was absolutely critical in the early days of Duck Commander. When we were dating, Willie and I painted Kay's kitchen cabinets for her for Mother's Day. She had a little tiny kitchen back then with not even a dishwasher, yet she cooked for the family and all the Duck Commander employees every day. There was so much grease on those cabinets from years of cooking, it was a miracle we ever got it all off to paint over it. Willie's love for his parents has always motivated him to do special things for them and to take Duck Commander to the next level, and they have always been very supportive and appreciative of him. Whether Willie paints Kay's kitchen, builds her something in the yard, cooks a great meal, or lands a big business deal, Kay has a special knack for bragging on him that makes him feel like a million bucks. She actually does that for all of us, and especially her boys. Sometimes people think that you should motivate your kids or employees by yelling at them when they fail or pointing out all the things they did wrong, but just the opposite is true. God created us to thrive on encouragement from others. Kay figured that out a long time ago. She has the gift of encouragement and gives that gift to those she loves the most.

KAY HAS A SPECIAL KNACK FOR BRAGGING ON HIM THAT MAKES WILLIE FEEL LIKE A MILLION BUCKS.

Whether it was in business or raising her family, Kay always managed to make it work even when times were hard and money was tight. Even though we have enough money now to eat big steaks, shrimp, and even lobster from time to time, we still love Kay's old-fashioned meals, like hot-water cornbread, dumplings, and fried squirrels. In a lot of ways, her home-cooked meals brought us comfort when we needed it most, and now they remind us of where we came from and how hard we worked to get where we are today, which none of us ever want to forget.

Hot-Water Cornbread

This is Southern cooking at its best, and nobody does it better than Miss Kay!

2½ cups yellow cornmeal (not self-rising)
1 teaspoon salt
1 tablespoon sugar
4 cups water, boiling
6 cups peanut oil

1. Mix cornmeal, salt, and sugar together.
2. Pour in boiling water, just until wet but not runny, stirring as you pour.
3. Heat oil in skillet.
4. Put your hands in ice water, because the mixture will be hot, then scoop out a small handful, pat out into a patty, then drop in skillet of hot oil. Fry until brown on both sides, then take out and put on paper towel. That's it! They're delicious!

Fried Squirrel

1 small, young squirrel
salt and pepper to taste
2 cups all-purpose flour
peanut oil, for frying

1. Skin the squirrel and cut into 7 pieces: 4 legs, back, rib cage, and head.
2. Season with salt and pepper, then roll in flour.
3. Fry in hot peanut oil until brown.

Boiled Squirrel

This is the best way to cook older squirrel (big ones)!

1 large, older squirrel
salt and pepper to taste

One 12-ounce can evaporated milk
½ stick of butter

1. Skin the squirrel, then cut in half.
2. Boil squirrel in water seasoned generously with salt and pepper for about 15 minutes.
3. Touch with fork to make sure it is tender, then take out squirrel from broth and add evaporated milk and butter. Allow to simmer while making your dumplings.

Dumplings

4 cups all-purpose flour
¾ teaspoon baking soda
5 teaspoons baking powder
1 teaspoon salt
3 tablespoons Crisco, Butter Flavor
2 cups buttermilk

1. Sift all dry ingredients.
2. Add Crisco and mix with a pastry blender.
3. Add buttermilk a little at a time, stirring the mixture until a soft ball forms (like the consistency of biscuit dough).
4. Lay out wax paper or a pastry sheet and sprinkle with flour.
5. Make dough into 4 balls and use a rolling pin to roll each ball out flat and thin If dough is too sticky add more flour. Cut into squares with a knife.
6. Bring squirrel broth to a boil. Make sure there is enough in the pot to fill at least half the pot. If there is not, add more water.
7. Drop dumplings into boiling broth a handful at a time. When they are all in, turn down heat to low, put lid on pot, and let simmer for 15 minutes.
8. Get out a bowl, add some dumplings and squirrel, and enjoy!

15

DUCK WRAPS

TWO ARE BETTER THAN ONE, BECAUSE THEY HAVE A GOOD RETURN FOR THEIR LABOR: IF EITHER OF THEM FALLS DOWN, ONE CAN HELP THE OTHER UP. BUT PITY ANYONE WHO FALLS AND HAS NO ONE TO HELP THEM UP. ALSO, IF TWO LIE DOWN TOGETHER, THEY WILL KEEP WARM. BUT HOW CAN ONE KEEP WARM ALONE? THOUGH ONE MAY BE OVERPOWERED, TWO CAN DEFEND THEMSELVES. A CORD OF THREE STRANDS IS NOT QUICKLY BROKEN.

—**ECCLESIASTES 4:9–12**

Someone once said to Korie that as the CEO of Duck Commander, I'm not accountable to anyone. But in reality, I'm accountable to everyone. If the company doesn't make it, then we're all out of work. And since most of our employees are also our relatives and friends, it's a heck of a lot of pressure to carry every day. I know the decisions I make affect everyone in my family, from Phil and Kay to Alan, Jase, and Jep and their families, as well as Korie and our children. Phil and Kay trust me to do the job because they know I recognize the burden and know I take the responsibility of running the family business very seriously.

It means a lot to me that my dad started this whole thing.

Phil launched Duck Commander and poured his heart and soul into it. It's his life's work. But I also think he would have never gotten the credit and recognition he deserved if we hadn't taken Duck Commander to another level. Changes had to be made, or Duck Commander would have suffered the same fate as a lot of other duck-call companies. Many of the guys who started out in the hunting industry when Phil launched Duck Commander in 1973 aren't around anymore. Several of them went through the same cycle: a father with a love for the outdoors starts a company, it has some success in the beginning, but if the next generation doesn't pick up the torch, and they just dwindle back down to where they first started, with a couple of guys making duck calls, or they fade away altogether. They still go to hunting shows, set up a little table, and sell their goods, but they haven't reached the success or had the longevity Duck Commander has. Now, there is certainly nothing wrong with setting up a table and selling your wares. In fact it reminds me of the old days for us. We were not big back then, but we had some good times at those hunting festivals.

When Korie and I took over the company, Phil told us that Duck Commander had begun to slide after its peak a few years earlier. Walmart sales were starting to go away and there was not a whole lot of traction in other stores, either. Buyers were starting to go to "full line" companies, which could sell them not only duck calls but also many other calls. It was harder and harder for companies who sold only one product to even get a sales meeting. Phil wasn't panicked or upset, he just felt that it was the life cycle of business and was proud of what he had accomplished up to that point. Duck Commander would have ended up being a very small business, probably only employing Phil, Kay, Jase, and Missy and maybe one other person, like it did in the early days. The ideas were getting fewer and fewer, the market was changing, Kay was stressed out, and Phil and Kay were just weary. I think Korie and I came at the right time and brought a lot of energy and excitement because we were young and had an entirely fresh look at it. Once the ball started rolling, other people became energized and the excitement was kind of contagious.

Every one of our employees at Duck Commander had an integral role in getting the company to where it is today. As I told you earlier, I'm a big baseball fan and Duck Commander is like a team. You have your flashier players, but you still need your utility men and middle relievers. You see people like Jase and Si on *Duck Dynasty* every week, but there are a lot of people doing really important jobs behind the scenes to make Duck Commander work.

When I took over, I was able to watch what was going on from afar and make some big changes, some that were popular and some that weren't. I had to fire some people and hired some people that others didn't think we needed. Everybody wanted to make more money than they were getting, and they thought they were probably going to get even less because we were bringing in additional people. One of the first hires I made that proved to be a really good one was Becky McDaniel, our accountant. After looking at Duck Commander's financial books, I realized Kay was spending about $35,000 a year on late fees, penalties, and finance charges. It wasn't Kay's fault; she was only trying to keep the company open when it was stretched to the max. Kay was doing the best she could and was simply overwhelmed. But in the end, hiring Becky was worth eliminating the monthly late fees and finance charges we'd been paying for so long. Becky has become an integral part of Duck Commander, doing much more than just accounting. She knows every part of the business and I can trust her to keep things rolling while Korie and I start new projects like making television shows.

Of course, it's never easy when you're related to most of your employees. You saw on the show what happened when I tried to put the guys through team-building exercises. They don't always listen to what I say or do what I want, but it's a lot more fun working with the people you care about the most. It also has its challenges. Like Uncle Si says, it's never a good family reunion when you start firing relatives.

LIKE UNCLE SI SAYS, IT'S NEVER A GOOD FAMILY REUNION WHEN YOU START FIRING RELATIVES.

My brother Jase is Phil's right-hand man in the blind and mine at Duck Commander. He went to seminary after high school, then worked for the church for a little while, but essentially came straight to work at Duck Commander. He loves ducks as much as Phil does and is the expert when it comes to duck calls. He takes what he does very seriously. He studies ducks and knows how to imitate their exact sounds. He doesn't settle for Duck Commander calls sounding okay. He wants them to be perfect. He'll spend the same amount of time tuning a call for a beginner duck caller who doesn't know what he's doing as he will for an expert caller who has been hunting for years. Making duck calls is one of his passions, and he just loves doing it. I think he especially likes the camaraderie of all the guys sitting around blowing a little smoke between blowing the duck calls. He doesn't like the stress of things changing and being different. Sitting in a chair and doing the same thing every day would drive me absolutely crazy, but I think that's part of what Jase likes about his work.

Korie: Jase lives right across the street from us, and he and his wife, Missy, have three kids: Reed, Cole, and Mia. Jase and Missy like to joke that our oldest son, John Luke, is like Kramer from *Seinfeld*. On nights when we're not cooking at our house, John Luke busts through their front door as soon as he sees the dining room light go on to join them for dinner. He seems to know exactly when Missy pulls the rolls out of the oven. Our baby girl, Bella, and their daughter, Mia, are great friends. We say Mia is like the ghost of our house. She appears in our house at all times. You'll turn around in your recliner, and she'll be standing there. As soon as we pull in the driveway, she's in our house, waiting to play with Bella. Our entire neighborhood is actually family. My parents are next door, along with four aunts and uncles and two grandparents. That's the absolute best thing about where we live. It's all about family.

I'm really proud of my youngest brother, Jep, who has grown up and become a good man. Jep was always like a little tree in a big forest. He was the youngest Robertson son, and his older brothers never lacked confidence. And of course, Phil was bigger than life, so Jep always kind of grew up in our shadows. Jep came along at a different time, too. When he was born, my mom and dad finally had a little bit of money. You know how poor people are when they get their hands on money. Everything had to be the nicest and the best for Jep, so he had a much different experience growing up than the rest of us. He didn't have to work like we did when we were younger, and I think a lot of things were handed to him. I think Jep probably needed more guidance and didn't get it. He ended up a little wayward and was kind of just hanging around.

When I took over Duck Commander, Jep was working at the company but wasn't really super ambitious and wasn't sure what he wanted to do with his life. Jep was my brother, so I was going to give him some breaks for sure, but I wasn't going to let him keep making the same mistakes and keep getting away with what he was doing. He was coming to work whenever he felt like it. I remember one time Jep was gone for like a month. Everybody thought that maybe he was out of town, but nobody knew for sure. I called Jep into my office when he finally came back to the warehouse. He was my brother, so I knew I couldn't fire him. But I couldn't allow Jep to keep making the same mistakes because it wasn't fair to our other employees and was bad for morale.

"Let me tell you something," I told him. "I ain't going to fire you. But what I am going to do is put a time clock in here. You're going to clock in and clock out every day. You're going to start out at your full salary. But if your time slip goes down, you're going to get less money. I'm not going to fire you, but if you're only making a thousand dollars per year, you're going to want to go work someplace else."

After a few months, Jep decided he wanted to go to work on the offshore oil rigs because he wanted to make more money. I thought it was maybe what Jep needed to do because he'd never worked anyplace other than Duck Commander. I thought maybe Jep needed to go find out what it was like to have a boss who wasn't part of his family.

"Hey, do what you've got to do, brother," I told him.

But the next day, I called Jep back into my office. "You've got to do what you've got to do," I told him again. "But let me tell you this: you're a stupid idiot if you leave this company. I'm fixin' to turn this thing around and you won't be here. You're going to miss out. Phil has four boys, and your last name is Robertson. There's an advantage you have in life just because you're Phil Robertson's son. You can take advantage of that working here, or you can go work in an oil field. They don't care what your last name is out there. You're going to lose every advantage you have in life and what Dad built for you. You're going to go trade it all for something like that?" I knew that if the dreams I had for our company came to fruition, I wanted Jep to be a part of it, and I couldn't just let him give it all up without saying something.

Fortunately, Jep didn't leave the company. We just had to find out what his talents were and take advantage of them. For a while, Jep decided that to make extra money he was going to start doing sales calls. I handed Jep a list of clients and told him to knock himself out. After two or three days, he came back into my office and said sales wasn't his cup of tea. But we found his gift. Jep has turned into an excellent cameraman. He shoots our Duckmen videos and does a lot of editing. Phil brags about how no one can capture ducks like Jep does. You have to be a hunter to do it, and Jep knows exactly how ducks fly and where he needs to be at all times to capture them on film. Plus, Jep isn't as outgoing as Jase and me, so he works well behind a camera. He loves to hunt but doesn't mind being a guy who sits and watches the action, and that's something Jase and I could never do.

WE JUST HAD TO FIND OUT WHAT HIS TALENTS WERE AND TAKE ADVANTAGE OF THEM.

Plus, I really like hanging out with Jep. He and I share a love for cooking and coming up with new recipes. He's the brother I would always choose first to accompany me on a road trip for a hunt or business deal. He's quieter than the rest of us, but his sense of humor is epic, and he is an awesome deer hunter. He accompanies me on many trips for deer and gets everything set up for me. I guess I have kind of prided myself on seeing value in people, no matter how big or small. When people are more outspoken about their talents, anyone can see the value, but for others you have to help them along to really unleash their potential. And, hey, life is too short to spend it with boring people. Jep and I have the same spirit of adventure. When we travel, Jase and Phil will just sit in their rooms, eat some ham and cheese, and do nothing. Jep and I always need to kick it up a notch.

Once on a duck-hunting road trip in California, Jase, Phil, Si, and the rest of the crew were gonna stay in this nasty little house with no TV and eat ham sandwiches every day. Jep and I refused and went to a casino to get a room. The best part was the casino had only one room left, and it was a suite and was the nicest one in the joint. The bad news was it was only available for one night. We took it. I went down to play a little poker to see if I could win enough money to pay for the room. Well, that didn't go like I planned. When I got back to the room, Jep was sitting in the oversized bathtub that was right in the middle of the main room, watching TV. We laughed so hard because we had never seen a bathtub in a living room before. We sat up half the night laughing about the other guys in that awful house while we lived it up. When they kicked us out the next day, we had to go find another place, and it was the worst motel I have ever stayed at in my life. The owners lived in the room behind the front desk. When I went to get ice, one of their kids got it out of their personal fridge. We went from the penthouse to the outhouse, but it sure beat sleeping on the floor at a crappy house with no TV. That's why I love running with Jep. When I feel like doing something crazy, he asks no questions and just says, "I'm in."

Korie: Jep and Jessica have four precious kids. They had three girls, Lily, Merritt, and Priscilla, then Jep had the boy he was hoping for, River. Bella and the girls love to play together. Mamaw Kay has the little girls spend the night together often and they have the best time, playing school, restaurant, or whatever. I think no matter how old our daughters get, we'll still call them the "little girls." And River is so cute with our Will. He looks up to him and thinks he's the best big cousin, and Will lets him play with all of his big-boy toys.

My oldest brother, Alan, only recently started working for Duck Commander. After high school, Alan moved to New Orleans and found some trouble. A guy beat him up with a crowbar and messed him up pretty badly. He moved back to Monroe and worked for Duck Commander for a few years. Kay and Phil always talk about how important Al was to the early years of Duck Commander. He and his wife, Lisa, lived in a little house right beside Phil and Kay's that later became the Duck Commander office for a while. Al and Lisa both worked for Duck Commander and helped to get it off the ground. Al eventually decided to go to seminary school and started working for a local church. Alan has been an incredible preacher for our church for nearly twenty-five years. He's still preaching and teaching now when he can, but it's great to have him back in the family business. When we started growing exponentially when *Duck Dynasty* came along, Korie and I

AFTER HIGH SCHOOL, ALAN MOVED TO NEW ORLEANS AND FOUND SOME TROUBLE.

started thinking about who we would need to hire to help us navigate the next steps and Alan was the only one who came to mind. We knew he was the missing piece to the puzzle. It's great to have all the brothers working at Duck Commander once again!

Alan's oldest daughter, Anna, has been working with us since she was in high school. After she graduated, she started working full-time and helps in shipping. Her husband, Jay, was a teacher and coach at a high school and up until this year he only worked for us in the summer. But we became so busy that we needed more guys who could build calls. Jay is a good hunter and has a knack for putting the calls together. If you have that skill and are kin, you got a good chance of being a Duck Commander employee.

Korie: I always say that what's worked well between the Robertson brothers is that none of them wants to do what another brother is doing, nor do they think they *can* do what another one is doing. There's no way Willie could do what Jase does. Willie doesn't have the patience to sit in a chair every day. It's not his personality. Willie couldn't do what Jep does, either. Likewise, Jase doesn't want the responsibility that Willie has because he wants to spend a lot of time hunting and fishing. He doesn't want to travel all the time going to the business meetings like Willie does. They all value each other's talent, and they each have their own special skills. Willie uses the team analogy, but I think of it like a band. If you take out one of the instruments, the song just

> doesn't sound as good. Everyone has their roles and they are all equally valuable. Thankfully each one really respects the others' roles in the group. Otherwise, working together would not be fun. I think what Willie brought to the family business was energy, innovation, direction, and motivation, which are attributes that a leader has to have. But Willie knows he couldn't have gotten Duck Commander to where it is today without his parents, brothers, and everyone else working for the company. A good band doesn't just consist of the lead singer.

Of course, Phil's brother, Si, has been working with us forever. Si served in the army for twenty-four years, including a stint in Vietnam. When Si retired from the army, he started putting reeds together for the calls. One of the first things I did when I took over Duck Commander was to look at our efficiency and our workload to see where I could eliminate waste. I found out Si was taking naps every day on Kay's couch! I went to Phil and told him it was a problem.

I FOUND OUT SI WAS TAKING NAPS EVERY DAY ON KAY'S COUCH!

"Look, I know he's your brother and he's my uncle, but he's not the kind of worker we need to have," I told Phil, while trying to make a good first impression.

I was trying to instill a new work ethic and culture in Duck Commander, and I couldn't have Si sleeping on the job!

"Don't touch Si," Phil told me. "You leave him alone. He's

making reeds and that's the hardest thing we do. Si is the only guy who wants to do it, and he's good at it. Si is fine."

Amazingly enough, in the ten years I've been running Duck Commander, we've never once run out of reeds. Six years ago, Si suffered a heart attack. He smoked cigarettes for almost forty years and then quit after his heart attack, so we were all so proud of him. Even before his heart attack, I wasn't sure about putting Si on our DVDs because I thought he would just come across too crazy. He cracked us up in the duck blind and we all loved him, but I told Jep and the other camera guys to film around him. Honestly, I didn't think anyone would understand what he was saying. When we finally tried to put him on the DVDs, he clammed up in front of the camera and looked like a frog in a cartoon just sitting there. He wouldn't perform. Finally, we put a hidden camera under a shirt on Si's desk. We were near the end of editing a DVD and showed a shooting scene to Si. He always takes credit for shooting more ducks than he really did. He's said before that he killed three ducks with one shot! We were watching the patterns hitting the water, and Si started claiming the ducks like he always does and going off on one of his long tangents. After we recorded him, we ran the DVD back and showed it to him. I think Si saw that he was actually pretty funny and entertaining if he acted like himself. We started putting Si on the DVDs and he got more and more popular. Now he's the star of *Duck Dynasty*!

Even though Si still takes long naps every day, he's making up for it on our DVDs. The naps don't bother me as much anymore, either, because I usually get back one-third of his paycheck in our Friday-night poker games. We begged Si to play poker with us for a long time, but he would never play because he said he loved it too much. Once Si finally showed up at our game, he never stopped coming. I guess he really does love poker that much. His wife, Christine, loves the fact that Si is getting out more and she's so proud of him. Si has one daughter, Trasa, and a son, Scott. After his heart attack, he decided he was going to start having a lot more fun and saw the bigger picture. In all the years Si has worked for us, never once has he ever really complained. He'll go off on his little tangents, but he's never come to me with a real gripe or a complaint. Phil has often said that Si is one of the best men he's ever seen. He's right; Si is as good as gold.

Some of my best friends work for us, too. Justin Martin, or Martin as we call him, played football at West Monroe High School. I pick on him, joking that he's the only man I know who looks dumb but is really smart and looks old but is really young. If you've seen him on the show, you know exactly what I'm talking about. He only lacks his thesis to complete a master's degree in wildlife biology, and he had a full scholarship to college. Martin is actually the only employee we have who ever worked in a sporting goods store that sold hunting products. He understands competitive pricing and inventory. I met Martin when he came to play poker at our house one Friday night. While on summer break from college, Martin was looking for some work. I was going out of town the next week, but I told him to come in and start calling sporting goods stores. About three days later, I received an e-mail from martin@duckcommander.com. The guy already had a Duck Commander e-mail with his name on it! I really thought he was only going to be with us for a few days and then go back to what he was doing. I never really hired him; he just ended up staying. But Martin is an excellent hunter—which gave him an advantage—and he knows all about animals. Martin will do anything for you, and he is my liaison in the blind. I'll give him new products that companies want us to try out, and he'll come back to me with everyone's feedback. Most important, Martin learned how to make our duck calls, which made him invaluable. Plus, he's another guy I enjoy hanging out with, and what's it all worth if you can't work with people you like?

I NEVER REALLY HIRED MARTIN; HE JUST ENDED UP STAYING.

John Godwin also works with Jase, Jep, and Martin in the duck-call assembly room. Godwin used to be in the rodeo and worked the graveyard shift at the local paper mill, which is the lifeblood of West Monroe. Godwin worked at the mill for sixteen years before he started working with us. John started going to Bible study at Phil's house and hung around long enough to get a job with Duck Commander. John is a big hunter and knows about calls. Phil has more than forty duck blinds on his property, and Godwin is the guy who sets up and organizes the decoys and makes sure everything is working properly. He's also Mr. Fix-It and can fix about anything, from the four-wheelers to the RV. But John is also smart enough to put in the accounting to Walmart and has overseen our shipping department for years. John and his wife, Paula, have been best friends with my oldest brother, Alan, and his wife, Lisa, for years. He's got a great attitude and is an overall great guy.

Paul Lewis, who was my best friend in high school, is our warehouse manager. Paul and I grew up playing basketball together, and he received a full scholarship to play at Southeastern Louisiana University in Hammond. Paul played against Shaquille O'Neal and LSU one time, and Korie and I were so excited watching him on TV. Shaq fouled Paul, and Paul made one of two foul shots. In 1995, Paul got messed up selling dope and was busted transporting drugs in Texas. He got himself into a lot of trouble and was sentenced to fourteen years in federal prison. Every Friday night while Paul was incarcerated, we got a collect call from a federal prison. I tried to visit Paul as much as I could, but they moved him to federal prisons in Arkansas and Texas, so it was hard. When Paul was released, we had him moved to a halfway house in Monroe. I told the judge from day one that Paul had a job as soon as he was released. Paul made a big mistake, but he was a great friend, and I wasn't going to give up on him. He got mixed up with the wrong people. We helped him get a truck and moved him into a trailer on Phil's land. He was married in Phil's yard, and I was proud to be his best man. He and his wife, Krystle, work for us; they have three children and they just bought a house in town.

Korie: Willie and Paul have talked about how they took two paths in life. They even spoke to a youth group at our camp last summer about how their lives turned out so differently. They told the kids about the two paths you can take in life, and Paul is a perfect example of what can go wrong. But Paul is also a great example of how you can change your life and how it's not over because you make a mistake. Paul told the kids about how scared he was during that time of his life. He said he had a gun and couldn't trust anybody, and how he feared it was either kill or be killed. Willie and I have talked about the milestones in his and Paul's lives, like the year when our oldest son, John Luke, was born or the year in which Willie took over Duck Commander. For Paul, those years came and went while he was in prison. Paul's life was put on hold for fourteen years because of a stupid mistake he made. But he learned from all of it. His attitude is incredible, and Paul remains one of our closest friends. We love him and his growing family.

Mountain Man came to us in an odd way. Our air conditioner was out and my housecleaner said she knew a guy who went by the name of Mountain Man who could fix it. She and I both shared a common interest in cooling the house down so I told her to get him over here. She warned me: "Now, he talks funny, but he know his air conditioners." When Mountain Man showed up, I learned she was right. The guy's speech was slower than pouring honey in January. We became friends and I invited him to watch while we made the pilot episode of *Duck Dynasty*. We were trying to lift a trailer in the air to hunt out of and I thought I could use all the redneck expertise we could get. He impressed the producers and they thought, "We gotta get this guy on the show somehow." In that same episode, Korie was having a garage sale and Mountain Man stopped by and bought my squirrel. And so a star was born. He now hosts his own radio show and enjoys people recognizing him. I think he likes the free food the best!

I like to say Duck Commander is a lot like duck wraps. Huh? No, really, it is. It's a bunch of things that may not seem like they belong together, but when they all come together they make something spectacular. Everyone at Duck Commander brings something special to the table, and rather than fighting against one another, we complement each other. Do we have our disagreements? Of course! But we don't take away from the unique flavors each one of us brings. We are all held together by a common love for family and for ducks, but more importantly we are fortunate to share a common faith. Our faith is the toothpick that holds the entire wrap together. If it wasn't for our faith in God, I can assure you, we would fall apart.

RATHER THAN FIGHTING AGAINST ONE ANOTHER, WE COMPLEMENT EACH OTHER.

How do you make a duck wrap? Take a duck breast, soak it well in brine, and then marinate it. You have to season it, split it, and then add in cream cheese, a sliver of real mozzarella cheese, and a half a slice of jalapeño pepper. Then you wrap it with thin (and cheap) bacon, and secure it all with a toothpick. Grill the wrap until the duck breast is medium-rare and the bacon is crisp. The finishing touch is glazing it with anything sweet. We all have our different twists and versions of it. All the employees of Duck Commander make up a great company. Some of our employees are sweet, some are spicy hot, and a few are a bit cheesy. Each one of us has our roles and jobs. When we put everything together right, we do amazing things.

Duck Wraps

Simply the best way for my taste buds to eat a duck. I wrap many things, but duck has such a good flavor. Play with it and add different types of "sweets" for topping. Honey is great, but there are others. If you bite into the first one and don't think it's done, don't panic; put them all in a pot and let them steam on low fire.

½ cup salt
10 cups water
8 to 12 duck breasts
1 package cream cheese
4 to 6 jalapeños
1 package Phil Robertson's Cajun Style Rub
1 pound thin-sliced bacon
honey

1. Dissolve salt in water in a large pot.
2. Soak duck breasts in salt water overnight in the refrigerator.
3. Cut jalapeños in half (take out the seeds).
4. Cut an incision down the length of each breast and stuff with cream cheese and one half of a jalapeño.
5. Coat each stuffed duck breast with Cajun Style Rub and wrap each with one slice of bacon, securing the wrap with a toothpick.
6. Cook wraps on an open grill until bacon is crisp and cream cheese starts to ooze out (it's okay for the wrap to be medium-rare; don't overcook or it will dry out).
7. Drizzle wraps with honey and cook for an additional 2 minutes.

16

BACK STRAPS

WHATEVER YOU DO, WORK AT IT WITH ALL YOUR HEART, AS WORKING FOR THE LORD, NOT FOR HUMAN MASTERS, SINCE YOU KNOW THAT YOU WILL RECEIVE AN INHERITANCE FROM THE LORD AS A REWARD. IT IS THE LORD CHRIST YOU ARE SERVING.
—COLOSSIANS 3:23–24

To tell you the truth, I *love* eating deer steak! Duck is good when you turn it into a gumbo or wrap bacon around it, but you really can't beat good ol' fried deer steak. It's so easy to make. You just cut off the back strap, soak it in milk, put it in an egg wash, add a little seasoning, coat it in flour, and then fry it up. My mouth is watering right now thinking about it. Starting Buck Commander was pretty much a no-brainer. Growing up, we did a little deer hunting so we could eat. But hunting deer wasn't Phil's first love, so we didn't do much of it. As I got older and started hunting on my own, I learned that I loved hunting deer. And like Phil, I was able to turn my passion into a successful business. After I took over Duck Commander, I was ready to branch out to something different. I knew that if I could somehow translate what we were doing with Duck Commander to deer hunting, the sky would be the limit. Let's face it: there are a lot more deer hunters out there than duck hunters.

Phil talked about getting into the deer market for quite a while, but it wasn't where his passion lay and nothing ever came of it. Jep actually did try it one time. He filmed a deer hunt, but it turned out awful. So Dad thought, "Oh well, let's just get back to hunting ducks." But I was young and full of energy and was primed and ready to start something new.

I loved the challenge of going into an entirely different market and learning everything there is to know about hunting a different species, so Buck Commander was born in 2006. For our new company to be successful, I wanted to follow the blueprint of Duck Commander. I knew hunting DVDs would be the most important products we offered. We had to produce DVDs that would make people laugh and say, "Wow!" at the same time. There had to be big deer, humor, and great personalities on the Buck Commander DVDs. I watched deer-hunting shows that were on TV at the time and thought much of what I saw was boring. I believed we could do better.

I LOVED THE CHALLENGE OF GOING INTO AN ENTIRELY DIFFERENT MARKET.

At the time I started Buck Commander, we were selling a ton of duck DVDs to Walmart. I thought it would be an easy transition to selling deer DVDs. Boy, was I wrong. When I tried to schedule a meeting with the deer-hunting buyer for Walmart, I couldn't even get him to return my phone calls. The big difference between ducks and deer was that Duck Commander *owned* the duck market. Deer were an entirely different beast. There was much more competition in the deer market. My whole plan seemed shot—or was it?

When Buck Commander finally got off the ground, we were able to build a great spin-off business that complemented Duck Commander. Fortunately, the Lord gave me what I was looking for—guys who were busy with their regular jobs for about eight months out of the year and then off just in time for deer season. Of all things, I found the people I needed in Major League Baseball players. Many major leaguers are avid hunters. I think it takes a lot of patience to be good at both: When you're riding a two-for-thirty slump, you have to remain patient and focused in order to hit your way out of it. When you're deer hunting, you might go three or four days without seeing a big buck. But you have to remain patient, knowing that there are some big deer out there.

Deer-hunting season takes place after the baseball season is over, so many major leaguers spend the off-season in the woods. I firmly believe that God is the one who put me with the folks I needed. My partners make a great living playing baseball in the summer, and they make some great hunting shows in the winter. I was convinced we could make better DVDs than what was already out there. I was also convinced that something as fun as deer hunting should never be portrayed as being something bland. Buck Commander set out to change things.

The first group of Buckmen included Russ Springer, who is from Alexandria (or Pollock for the locals), Louisiana, and pitched for nine major league teams from 1992 to 2010; David

Dellucci, who is from Baton Rouge, Louisiana, and was an outfielder for seven major league clubs from 1997 to 2009; and Mike DeJean, who is also from Baton Rouge and pitched for five MLB teams from 1997 to 2006. It was a coincidence that each of the first Buckmen was from my home state of Louisiana. Maybe it was because Louisiana guys are willing to take crazy chances. Word began spreading through the major leagues that something big was happening in the deer-hunting industry with baseball players, and these guys were the first ones to step up to the plate. Adam LaRoche, who was then a first baseman for the Atlanta Braves, was the next player to join the team, and he brought along Braves third baseman Chipper Jones. Chipper was a good friend of Matt Duff, who pitched for the St. Louis Cardinals in 2002, so they joined together.

Like a baseball roster, there has been some turnover with Buck Commander from season to season. My current partners are some of my closest friends: LaRoche, who is now a first baseman with the Washington Nationals; former major league pitcher Tom "Tombo" Martin; Los Angeles Angels outfielder Ryan Langerhans; and country superstars Jason Aldean and Luke Bryan.

Ryan grew up hunting deer in Texas and was teammates with Adam in Atlanta. Tombo grew up in the Florida panhandle and pitched in the majors for thirteen seasons, most recently with the Colorado Rockies in 2007. They are just really super guys who have become good friends to me over the years.

Adam is really the guy who helped me save Buck Commander and Duck Commander. Dave LaRoche, his father, pitched for the Los Angeles Angels, Minnesota Twins, Chicago Cubs, Cleveland Indians, and New York Yankees during the 1970s and early 1980s. His younger brother, Andy, was a third baseman for the Los Angeles Dodgers, Pittsburgh Pirates, and Oakland A's from 2007 to 2011. Adam was born in Orange County, California, but grew up in Fort Scott, Kansas, where there's some really big whitetail deer. Hunting and fishing have always been in Adam's blood. He loves being outdoors as much as he loves playing baseball.

When Adam was a rookie with the Braves in 2004, he lost his lucky Duck Commander hat. You know how baseball players are about their superstitions. Adam *had* to find a replacement hat. He went to the Duck Commander website and didn't find one, so he called our headquarters, and Jase answered the phone. Adam told him he was a Major League Baseball player.

"Huh, I've never heard of you," Jase told Adam. "We don't sell that hat anymore, but I think I might have one in my closet."

A couple of weeks later, Adam received a worn-out, sweat-stained Duck Commander hat from Jase in the mail. I became friends with the Rockies' first baseman Todd Helton, who is another avid deer hunter, at about the same time Adam called the Duck Commander office. Helton invited me to one of his games against the Braves at Turner Field in Atlanta in September 2005. The Braves had wrapped up their fourteenth consecutive division title the night before. Adam found out I was at the game, and I met him at home plate during batting practice. Not many people can say they met their future business partner at home plate at Turner Field.

Adam was a big hunter and told me he grew up watching Duck Commander videos. We quickly became friends and started hunting together. I was traveling a lot, getting Buck Commander off the ground, hunting all over the country with my partners and friends, Helton and other fellow Rockies players like Aaron Cook, Danny Ardoin, and Brad Hawpe.

I will never forget being on a deer hunt in Iowa with Hawpe and Ardoin. We drove through one of the worst snowstorms I have ever seen. We must have seen two hundred cars on the side of the road. You couldn't even see the exit ramps off the interstate because the snow was so heavy. It was a tense car ride. After finally making it to the camp, I got so sick I had to stay in my room the whole time. We didn't kill one deer on that trip. That's when I realized making deer-hunting videos might be a little harder than I thought!

After Adam was traded to the Pirates in 2007, Korie and I took our kids to Disney World in Orlando, Florida. We were walking around the Magic Kingdom when Adam called and told me to meet him in Tampa. He was going to drive from Bradenton, Florida, where the Pirates were having spring training. Adam had a tee time and wanted me to play golf with him. I was always up for an adventure, so I let Korie know I was going. She gave me that classic look I've seen many times before, but knew I had to go.

Korie: We were on family vacation at Disney World with four young kids, literally in the line for Splash Mountain. Willie hates waiting in lines, so I wasn't really surprised when he jumped at Adam's offer. I had never met Adam, but I knew that Willie liked him a lot, and they had talked about his being a part of Buck Commander. While the golfing trip would be fun, it could also be an important business meeting for Buck Commander, but really? Forget the fact that I was going to be left alone at Disney World with four kids. He had to get to Tampa and we didn't have a car! Willie would figure it out, though. He always does, and the kids and I had a great time that day at the park.

I was wearing running shorts and a T-shirt. I jumped in a cab outside Disney World and told the cabbie to drive to Tampa. The cabbie started looking at his fare chart to figure out how much it was going to cost. "Turn your meter on, son," I told him. "Let's get there."

"TURN YOUR METER ON, SON," I TOLD HIM. "LET'S GET THERE."

After more than two hours in a cab, it cost me $360 to get to Tampa. Adam was standing outside this super-nice country club waiting for me with the golf pro. "This is your friend?" the pro asked. "We're going to have to get him some clothes."

I dropped another hundred dollars on a collared shirt. But the expenses were well worth it because during dinner, Adam told me he wanted to invest in Buck Commander and become a partner in the company. I was really happy to have him on board, and Buck Commander probably wouldn't have survived without him. Again, God's timing is always perfect.

When we were finished with dinner, Adam broke the news that he couldn't take me back to Orlando because he had a spring-training game the next morning and had to be at the park very early. He still had a good drive to get back to Bradenton, so I was going to have to figure out how to get back to Korie and the kids. When we couldn't find a cab to take me back to Disney World, Adam walked up to a hostess at the restaurant and offered her a hundred dollars to take me back to Orlando. He even called Korie and asked her if it was okay for another woman to drive me back.

Korie: I was just happy Willie was going to make it back. It was getting late, and I was worried he might have to spend the night in Tampa. I told Willie to hurry back and meet us at Epcot. The park was open till one A.M. that night and the kids and I were still going strong.

I ended up riding back to Orlando in an old Honda Civic with a waiter and waitress from the restaurant. The car's radio didn't even work, so these eighteen- and nineteen-year-old kids were wearing iPods, singing and smoking the entire way. I was sitting in the backseat, wondering how in the world I get into these situations. Fortunately, I arrived at Epcot shortly before midnight and was able to ride Soarin' with the kids.

Korie: I was so happy to see Willie. I was carrying Bella, who was asleep in my arms, and pushing Will in a stroller. There were still a few rides we hadn't gotten to, and John Luke and Sadie weren't ready to stop. My back was killing me, so when Willie walked up I couldn't have been more excited. I passed Bella over to him and we closed the park down!

It ended up being a really great day and set the stage for Buck Commander. It was classic Adam. I think sometimes we do this kind of stuff just so we'll have a great story to tell. He and I have had some epic adventures. In the early days, Adam and I, along with Langerhans and a few other buddies, got into a massive food/forty-ounce-drink fight outside of a restaurant chain in Texas. Adam was buying drinks at a drive-through window and was throwing them at us in the truck behind them as fast as he could!

SOMETIMES WE DO THIS KIND OF STUFF JUST SO WE'LL HAVE A GREAT STORY TO TELL.

Adam is a great friend—he's like another brother to me. What I've learned from Adam, more than anything else, is to have *confidence.* For Adam, if you can think of it, you can do it. That motto has led to some crazy late-night arguments, where I find myself being the practical one! But I love that he's a big thinker and that he pushes me to step across that line. Adam is also a great connector. He makes friends and holds on to them. That's how Jason Aldean and Luke Bryan became involved in Buck Commander. Adam met Jason when he sang the national anthem at a Braves game in 2005. He met Luke the same year, when Adam and a bunch of his teammates went to see him play at a bar in Atlanta. They arrived after the show was over, but Luke came out and played a two-hour set just for them.

Growing up in the South, Luke and Jason have both always been hunters. Jason grew up in Macon, Georgia, and started pursuing a music career immediately after high school. Luke grew up in Leesburg, Georgia, and is not only a great singer and performer but also an awesome writer. Now Jason and Luke are both producing platinum albums. They're pretty much as big as you can get in the music industry, and I'm so happy for both of them. Jason has done everything you can do in country music. He's never afraid to take a chance and do something different. Jason does it his way, and I like that about him. I just recently surprised Luke in Nashville and showed up for his platinum party for *Tailgates and Tanlines*. In person, Luke is exactly like he is onstage: the life of the party and a blast to be around. He's also the kind of guy that really cares about his friends and has given me some really great advice as the success of the show has taken off. I don't give him the satisfaction of knowing I'm actually taking his advice, but I am listening.

On our deer-hunting trips for our show *Buck Commander Protected by Under Armour* on Outdoor Channel, Luke and Jason will pull out their guitars while we're sitting around a campfire. It's absolutely the most fun part of our time at deer camp. One of my favorite things to do is to see their live shows. Luke and Jason have put on charity concerts in Adam's hometown of Fort Scott the last few years before we go on our big hunt. It's great fun having all of our friends there together, enjoying some great music and doing something for the community. Adam and his wife, Jenn, are the kindest, most down-to-earth people you will ever meet. Korie and I are proud to have them as some of our closest friends.

Both Luke and Jason have pulled me up onstage with them all over the country. Once I took Jason his guitar during the show and knelt down, lifting it up to him with my head bowed. He was cracking up, shaking his head at me as he took it. In Little Rock one night, Luke actually offered me the microphone during a song. It may have been the only time in my life I refused an open mic, but I didn't know the song and didn't want to get up there and butcher it. Jason got me up onstage with him recently at Bayou Country Superfest in Baton Rouge, Louisiana. He asked me what song he was about to play and gave me the hint that it could have been written for my family. My mind was racing, and I sheepishly said "Hicktown." And, yes, thankfully, it was the right song. I told him next time, he oughtta give me a heads-up when he's going to call me out in front of fifty thousand people so I make sure I get it right! I still gotta get up with Jason's deejay, DJ Silver, and perform with him. It's on my bucket list.

Once my friend Colt Ford got me onstage at Rabb's in Ruston, Louisiana, and wanted me to sing a song with him. The only problem was when I got up onstage I had no idea what song he was playing. I danced and tried to fake it. The crowd's beer intake must have helped me out because I don't think they even noticed. The funny part is the song was "Dirt Road Anthem," a song Aldean took to number one later that year. When Colt came and performed in West Monroe a few years later, he called me up again. He handed me a mic and the band started playing the same song. Believe me, I didn't miss on that one! I sang most of the song from on top of a speaker about four feet in the air. It was a really fun night, for sure.

My involvement in Buck Commander has allowed me to do some pretty cool things. I go to baseball stadiums across the country to see my buddies play. I even held the finish line in the sausage race at Miller Park in Milwaukee. Earlier this year, I threw out the first pitch at a Louisiana-Monroe baseball game, which was cool to get to do at my alma mater. I was also invited to throw out the first pitch for the Mississippi Braves in Jackson, Mississippi, by my buddy Phillip Wellman, who managed them at the time. Wellman had the most classic confrontation with an umpire ever, when he crawled around the field and threw fake grenades. I pick at him all the time about that, as I'm sure all his other buddies do. He's an awesome guy.

I got to take batting practice with the San Angelo Colts in San Angelo, Texas. It's a small independent team that Tombo was pitching for when he was trying to get himself back in shape to make another run at the majors. I thought I was going to die at that game because it was 112 degrees. I realized how hard those ball players work and what good shape they are in. I had fun though, and I chased the mascot down at the end of the game. I remember thinking, "I hope this is not a girl under the costume."

The Atlanta Braves have called me a couple of times. I thought I was going to get to throw out the first pitch at one of their games, which is something I've always wanted to do. But the marketing guy asked me to sing "Take Me Out to the Ballgame" during the seventh-inning stretch. When he said that, I could feel the blood rushing out of my body, and I panicked. The guy kept talking to me, and I finally said, "Wait a second, did you just say *sing*?"

Korie told me, "Oh, you can do it. You sing all the time."

"Not to forty thousand people!" I told her.

It was "Field and Reels Outdoorsman Night" at Turner Field, so I seemed like the right choice to sing, I guess. I must have done okay because they asked me back again the next year. After the song was over, I danced on the dugout while they played "Thank God I'm a Country Boy."

The Braves brought me back the next year to sing again, and right before the opening pitch, I participated in a closest-to-the-pin golf contest with first baseman Ryan Klesko and infielder Brooks Conrad. Conrad hit his ball within about twelve feet, and Klesko hit his to about fifteen feet from the pin. I stood over my ball and could feel the blood leaving my body. I started thinking about everything that could possibly go wrong. I had a vision of shanking the ball right into the dugout and knocking Braves pitcher Tim Hudson out for the season. Before I started to swing, I told myself, "Whatever you do, don't miss this ball!" Of course, my hips flew too fast and I pulled the ball. I crushed it to where the Arizona Diamondbacks were warming up—which was nowhere near the pin—and catcher Miguel Montero caught it. That was a little embarrassing, but I thought it could have been a lot worse.

I STARTED THINKING ABOUT EVERYTHING THAT COULD POSSIBLY GO WRONG.

One time, I was meeting with my friend Lacey Biles with the National Rifle Association in Washington, DC, and Adam was playing for the Arizona Diamondbacks. I went to the game with him and was on the field for batting practice. Stephen Strasburg was pitching for the Nationals, and I couldn't wait to see Adam hit against him. I jumped the fence right before the game and was sitting in a section of seats right behind home plate. An usher told me I couldn't sit there because I didn't have a ticket. While I was arguing with the usher and trying to explain that my friend Lacey from the NRA was not there yet and had my ticket, Adam took Strasburg deep for a home run. I only saw the ball in the air. I wanted to knock that usher's teeth out. He told me I had to stand up until my ticket arrived and to not eat the food that came with the ticket. I took some joy in knowing I had already eaten three times. A few innings later, troops of soldiers came to where I was standing. They were going out on the field to be honored. Someone recognized me and invited me to stand with them, which was a huge honor. Adam told me later he looked up and saw me on a JumboTron standing with our troops.

Conversely, when I was at a Philadelphia Phillies game one time, they threw my face on the JumboTron. I covered my face with a hat when I saw it, thinking it would be funny. Of course, the fans in Philadelphia booed me. "Show your face, you blankedy-blank!" they yelled at me. You gotta love the Philly fans; they booed Santa Claus and they booed me.

In 2008, I went to St. Paul, Minnesota, to meet with Kyle Tengwall from Federal Premium Ammunition. Kyle called me and told me they couldn't find me a hotel room because the convention was in town. "What convention?" I asked him. He told me it was the Republican National Convention.

"Let's go," I told Kyle.

"Willie, you can't just go," he said. "You have to be a delegate."

"Give me an hour," I told him.

Within one hour, I had a floor pass to the Republican National Convention, thanks to my good friend Rodney Alexander, my district's congressman. While I was on the floor, several people took pictures of me, and I was starting to think I'd become a pretty big deal. What I didn't realize was that I was standing next to Mitt Romney, who was the governor of Massachusetts at the time. A few hours later my mom called me. "Willie, am I watching you on Fox News standing with Megyn Kelly?" she asked.

"Yep, who else looks like I do?" I told her.

She and Dad didn't even know I was at the convention. Kyle and I, along with Anthony Acitelli, or Ace as we call him, have had some classic trips. We've played golf at Pebble Beach in

California, attended the Masters golf tournament, and even played golf with PGA Tour pro Boo Weekley and Larry the Cable Guy. We were at the Masters, and my friend David Toms came over. Toms has hunted with us before, and we talked for like five minutes *while he was playing the Masters*! Kyle and I were cracking up at everybody's face looking at us. Right after Toms left, a guy ran up to me and asked, "Are you Gregg Allman [of the Allman Brothers Band]?" You can't make this stuff up.

Of all the crazy experiences, though, the one that really sticks out happened south of Nashville in a Walmart parking lot. My buddy Carter Smith and I took an RV to a hunting show. Carter dropped me off at Starbucks and went to Walmart for supplies. We planned to meet back at the RV. Now, if you've seen our RV, you know it has our pictures all over the side of it. I had a bag of stuff I'd bought and a cup of coffee. But when I got back to the RV, I realized Carter locked it and I was going to have to wait until he came back. I sat on the curb and waited. A guy pulled up to me and said, "Hey, man, you okay?"

"Yes, I'm good," I said, though I was a little confused.

"You need anything? Food or anything?" he asked.

Finally, I realized he thought I was homeless or just down-and-out. I'm sure my long, scraggly hair and beard were his clues. I just started smiling, and he finally looked over at our RV.

"Is that your picture on that RV?" he asked.

"Yep, I'm waiting on my driver," I said.

"I guess you are all right then," he replied.

I took no offense at his thinking I was homeless. He was a nice, kindhearted guy who thought I might be in a bad spot.

I guess no matter how big-time you think you are, there's always someone there to remind you that you're not too far off from looking like a homeless person, or maybe even one of the Allman brothers!

HE WAS A NICE, KINDHEARTED GUY WHO THOUGHT I MIGHT BE IN A BAD SPOT.

I've told you these stories not to say, "Look what I've done," but to say, "Look what God's done." I give Him all the glory. From being a kid who was on free lunches to today, a lot of good things have happened in my life. I've had a few tough times as well, but mostly I'm just happy to be here. I look around and think, "Wow, I'm eating the back strap off a monster deer that I killed in Kansas hunting with my best buddies." Life is good!

Fried Back Straps

This one is a simple one. Hard part is getting the meat, but that's also the most fun part. Back straps, for all you yuppies, are the back meat on the deer right along the spine. When cleaning a deer, it's the easiest part to cut off, so go ahead and do this the same day you harvest your deer. When my children find out I got a deer, they know *I will be frying that night, no matter what time it is. If the deer is old or mature, you can add a step to make it very tender.*

1 back strap
milk (enough to cover the meat)
a few shakes of Worcestershire or any meat marinade (we have our own)
2 eggs, beaten
2 cups flour
peanut oil (enough for 4 inches in the pot; make sure meat is covered)
Phil Robertson's Seasoning to taste

1. Cut back strap into thin steaks the width of your pinkie.
2. Mix milk and marinade and put in a plastic bag or bowl with back strap.
3. Put in fridge for an hour or two. (I shake up the bag during the process.)
4. Pull pieces out of bag or bowl and pat dry with paper towel.
5. Wash in egg.
6. Dip in flour.
7. Place in hot peanut oil; fry until brown.
8. Season with Phil Robertson's Cajun Style Seasoning as soon as it comes out of the grease
9. Taste. If it's good and tender, make your sauce (recipe follows), dip, and go ahead and eat. If tough, then do this:

    - Stack in big black skillet with onion, mushrooms, garlic, and sausage if you're feeling sassy.

- Put in oven at 300 for around 45 minutes. Should be very tender.

My super-special, super-simple back strap sauce:

1 cup of mayonnaise
2 squirts of mustard
1 shake of Worcestershire
1 teaspoon of horseradish (or more if you want it spicy)
Simply mix these ingredients together to make the sauce.

17

DUCK AND DRESSING

"I LOOKED INTO IT AND SAW FOUR-FOOTED ANIMALS OF THE EARTH, WILD BEASTS, REPTILES AND BIRDS. THEN I HEARD A VOICE TELLING ME, 'GET UP, PETER. KILL AND EAT.'"
—ACTS 11:6–7

Nowadays, people often ask me what it's like hunting with my dad. We've actually had offers of tens of thousands of dollars from people who want to spend a day in Phil's blind. It always amazes us because when we were growing up, duck hunting was our everyday life. When we were kids, we were always in the blind with Dad. I don't remember my first hunt or the first duck I killed, like other young hunters. It was a different time and Phil wasn't exactly a traditional dad. He didn't take pictures of our first duck. It wasn't sentimental; it was just life. We hunted and fished because we wouldn't eat if we didn't. Phil's number one concern was always safety. If you were careless with a loaded gun, you would not come back to the blind. You'd be stuck at home with Mom the next time.

Also, you had to be prepared because Phil wasn't gonna baby you out there. If you didn't wear the proper clothes, you were gonna freeze your butt off. And I did many times! You had to get your stuff together as well: shells, guns, and whatever you needed. I will never forget a time when I was about ten and we were all going on a dove hunt. It was opening day, and we were all excited. I was shooting a .410 shotgun, but I could only find one shell. Since we were leaving early in the morning, Phil let me know we wouldn't be able to stop at a store because none of them would be open that early in the morning.

"You better make that shot count," Phil told me.

So I shadowed Phil during the entire hunt, watching him drop 'em. I ran to fetch the birds for Phil, and if any were still alive, he would pinch their heads. With one flick of Phil's wrist, the dove's head separated from its body. I was fascinated and yet a little freaked out. You can't be sensitive when you're hunting with Phil. I kept throwing my shotgun up to shoot, but I knew I had only one shot. Finally, about eleven o'clock in the morning, I saw my opportunity. I told Phil I was gonna take my shot. He was supportive and told me to make it count. Boom! Wouldn't you know I smoked the dove? I couldn't believe it. I went one-for-one with only one shell. As I turned to look at my dad with the biggest smile ever, I noticed he was putting his gun down. He'd shot at the exact same time. He wanted to make sure my shot counted.

WITH ONE FLICK OF PHIL'S WRIST, THE DOVE'S HEAD SEPARATED FROM ITS BODY.

"Good shot, Willie boy, put your safety back on," Phil told me.

I didn't know why the safety mattered since I only had one shell, but he wanted to instill the practice in my brain. We'll never know who hit that bird, but believe me, I told Jase that I got it for sure.

When hunting with Phil, the number one rule was always to follow the laws and regulations of the sport. He wouldn't allow anyone to do anything illegal when it came to hunting. You had to have a license, wait for legal shooting times, and respect the rules of duck hunting. And safety checks were constant—and still are when we're in the blind. Guns have to be put in a place where they will not fall over accidentally, even if a dog runs through the blind. Phil still tells us stories of when guys would come to him with one leg missing and blame their dogs for getting shot. When a dog accidentally knocks your gun down, it can step on the safety and its claws can pull the trigger. You wouldn't believe how many people have been shot accidentally. Phil even invented a safety gun boot to put in a duck blind so it would never happen to us.

As far as the duck-blind rules, they are sort of unwritten in Phil's blind. He always does most of the calling. You wouldn't dare pull out your duck call and start wailing. He'll let you call a drake whistle, but not a hen call. In fact, Jase had to wait several years before he could call with him. And you really only need about two good callers in a blind. People ask me, "Why don't you call in the blind?" I ask them, "Would you call with Phil Robertson in your blind?"

It's like pinch-hitting for Albert Pujols. It doesn't make sense when you have the best duck caller in the world in your blind. The benefits of not screwing up are better than those of taking a chance on doing something stupid. Believe me: if you mess up, you're going to hear about it. I never will forget when we had about twenty-five mallards almost in the hole. They were on their third pass down when the text message alert on my phone went off. After my phone buzzed, the mallards decided not to come in. Phil looked down the row of guys with a look that was a mixture of craziness, agony, and Satan himself.

"What was that?" he hollered.

Now, there was no way I was gonna fess up.

"I heard something!" Phil yelled again.

I didn't feel like trying to explain to him that there was no way the ducks heard my phone from sixty yards away, so I didn't say a word. I'm glad waterboarding isn't allowed in the blind, because ol' Phil would have filled our faces with water to find the culprit. There is always a lot of pressure to have 100 percent success. If we get four out of six ducks, we'll sit there and debate for the next two hours why we didn't get all six.

Most of the quality time I spent with my dad was in the duck blind. When I was young I didn't appreciate what it took to be so successful at the sport. We just knew that it was what Dad loved and you had to respect that. No matter what the weather was like, whether it was rain, sleet, or snow, Dad was out in the blind. I didn't hunt nearly as much when I was in high school because I was into sports and girls. It wasn't until I came home from college that I really started to understand how special duck hunting is. I grew up in and around the business of duck hunting, so it wasn't as cool for me as it was for other guys.

MOST OF THE QUALITY TIME I SPENT WITH MY DAD WAS IN THE DUCK BLIND.

My most memorable hunts happened when I was older. We were in Arkansas one year, and it was a slow day. I talked Phil into moving to an area where we saw ducks going down. We decided to take a small crew—Phil, Jase, a camera guy, and me. The mallards were pouring in like we had been seeing all morning, so we didn't even have to call that much. It was just one of those spots where the ducks wanted to be. We each grabbed a cypress tree and spread out. We limited out in like twenty minutes, all green heads! It was a special hunt.

On another memorable hunt, a lone mallard came in. Jase told Phil, "Let's let Willie take this one." Now, I know why he said it. Jase was convinced I would raise my gun and miss. Well, I raised my gun and folded it. Phil looked at Jase and said, "Ol' Willie's been practicing." We laughed and talked about my shot the entire morning.

My favorite duck is an American wigeon. I just think they are prettiest. We don't get a whole heck of a lot of them on our land in Louisiana, so we went to New Mexico to do some duck hunting. We scouted in the mornings on bluffs and looked at the potholes to see if they had birds in them. If we found ducks, we made our way down and hunted them. We found tons of wigeon there, and I loved it. It was a different type of hunting; we all like being in different environments. We also saw sandhill cranes, and those suckers came down like helicopters. Phil tried to bite their heads and that was a mistake. Sandhill cranes' heads are much harder than the heads of the ducks Phil was used to. He nearly broke his teeth! But let me tell you something, they are some of the best birds I have eaten in my life. They call them the "rib-eye of the sky," and they're right. I also went and visited the UFO Museum in Roswell, New Mexico, while we were there. I couldn't talk Jase or Phil into going with me, so I took our camera guy Jeremy Helm. It was, well, let's just say, strange.

We mostly duck-hunt in Northeast Louisiana in flooded timber. Phil has always believed a duck in flooded timber is the hardest duck to hunt. Usually, they've already fed and are looking for a place to sit and rest. Of course, there are a lot of other things that can get them in the timber besides us, so the ducks are always a little skittish.

Honestly, hunting in the timber is the only way we could have filmed our DVDs all these years because it allows us to hide our equipment. I don't think people realize how much equipment and personnel we have to hide when we hunt. There are sound guys, wires, camera guys, directors, gaffers, and a whole bunch of other equipment. We stick people in trees and anywhere else where we can hide them. Plus, one of the things we always try to capture on film is a duck with a background. Think about when you look up and the sky is your background; you lose perception on how far away everything is. But when there is a tree behind the duck you can tell the distance a lot better. If we shoot a duck at twenty yards, it looks like forty yards on TV. So we have to get the ducks as close to us as possible because it looks the best and it also helps your chances of getting them. We don't do much pass shooting. It's fun, but it doesn't look good on film; the ducks look like little dots. It's way more fun trying to get a big group hovering over your decoys—and it looks better on film too. But it's hard because the closer the ducks get to you, the harder it is to get them to commit. A duck has way better eyesight than a human. You gotta remember they came down all the way from Canada, so by the time they get to Louisiana, well, they've seen just about everything.

If you've ever been duck hunting, you know there's a lot of idle time involved in the sport. You're basically at the mercy of the ducks, weather, and God. Being Robertsons, we figured the best way to spend our free time in the blind is by cooking. There's only one chef in the blind, and several of us take turns. Everyone tries to outdo everyone else when it comes to cooking. Phil likes to say that everything tastes better in the blind—even sardines. Over time, as the blinds got bigger and bigger, so did the kitchen. Now we have a fully operational kitchen in the blind we call the "Big Blind," complete with a cooktop, boiler, and mini fridge. Most of the time, breakfast includes eggs, bacon, biscuits, and mayhaw jelly. But that's only the start. On

BEING ROBERTSONS, WE FIGURED THE BEST WAY TO SPEND OUR FREE TIME IN THE BLIND IS BY COOKING.

other occasions, we've eaten deer, dove, quail, ham, pot roast, steaks, and spaghetti for lunch in the blind. We even boiled Alaskan king crab legs one time. It's a wonder anyone came back out to shoot ducks that day.

Of course, you never know what the chef is going to come up with out in a blind. Uncle Si likes to say he's the MacGyver of cooking. Si says if you give him a piece of bread, cabbage, coconut, mustard greens, pig's feet, pine cones, and a woodpecker, he'll make a delicious chicken pot pie! My favorite duck to eat is a wood duck, or woodie, as we call 'em. They're acorn eaters, so their meat is very clean and tasty. Most of 'em are local ducks, and they live in trees. Our place is full of 'em and you can now harvest three a day (it used to only be two). They typically fly at daylight and fly really crazy, darting and dodging to avoid trees as they fly through. They also don't fly very high in the air and stick to the treetops. Wood ducks are hard to call, although I have seen us peel 'em in from time to time. They squeal and make a noise in the air, but when they sit they have a different set of sounds. We always try to mimic the sitting sound so they think their buddies are on the water in front of us. They really don't leave the woods much, which I guess is why they have their name. They are some of the most beautiful ducks, but I just love the way they taste. They're my favorite ducks to eat hands down.

Growing up like we did is scary to think about now. We did some dangerous things; there's really no other way to say it. I shudder to think of my kids doing the things we did back then. It was a different time. I always feel like I came up in the last days of the good ol' days. Now you would never think of letting your children do what we did. There seems to be so much fear nowadays. We're concerned about lawsuits and predatory people, and I guess we know more about our surroundings and it's caused us to see danger everywhere. When I was a kid, we always rode in the back of the truck on the way home from town. No one ever thought about what would happen if we got in a wreck or if one of the kids simply fell out. I drove for years without a license. We just survived. I guess God was looking over us. He had a plan for my family. He always provided for us, and we always gave Him the glory for what we had, and we still do.

I believe our faith is what sets us apart. It's not about our beards, our success, or our hunting skills. It's the Lord. He keeps us in line. That's why we don't fight and bicker much, like a lot of families do. And when we do, we forgive one another because the Lord forgave us. That's why we don't let our own selfish desires pull us apart. We not only read the Bible and study it, but we actually live by it. We believe that what's in the Bible is the truth. We live our lives trusting that God's promises are real.

When Phil came to the Lord and began to live differently, we witnessed it happen. We saw how Phil turned his life over to God and how it changed him and our family for good. We had a crazy life growing up, but I wouldn't change any of it. My parents may not have been the best parents in the world all the time by parenting experts' standards, but they did the absolute best they could in the circumstances they were in.

And despite the obstacles, they set the bar high for us. I am so proud of them and all they've accomplished. I am proud of each of my brothers, and I have a super relationship with each of them. I really love getting to see them every day at work. I realize that so many people will never know what that's like.

WE HAD A CRAZY LIFE GROWING UP, BUT I WOULDN'T CHANGE ANY OF IT.

I am the most proud of my children and my wife, Korie. Without her, none of this would have ever happened. She took a chance on a cute boy with dimples in whom she saw potential. Our life together has never been boring. We endured hard times with hopes and dreams of doing the inconceivable. We were content when we had very little and when we had a lot. Our kids are strong, spiritual, and well disciplined. They will have their hopes and dreams as they grow, and I will be right there beside them cheering them on.

Sure, the Robertson family has its flaws, but we're pretty good at quite a few things—like duck hunting, frog catching, fishing, and selling worms. But most important, we're really good at being a family. Like I say in one way or another at the end of each episode of *Duck Dynasty,* at the end of the day, we're a family first, and everything else is just not worth getting that worked up over.

We've enjoyed showing our family to the world through the TV screen. Best of all, it's actually fun for us to watch the show, because the Robertsons always find a way to laugh at themselves. We're the ones laughing the hardest when one of us does something stupid, which, as you can see, happens quite often!

My advice is: Don't take yourself too seriously, laugh a lot, enjoy your time with family, and appreciate the unique talents of others. Trust in God, love your neighbor, say you're sorry, forgive, and work hard. Sit down to a good meal, turn off your cell phone, respect your elders, and, of course, get out in the woods and enjoy some good ol' frog legs. That's the Robertson way!

Duck and Dressing Recipe

A classic at the Robertson household, this is our Thanksgiving meal at Phil and Kay's house. Ducks are as fresh as daylight that same morning. It is a hard one to perfect. We only eat this a few times a year, and not because we don't love it; we just do it for special occasions. If you don't have any ducks, try this dressing with turkey next Thanksgiving. I promise it'll be the best you've ever eaten.

5 or 6 ducks
salt and pepper to taste
1 bay leaf
8 hot dog buns
2 bundles green onions
1 bell pepper
2 celery stalks
1 stick butter
a 9-by-12-inch pan of cornbread
1 sleeve of saltine crackers
2 eggs, whipped
½ cup evaporated milk
1 teaspoon sage
Phil Robertson's Cajun Style Seasoning Original

1. Place cleaned ducks into a large pot. Then add salt, black pepper, and bay leaf, and fill pot with water. Boil for 2½ hours.
2. Bake hot dog buns for 2 hours at 225 degrees.
3. Dice green onions, bell pepper, and celery. Sauté your vegetables in half of the butter on medium-low heat.
4. After your hot dog buns are done, take a very large roast pot and dump your buns, cornbread, and saltine crackers into the pot. With your hands, crumble the bread mixture into a fine consistency.
5. When your ducks are done boiling, remove them from the pot and pour a third of the broth into crumbled bread mix.
6. Stir until it reaches a paste consistency. Add vegetables.

7. Add broth until you get a thick but pourable consistency.
8. Add eggs and evaporated milk to your dressing mix and stir.
9. Add sage.
10. Place ducks lightly on top of dressing. Sprinkle Phil Robertson's Seasoning on top of ducks. Lightly coat ducks with rest of butter.
11. Bake duck and dressing at 375 degrees for 25–30 minutes.
12. Enjoy!

Acknowledgments

We feel blessed beyond measure to have been able to put our life into a book. Really, how many people get to do that? It doesn't just happen, though. Our sincerest thanks to John Howard, not only a great father and father-in-law, but also an excellent book agent who knew we could do it and helped us work through this process with lightning speed. We want to thank our editor and friend, Philis Boultinghouse, who sweetly encouraged us along the way. Also Amanda Demastus, who kindly kept us on schedule, not always an easy task. Thanks to Mark Schlabach, who helped with the writing process. A special thanks to our assistant, Angila Summitt, who, along with the other things she does for us daily, helped us gather and choose the pictures to include in the book. Narrowing your entire life to just forty pictures is tough! Thank you to A&E for believing in us and allowing us to show our crazy family to the world. Thanks to our children for being patient while we added one more thing to our already busy lives. Thanks to our big family: our brothers, sisters, aunts, uncles, nieces, nephews, and cousins with whom we are blessed to be able to work hard and play hard. And last but certainly not least, thanks to our parents who gave us this story with a life well lived and who continue to be an integral part of our story and our lives. We couldn't do it without you.

SI-COLOGY 101

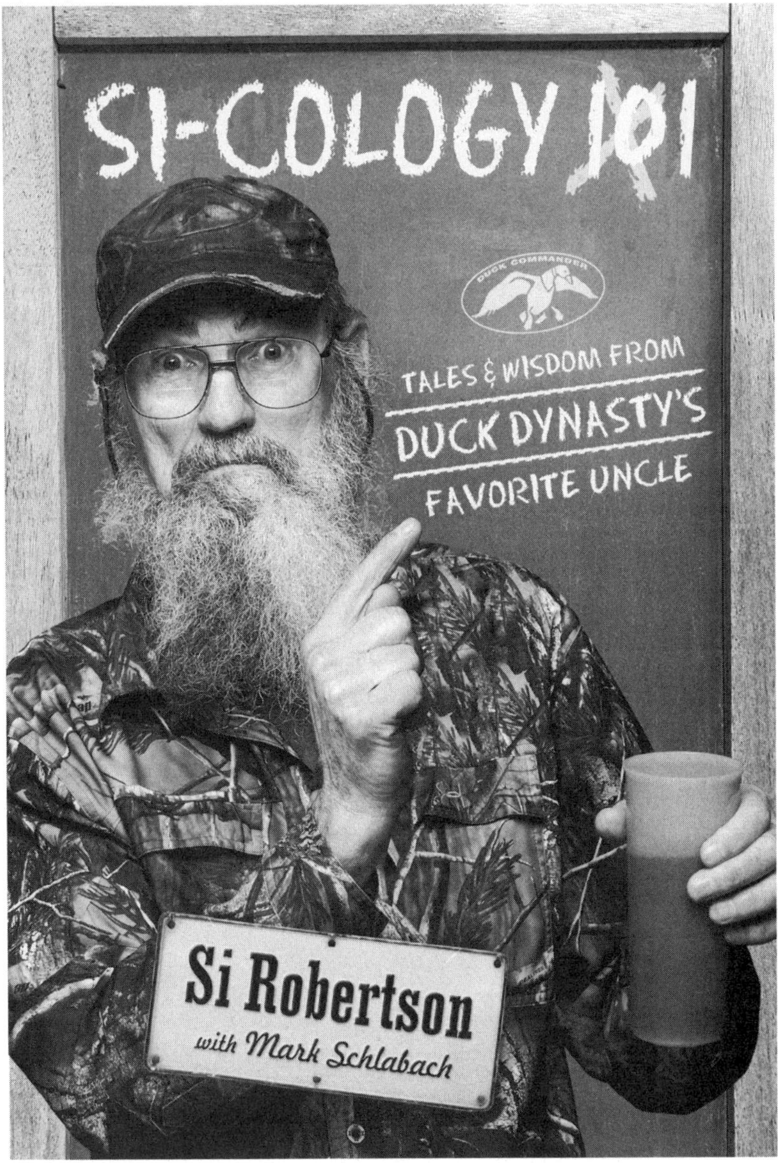

SI-COLOGY 1

TALES & WISDOM FROM DUCK DYNASTY'S FAVORITE UNCLE

Si Robertson

with Mark Schlabach

HOWARD BOOKS
A DIVISION OF SIMON & SCHUSTER, INC.
NEW YORK NASHVILLE LONDON TORONTO SYDNEY NEW DELHI

Howard Books
A Division of Simon & Schuster, Inc.
1230 Avenue of the Americas
New York, NY 10020

First Howard Books hardcover edition September 2013

HOWARD and colophon are trademarks of Simon & Schuster, Inc.

For information about special discounts for bulk purchases, please contact Simon & Schuster Special Sales at 1-866-506-1949 or business@simonandschuster.com.

The Simon & Schuster Speakers Bureau can bring authors to your live event. For more information or to book an event, contact the Simon & Schuster Speakers Bureau at 1-866-248-3049 or visit our website at www.simonspeakers.com.

Designed by Davina Mock-Maniscalco

Manufactured in the United States of America

10 9 8 7 6 5

Library of Congress Cataloging-in-Publication Data

Robertson, Si, 1948–
Si-cology 101 : tales and wisdom from Duck Dynasty's favorite uncle / Si Robertson.
—1st Howard Books hardcover edition.
pages cm
1. Robertson, Si, 1948– 2. Television personalities—United States—Biography.
I. Title.
PN1992.4.R5355A3 2013
791.4502'8092—dc232013018290
[B]

ISBN 978-1-4767-4537-4
ISBN 978-1-4767-4539-8 (ebook)

Contents

Contents

SI-COLOGY 101

"You can't spell squirrel without Si, and that's me!"

MY PARENTS ABSOLUTELY RUINED me. One of the lessons they always preached was to tell the truth no matter what. The Bible says we should always be honest, and that's one of the virtues I've tried to live by. I grew up to be an honest man who always told the truth to my teachers, coaches, sergeants, and bosses. Hey, I was like George Washington—I could never tell a lie! I can't even cross my fingers behind my back, Jack!

I believe lying is a learned skill. Some people are good at it, while others aren't. I've always been a lousy liar. The key to being a good liar is to know when you can get away with it and when you can't. You have to keep a straight face if you're going to lie, and I could never stop smiling when I tried. My palms would get sweaty, and I'd lose my composure and start to stutter. Hey, I even grew a long beard so people couldn't call me a

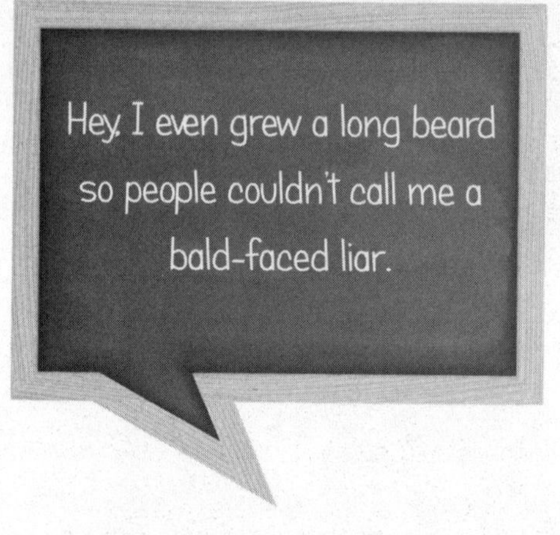

bald-faced liar. Still, as much as I tried, I couldn't tell a lie!

My older brother Phil always told me that my nose would grow longer than Pinocchio's if I was ever dishonest, and I figured my nose was already big enough. Some people are great at lying. Poker players are great liars, and most politicians will never get elected if they can't lie. Hey, how do you know if a politician is lying? His lips are moving! Some great Americans were undone by not telling the truth: Bill Clinton, Richard Nixon, Lance Armstrong, Mark McGwire, the guys from Milli Vanilli, and Pete Rose, to name a few. I don't want to end up like them, so I always tell the truth. Hey, do you know what happens to a liar when he dies? He lies still, Jack!

My twenty-four years in the army would have been *much* easier if I'd told only a couple of white lies. I got myself into so much trouble in the military by simply telling the truth. I was passed over for promotions and given crummy assignments because I was always honest. If I'd told a few little lies, I might have left the army as a four-star general!

Well, I'm always honest, so I have to tell you about the time I tried to tell a lie while I was in the army. Hey, even the best of us slip up every once in a while! During my first year in Vietnam, I actually tried to lie to my commanding officer. I was extremely homesick and was desperately trying to get a furlough back to the United States. One day, I walked into my sergeant's tent.

PROLOGUE

"Sir, might I have a word with you?" I asked very politely.

"What is it, Private Robertson?" he said.

"Well, sir, my wife is extremely ill and the doctors can't figure out what's wrong with her," I said. "I really need to fly back to Louisiana to check on her. I think she might die."

"Robertson, I have some good news for you," he said. "We received a telegram this morning from your wife, and she's been released from the hospital. Everything's going to be fine. There's no reason for you to go home."

I scratched my head in disbelief.

"Sir, with all due respect, I have to tell you that we must be the two biggest liars in Vietnam," I said. "I don't even have a wife!"

Hey, if I've learned anything from being a part of *Duck Dynasty* it's that you can't believe everything you see or read. It always amazes me that if people see something on TV or read it on the Internet, they instantly believe it's true.

I remember going to church on a Sunday morning not long ago, and a little old lady walked up to me before the service started.

"Si, I'm so sorry about your vision," she said.

"Hey, what are you talking about?" I said. "My vision is perfect. It's forty/twenty!"

"No, you're blind, honey," she said. "I saw it on TV. It was on *Duck Dynasty*."

Hey, no matter what I told the lady, she thought I was blind! She even asked me if I needed to be escorted to a pew!

When Phil and I were making an appearance last summer, a pretty lady walked up to our table and said, "Here I am."

"Who are you?" I asked.

"I'm the lady that just drove three hundred and fifty miles to marry you," she said. "I'm ready. Let's go."

"Well . . . that's an interesting proposal, but there's someone I know who might object."

"Who's that?" she asked.

"Hey, I'm sorry, darlin'," I said, "but I've been happily married for more than forty years. I don't think my wife would like it if I got hitched to you, too."

"You mean I drove all this way for *nothing*?" she said. "Would you at least sign these T-shirts?"

Hey, you wouldn't believe the number of marriage proposals I get every week. Women send me letters, cards, e-mails, flowers, razors, and candy. For some reason, the women across America think I'm an eligible bachelor. Hey, sorry, ladies, I've been married since 1971!

It amazes me what people will say about you sometimes. A few months ago, the phone started ringing at my house one afternoon. All of my relatives and friends started calling me to make sure I wasn't dead! People were even calling Phil's house to make sure I was okay. Apparently, someone had advertised that I would be appearing at a festival in Louisiana. When a bunch of people showed up to see me and I wasn't there, one of the vendors at the festival told them that I'd been killed in a car wreck! Naturally, everybody thought I was dead. The news of my tragic demise spread like wildfire across the Internet! Hey, news flash, people: I'm still here!

As you read this book, there are a few things that you have to understand: 95 percent of my stories are truthful. Every member of the Robertson family has the God-given gift of storytelling. Hey, when you've sat in a duck blind for more than half of your life, you have to figure out some way to pass the time! It's better than looking at Willie and Jase for six hours! Many of the stories I like to tell happened when I was a young boy or when I was in Vietnam. My family members shared some of the stories over the dinner table, and other soldiers in Vietnam passed some of them on to me. At my age, a few of the details are cloudy, but I'll recollect the coming stories as best I can. Hey, just remember it isn't a lie if you think it's true! It's up to you, the reader, to figure out what's true and what's fiction. Best of luck with that, Jack! May the force be with you.

Hey, another thing you have to know: my stories are kind of like my vocabulary. You might have noticed I like to say "hey" quite a bit. "Hey" can mean anything. It can mean "yes," it can mean "maybe," and it can mean "no." Hey, it could mean "next week." The bottom line is, you have to understand "hey" to understand me.

And if you know anything about Silas Merritt Robertson, you know I'm a hard rascal to figure out.

"The naked truth
is much better
than the best-dressed lie."

Chapter 1

Birthday Suit

LIKE EVERY OTHER HUMAN on earth, I came into this world in the buff. According to my brothers and sisters, I stayed that way throughout much of my early childhood. For whatever reason, I never liked to wear clothes when I was a boy, so I ran around our farm buck nekkid. I guess I figured since God brought me into this world in my birthday suit, I might as well wear it. Hey, some people have it, and some people don't. I've always had it, Jack!

When I was born on April 27, 1948, my parents, Merritt and James Robertson, were living in a log cabin outside of Vivian, Louisiana. The cabin was really rustic; we used an outhouse and didn't even have hot water to take baths. I was the youngest of five sons: Jimmy Frank was the oldest boy, followed by Harold, Tommy, and Phil. I had an older sister, Judy, and then my younger sister, Jan, came along a few years after I was born.

Our log cabin sat on top of a hill and was surrounded by about four hundred acres. Marvin and Irene Hobbs, Momma's brother-in-law and sister, lived at the bottom of the hill. They had several kids: Billy, Mack, Sally, and Darrell, who were our first cousins. When Momma and Daddy played dominoes at the Hobbses' house, Jimmy Frank was put in charge of the younger kids. Our cabin became a prison, and Jimmy Frank was the warden. He'd walk outside the cabin, as if on patrol, making sure none of the younger kids escaped, so we always called him the warden! We younger kids wanted to go to the Hobbses' house to play with our cousins, but Jimmy Frank was under strict orders to keep us inside.

There were only two windows in the cabin, and they were our routes of escape. As the warden marched around the log cabin, one of us captives would watch him through the cracks in the walls. When he made his way around the right corner of the house, we'd all jump through the window and run down to the Hobbses' place. At least there weren't any sirens when we made our getaway!

My daddy started working in the oil industry when he was young, first as a roughneck, then as a driller and tool pusher, and eventually he became a drilling superintendent. It was really hard work, but I never heard him complain about it. It was an honest living, and even though we never had a lot of money, we always had enough food to eat, which mostly came from the fields and gardens on our farm. And with so many kids around, we were never bored and always seemed to find something to keep us busy.

When I was a little bit older, we left the log cabin and moved to Dixie, Louisiana, which is about fourteen miles north of Shreveport. We made the move because Momma suffered a nervous breakdown and was diagnosed as manic-depressive. Living in Dixie made it easier for her to get the treatment she needed; she spent a lot of time in hospitals and the state mental institution. I loved my momma dearly, and my brothers and sisters always say I was her favorite child. Hey, what can I say? I've always had that effect on women!

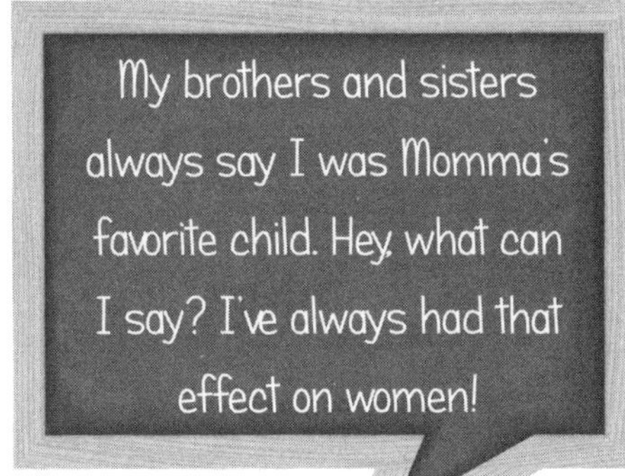

A lot of my fondest childhood memories occurred in Dixie. I can still remember the day we drove to our house for the first time. We unloaded out of a 1957 Chevrolet and a couple of kids from the neighborhood walked up. We introduced ourselves to the boys, and the only way I can describe them is, well, they were geeks. We wandered around the yard, exploring the place, and noticed a big patch of woods about two miles from the railroad tracks in front of our house. We asked the boys, "Hey, what's over there?"

"We have no idea," they told us.

"What do you mean you have no idea?" I asked them. "Have you not been over there?"

"No, we've never been over there," one of them said.

The next thing they knew, Tommy, Phil, and I were racing across the railroad tracks and into the woods. We drove the farmers around our house slap insane by hunting on their land without permission. One of the farmers loved to chase us out of the woods in his pickup truck. Every time we heard his pickup coming, we'd take off running like deer through the woods. We hid behind logs and in underbrush, looking for his truck at the top of a hill or in the pecan orchard. It was like Wile E. Coyote chasing the Road Runner. He never did catch us.

Years later, we found out that chasing us was one of the farmer's favorite things to do. Momma sold Avon cosmetics for a while, and one day she was at the farmer's house selling products to his wife. Momma apologized to the farmer for our hunting on his land, but he told her we were allowed to hunt on any of his property. Momma thanked him and was getting ready to walk out the door.

"Hey, wait a minute," he said. "Don't tell them."

"Well, you gave them permission," she said.

"Oh, yeah, they can hunt on all of my land whenever they want," he said. "But don't tell them I gave them permission. If they know they have my permission, they won't run from me."

That farmer loved the chase. We ran from him for about fifteen years and didn't even have to!

Phil, Tommy, and I were always hunting or fishing. One of the best things we did happened when the sun went down. When Phil was ten years old, he got an air rifle for Christmas. I was eight and got a Daisy BB gun. We spent every day going around the neighborhood, shooting anything we could kill. When the sun went down, we got our flashlights and shined them under the awnings over the windows of our neighbors' houses. Birds loved to fly up there and go to sleep. Guess what? We loved to shine our flashlights on the birds and shoot them! Every night, our neighbors would be awakened by the *clank! clank! clank!* sounds.

Imagine their surprise when they opened the curtains and saw a bare-bottomed gunman!

DUCK COMMANDER

"I like a dog that fits my personality: well-groomed, handsome, a natural-born killer, and one that doesn't mind taking a nap once in a while."

Dynamic Dog Duo

Mark Twain once said the difference between a cat and a lie is that a cat only has nine lives. Hey, let me tell you something: where I grew up, cats didn't have nine lives—they generally had just one! There weren't many second chances when the Robertsons were involved!

We always had a lot of animals around our house, whether it was chickens, cows, pigs, rabbits, or horses, but I had two favorite family pets. Maimey was a Wiedemeyer—or a Weimaraner as they call them—and she was a good hunting dog. Bullet was a cur, a Louisiana Catahoula leopard dog, which is a fancy way of saying she was a mutt. The breed is actually named after Catahoula Parish on the Ouachita River, which runs in front of the house where Phil and Kay live today.

The Catahoulas are believed to be the first dogs bred in

North America; some people even suspect that Native Americans bred their dogs with the molossers and greyhounds that Hernando de Soto brought to Louisiana in the sixteenth century. Curs really aren't true hounds, but they're great hunting dogs and terrific at tracking wild boar. Many of them have spotted coats, and nearly all of them have distinctive marbled glass eyes. Bullet had one glass eye and a black and yellow coat. We always knew our toast was perfect when it was the color of Bullet's coat.

I remember the day Bullet died. A truck hit him on the road in front of our house. Phil and I saw it and were crying as we climbed onto the school bus. By the time we got to school, everybody on the bus was crying and then everybody in our class was crying. All the kids knew Bullet because they were always hanging out at our house.

Maimey was a much bigger dog than Bullet and had a slick silver coat. Now, one of the problems with the Weimaraner breed is that the dogs are typically stubborn and not very smart. But Maimey was quite the exception. Not only would she listen to our commands, she would even talk to us on occasion!

In fact, Maimey was Momma's alarm clock when we were young. Every morning, Momma would wake up early to cook us breakfast before we left for school. While Momma was cooking eggs, bacon, and buttermilk biscuits, she talked to our dogs.

"How are you this morning?" she would ask them. "Are you having a good day?"

Even though none of us believed her, Momma insisted the dogs talked back to her.

When it was time for us to wake up for breakfast, Momma would send Maimey to our room.

"Okay, wake them up," Momma told her.

Maimey liked to leap into our beds and put her cold, wet nose on our faces to wake us. Once she received Momma's command, she'd take off running around the corner in the kitchen and then sprint down the long hall to our beds. Most of the time, we heard Maimey's claws scratching the hardwood floors before she jumped on our beds. This was our fair warning to pull the quilts over our heads. Our house was always cold in the winter—there were only a few floor heaters scattered through the shotgun house—and Maimey's nose was ice-cold after being outside. Once Maimey found an opening in the blankets, she'd root her way under them and there we were—jumping out of bed!

It was impossible to keep Maimey out of the house. When we tried to put her outside, she'd open the front door. I guess she learned to open it by watching us turn the doorknob; she finally realized she could do it with her paws. When Maimey was ready to come inside, we'd hear scratching on the doorknob and then she'd waltz into the front room!

By the time we moved from the log cabin to our house in Dixie, Louisiana, Jimmy Frank and Harold were in school at Louisiana State University in Baton Rouge. One night, Tommy, Phil, and I were sitting at the dinner table with Pa and Granny (that's what we called my parents after their first grandchildren were born). It was one of the rare occasions when Maimey was outside.

As soon as we started eating dinner, the front door opened

and Maimey came running in. She looked at Momma and growled something I didn't understand.

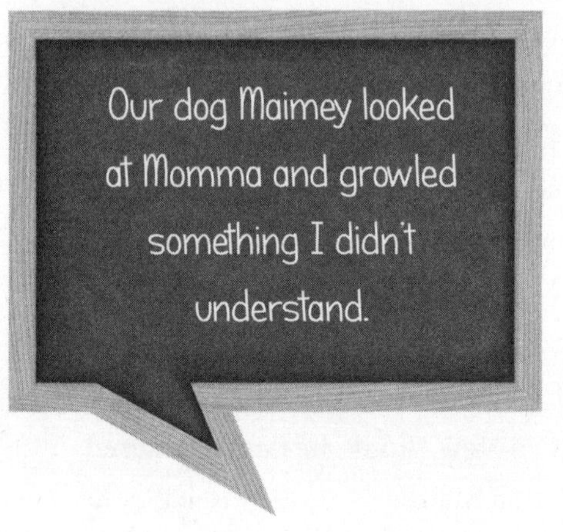

"What did she say?" Momma asked us. "I think she just said, 'Harold is home.'"

A couple of minutes later, we heard a car door shut and then Harold walked in through the front door.

My brothers and I were dumbfounded. Nobody said anything as we looked at each other.

"Hey, I've been telling you I talk to her all the time," Momma told us. "And she talks back to me."

Finally, I believed her.

When Daddy worked as a driller, he was on the graveyard shift and some of his workers would occasionally come to our house before their shift. One night, one of our distant cousins, Wade Childs, was sitting in a dark green chair next to the fireplace. He didn't know it was Maimey's bed. Our front door was glass, so we could see through it from top to bottom. Wade was facing the door and saw the knob turning. Since it was nighttime, he couldn't see Maimey because of her dark coat.

Wade must have thought a ghost was opening the door. His eyes got bigger and bigger, and then Maimey walked through the door. She walked straight toward him and sat in front of the chair.

Then she started growling at him. She didn't bark; it was only a low growl in her throat.

"Merritt!" Wade screamed. "Merritt!"

Mamma walked in from the kitchen and asked him what was wrong.

"I didn't do anything," he said.

"Oh, you need to get out of her chair," Momma told him. "She's telling you she's ready to go to bed."

Wade got out of the chair, and Maimey jumped into it. She sneezed and spun around three times before taking a seat.

Before Maimey started to snore, I swear I heard her say, "Sleep tight and don't let the bedbugs bite."

Whenever we went hunting and fishing, Bullet and Maimey were always with us. They were great at retrieving ducks, doves, quails, squirrels, or whatever other game we were hunting. But Maimey had more of a thirst for blood.

Every morning when we went outside to wait for the school bus, Bullet and Maimey would sit and wait with us. Bullet would lie down on the ground, but Maimey would run across the railroad tracks in front of our house and into a big mess of dewberry bushes. She wouldn't be gone three minutes but always came back with a rabbit in her mouth. She did it every morning, Monday through Friday, without exception. Maimey would come back, lie down, eat the head off the rabbit, and leave the rest. Don't know why she didn't eat the body, but that's what she did. Every day when we came home from school, Momma would tell us to get the rabbit carcass off the front porch. I knew rabbits liked briar patches, but I couldn't believe how many rabbits were over there!

Bullet was named exactly right, because he was *fast*. He was like a cheetah chasing antelope running through the woods. Maimey was a bigger dog than Bullet and wasn't quite as swift. Together, though, they were the dynamic duo and the greatest cat-killing team I have ever seen.

Bullet was adept at getting in front of a cat and keeping its attention while Maimey would sneak up from behind and pounce. She would break its neck before she was ever clawed. Bullet was fast, but he wasn't as quick as a cat. There were several times he came home covered with cat scratches.

Our friend Tommy McKenzie's grandmother Mrs. Wilson lived next door to us in Dixie. Purple jasmine grew over the back door of her house. When it bloomed, it was beautiful and you could smell the flowers all the way from our house. Mrs. Wilson also had forty Siamese cats. Now, I'm not much of a cat person, but I have to admit her cats were something to look at. Their coats had different colors, and she spent a lot of time grooming them.

When I left to join the army at nineteen. Mrs. Wilson had only two cats left! Bullet and Maimey killed nearly every one of them.

Hey, when I left to join the army at nineteen, Mrs. Wilson had only two cats left! Bullet and Maimey killed nearly every one of them. The lone survivors lived at the top of a big walnut tree in her backyard. The only time we saw those two cats was when we looked up the giant tree. The two cats were always sitting at the tip-top of it. Talk about survivors! Those cats knew that if their paws ever hit the ground, they'd be goners.

Out of Mrs. Wilson's forty cats, Maimey and Bullet killed thirty-eight of them! Mrs. Wilson would walk over and say to Momma, "I don't know what's happening to my cats. They keep disappearing."

Fortunately for us, Mrs. Wilson was about half deaf. Whenever anyone asked her about living next door to us, she always said, "Oh, they're the sweetest boys. They never make any noise. They're the quietest people you'd ever want to be around."

Hey, you know what they say: *See no evil, hear no evil, speak no evil!*

"Once I reached down to pet a little dog and when I did, it was a five-pound squirrel."

Redneck Pets

When we lived in the log cabin near Vivian, Louisiana, there were two big hickory trees in the front yard. If you've cracked open a hickory nut before, you know there is a green nut inside. Once you crack the thick shell or it pops off once it's ripe, the nut is as hard as a brick! My brothers and I had wars throwing those things at each other, and they really hurt! If you were ever hit in the head, it left a goose egg on your noggin!

Until we were old enough to get a BB gun or some kind of firearm, we made slingshots and used the hickory nuts as ammunition. We'd take the inner tubes out of old tires and cut strips from them to use as slings. We found trees with forked limbs and tied the slings to the limbs with string. If you wanted a six-gun, you used a limb that was about six inches long. If you wanted to be like Wyatt Earp and have a long barrel, you made it twelve inches. Then we took the leather tongues out of old shoes and put the rocks and hickory nuts inside—for easy storage and carrying, ready to fire from the slings.

We killed plenty of game with the slingshots, from squirrels to rabbits to blackbirds. We also made our own bows and arrows before we had rifles. We used thick reeds as our arrows, sharpened them, and then tied broad rocks to them for arrowheads. Anything that walked or flew was fair game! Momma raised chickens at our house, and they were always running around our backyard. One day, Phil and I were messing around in the yard with our bows and arrows when one of Momma's chickens ran across the yard in front of us. Bad move, Jack! When the chicken made its way back to the other side, Phil fired an arrow and missed. On the second try, he hit the chicken right in the head.

Phil and I grabbed the dead chicken and went down to the creek that ran behind our house. We plucked the chicken, built a fire, and roasted it for lunch. We knew we had to eat the evidence before Momma found out! We never told Momma we killed her chicken, but she knew one of them was missing. She figured a fox or stray dog killed it.

Chickens weren't our only casualties. We used to hunt squirrels with our slingshots and bows and arrows—they've always been my favorite game to eat. But one time we found a baby squirrel that was still in its nest. Now, even I have a soft spot in my heart when it comes to young critters. We brought the baby squirrel home and fed it with an eyedropper. Somehow, the squirrel survived and became one of our pets. It crawled up on our shoulders and nibbled our ears every once in a while. Momma even allowed it to stay inside and roam around the house.

We managed to keep the squirrel until the day Momma

bought a new sofa for our living room. After we moved the sofa into our house, the squirrel crawled underneath it and wouldn't come out. It ate a hole through one of the boards and built a nest under the cushions. Every time someone sat on the sofa, a spring popped him in the butt because the squirrel had pulled out all of the cotton. I'd never seen my momma so mad! Needless to say, the squirrel was banished from the house and never allowed to come back.

Being rednecks, squirrels weren't our only exotic pets. One day, Momma sent Phil and me to the store to buy a gallon of milk. On our way, we saw a flock of pigeons sitting on the roof of a cotton gin. We looked around and found a handful of flat rocks—we called them sailers—to hurl at the pigeons. Sailers are the best rocks to throw; if you throw them on water, they're really good skippers.

"You throw first," I told Phil.

"Nah, you throw first," he said. "When you throw, they're going to jump up and then I'm going to get me one."

I wound my arm back like Nolan Ryan and fired a rock at the pigeons. I knew I was fixing to nail one because I'd found the perfect sailer. As the rock made its way toward the cotton gin, I could see the pigeons getting anxious and fidgety. As the rock started its descent, they got *really* nervous. It was like artillery falling from the sky. You know what they say about nuclear war: all pigeons are cremated equally! Just about the time the pigeons jumped up off the roof, my rock nailed one of them.

Phil and I ran to the cotton gin and picked the pigeon up off the ground. My rock had hit him squarely in the head and somehow twisted his head around. The pigeon was looking straight back! The rock snapped his neck, but he wasn't dead!

We had a pigeon coop at our house, so Phil and I carried the bird home, along with the gallon of milk. I put the pigeon in the coop, where it always sat on the top perch, his chest facing our house and his head looking behind him. I named the pigeon Eagle. Every morning, I went to the coop to pet Eagle and feed him. When I took Eagle out of the coop and threw him into the air to fly, he flew straight into the ground and rolled over. How can you fly if you can't see where you're going? Phil and I used to throw him up into the air just for the fun of watching poor Eagle.

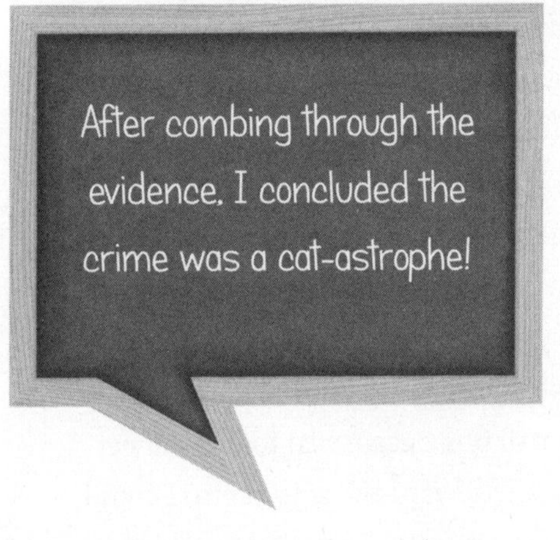

Now, we found Eagle before Bullet and Maimey, our family dogs, ravaged Mrs. Wilson's prized collection of Siamese cats. One morning I woke up and went to the coop to feed our pigeons. As I walked down the hill, I was immediately struck with terror to see there had been a mass murder. There were blood and feathers everywhere in our pigeon coop! There were half-eaten carcasses lying on the floor.

I set out to solve the crime. It's obvious that you can't spell "NCIS" without "Si"—and that's me! After combing through the evidence, I concluded the crime was a cat-astrophe! Out of twenty-five pigeons, Mrs. Wilson's cats had killed every one—except Eagle!

Eagle was still sitting on the top perch, his chest facing me and his head looking the other way. The only thing I could figure was that the cats were superstitious and were afraid to kill him.

Or maybe Eagle had eyes in the back of his head and managed to fend for himself!

"When you were born
and they were handing out brains,
you thought they said 'trains.'"

Book Report

After Jimmy Frank and Harold left for college, Tommy, Phil, and me went everywhere together. We were inseparable. I'm not sure Tommy and Phil wanted to drag their little brother everywhere they went, but Momma didn't give them much choice. If they were leaving to play football, going fishing or hunting, or going to town, Momma always told them, "Take little brother with you."

Tommy, Phil, and I were like stair steps everywhere we went. Tommy always walked in the front, and he was about four inches taller than Phil. I walked behind Phil, who was four inches taller than me. Since I was the youngest brother, I always brought up the rear.

When Momma would get tired of us, she'd load us up in our Ford Falcon and drive to Belcher, Louisiana, which was about ten miles from where we lived and was where we went to middle school. She'd drop us off at the Red River levee and say, "Go catch us a mess of fish; I don't want to see y'all until supper time."

Basically, Momma was letting us know that she was tired of us and needed a day off. Hey, if I spent most of my adult life around five boys, I'd need a vacation every once in a while, too!

When Momma dropped us off, we'd follow the river back toward our house. We'd usually float down the river on a log for about five miles, get off where the river started to make an S-curve around a bend, and then walk the last two or three miles to our house. We were always exploring that river, like we were in a Huckleberry Finn adventure.

If we were at the river, we were usually fishing. We used throw lines on the river, and it was a three-man operation. We used a brick and nylon rope with hooks. We could make the throw line however long we wanted to make it, as long as it was short enough for us to control. We usually went with twelve hooks on each throw line. We cut a thick branch off a willow tree, and drove it into the ground. Then we tied the throw line to the top and bottom of the branch. Before we were ready to fish, two people had to catch live brim and carry them in a washtub full of water.

One of us was in charge of throwing the brick and rope into the water, making sure not to hook ourselves in the process. After we hooked ourselves several times, we finally used our brains and learned to make the rope between the last hook and brick long enough so it wouldn't hook us. While one of us was throwing the brick into the water, somebody else had to hold the rope at the willow branch, making sure the throw line didn't slap the water and knock the bait off the hooks. The third person was in charge of making sure each of the twelve hooks always had fresh bait on it.

Usually, we set out four or five throw lines on the river at once, so we'd have as many as sixty hooks in the river at the same time. Let me tell you something: there's not a finer sight than seeing a willow branch shaking back and forth because there are so many fish on your throw line. We used to get so excited running to the lines, pulling in fifteen-pound blue catfish. We also caught Opelousas catfish and high-fin blue catfish. We'd come home with three washtubs full of catfish. It was fish-fry time! The whole neighborhood would come over to eat when they smelled the grease at the Robertson house.

> There's not a finer sight than seeing a willow branch shaking back and forth because there are so many fish on your throw line.

We supplemented whatever Momma and Daddy bought at the grocery store with catfish, crappie, white perch, and the game we killed in the woods.

Our fishing trips became legendary among our friends. During high school, we were required to read a book, write a book report, and then stand in front of the entire class and give an oral report on what we read. I was prepared to give a report on *The Adventures of Tom Sawyer*. But when I stood up in front of my class, one of the other students said, "No, no! We've already read *Tom Sawyer*. We know Si and Phil skipped school last Thursday. We want to know what they did last Thursday!"

I looked at my teacher, Mrs. Jones, and asked, "Well, what do you think?"

"Tell them what you did last Thursday," she said. "But know this: it better be good, because I am grading you on this."

So I proceeded to tell my class what I did the previous Thursday.

Momma woke up early like always last Thursday and fixed us a good breakfast. But then she changed her mind and decided Phil and me weren't going to school.

"I'm hungry for fish," she told us. "I want y'all to go catch me a mess of crappie."

Phil and I started jumping up and down. Any day at the lake was better than spending a day at school. So Phil and I sat in the front room of our house, looking out the window for the school bus with our noses just above the windowsill. The bus stopped right between the shrubs in front of our house, and the bus driver opened the door and then blew the horn. Momma walked out and waved her on.

Phil and I gave the bus driver just enough time to turn left at the end of our street, and then we ran out the back door to get our cane poles, washtubs, and bait. We jumped in the Falcon and drove fifteen miles to an oxbow lake on the Red River. We climbed into a boat that the man who owned the lake allowed us to use, and we were ready to catch some crappie.

But when we got out on the lake, there was a north wind of about thirty miles per hour. It was a bad day to be fishing on open water. The lake had once been a channel of the Red River, but now it was landlocked and there were no trees to block the wind. It was wide open, and we were paddling against winds of thirty miles per hour.

When we finally reached our favorite spot to fish, Phil and I realized a commercial fisherman had recently been there. We saw two sticks in the water, about one hundred and fifty yards apart, and we knew that was where he'd tied off his net. Phil and I threw our lines into the water right there, and as soon as our shiners hit the water, we each caught a pound-and-a-half crappie. By the time we had the fish in our boat, we were one hundred and fifty yards away from the sweet hole. So we paddled against thirty-mile-per-hour winds again, and then dropped our lines in the water and caught another fish. We looked up and we were one hundred and fifty yards away from the sweet spot again!

Finally, after about the third time of doing this, Phil said, "Hey, this isn't going to work. One of us is going to have to paddle to keep us here while the other one fishes."

Of course, I was the youngest, so I became a three-and-a-half-horsepower human trolling motor to keep Phil between the sticks.

Phil sat there and caught about seventy-one more crappie. We ended up with seventy-five crappies in our boat and then had one heck of a fish fry that night.

After I finished telling the story, all of the kids in my class clapped. One of my buddies said, "That's what I'm talking about."

I stood up from my chair and looked at my teacher. "C-minus," she said.

"C-minus?" I asked her. "Have you lost your mind? Seventy-five white perch in thirty-mile-per-hour winds, and I was the motor! You're giving me a C-minus?"

She looked at me and shook her head.

"Hey, woman," I said. "I've got a news flash for you: That is an A-plus!"

DUCK COMMANDER

"Hey, fear is a **healthy thang.**"

Unidentified Walking Object

There are only a few things in this world I fear: poisonous snakes, losing my iced tea cup, not being able to take a nap, and being left alone in the dark. Hey, I'm man enough to admit that I'm afraid of the dark. I like the world better when it's light outside; you can see what's in front of you or, more important, what's lurking behind you. I'm not actually afraid of the dark—I'm scared of what's in it, Jack!

I'm not exactly sure when I was diagnosed with achluophobia—the fear of darkness—but I've always been afraid to be left alone in the dark. Growing up in the Robertson house, my older brothers always teased me about being scared of the dark. I spent many nights in bed with the covers pulled over my head while Tommy and Phil tapped on the walls or made scary noises to frighten me. I don't like to watch horror movies and didn't even like to go trick-or-treating when I was a kid, unless we were back at our house before the sun went down! I always checked to make sure the doors and windows were locked—and the closets were clear—before I went to bed, and I even slept with a nightlight until I left for Vietnam. Now I sleep with the TV on in our bedroom. I still don't like the dark!

Whenever we went fishing or frog gigging at night when we were kids, Tommy and Phil liked to run off and leave me alone in the woods. I always feared that a grizzly bear, Sasquatch, or a fifty-pound squirrel was going to eat me. Hey, you probably didn't know squirrels could grow that big, but I've seen them! They have razor-sharp teeth and don't look anything like the cute squirrels that eat nuts. They're man-eaters and like to gnaw on human bones! They'd probably like nothing more than to eat the hunters who are trying to shoot them, including me!

I've been afraid of the dark for as long as I can remember. One night, Momma asked me to go outside to get her shoes, which she'd left on the front steps of our log cabin.

"Momma, I don't want to go outside," I told her. "It's dark out there."

Momma smiled and said, "Silas, you don't have to be afraid of the dark, son. Jesus is out there. He'll watch over you and protect you."

"Are you sure he's out there?" I asked her.

"Yes, Silas, he's always with you," she said.

So I mustered up the courage to crack open the front door. I stuck my head outside. It was pitch-black, and I could hear the grizzly bears and fifty-pound squirrels stirring in the woods around our house.

"Jesus?" I asked, while praying he would respond to my plea. "If you're out there, can you hand me Momma's shoes?"

Well, Jesus never handed me her shoes, so I'm still afraid of the dark.

Momma always told me my fear of darkness would go away once I got older, but it only seemed to get worse over the years. When I was in the fourth grade, Tommy, Phil, and I went frog gigging one night. After we'd gigged a bagful of bullfrogs, we started to make our way through the dark woods back to our house to clean them. We were walking in a straight line, like we always did, with Tommy in the front and Phil in front of me.

As we were walking through the woods, I kept hearing something walking behind me. Tommy had the flashlight, so I was trying to make sure that I kept Phil in sight. I didn't want to be left alone out there! No matter how fast I walked, I kept hearing footsteps behind me. After I heard the footsteps once more, I turned around and looked but didn't see anything. I figured I was only imagining the sounds because it was so dark in the woods and, hey, I was scared.

The next time I turned around, though, I saw a pair of yellow eyes looking right at me! The eyes were glowing in the dark!

I tried to muster up enough courage to scream, but my mouth

was as dry as the Sahara Desert. I sat there in the woods, shaking and trembling in my boots, wondering what was about to eat me for dinner. Suddenly, I remembered a Bible verse Momma read to me. It was Isaiah 41:10:

So do not fear, for I am with you; do not be dismayed,
for I am your God. I will strengthen you and help you;
I will uphold you with my righteous right hand.

I reached out for God's right hand but couldn't find it. So I looked for the next-best thing: Phil's shoulders! I took off running and ran right into Phil's back, and then he fell into Tommy. We fell into a clump on the ground.

"Hey, hey!" Tommy yelled. "Si, what's going on?"

"There's something behind me!" I screamed. "It's Sasquatch!"

Tommy shined the flashlight back to where I'd seen the unidentified walking object. We didn't see anything.

"You're imagining things," Phil told me. "You're such a sissy."

But when Tommy shined the light back to the spot again, we saw a big blur run past us. It jumped into a large culvert to our left.

"I told you there was something back there!" I said.

We slowly tippytoed toward the culvert and shined the light down into it. We didn't see anything, but we were suddenly overcome by the putrid scent of a skunk. It smelled awful.

"Si, it was only a skunk," Phil said.

To this day, Tommy and Phil still contend I only saw a very large skunk.

Hey, I don't know about you, but I've never seen a skunk that walks upright and is four feet tall! Even now, I still have no idea what the unidentified walking object really was. It had eyes that glowed in the dark and walked just like we do. It fell in line right behind us as we walked through the woods!

Maybe it was a four-foot skunk. We grow them pretty big down in Louisiana. Or maybe it really was Sasquatch and he badly needed a bath!

"He's like a snake in the grass.
Hey, if you chop its head off,
It'll still bite ya!"

Snake Bit

One of the biggest hazards of living in Louisiana is that nearly forty different species of snakes are here. Where I live, snakes hide under rocks, logs, floor mats, and pillows. Hey, they even sleep in your boots! If you're not careful, they'll crawl into your pocket when you're walking to the duck blind and back. Heck, I have to check my gun barrel every time I shoot to make sure a snake didn't crawl into it. As you may can guess, I don't like snakes. The only good snake is a dead snake! If anyone tries to mess with me when it comes to snakes, they're going to have a fight on their hands.

Given as much time as I've spent in the woods hunting squirrels, birds, deer, and other game, along with being on the water fishing and shooting ducks, the odds were pretty good I was going to be bitten by a snake. In fact, I've been bitten by a snake twenty-seven times in my life, to be exact. Over the years, water snakes, pine snakes, blind snakes, brown snakes, garter snakes, ribbon snakes, rat snakes, racers, and king snakes have bitten me. Hey, I don't blame the snakes. That's what a snake does—they're snakes!

Looking back, it's amazing that a poisonous snake never bit my brothers or me. I guess Momma was right; someone was always watching over us. Northwest Louisiana, where we grew up, is one of the few places in the United States that is home to all four of the venomous snakes of North America: the copperhead, cottonmouth, coral snake, and rattlesnake. We're even blessed to have two kinds of rattlesnakes: the canebrake and the eastern diamondback. Boy, aren't we lucky?

You always have to be on the lookout for snakes. You never know when one is going to be lying in the path of your next step as you're walking through the woods or swamp. Fortunately, Phil detests snakes as much as I do, so there are always two sets of eyes scanning the ground for them.

My brothers and I had plenty of close calls when we were kids. One day, while we were running on a sandbar on the Red River, Tommy stopped dead in his tracks. What followed next was like something out of a cartoon. Phil bumped into Tommy, and I ran into Phil's back. It was like dominoes falling over. We landed about six inches from a big snake.

"Whoa, whoa!" Tommy screamed. "It's a king cobra!"

We looked down and saw a big black snake on the ground. It was standing on its tail with its head flared up. The king cobra was staring straight at us and looked ready to strike and send us to our graves.

We stepped back and the snake backed down. It coiled up on the ground, and its head returned to normal.

"Nah, I've seen a picture of one of these snakes in a book at school," Tommy said. "It's not a king cobra snake. It's a hognose snake."

Since it wasn't a king cobra that could kill us with one strike, Tommy caught the snake with his bare hands. It kept flaring its head at us while we played with it. It was a bad-looking thing! When it calmed down, its head looked like it had a pig's nose with big nostrils. But when it flared up, it was wicked-looking!

One summer, we learned we could sell dewberries for about five dollars per gallon bucket, so we went into high gear gathering them. We went anywhere to find them. Dewberries are closely related to blackberries and raspberries, but they're bigger and grow on trailing vines that look like weeds. We sold them to women who used them to make cobblers, jams, or pies. We always saved enough for Momma to jar or turn into a Sunday cobbler. Five dollars a bucket was a lot of money for boys who never had much money in their pockets, so we searched for them day and night. We kicked it into high gear, Jack, and we went to picking dewberries fast and furious.

After a few weeks, we tapped out our sweet holes, so we went searching for more brambles of dewberries. We walked down the levee at the Red River, looking for dewberries along the bank. At the bottom of the incline, Tommy spotted some dewberries.

"Hey, we have to get down there," Tommy told us. "If there are dewberries down there, they're going to be big because they're close to the water."

Sure enough, we found some dewberries. We were on one knee wading through the water, picking dewberries at the edge of the river. They were as big as fifty-cent pieces! I was counting the money we were going to make in my head. Phil and I filled our buckets in about three minutes.

When Phil and I were finished, we walked back to the top of the levee, which was about six feet above the water at a forty-five-degree incline. Phil looked down at Tommy, who was still on one knee. Right above him on the bank were two big black rings with a white spot in the middle of them. The rings were four inches from Tommy's leg. It was two cottonmouth water moccasins, which are some of the meanest and deadliest snakes you'll come across. The snakes were about as big as my arm, about four inches in diameter. They looked like they could kill an eight-hundred-pound bull!

"Tommy, look down at your right knee!" Phil yelled.

I heard Tommy scream, and then the next thing I knew, Tommy was standing between Phil and me! Both of our mouths just dropped open. He jumped six feet from the water to the top of the hill!

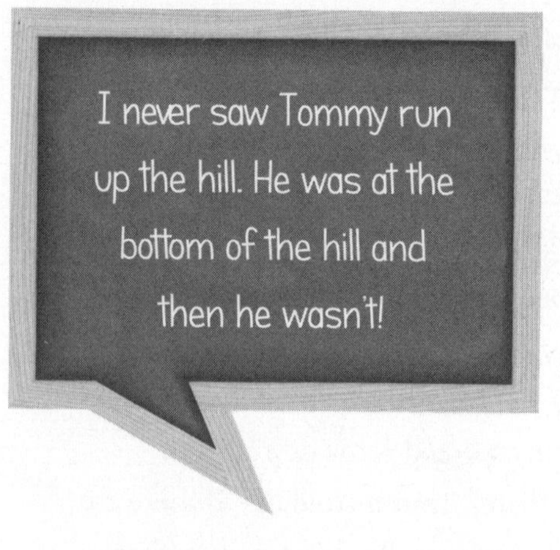

I never saw Tommy run up the hill. He was at the bottom of the hill and then he wasn't!

After catching our breath, we found big sticks and killed the two snakes.

"Hey, I've got to figure this out," Tommy said.

Tommy is smart and always has to have a logical reason for why something happens. He went back into the water where he was kneeling, jumped up, and ran up the hill. It took him about six seconds. He tried to jump out of the water, but he could only jump about three feet. Then he went to the top of the hill, ran down, and jumped, but it wasn't much farther. No matter how much Tommy tried, he couldn't duplicate the feat.

Now, I've read several stories about hysterical strength and how adrenaline allows humans to do things they normally couldn't do. In 2011, a University of South Florida football player named Danous Estenor lifted a 3,500-pound Cadillac Seville off a tow-truck driver who was pinned under its rear tire. In 2006, an Eskimo woman named Lydia Angiyou distracted a 705-pound polar bear long enough for hunters to arrive and rescue her seven-year-old son and two other children. And in 1982, a Georgia woman named Angela Cavallo lifted a 1964 Chevrolet Impala off her son after two jacks fell. Now, that's a muscle car!

I don't know what the Olympic record is for the standing broad jump, but my older brother broke it that day. Those two cottonmouth water moccasins put springs in his knees!

"You put camouflage on anything and it automatically becomes cool."

Floating Log

Hey, remember what I said about snakes being everywhere in Louisiana? News flash: snakes aren't even the state reptiles of Louisiana! It's the alligator. If you're walking through a swamp, lake, or river and don't step on a snake, chances are you'll step on an alligator. Bad news, Jack! The alligator is one mean sucker and, hey, it's a cold-blooded animal. I've seen alligators that are twenty feet long and weigh more than one thousand pounds. They'll eat fish, rats, crabs, birds, beavers, muskrats, raccoons, ducks, deer, and Milo the family dog. In Vietnam, I once saw an alligator wipe out an entire village on the Dong Nai River. It wasn't a pretty sight. A snake's bite might kill you, but it sure beats getting locked in the jaws of death!

Alligators live to be about fifty years old in the wild, and there's a reason they've survived for so long. They're the baddest predators in the swamp! They'll go through nearly three thousand teeth killing their prey before they die. When one tooth falls out, another one grows in its place. Nothing else has the courage to mess with them. Hey, how many arms does an alligator have? It depends what it ate for dinner, Jack! There are nearly two million alligators living in Louisiana, and I suspect more than half of them reside in our duck holes.

I've been running from alligators since I was a young boy. Momma taught me early that I could become an alligator's appetizer if I wasn't careful. We've never really hunted alligators, because we don't like to mess with them, but we're always mindful that one might be lurking close by when we're in the duck blind. Some time ago, I decided I wanted a pair of alligator boots. But every time I killed an alligator, it wasn't wearing any shoes!

Alligators are about the only game we haven't hunted—unless we had to. We never had much money growing up, but Daddy always made sure we had ammunition and guns for hunting because we wouldn't have much meat to eat if we didn't kill game. There were two guns in our house for us to use: Daddy's Browning semiautomatic sixteen-gauge shotgun and a Remington .22 that belonged to our uncle Al Robertson, which somehow wound up in our house. It was a bolt-action with a seven-shot clip. During duck season, we always managed to find a second shotgun to use.

When duck season opened my sixth-grade year, Daddy went out and bought us a couple of boxes of shotgun shells, like he did at the start of every season. Phil was in the eighth grade and was fourteen years old. On opening day, we jumped in the Ford Falcon, and Phil drove us—without a driver's license—to the duck hole, which was about fifteen miles from our house at Horseshoe Lake in Gilliam, Louisiana. Horseshoe Lake was one of our favorite holes to hunt mallard ducks. There were a bunch of willow trees growing at one end of the lake, and when the water level was high enough, mallard ducks sat in the hole. Phil knew the river was high, so it was time to go shoot mallard ducks.

"Let's go whack 'em," Phil said.

While we always had shotgun shells and guns to use, we were too poor to buy waders, which keep you dry when you're walking through the swamp to get to the duck hole. Blue jeans and tennis shoes were our waders! That's what we wore to wade through chilly water, regardless of what time of year it was. Hey, what do you get when you throw blue jeans and tennis shoes into a lake? A wet suit, Jack, and it made for some long days in the water!

When we arrived at Horseshoe Lake, we started to wade through the swamp. The water was about waist-deep, and it was early January, so the water was probably only twenty degrees. It was cold! After a few steps, Phil noticed a log sitting to the left of us.

"Hey, watch out," he told me. "Don't trip over that log."

I walked past the log and didn't think much of it.

After we found a spot in the duck hole that would conceal us—this was long before we started building duck blinds—we stood shaking in the water and waiting for the ducks. Fortunately, we had to wait only a few minutes before a flock of mallards came into sight. Phil called them over and they sailed right over us.

Boom! Boom! Boom! Boom!

We knocked down four mallard ducks, two apiece, on the first pass. Being the youngest brother, I waded through the ice-cold water and retrieved our kill. On my way back to the blind, Phil reminded me not to trip over the log.

"Hey, watch it," Phil said. "There's that log again."

"I see it," I said. "I'm not blind."

After a few more minutes, another bunch of mallards came into view. We both had guns, so we had three shots apiece. Phil called the ducks—he was really good at doing it even when he was young—and they flew right over our blind again. We each brought down three more ducks.

"Hey, there's a cripple over there," Phil said. "Shoot it again."

I looked to my left and there was a big mallard drake floating in the water by the log. He was still moving. I was closest to the wounded duck, so I aimed to shoot him again. But then I saw that the duck was facedown in the water, so I figured he was close to dying, so I wasn't going to waste another shell on him.

"Shoot him!" Phil yelled.

"Hey, he's dead," I said.

"No, he's not," Phil said. "Shoot him again!"

"Hey, trust me, he's deader than a lobster in butter sauce," I said. "I'm five feet from him. He's not going anywhere!"

That duck was spinning in the lake like water does when you're draining a bathtub. All of the sudden, the duck started spinning faster and faster. And then the big mallard drake was gone! It popped under the water like a cork does when you hook a two-pound crappie.

Then that twenty-foot log started moving! It sucked the mallard drake about two feet under the water! I looked at Phil and said, "Whoa, that log is an alligator!" We'd been walking around that stupid thing for thirty minutes!

Hey, news flash: we didn't walk on water that day, but we got out of it!

See ya later, alligator!

"I'm the master of distractions!
A couple of hand gestures and—*bam!*—
I'll pull the underwear clean off your butt!"

Dancing with Wolves

YOU'VE GOT TO UNDERSTAND one thing about me: I had four older brothers and one older sister. I was the baby boy of the Robertson family. All of my life, wherever I went, people were always comparing me to my older siblings. If I did something wrong in school, one of the teachers would undoubtedly say, "Well, good grief, Harold wouldn't have done that." If I did something foolish at church, my Sunday school teacher might say, "Well, goodness, Si, Judy wouldn't have done that."

Hey, news flash: I'm not Harold and I'm not Judy! I'm Silas Merritt Robertson! Growing up, I had an identity crisis because I was always being compared to someone else. All of my life, all I ever heard was "You're not doing it like so-and-so used to do it." Hey, guess what? I'm not so-and-so! I'm me!

My older brothers are the reason I'm afraid of the dark and

still have separation anxiety to this day. We'd go into the woods to hunt or play hide-and-seek, and they'd run back to our house without telling me. They'd leave me in the woods alone, and they especially liked to pull the trick when it was dark. I would cry, "Hey, where did y'all go? Hey, come back! Please come back!" But even when it was light outside, I didn't like to be left alone. Hey, would you want to be left alone with the thoughts being pondered in this head? My mind, it's wide open. It's like a hollow tunnel of air!

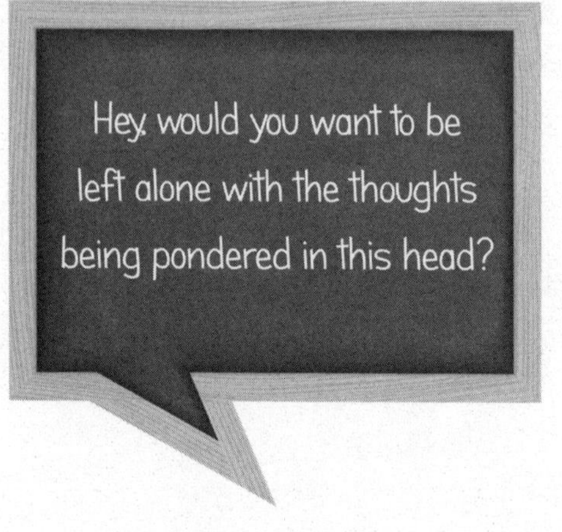

When Phil was in high school, he came home one Friday and said he and a couple of his football teammates were going camping on the Red River. They were going to go fishing the entire weekend and wouldn't be home until Sunday. Of course, the first thing out of Momma's mouth was, "Take your younger brother with you." Andy Yarbrough and another football player came by our house to pick up Phil and me, and they made me ride in the back, while the three of them planned our trip in the cab.

They decided I was going to drive our boat across the Red River to a camping site on the other side and wait for them to get there. We pulled up to the Red River and put our boat in the water, and then they showed me how to crank the motor.

"You see that big log on the riverbank over there?" Phil asked me. "Drive the boat over there, tie it up good, and don't let it get away. We're going to drive the truck the long way, go across the bridge, and come in the back way to the woods. When you get to the other side, you'll see a trail. Follow it up the hill and you'll find the campsite. We'll see you in a little while."

"How long before you get there?" I asked him.

"We'll get there before dark," Phil said.

I told him as long as they were there before dark, I'd do it. I was in the ninth grade and was still afraid of the dark!

They left in the truck, and I motored the boat across the river just as the sun was starting to set. I parked the boat, tied it down, and then walked down the trail Phil told me about. I walked into the woods and quickly realized there wasn't a house or another human being within forty miles of me. I was in the wilderness. I had no idea where I was, but I somehow found the campsite, which was about a fifteen-foot circle slap in the very middle of the woods.

I sat down and waited for Phil and his buddies to get there. After about twenty minutes, I noticed the sun was going down over the horizon. It was barely visible. Darkness was coming—and it was coming quickly! I was getting more nervous with every passing second.

Suddenly I heard a ruckus behind me. It was a pack of wild wolves! Along with being terrified of the dark, I was also afraid of wolves. They were actually coyotes, but we called them wolves. When you have wild dogs that are capable of dragging down large cattle and killing full-grown bulls, they are *wolves*.

I was trying to keep my composure, but the sounds of the wolves were getting closer and closer. I stood up and looked behind me, and I saw one of the wolves poke its head out of the brush! It was looking right at me! I looked to my right and saw tire tracks going up the other side of the woods. As I pondered what to do, I saw another wolf stick his head out of the brush and then another one. I knew I was in trouble, so I took off running down the barely visible road. Hey, Fred Astaire's got nothing on me, but I wasn't about to be dancing with wolves! After I took off running, the wolves jumped in behind me and were yelping. They were getting louder and louder. I knew there were a bunch of them behind me but I was too afraid to look back. I felt like Little Red Riding Hood running through the woods to Grandmother's house!

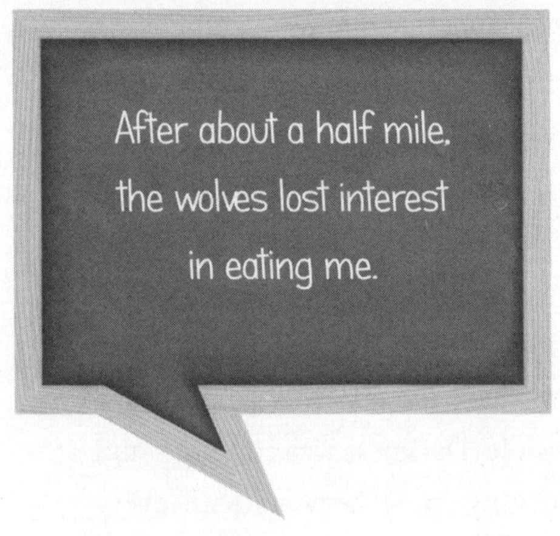

I was running in second gear and my legs were already burning. But I knew if I slowed down, they were going to catch me. I shifted to third gear and thought, *Goodness, I've never run this fast!* But the wolves were gaining on me, and I could almost smell them when the road turned from dirt to gravel. The wolves were getting even closer, so I switched it to fourth gear. Then the dirt road switched to pavement, and I figured I'd better run with whatever I had left in my tank. So I put the pedal to the metal and sprinted at full throttle. I put the hammer down and was running in fifth gear!

After about half a mile, the wolves started losing ground, and then they lost interest in eating me altogether. If someone had timed me with a stopwatch, I would have set every world record from forty yards to ten miles! From a sprint to a marathon, I was moving, Jack!

When I stopped running, I bent over and tried to catch my breath. My lungs were burning and my shirt was drenched in sweat. *Good grief, it's hot,* I thought. Then I smelled burning rubber. I figured some farmer was using tires to start a brush fire.

But then I looked down, and the rubber soles of the tennis shoes I was wearing were on fire. They were ablaze in flames!

Fortunately, it had rained the night before, so I stepped into a mud puddle and extinguished both of my shoes before my feet were badly burned.

Hey, where there's smoke, there's fire, and I wasn't going to stick around just to be burned—or eaten!

“I sting like a butterfly
and punch like a flea!”

Bumblebees

While I was growing up, my favorite thing to eat for breakfast during the winter was Momma's homemade buttermilk biscuits with honey. Boy, were they good! It's hard for me to get much sweeter, but I just love the pure taste of honey. Now my wife tells me all the time, "I need honey, honey." Look, when you get honey in your beard, it literally stays there for two weeks. When my wife kisses me, she's like, "Oh, that was good." She doesn't even know why. She just thinks I'm sweeter than most males.

When I was seven, I was sitting on our front porch one day with Phil and Daddy. We looked over at Mrs. Wilson's house next door and saw a swarm of bees that had flocked on the purple jasmine over her back door. The swarm of bees was as big around as two basketballs.

"Hey, we're fixing to have us a beehive," Daddy said.

He told Phil and me to get two chairs out of the kitchen while he went to get a hammer. We walked into the backyard, where we had a one-room shed. Daddy took the hammer and knocked a knot out of a pine board on the side of the shed. Then he took a saw and cut a board out of the shed. He cut two two-by-fours and nailed them to the inside of the shed, which is where the bees could build a honeycomb. He nailed a board back on the shed, which could easily be taken off and put back on to get access to the beehive whenever we wanted.

"Get one of those chairs and come with me," he told us.

We walked over to the purple jasmine and put the chair in front of it. Daddy told me to stand on the chair.

"What do you mean get on the chair?" I asked him. "Those bees are fixing to tear me up."

"Boy, get up here on a chair before I take off my belt and tear you up," he said. "If you don't get up here, you're going to get torn up one way or the other."

I figured the bee stings wouldn't hurt as bad as Daddy's belt, so I climbed on the chair. Daddy cut one end of the vine with his pocketknife and handed it to me.

"Be careful," he said. "Don't be shaking the vine and moving it around or we will get stung."

Daddy cut the other end of the vine and told Phil to take the chair back to the shed and put it next to the other one. Then we carefully carried the vine with the hive hanging from it to the chairs. We slowly sat the vine on the chairs, with thousands of bees swarming around it. I didn't even know bees liked jasmine. I thought their favorite flowers were bee-gonias and honeysuckle! Hey, what do I know?

"Go get me another chair," Daddy said.

I brought him another chair, and he sat down and waited. Finally, the queen bee rolled up to the top of the vine, and Daddy flicked her into the hole in the shed. Within a matter of seconds, every one of the other bees followed her into the hole.

For the next ten years, whenever we wanted honey, we went to the shed, pulled the two nails out, and robbed the honeycomb.

One time when it was time to rob the beehive, Phil walked out wearing two pairs of blue jeans, three football jerseys, a pair of gloves, and a homemade screen-wire helmet that went down to his shoulders. Phil was convinced he couldn't be stung!

We didn't trust him, so Momma, Tommy, and me sat in the kitchen watching him through the window. Phil took the nails out and pulled out the board but didn't know there was a large honeycomb on the back of the board he had just pulled out! He threw it to the ground and it landed faceup! Within a matter of seconds, you couldn't see Phil's legs. They were covered in bees! He took off running, swatting the bees with every step. I don't know how many times he was stung, but it was a lot, Jack!

Whenever we robbed the honey, we cut out the honeycomb, leaving just enough for the bees to survive. By the time we were done squeezing the honeycomb, we'd have about three gallons of honey, which lasted for nearly a year. It was another way we lived off the land.

Phil wasn't the only one stung by bees. When Phil was in the eighth grade and I was in the sixth, we went squirrel hunting one day. As usual, Phil was walking in front of me, and we were about to cross under a barbed-wire fence. As Phil crawled under the fence, he grabbed ahold of a fence post, which was rotted from the ground up. As soon as he grabbed the post, bumblebees started swarming out of it. Phil took off running, but I was already making my way under the barbed wire before I noticed them. I panicked and unknowingly ripped my blue jeans clean across my rear. I took off running behind Phil, with the bumblebees chasing us.

As I was running, I remembered something Momma told me: if bees are chasing you, you're supposed to fall down and lie still, because they follow your vibration. So I fell down and played dead. Unfortunately, I didn't know my jeans were ripped. There was now a full moon in the middle of the day! I looked up and it was like World War II, with Allied fighter pilots bombing Germany. My white underwear was showing, and the leader of the bees said, "Boys, there's our target!" They must have had advanced targeting systems, because they didn't miss! Trust me, it didn't take them long to get me off the ground. I was running and crushing my underwear at the same time.

When I got home, Momma said, "Well, drop your drawers." When I did, she busted out laughing.

"Hey, it's not funny," I said.

"If you could see it from my angle, it's funny," she said. "That's the biggest your butt has ever been."

Momma sat in the kitchen and pulled twenty-seven bee stingers out of my rear while she and Phil laughed.

Look, what's worse than being a fool? Fooling with a bee, Jack! Like the Beatles sang, let it bee!

"Jack, I can hurt you,
physically and metaphysically."

Chapter

10

Kamikaze Pilot

When Phil left to play football with Tommy at Louisiana Tech University in Ruston in 1964, Jan and I were the only kids left in the house with Momma and Daddy. I was older than Jan, but I didn't pick on her because my older brothers picked on me so much. I didn't think it was the right thing to do, because she was a girl. If she had been a boy, I'm sure things would have been much different.

After Phil left for college, I still had to finish my junior and senior years at North Caddo High School in Vivian, Louisiana. I was a pretty good football player in high school, but there was this problem: I weighed one hundred and thirty-five pounds when I was soaking wet. If I had weighed one hundred and sixty or one hundred and eighty pounds, like Tommy and Phil, I would have gotten a scholarship to Louisiana Tech, there's no doubt in my mind.

We grew up playing football in our backyard. We even had goalposts at one end, which Jimmy Frank and Harold made from a couple of oak-tree uprights and a sweet-gum crossbar. Our football field was about thirty yards long and half as wide. We played two-hands-below-the-waist touch football year-round. Jimmy Frank managed to bring home a few old footballs from his high school team, so we were always playing in the backyard.

I played quarterback during my freshman and sophomore seasons at North Caddo High School and then moved to end on offense, and cornerback and linebacker on defense. Tommy and Phil were really good football players—they played quarterback and halfback and were all-district and all-state players—so I had a pretty big legacy to live up to. I wasn't very big, but I was crazy enough and dumb enough not to know that the guy I was trying to tackle was twice as big as me! I didn't care how big he was—I was coming in there like a torpedo! I was a kamikaze pilot on the football field. I was the meanest and craziest one-hundred-and-thirty-five-pound player on the field! Because my older brothers picked on me growing up, I didn't have a problem taking on guys who were bigger than me.

I was crazy enough and dumb enough not to know that the guy I was trying to tackle was twice as big as me!

I really enjoyed playing football and probably got the most from my God-given abilities. I played in a couple of games as a senior in 1965, but then I broke my arm in a car accident and missed the rest of the season. When the season was over, my coach called me into his office and told me he could get me a tryout as a walk-on player at Louisiana Tech. He told me if I was good enough to make the team and worked hard to get bigger and stronger, the Louisiana Tech coaches might even be willing to give me a scholarship a couple of years down the road. My coach told me he thought I was talented enough to do it. When my coach was finished talking, I busted out laughing.

"Hey, I've been in the Louisiana Tech locker room with Phil and all those boys," I told him. "Excuse me, I've been in the locker room with Phil and all those *men*. I weigh one hundred and thirty-five pounds. I love the game, don't get me wrong, but I'm not stupid. I might not be the sharpest knife in the drawer, but I'm not the dullest one, either. I love football, but I'm not getting on the field with those men."

What I didn't tell my coach was that I wasn't even sure I wanted to go to college. I wasn't sure that four more years of school was the right thing for me. I'd had enough of going to class five days a week. Some parents get all bent out of shape because their kids don't want to go to college. Look, college isn't for everyone. I tried college ten times and never liked it. To me, college is an endurance test. You put up with four or five years of crap just for someone to hand you a piece of paper that says you have some sense.

Hey, news flash for all you people: I got sense without the paper! And I didn't have to endure four or five years of crap for someone to tell me I'm smart!

During the second half of my senior year of high school, we moved to Gonzales, Louisiana, because Daddy took a job there. I graduated from East Ascension High School in May 1966 with a bunch of strangers. It was terrible. Moving during my senior year really ruined my high school experience. I didn't get to graduate with the friends I grew up with, and we moved too late for me to make close friends with kids at my new school.

Right after high school, I went to work for Daddy as a welder's apprentice on an oil rig. It was grueling work. I did okay on the smaller rigs, but once we were on the bigger rigs, it was too much for me physically. I wasn't as strong as Phil and Tommy and didn't have their stamina. It didn't take me long to figure out that the off-shore drilling business wasn't for me.

A couple of months after high school ended, Momma informed me I was going to college, whether I wanted to go or not. While we never had much money, every one of my brothers and sisters graduated from college. Most of them even went back and received master's degrees.

"No, I don't want to go to college," I told Momma. "I don't want you and Daddy wasting your money."

"No, you're going to college," she said. "You don't have a choice."

"What don't you understand?" I asked her. "I'm going to go to college and do nothing but party."

Momma smiled at me and said, "Well, have a good one, because you're going to college."

I asked Momma why she wanted to waste her money on sending me to school.

"Because when you're out there digging ditches, I don't want you to say it was Mom and Dad's fault," she said. "We're giving you the opportunity to go to college."

Like it or not, it was up to me to make the most of it.

DUCK COMMANDER

"I'm like an owl.
I don't give a hoot."

The roe deer in Germany aren't nearly as big as the white-tailed deer we have in the United States, but they're just as tasty!

C Is Always the Best Answer

When I enrolled at Louisiana Tech in the fall of 1967, there were four Robertson brothers attending the same school. Tommy and Phil were playing on the football team, and Harold came there to get a master's degree after earning a bachelor's degree at Louisiana State University. It was like a family reunion.

While my older brothers were at Louisiana Tech to actually get an education, I went there for three quarters and did nothing but party for two of them. Hey, I told Momma that's what I was going to do, and I'm a man of my word!

I rarely went to class because I didn't have much interest in getting a college education. My partner in crime was Miss Kay's cousin Charles Hollier. We called him Tinker Bell, and he was flunking out of school, too. We pretty much had our own fraternity—Kappa Tappa Kegga. If I wasn't working at the mess hall or hunting and fishing with Phil and Tommy, I was drinking beer with Tinker Bell. He wasn't nearly as bad as I was about the partying. It didn't take me long to figure out there was always a party somewhere at college if you looked for it, and I usually took the time to find one!

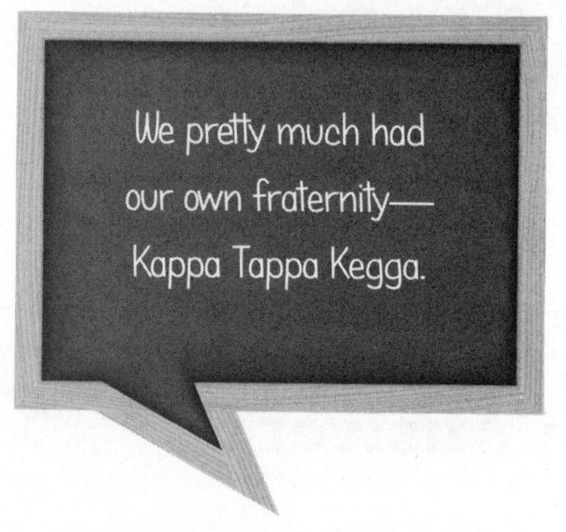

Every weekend, we had a get-together at either Tommy's house or Phil's. Both of them were married, so Miss Kay or Tommy's wife, Nancy, would cook us a big meal. They lived next to each other at the Vetville apartments, which the school built in 1945 to accommodate married veterans coming home from World War II. The red brick apartments were located on South Campus, about a mile from the main campus. Phil's front yard was always littered with fishing boats, motors, duck decoys, and on occasion, animal carcasses. His neighbors loved him!

During one gathering near the end of my third quarter at Louisiana Tech, Harold, Tommy, and Phil started getting on my case about not going to class. They were calling me stupid and lazy, and one of them said I wasn't smart enough to finish college.

"No, you're wrong there," I told them. "Being intelligent has nothing to do with this."

It's true that I was flunking out of school, and I'd only been there for a few months! I was already on double-secret probation with the dean as a freshman, and there wasn't much margin for error before I'd get thrown out of school. I really wasn't too worried about it. I made it to just enough classes so they couldn't kick me out of school for truancy, but I didn't expend much energy in studying for midterms and final exams.

With only a week to go in my third quarter, Tinker Bell came to me and asked me if I knew anyone who would give us the lecture notes for our classes.

"If I flunk out my daddy is going to kill me," Tinker Bell said.

"What do you think we can do about it now?" I asked him. "There's only a week until our finals, and we haven't been to class in a month."

"Hey, if you can get the notes, we'll hit the books," he said.

So I found a couple of girls who gave me copies of their notes from our classes. Hey, have you ever known a woman who could tell me no? Over the next four days, Tinker Bell and I studied seventy-four hours in a row. We never went to sleep! We went to the store and bought eight cases of soda pop. Look, I discovered that soda pop makes you drunk if you drink enough. This was back when they still used real sugar in sodas. We drank so many soda pops while studying that we were wired for four straight days. Hey, when we were done studying, I couldn't remember the last time I'd blinked! If someone had given me a cup of decaf coffee, I might have slipped into a coma! Thank goodness they hadn't invented Red Bull yet!

The day of my final exams, I did fine in my first three classes. I breezed through the final exams and was as alert as a one-legged man walking through a minefield in Vietnam. I was still wired from the caffeine. My last final exam was late in the afternoon and it was one of my least-favorite courses: Romance languages. Hey, what more could the professor have taught me that I didn't know already?

Look, the final exam was about one hundred questions. I answered about fifteen of them, and the next thing I knew the professor was shaking me! I fell asleep in the middle of the test!

"Wake up," he told me. "You don't have but ten minutes left to finish."

There was one thing in my favor: the test was multiple-choice! I didn't give a flip anyway, so I went through the answer sheet, filling in bubbles with my no. 2 pencil all the way down. The test sheet looked like an Etch A Sketch when I was done! Fortunately, I remembered that C is always a good answer! It took me only five of the ten minutes to complete the exam. I handed it to the professor and skipped out of the classroom.

I figured I had probably taken my last college exam, so I gave Tommy one hundred dollars to buy us some steaks. Phil and Tommy were going to grill steaks for us the next day at an end-of-the-quarter party at Tommy's house. I had a job in college, so I usually had a few more bucks than my brothers. I worked in the freezer department of the university's cafeteria. The cooks prepared turkeys and then sent them down to us to wrap and freeze. When the cooks were ready to serve the turkeys to students, they'd thaw them out and warm them up. One day, I went to work without eating lunch. Every time a turkey came down, I picked a little piece of meat off it. Hey, when you've picked forty turkeys, you've had a full meal!

At the end of the day, the foreman called us together.

"Hey, if you're hungry, take some time and go upstairs and eat," he said.

Then he walked us into the freezer. There was a bare turkey

carcass sitting there. It was so naked I wanted to find it some clothes! Its breasts were sticking out and its legs had been picked to the bone! I guess I was a little hungrier than I thought!

Fortunately, the boss man didn't fire me. It was a good job, and I always had a little money in my pockets when I was a student.

When I arrived at Tommy's house the next day, Nancy wouldn't open the front door for me. She was looking through the peephole, and then she started ranting and raving at me. The woman went slap insane!

"What is your problem?" Nancy said.

She worked in the registrar's office at Louisiana Tech, so I figured she'd seen my grades. I knew I'd be on the next bus back to Gonzales, Louisiana, when Momma and Daddy found out I'd flunked out.

"Are you going to let me in?" I asked her.

She stood behind the door and hollered at me for the next five minutes.

"Hey, look, if you don't open the door, I'm going to go back to the dorm," I said.

She opened the door and screamed, "No, you're not. Get in here and sit down!" She pointed her finger at me and said, "Did you go check your grades?"

"No," I told her. "I couldn't care less what my grades are, because I'm not coming back."

She proceeded to chew my butt out for the next hour.

"You really didn't go look at your grades, did you?" she asked.

"No, I know I flunked out," I told her. "I don't care what my grades are. I know one thing—college is not for me."

By then, Tommy, Phil, and Harold were there, and they

started in on me as well. They were calling me stupid and lazy again.

"Hey, y'all might as well get off of that," Nancy told them.

"What do you mean?" Phil asked her.

"He partied for six months and never went to class and nearly made the dean's list," Nancy said. "He was three points from making an A average! He's obviously not too dumb!"

Hey, I told you C is always the correct answer.

DUCK COMMANDER

"One time in Vietnam, I saw a grizzly bear riding a scooter."

Big Oaf

EVEN THOUGH I EARNED my way onto the list of possible candidates for Louisiana Tech University's honors program, I didn't return to school for the next academic quarter in the spring of 1968. I knew going into my freshman year that college probably wasn't for me, but I gave it the old college try, and, hey, I proved to my older brothers that maybe they weren't smarter than me.

For whatever reason, I couldn't get into the routine of going to college. One of the things that really turned me off about higher education was that I met a lot of guys who had college degrees, and they told me they spent most of their time in classes like basket weaving and pottery. Then they'd tell me they majored in psychology! Hey, if you're going to become a psychologist, why are you learning how to make a basket and an ashtray? It doesn't make any sense to me. Some of the smartest people I know have sixth-grade educations and started working in the seventh grade because their families needed them to work. Conversely, some of the most educated idiots I've ever met have a master's degree or PhD. They couldn't pour urine out of a boot with the instructions written on the heel!

Breaking the news to Momma and Daddy wasn't easy. Even though I'd warned them about what was probably going to happen if they sent me to college, I knew they would be disappointed because each of my brothers and sisters was in school. They wanted me to have the same opportunity, and I'm sure they made some big sacrifices to make it happen. I think they might have even mortgaged the family farm to pay my tuition.

I broke the news to Daddy when we were driving to a duck hole one morning during Christmas break.

"Daddy, I ain't going back to school," I told him. "I know you and Momma really want me to go, but it ain't for me."

Daddy looked at me and sadly shook his head. I could see the disappointment in his eyes.

"Si, after all the sacrifices your mother and I made over the last few months to come up with the money to send you to college, you still say 'ain't,'" he said.

That was the end of our conversation.

After three quarters of college, I decided it was time for me to major in Si-cology. I was ready to get on living my life and finding my place in the world.

Of course, I knew Uncle Sam probably had other ideas for me. Phil, Tommy, and Nancy warned me that if I dropped out of college, I would probably get drafted into the military and be sent to Vietnam. American military advisers had been involved in the

Vietnam War since 1950, and then our involvement escalated in the early 1960s. The number of American troops in Vietnam tripled in 1961 and tripled again in 1962, and then U.S. combat troops were first deployed there in 1965 to fight the Vietcong and the spread of communism.

After Congress passed the Military Selective Service Act of 1967, if you were a male, at least eighteen years old, single, and not in college, you were going to Vietnam. Hey, I was four for four, Jack! Two weeks after I withdrew from Louisiana Tech, my draft papers arrived at my parents' house. I opened the letter and it basically said, "Uncle Sam wants you—right now!" A few weeks later, I reported to the army recruitment office in Shreveport, Louisiana, where they gave me a physical and determined I was fit to serve my country. Was there ever any doubt?

I went home to Dixie for about a month, and then I boarded a train in Shreveport in April 1968 for basic training at Fort Benning outside Columbus, Georgia. As soon as I stepped off the train, the drill sergeants were in my face screaming, "Get down, maggot!" My basic training lasted eight weeks, and it was miserable. It was the start of a hot, sticky Georgia summer. Hey, it was so hot and humid that I saw trees fighting over dogs. That's how thirsty they were! Even the squirrels were using suntan lotion! Growing up in Louisiana, I was used to

the heat and humidity, but it's a lot more unbearable when you're going through basic training.

My basic training was especially hard because I had two drill sergeants with completely different personalities The first one lasted only a couple of weeks and left because of a death in his family. I didn't even know the man, but it wasn't very long until I was missing him more than my momma! After he left, a bunch of us were sitting on the barrack steps waiting for the next guy who was going to make our lives miserable. We saw a taxicab coming down the main road in the base, and there was something wrong with it. Most automobiles are equally balanced on four tires. But this taxi was leaning heavily to the right side! It looked like the right side of the taxi was going to grind the asphalt on the road!

When the taxi pulled up in front our barrack, King Kong climbed out of the backseat. My new drill sergeant was about six feet eight inches tall and weighed four hundred and fifty pounds! He was wearing a Smokey the Bear hat that I could have taken a bath in! The guy was enormous! He was a huge man! His name was Sergeant Oliver, but we called him the Big Oaf behind his back. It seemed that his objective was to make my life as painful as possible.

While the Big Oaf was determined to break me, I will give him credit for one thing. Fort Benning is an army Ranger base. Look, you do not walk on a Ranger base—you run everywhere! We ran to the mess hall, showers, latrines, barracks, and everywhere else we went. We ran while brushing our teeth! You did not walk; you did the airborne shuffle, which is running. As large as the Big Oaf was, he actually ran right next to us everywhere we went. You had to respect the man for that.

Big Oaf

One day in basic training, the Big Oaf woke us at five A.M. and informed us we were going on a ten-mile run. We ate breakfast and then loaded our packs onto our backs. About an hour later, after most of us had puked up our breakfast, the Big Oaf yelled, "Men, you're doing a great job. We've already covered five miles!"

I guess we felt like the end was in sight, because we picked up our pace. About an hour later, as we were really beginning to feel the weight of our packs, the Big Oaf yelled, "You're doing fine, men. Just fine! We should reach the starting point any minute now!"

As much as he tried, I was never really intimidated by the Big Oaf. Since I was from a large family and had so many older brothers, people getting in my face and yelling at me never really bothered me. But some guys couldn't handle it, and their lives were miserable during basic training. I always thought the hazing was funny, but my drill sergeants never found it to be very humorous. They didn't like that I was laughing or smiling the entire time. Somehow, I made it out of basic training alive.

On the day I graduated from basic training in June 1968, we were wearing our dress greens on the drill fields as we waited for the ceremony to start. The Big Oaf got in my face and was screaming at me again. It was almost as if he wanted one more shot at me. He started yelling, and, of course, I busted out laughing. I couldn't help it. It made him so mad. He yelled his favorite words: "Drop, maggot!"

I stood there and laughed at him.

"Hey, I'm in my dress greens," I told him. "I'm not getting down and getting dirty. You're out of your mind."

The Big Oaf looked at me in disbelief.

"Am I hearing you say what I think you said, Private Robertson?" he asked.

"Yeah, I ain't getting down and dirty," I told him.

"Am I going to have to put you in the front, leaning, rest position, maggot?" he asked.

"Are you serious?" I said.

"Dead serious," he yelled.

So I dropped and did twenty-five push-ups. I jumped up and was smiling again.

"Wrong answer, maggot!" the Big Oaf yelled.

I dropped down and gave him twenty-five more. I was in the greatest shape of my life, so it wasn't a problem, but I was obviously still as stubborn as a mule.

It took three hundred push-ups before the Big Oaf finally wiped the smile off of my face.

With my deployment to Vietnam right around the corner, I feared I wouldn't be smiling for much longer.

DUCK COMMANDER

"Your beard is so dumb,
it takes two hours to watch *60 Minutes*!"

Passing the Test

ONE OF THE MAIN reasons I left college and went into the military was because I didn't want to have to attend class—and I really didn't like taking tests. What's the first thing the army did with me once I graduated from basic training?

Uncle Sam gave me a test!

To assemble an effective fighting force, the United States Army believed it needed the right kind of man as well as the right kind of equipment in Vietnam. Hey, it didn't take the army long to realize it had the right kind of man on its hands, but it had to figure out what kind of equipment to put in my hands to make me a killing machine. When I joined the army, there were over three hundred occupations available. The army wanted to make sure it didn't waste my talents and abilities, so it gave me a long test to determine how I could help America the most.

Fortunately for me, it was a multiple-choice test!

Before the army assigned me to a unit, I was required to take the Army Classification Battery (ACB), which graded incoming soldiers in areas such as electronics repair, general maintenance, mechanical maintenance, clerical skills, radio code, surveillance and communications, and, of course, combat. If a soldier scored well in electronics repair, he would probably be assigned to something like missile or air defense repair. If a soldier scored well in general maintenance, he might be assigned to areas like construction and utilities. Someone who scored well in combat might end up in the infantry or armor units, and high marks in clerical skills usually correlated well to desk jobs.

Shortly after I was assigned to Advanced Infantry Training at Fort Lee in Virginia in the fall of 1968, I took the ACB for the first time. Hey, I can recite the alphabet after drinking a twelve-pack of soda pop while blindfolded and standing on one leg, so I knew the army's test wouldn't be a problem. A few days after I completed the test, my commanding officer called me into his office.

"Hey, Robertson, your smoke-blowing days are over," he told me.

"What are you talking about?" I asked him.

"The ole country-boy act you've got going isn't going to cut it anymore," he said. "You're in the top five percent in the world."

"What world are you talking about?" I asked.

"What don't you understand?" he said. "You just scored higher than ninety-five percent of the army on the ACB. You're on the fast track."

Now, you have to understand one thing: people were bombing the ACB worldwide in the army in 1968. It was a big scandal throughout the military, and the Pentagon couldn't figure out if the test was flawed or if its troops really weren't that smart! A seventy was considered a passing score on the ACB. I scored a sixty-nine! Somehow, I was still better than nearly everybody else entering the army at the time.

When I saw my test results, I was surprised to see the areas in which I scored the highest. I scored extremely high in architecture and engineering, followed by clerical, mechanical maintenance, and surveillance and communications. As I sat there looking at my scores, I pondered what my vocation was going to be in the military. Would I be a spy? Hey, I'm kind of like Victoria. She has her secrets and so do I! Need a secret Santa? I'm your man! The Vietcong would never detect me behind enemy lines. I'm the master of distractions! A couple of hand gestures and—*bam!*—I'll pull the underwear clean off your butt!

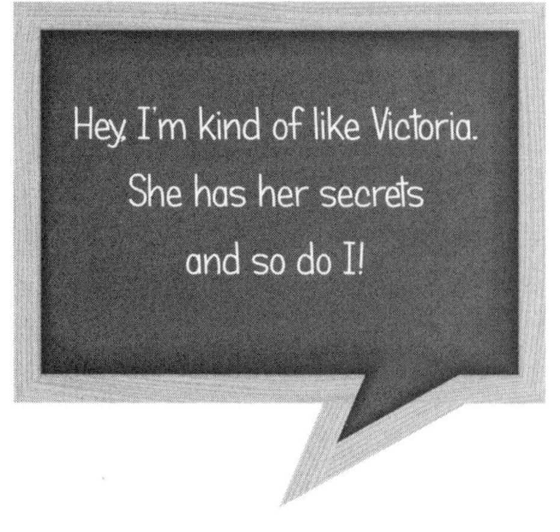

While espionage sounded enticing, so did the possibility of being a mechanic or engineer. My brothers and I were always building and fixing things when we were growing up. If our bicycles or boat motors broke, we had to fix them because we sure weren't getting new ones. We built forts, bridges, duck blinds, and dams when we were young. How much different could Vietnam really be from Louisiana?

I even thought about going into the military police or becoming a cook. Hey, I'd rather eat my cooking than what I ate in Vietnam. I am the MacGyver of cooking. If you bring me a piece of bread, cabbage, coconut, mustard greens, pig's feet, pinecones, and a woodpecker, I'll make a great chicken pot pie. One time I cooked a big pot of soup. The label on the packaging said to empty the entire contents into the broth. Well, Miss Kay got a twenty-cent coupon in her bowl of soup. At least she saved some money on her next trip to the grocery store!

There were so many career choices in the army, and it was difficult to pick only one.

At first, the army sent me to sniper school after I graduated from Advanced Infantry Training. I guess they figured if I could shoot squirrels and ducks, I could hold my own on the battlefield and shoot Charlie. But I was only in sniper school for about a week. After a few days, I asked one of the instructors, "Hey, when are we going to shoot?" He told me we had three more weeks of classes before we would get our rifles. Well, you know how I am about attending classes.

"Uh-uh," I told him. "Send me to a unit."

Now, just because the army gives you a test doesn't necessarily mean it's going to put you in a job that best utilizes your skills. The army tried to put people in areas where they could help it the most, but they weren't always good at doing it. If the army had a truck driver and a computer engineer, you would think the former would drive a truck and the latter would work with computers. Uh-uh, not in the army. No, let's switch it. The truck driver worked on computers and the computer engineer drove the truck. The army liked to break a man down and mold him into what it wanted. It didn't make any sense, but that's how they did it.

I was assigned to be a readiness noncommissioned officer (NCO) in the areas of materials supply and accounting. My job was supervising supply requests, receipt, and storage, and maintaining an account of individual and organizational equipment. I was like the equipment manager of the army. If a soldier wanted something in Vietnam, he had to come see me. Need a new pair of socks? I'm the man to see. Need ammunition for your M16? I'm the guy. Most days, it was a pretty smooth process when soldiers came to see me. But if I was having a bad day, hey, all bets were off. Grab a Snickers bar, because you're not going anywhere for a while, Jack!

I was also involved in the day-to-day operations of transporting soldiers, mobilization planning, maintenance, pay, and guard duty. I was basically the commander's right-hand man. I did whatever he told me to do. Now, I did not wear hard stripes. There were hard-striped soldiers in Vietnam and there were specialists. A hard-striped soldier specialized in combat and war; a specialist was someone like the military police or a medic. We were specialists in something other than actual fighting. Everybody in the army was trained to fight, but some of us were put in areas of support off the battlefield.

After I graduated from Advanced Infantry Training, they sent the notice of deployments to our barrack. Obviously, everyone was hoping to avoid Vietnam, but I always knew that was where I was going to be deployed. I didn't know why, but I knew in the bottom of my heart that's where I was going. Well, guys with last names that started with A to R were sent to Germany. Somehow the list of last names beginning with R ended before Robertson. Then I and every guy with a last name after mine were sent to Vietnam. I was the only soldier from my company who was immediately deployed to Vietnam. Later, I found out the guys who went to Germany were only there for a couple of weeks of training and then were sent to Vietnam.

A couple of weeks before I was scheduled to leave for Vietnam, a few of my buddies and I went to see a movie during a weekend pass. John Wayne had just finished making a war movie about Vietnam. It was called *The Green Berets*. It was about an army colonel who picked two teams of Green Berets to complete a dangerous mission in South Vietnam. We went to see the movie at a theater, and it scared every one of us. Even though the movie was fictional, the images looked real to me. It was the first time I'd seen war. I knew Vietnam was where I was fixing to go, and it didn't look like a very nice place. In fact, it scared me to death.

DUCK COMMANDER

“Hey, I gotta work
with what I’ve got.
It’s called improv-isavation.”

Chapter 14

Good Morning, Vietnam!

MY FEET HIT THE ground in South Vietnam on October 19, 1968. Several guys told me their stories about flying into Vietnam, and a lot of them were pretty wild and scary. They told me about being bombarded with rockets and missiles as their jets landed. My arrival was pretty uneventful. We flew into the Can Tho airfield and climbed off the plane. It was eerily quiet until somebody said, "Welcome to Nam."

Perhaps the thing I remember most about arriving in Vietnam is being overwhelmed by the smell of fish. Now, I grew up on the river, and my brothers and I were always fishing or cleaning fish, but this was different. I smelled fish everywhere I went. The South Vietnamese ate a lot of fish, and commercial fishing was one of their major sources of income. It wasn't necessarily a bad smell, but it was the only thing you could smell! Hey, how do you stop a fish from smelling? You cut off its nose, Jack! I was ready to cut my nose off after only a couple of weeks in Vietnam. When I returned home after my twelve-month enlistment, I couldn't stand the smell of fish. I couldn't even stomach the smell when I went to Phil's house on the Ouachita River years later. It's one of the reasons Phil gave up fishing altogether after he quit working as a commercial fisherman. Phil was around fish so much as a commercial fisherman that he didn't want to be near them after he quit. I'm the same way when it comes to fish, even more than forty years after I left Vietnam.

Can Tho is the largest city in the Mekong Delta and is about seventy-five miles southwest of Ho Chi Minh City (which was called Saigon when I was in Vietnam). It sits near the Mekong River and is the delta's commercial hub. Today, Can Tho produces about half the country's rice. Rice paddies, low-lying marshes, and mangrove swamps surround the city, as does a vast system of natural and man-made canals. There were floating markets where you could buy fish, fruits, and vegetables. I'm sure it's a beautiful city now, but it wasn't very picturesque when I was there, at least not to me.

While I was deployed to Vietnam, I lived in a three-story hotel in downtown Can Tho. The army base in Can Tho wasn't big enough to have barracks to house all of the troops, so a bunch of soldiers stayed in hotels with names like the Pink Palace, Cheap Charlie's, and the Mekong Hotel. From what I remember, the hotel I stayed in was far from a palace, and I'm sure the rent was pretty cheap for Uncle Sam.

Fortunately for me, I arrived in Can Tho about nine months after the Tet Offensive. On January 31, 1968, the Vietcong and North Vietnamese launched a series of surprise attacks against

South Vietnam, American forces, and our allies during what was supposed to be a two-day cease-fire during the Tet lunar new year celebration. More than seventy thousand North Vietnamese and Vietcong troops attacked more than one hundred cities and towns in South Vietnam, including the Can Tho airfield, which is where I primarily worked.

It took American forces about three days to clear Can Tho of Vietcong troops. Although U.S. and South Vietnamese forces fought back most of the attacks, the Tet Offensive was a major turning point in the Vietnam War. The North Vietnamese and Vietcong put the U.S. on notice that they were more organized and stronger than we suspected.

In a civil war like was happening in Vietnam, it's hard to figure out who's fighting for what side. What most people don't understand about the military is that if you go to a foreign country, sometimes they don't speak your language and don't want you there. In other words, most of the people there don't like you. Hey, I wasn't trying to make friends in Vietnam. My only goal was to complete my twelve months and get back to Louisiana as quickly as possible.

Although I was there for only one year, it was a really difficult time in my life. It was the first time I'd been away from my parents, brothers, and sisters, and I was thousands of miles across the Pacific Ocean from home. I wasn't quite sure why we were fighting in a land so far from home, but I was bound and determined not to get myself killed while I was there.

One of the things I remember most about being in Vietnam is watching movies on the roof of the hotel where I was living. We had a movie projector set up and we sat and watched movies nearly every night. When I first got to Vietnam, I sat on the roof and watched guys going out. They'd leave sober, but then they'd come staggering back drunk a few hours later. I always thought, *That's not going to be me*. But a few months later, guys sat on the same roof and watched me come back stumbling drunk.

Believe me, it was easy to find a drink in Can Tho if you wanted one. Of course, you had to be careful where you went because the Vietcong also used Can Tho as an R & R spot. Charlie would dress like a Vietnamese peasant and walk right into town for some rest and relaxation. Most of the watering holes were filled with bar girls, some of whom made so much money from American troops that they bought estates in the countryside! You could find a drink and a girl whenever you wanted for the right price.

It was the only time in my life when I drank heavily. Now, I partied during my short stay at Louisiana Tech, but it was different in Vietnam. I was largely drinking to forget where I was. When you're in a place like Vietnam, you get to a point where you don't care anymore. You're in a place that's foreign to you, and you know for a fact that many people there hate you and will kill you if they get the chance. It really does something to your mind to know that many of the people living around you don't like you and want you to die.

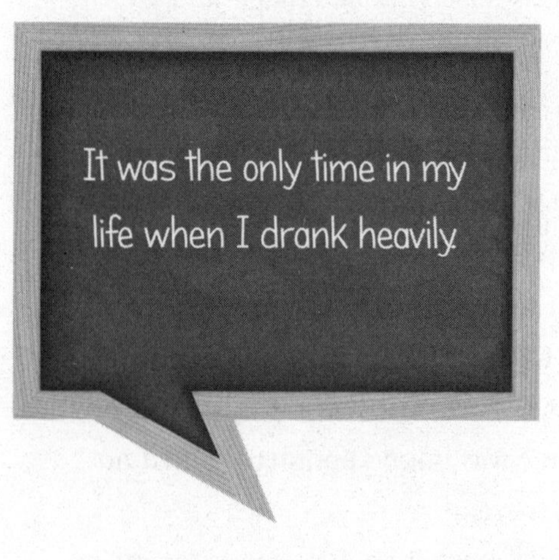

Believe it or not, I came close to killing two people in Vietnam. Shortly after I arrived there, I was on guard duty in a tower at the airfield. I had an M14 rifle and a slingshot. Guess what Vietnamese children liked to do for fun? They liked to throw rocks at the American guards in the watchtowers. I kept a handful of rocks in one of my ammunition pouches just in case I became a target. One day while I was on guard duty, a rock nailed me on the side of my head. I touched my hair and my hand was covered in blood. I thought I'd been shot! I looked down and saw a Vietnamese boy laughing and pointing at me. I clicked my gun and started to aim to shoot him. Thankfully, I came to my senses and didn't do it. The next time I was hit by a rock, I returned fire with my slingshot. Before too long, I was having regular slingshot wars with the Vietnamese children around our airfield. It didn't take them long to figure out that I was a better shot than them!

The other time I nearly took a life, I was waiting for a truck to pick me up and felt a tap on my kidney. I turned around and saw a huge snake staring right at me. A Vietnamese woman—we called them momma-sans—had a boa constrictor wrapped around her neck. It was big enough to eat her if it wanted. "You want to buy the snake?" she asked me. I grabbed my gun and was fixing to shoot her and the snake! I'm not sure if I could have ever shot Charlie if I had to, but I was ready to shoot her!

Here's how bad it got for me during my twelve months in Vietnam: A buddy and me came up with the brilliant idea of us volunteering to be door gunners in helicopters. At the time, the life expectancy of a door gunner in Vietnam was about three days. When one was killed, the army put another soldier in his place. It was about the most dangerous job in the war, and my buddy and I were getting ready to volunteer for it! Fortunately, I came to my senses before we signed up. I must have been insane to even be thinking about it!

I drank so much beer and whiskey in Vietnam that I decided I would quit drinking alcohol altogether once I returned home. I saw what alcohol was doing to me in Vietnam and realized I needed to stop for good.

But I had to make it home alive for that to happen.

DUCK COMMANDER

"I don't like uniforms. Hey, right now I want to kick my own butt!"

Chapter 15

Deuce and a Half

SHORTLY AFTER I ARRIVED in Vietnam, some of the soldiers who had been there for a while gave me a few tips on how to survive. One of the most important things they told me was to make sure all of my personal belongings were locked down at all times because the Vietnamese loved to steal from Americans. Now, Momma and Daddy had taught me that stealing was a sin—"Thou shalt not steal" is one of the Ten Commandments—so I found it hard to believe that the nice Vietnamese people would steal from the very people who were sent there to protect them.

"What are you talking about?" I asked one of the soldiers.

"These people will steal anything and everything," he said.

"Hey, I don't believe you," I said. "Give me an example."

"These people will steal your radio and leave the music," he said.

"Now, that's a thief!" I told him.

It didn't take me long to figure out he was telling the truth. One of my daily duties in Vietnam was to drive troops from our hotel to the Can Tho airfield in the morning and then back to the hotel at the end of the workday. I transported the troops in a two-and-a-half-ton cargo truck—we called it a deuce and a half—and it didn't have a canvas over the bed or rails on its sides. The army started using the M35 family of trucks in 1949 and utilized them all the way through Operation Iraqi Freedom. Obviously, they were good, dependable trucks. The truck had a ten-tire configuration, so it could carry as much as twenty thousand pounds of cargo on the road. It was a very versatile truck in a war zone.

One day, before I made the drive back to the hotel, which was only about one mile, I walked around my truck and gave it a thorough inspection. I was required to inspect the truck every time I climbed behind the steering wheel to make sure it was working properly and hadn't been booby-trapped by the Vietcong. I saw that each of the ten tires was there and was inflated properly and didn't notice anything else suspicious. After I gave a thumbs-up, the troops loaded up in the bed of the truck, and I pulled out to drive back to the hotel. But on this particular day, for whatever reason, there was a lot of traffic in downtown Can Tho, so the drive took a little longer than usual. Even though the traffic was crazy, I never had to completely stop and probably didn't drive less than ten miles per hour.

I arrived at the hotel and the troops started to unload. I locked up the steering wheel, locked the doors, and then started to walk to the hotel.

"Hey, Robertson," one of the soldiers yelled to me. "You're missing a tire."

"Yeah, sure," I said.

"No, seriously, you're missing a tire off the back," he said.

"Good grief," I said, knowing the soldier was probably trying to play a trick on me.

I walked back to the truck and saw a lug nut sticking out of where one of the dual back tires used to be. Someone stole a tire while I was driving back to the hotel!

"Y'all didn't see anything?" I asked a few of the soldiers, who had gathered around the truck.

"Nah," one of them said. "We didn't see anything."

"Hey, look, all of the tires were on this truck when we left the airfield," I said. "I never stopped. Y'all were sitting in the back. You didn't see anything?"

"Nope," one of them said.

"Something's not right with this picture," I said. "You're sitting above the tires, you idiots. You had to have seen or heard something!"

"Nah, we didn't hear or see anything," one of them said.

I sat there looking at the lug nut while scratching my head and trying to figure out what had just happened.

"The lug nuts must have been loose," one of them said. "The tire must have fallen off."

We didn't have loose lug nuts on a deuce and a half. When we put tires and lug nuts on a deuce and a half, we had to stand on the tire iron to make sure they were tight. There wasn't any way the lug nuts were loose.

The only plausible explanation was that a Vietnamese person

stole a tire while I was driving down the road! NASCAR pit crews don't work that fast, Jack! I know it might be hard to believe, but it's exactly what happened!

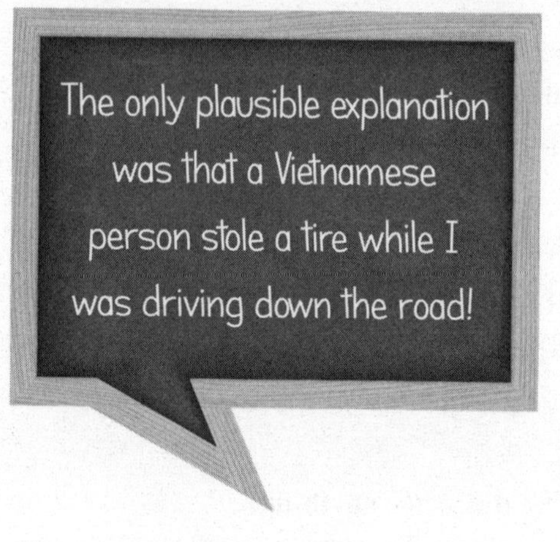

Now, I've never had much patience for thieves. A thief is someone who is too lazy to work for what he wants, so he'll steal from someone else. I've read about smart thieves and not-so-smart thieves. In the Czech Republic last year, a band of thieves stole a ten-ton bridge! They arrived at a depot and informed the workers they'd been hired to disassemble the bridge to make way for a new one. The thieves walked away with millions of dollars in scrap metal before anyone figured out the bridge wasn't supposed to come down! Now, that's a thief, Jack!

Last year, a man snatched a woman's purse while she walked through a park in Georgia. When police located a man matching the suspect's description, they put him into a police cruiser and returned to the scene of the crime. Police told him to exit the vehicle and face the victim for an ID. He looked and her and said, "Yeah, that's the woman I robbed." Hey, at least he was honest!

The Lord tells us we're supposed to love everyone, so I don't hate thieves. I guess there's even a place in heaven for them. At least I can respect their ingenuity, and they're still more likable than most of the attorneys I've met.

One day, a teacher, a petty thief, and a lawyer died and went to heaven. St. Peter met them at the gates and said, "Sorry, heaven's about filled up, so you'll have to answer a question correctly to come in."

St. Peter looked at the teacher and asked, "What's the name of the famous ocean liner that sank in the Atlantic Ocean after hitting an iceberg?"

"The *Titanic,*" she said.

"Correct," St. Peter said. "Come on in."

Then St. Peter turned to the thief.

"How many people died on the ship?" he asked.

"Ooooh, that's a difficult question," the thief said. "But I saw the movie, and I think the answer is about one thousand and five hundred."

"Close enough," St. Peter said. "Come on in."

Finally, St. Peter turned to the lawyer.

"Name each of the deceased," he said.

Hey, let me tell you how bad the Vietnamese were about stealing. One of the army's platoons had set up shop on a mountainside above a village in the Mekong Delta. They were on a reconnaissance mission, going from village to village to determine whether Charlie had infiltrated them or not. For whatever reason, they kept burning up power generators and losing electricity at their base camp. They couldn't figure out what was happening. No matter what they did, they were burning up brand-new generators every night! The motor officer was yanking his hair out trying to figure it out. Every night before they turned them on, they checked the oil and made sure they were operating correctly, but they kept burning up in the middle of the night.

Finally, one of the officers decided he was going to get to the bottom of it. The generators usually ran on two hundred and twenty volts, but you could convert them to four hundred and forty volts. One night, the officer shut down the generators and switched them to four hundred and forty volts. After he turned the generators back on, the village became extremely bright. It looked like the Las Vegas Strip! All of the sudden, it sounded like fireworks. TVs, radios, and all the other appliances in the village were blowing up! It looked like a firefight in the bush.

The officer sent a few soldiers down the hillside and they discovered a string of extension cords that probably covered two miles from the generators to the village! Every night, one of the Vietnamese villagers snuck up the hill and plugged the cord into the generators. The Vietnamese watched TV all night on Uncle Sam!

Now, that's a thief, Jack!

DUCK COMMANDER

"I'm like Aretha Franklin.
Don't get any R-E-S-P-E-C-T
round this joint!"

Chapter 16

Guard Duty

One of my first jobs in Vietnam was working in a warehouse in the back of Can Tho Airfield. Every chance I had, I rode in a rough-terrain forklift with the guy who was operating it. I rode with him for about six months to learn how to drive it. I figured if something happened to the guy who was driving it, I'd be next in line to jump into the driver's seat. Driving the forklift would keep me out of harm's way if nothing else. Hey, I might have been born at night, but it wasn't last night, Jack!

Mostly, we loaded and unloaded supplies from cargo planes and moved crates to where they needed to be. But every now and then, we'd get in a Jeep, deuce and a half, or five-ton cargo truck that had been shot up by the Vietcong. Our job was to go over the vehicle and strip it down, taking every working part we could possibly use. We'd set aside the tires, wheels, motors, batteries, transmissions, carburetors, water pumps, and any other parts we could salvage. Normally, only the metal frame of the Jeep or cargo truck was left. We'd pick up the truck or Jeep frame with the forklift and drop it into a pond at the back of the airfield.

Well, as I suspected, the guy who was driving the forklift left Vietnam when his enlistment in the army was over. A sergeant came up to me and said, "Hey, we need somebody to drive the forklift. Do you know how to do it?"

"Hey, can you crank it?" I asked.

"I've been watching you ride around with him for six months," the sergeant said. "You never saw him crank it?"

"Nah, I never saw him do it," I said. "Do you want me to do everything around here?"

So the sergeant climbed into the forklift and cranked it up.

"Get out of the way," I told him.

From that day forward, my job was to drive the rough-terrain forklift in the warehouse and motor pool at the airfield. Some nights, I also had to take my turn on guard duty at the airfield. I usually guarded the motor pool, where they kept the Jeeps, trucks, and other vehicles we used in the army. The motor pool extended all the way to the edge of the pond where we dumped the stripped truck and Jeep frames.

Guard Duty

One day, we had a brand-new deuce-and-a-half diesel engine come to us in a metal box. New engines were like gold in Vietnam. Most of our vehicles were pretty outdated, so it was rare that we acquired new equipment. The technicians in the motor pool took the engine out of the box, hooked a battery to it, and cranked it to make sure it was running properly. Then they bolted it back down because they planned to put it in a deuce and a half the next morning.

That night, a buddy and I were on guard duty. We had to cover a pretty big compound, so we started the night walking the fence in opposite directions. About an hour later, we hooked back up again for a cigarette break.

"You see anything?" I asked him.

"Nah, I didn't see anything," he said.

"Nah, me neither," I said.

Suddenly, we heard some noise coming from the motor pool area. I called the watchtower and told them to pop a flare over the motor pool. They fired a flare and it lit up the entire area. We scanned the motor pool and didn't see anything. We checked under and inside every vehicle to make sure Charlie wasn't hiding anywhere. We didn't find anything suspicious.

I called the watchtower again and told them to shoot a flare over the pond. I wanted to make sure our suspects weren't swimming back across the pond, which separated the American army compound from the South Vietnamese military base.

When a flare lit up the sky again, I looked out at the pond and saw the brand-new deuce-and-a-half engine floating on the water. There was a Vietnamese person swimming on each side of it. The two men were swimming with one arm while holding the engine with the other. They were stroking their free arms kind of like the Olympians do in the butterfly stroke.

Now, you have to understand that this was a 478-cubic-inch engine that probably weighed close to 1,650 pounds. I looked closer to see if the engine was floating on a raft but didn't see one. I looked to see if the Vietnamese had magically built a bridge across the pond but didn't see one.

As my buddy and I watched the Vietnamese in amazement, they stroked the engine all the way across the pond. The pond was more than one hundred yards wide!

I'll never forget the expression on my buddy's face after the Vietnamese reached the other side of the pond. Neither one of us said anything, but he had the dumbest look on his face. Then he smiled.

After I picked my jaw up off the ground, I asked him, "What did you see?"

"You first," he said.

"Let me start this conversation out this way," I said. "Did you see any kind of flotation device around that diesel engine?"

"Nah," he said.

"Are you sure you didn't see any kind of flotation device?" I asked him again.

"Uh-uh," he said.

"Well, how many people did you see?" I asked.

"One on each side," he said.

"Did you see any kind of raft?" I asked him.

"Nope," he said.

"Did you see any kind of bridge?" I asked.

"Nope," he said.

"Well, how are we going to report this in the morning?" I asked him.

"I'd rather not report it," he said.

"Hey, they're going to be missing that diesel engine in the morning, and then they're going to come looking for us," I said. "They're going to ask us why we weren't doing our jobs while we were on guard duty. We're going to have to report it. A brand-new diesel engine just doesn't get up and walk away."

"I don't know what we're going to say," he said.

"All I know is we can tell the truth," I said. "Did you see one Vietnamese on both sides of the engine?"

"Yep, that's what I saw," he said.

"Well, that's what we're telling them," I said.

"Sounds good to me," he said.

I knew no one was going to believe us.

When I gave my report to the officer in charge the next morning, he said, "Hey, y'all were smoking weed, weren't you?"

"I don't smoke weed, sir," I told him.

"Well, then you were drunk," he said.

"Hey, on a bad day, you might have me on the alcohol use because I keep a fifth of liquor in my pocket," I said. "But I don't drink while I'm on guard duty."

Well, after my buddy and I were interrogated for the next few hours, they finally believed our story, or at least they couldn't come up with another plausible explanation as to what happened to the engine.

My commanding officer sent two MPs in a Jeep to the other side of the pond. Much to their amazement, they found the deuce-and-a-half engine inside the South Vietnamese military compound and brought it back to the American side.

All these years later, I'm still not exactly sure how deep the water was in the pond. Day after day for six months, I watched Jeep and truck frames get dropped into the pond, so it was obviously pretty deep water.

What I do know is the pond was deep enough for fifty Vietnamese soldiers to stand on each other's shoulders and carry a diesel engine for more than one hundred yards.

And, boy, the Vietnamese sure can hold their breath.

DUCK COMMANDER

"A beaver is like a ninja— the suckers only work at night and they're hard to find."

Chapter 17

Leave It to Beavers

HEY, MY HAT IS off to the Vietnamese. They're some of the most resourceful people I've ever seen. In a lot of ways, they were like beavers: they worked only at night, they were relentless, and they didn't stop working until the job was finished. Hey, it's hard to capture or kill something if it only moves at night. Beavers are hard to kill and so were the Vietnamese. It's the reason the Vietnam War lasted so long; the North Vietnamese and Vietcong continued to fight us even though they were grossly outmanned. They didn't think they could lose, and they took advantage of their natural surroundings.

Look, you know what's un-be-beaver-able? In 2010, scientists discovered that beavers had constructed a dam of trees, branches, grasses, and mud in Alberta, Canada, that was more than half a mile long! The dam is located in a remote part of Wood Buffalo

National Park, and park rangers didn't even know it was there until scientists saw it on satellite images from outer space! Scientists say the dam is the largest in the world and that the beavers have probably been building it since the 1970s.

Hey, you know how I feel about beavers. I believe they're the pelted plague. The furry rodents are nothing more than log-chewing, water-slapping, flat-tailed rascals! Phil and I always have problems with them on our hunting land. They're our bucktoothed archnemeses. Beavers like to dam up water, which prevents it from reaching the land around our duck blinds. Look, it's pretty simple: if there's no water, there's no ducks. So there are few things that are more enjoyable to me than blowing up a beaver dam. It's like I tell Phil: hey, give them a kiss for me—the kiss of death!

I didn't know why beavers have flat tails until I went to Vietnam. Shortly after I arrived there, one of the American soldiers warned me to never go into the jungle at night. Now, I wouldn't have been caught dead in the jungle even during daylight, but I was curious to know why I shouldn't go in there at night.

"Because elephants jump out of the trees at night," he said.

Hey, now you know why beavers have flat tails. They go into the jungle at night, Jack!

While I despise beavers, I also respect their work ethic and determination. Do you know how hard it is to build dams and lodges? A lodge is a hollow mound of sticks, stones, and mud, and beavers live and sleep inside of them. Beavers usually build them on the banks or islands of a stream or river. The entrance to the lodge is underwater, so beavers first build a dam across the river to prevent the entrance from freezing during the winter. Hey, when two beavers walk into the house, the first one always tells the other one, "Hey, shut the dam door!"

Beavers work together to build their dams and lodges, kind of like we do when we're building duck calls. It's a collective effort. With their long, sharp teeth, beavers chew through thick trees. Hey, beavers are even smart enough to make sure the trees always fall toward their dams! They drag tree limbs with their teeth and push logs to the dam with their noses. Beavers even roll large stones on the logs to keep them in place. Hey, you want to talk about some busy beavers!

When the beavers are finished constructing a lodge, they cover the walls with mud to insulate them and keep out predators, whether it's foxes, wolverines, snakes, bears, Grizzly Adams, coyotes, or Daniel Boone. If a predator manages to break its way into the lodge, the beavers are able to escape through a secret exit. See, when beavers first start building a lodge, they burrow a secret tunnel on the other side of the river, which leads back to their lodge underwater. Now, tell me beavers aren't smart!

When I was in Vietnam, it was like we were fighting some really mean beavers. They were ferocious, Jack! One of the first things American troops did when they built a new camp in the Mekong Delta was bring in engineers and bulldozers to clear about two hundred yards of bush for a firing zone. If the Vietcong attacked them, they wanted a clear area to fire mortars, grenades, or whatever else they wanted to repel them. As soon as the firing zone was cleared, the Americans built bunkers around the perimeter, giving our troops shelter and protection in case we were attacked. Well, at one forward base, the American troops dug bunkers around the perimeter just before dark. When they awoke the next morning, they discovered the Vietnamese had dug a bunker in front of every bunker they'd made! Their bunkers were even finished with roofs, hot tubs, and satellite dishes! Our bunkers were only holes in the ground. I

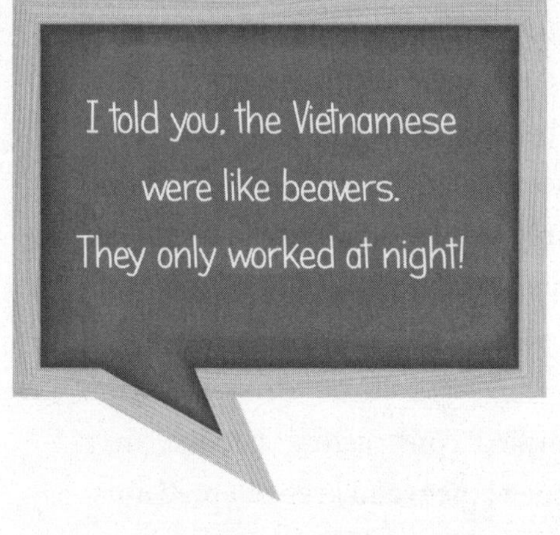

told you, the Vietnamese were like beavers. They only worked at night!

And, hey, you want to talk about smart! One of the American military's main objectives during the Vietnam War was to blow up bridges along the Ho Chi Minh Trail to cut off the Vietcong's supply lines. The Ho Chi Minh Trail ran from North Vietnam to South Vietnam, snaking through neighboring Laos and Cambodia along the way. Our air force flew over the trail and bombed bridges, wiping nearly every one of them out. After a few months, the Americans realized the Vietcong were still moving supplies along the Ho Chi Minh Trail. They were still getting materials to South Vietnam, even without the bridges.

Well, a few high-ranking officers assembled a couple of Special Forces teams for a reconnaissance mission to find out how the Vietcong were doing it. After a few weeks of hiding in the bush, the Americans saw a trail of truck lights coming. The trucks were barely visible coming down a mountain. When the trucks pulled up to a river, they just kept coming, even though the bridge had been wiped out! The trucks drove through the water and came out on the other side. Hey, the Vietcong built a bridge about three feet underwater. The U.S. Air Force couldn't even see the underwater bridges to blow them up.

And you want to talk about bold! One time, the Vietcong dug a tunnel under an American headquarters in Vietnam and listened to our high-ranking officers giving commands. The Americans were preparing to sweep an area where there were more than 100,000 Vietcong troops. But when American troops swept the area, there wasn't a soul in sight. Hey, the Vietcong listened to our orders and got everybody out. When the Americans left, the Vietcong moved back in. When I left South Vietnam in October 1969, there were two battalions of North Vietnamese army troops working the area around Can Tho. A gunship finally located one battalion moving across an opening, but there was still a second battalion on the loose. And we could never find them!

Sometimes the North Vietnamese were right under our noses and we didn't even know it! In the Seven Mountains region of the Mekong Delta, American troops kept bombing a mountain to drive out Vietcong forces. But every time the Americans sent in a recon patrol, they took heavy fire and had to retreat. So the Americans sent in more B-52 bombers, artillery fire, and rockets. They hammered the mountain day after day for a couple of weeks, but American troops kept taking fire when they tried to capture the mountain. After bombing it every day for three months, the Americans finally took the mountain. When American troops went inside a cave in the mountain, they found a ten-story hospital inside! There were operating rooms, recovery rooms, and offices for the North Vietnamese and Vietcong troops that came through the area. There was an American airfield right around the corner from the mountain, but we never even knew the hospital was there! Good night!

Hey, at least beavers slap the water with their tails to let us know they're there.

"I don't know any redneck who's not into fun. That's their middle name: Red Fun Neck!"

Chapter 18

Black Market

While I was in Vietnam, I became sort of a psychologist for several of the soldiers from Bravo Company, who were the infantry and foot soldiers. They were some of the bravest soldiers in Vietnam and always seemed to be in the line of fire. Well, the army liked to give the guys who'd been beating the bush for eleven months a couple of weeks to cool off before they shipped them back to the United States. I guess Uncle Sam figured there wasn't any better place to do it than my hotel room. There was always an empty bunk in my hotel room in Can Tho, and a lot of the guys from Eleventh Bravo ended up staying in my room for a couple of weeks.

Hey, while they were cleansing their minds and relaxing, they liked to tell a lot of their stories to me. My empty bunk became Dr. Phil's sofa! I listened to their stories with an inquiring mind, and a lot of guys liked to bounce their fears and problems off of me.

You wouldn't believe some of the stories I heard! One guy showed up and stayed in my hotel room for three weeks. We became pretty good friends, and he told me about how the Vietcong attacked their camp one night. He said three of their guys were badly hurt during the attack, and the medic immediately started treating their wounds. The medic attended to one guy, leaned him up against a tree, and then started patching up the next guy.

Well, after the medic patched up the second guy's shoulder, he moved on to the third guy, who was shot in the leg. All of a sudden, they heard the second guy screaming. A tiger had attacked him and was dragging him back into the jungle! The medic and the other two guys started shooting at the tiger and scared it back into the bush. It was one of the most frightening stories I heard in Vietnam.

Fortunately for me, I avoided most of the dangerous missions in Vietnam. But one day, my colonel came to me and closed my hotel room door.

"This conversation never took place," he said.

Uh-oh, I thought to myself. *I'm in trouble now.*

The colonel reached into his pocket and handed me three thousand piastres, which was Vietnamese money.

"Go get me a Jeep engine," he said.

"Say what?" I asked. "Why did you come to me? What do you expect me to do?"

"You have the money," he said. "Go find me a Jeep engine."

Hey, I didn't know what to do. I went and found one of the guys staying in my room. He'd been in Vietnam for more than three years and was always downtown. He spoke good Vietnamese, so I figured he knew a bunch of the locals and where to find a Jeep engine.

"Hey, Kelly," I said. "Look, I need to go get a Jeep engine. Can you help me?"

"Sure, I know where to go," Kelly said. "No problem. When do you need it?"

"Now," I said.

"What are we going to drive?" Kelly asked.

"Hey, I guess we'll take the deuce and a half," I said. "We're going to need somewhere to put the engine."

"Meet me in the lobby in an hour," Kelly said.

An hour later, I met Kelly in the lobby and we loaded up in the deuce and a half. We drove downtown, and he told me to pull the truck into a narrow alley.

"Hey, this truck won't fit into the alley," I said.

"Sure it will," he said. "Pull the truck all the way to the end."

Sure enough, the truck fit into the alley with only a couple of feet to spare on each side. When we reached the end, Kelly jumped out and disappeared for a few minutes. He came back with a short Vietnamese man.

"Get out," Kelly told me.

I jumped out of the truck. The Vietnamese man proceeded to blindfold Kelly and me.

"Where are we going?" I asked.

"You don't need to know," the Vietnamese man said.

Over the next several minutes, we walked through a maze of alleys and doorways, and then they loaded us into a car. We drove around Can Tho for about thirty minutes. I knew I was going to die when we stopped!

When we finally stopped, I heard a door open. We walked

into a building, and then someone took our blindfolds off. When I opened my eyes, the only thing I could see was hundreds of large green containers. "Property of the U.S. Army" was stamped on the side of every container! There were engines for Jeeps, helicopters, and trucks lined up against the wall for nearly three hundred yards. It was like an auto parts store. They had whatever the army needed because they'd stolen it from us.

"We need a Jeep engine," Kelly said. "Give them the money, Robertson."

"Hey, this ain't the deal," I said. "I want to see the Jeep engine on our truck. You sure are a trusting soul. We don't even know where we are."

"Just give them the money," he said. "The engine will be on the back of the truck when we get back. I've done this before."

Against my better judgment, I handed the Vietnamese man the money, knowing I'd never see it or him again. And I knew there wouldn't be an engine on our truck, either.

Well, they blindfolded us again and drove us back to our truck. When I opened my eyes, I couldn't believe it when I saw a Jeep engine in the back of it.

The Vietnamese man shook my hand and said, "Nice doing business with you!"

Hey, now I buy everything through the black market: designer jeans, boots, high-definition TVs, toasters, kidneys, livers, and Swatch watches. It's the only way to do business!

I'll never forget the time a Bravo Company soldier stayed in my room for a couple of weeks shortly before I was sent home. The only things the guy carried with him were an M16 rifle, ammunition, and a small rucksack that had pineapple grenades hanging from it. I was beginning to wonder how crazy the guy actually was. One night, the guys staying next to us—our rooms were only separated by thin partitions—got drunk and started getting rowdy. They were throwing beer cans and boots at us. The guy staying with me started to get really upset. He'd been chasing Charlie for nearly a year, while trying to stay alive, and the last thing he wanted to deal with was a few drunks! Well, when a boot hit the mosquito net over the guy's bed, he nearly lost it. He went next door and told them to settle down.

A few seconds later, the guys threw another boot at him.

The guy staying with me reached under his bed, grabbed a pineapple grenade, and popped the pin. Then he threw it over the partition into the next room! Hey, I was lying against the wall to the other room. I grabbed my thin mattress and wrapped my body in it. I was expecting the grenade to explode and blow me into the next room! When the grenade landed in the next room, it sounded like something out of a cartoon. The three guys over there started scurrying for cover. I thought they were all going to die!

The guy staying with me reached under his bed, grabbed a pineapple grenade, and popped the pin.

Well, the guy in my room was standing in our door, laughing his butt off. I thought he was slap insane! He walked into the next room, grabbed the grenade, came back, and threw it at me.

"Hey, it's a dud!" he said. "They reacted the same way Charlie does when I throw one into their bunker. There's one big difference, though. The Vietcong doesn't get to run. When I throw it into their bunker, I mow them down as they scurry out!"

I looked at him and said, "Man, you're about half a bubble off. You're not right."

I'm telling you: Vietnam did something to your mind if you were over there too long. Another guy who stayed in my room had been in Vietnam since the war started. He was on his sixth tour of duty. He was going home for leave and coming back for a seventh tour!

"Hey, man," I told him. "You've done your part for your country. You've done your share and five other guys' shares. You have a wife and two beautiful daughters. Go home and stay there! Good grief."

"Hey, I'm going home for thirty days to enjoy my family," he said. "Then I'm coming back here and kill some more Vietcong."

"Man, you're not right," I said.

"If my mind was a computer chip, I guess there might be a few blips on it," he said.

Hey, I guess I'm lucky my brain was faulty before I even went to Vietnam.

DUCK COMMANDER

"As someone who travels
with a gallon of tea,
I've got to make a lot of pit stops."

Chapter 19

Iced Tea Glass

BELIEVE IT OR NOT, we actually had pretty good food in the army. There was one cook in Vietnam who baked some of the best cinnamon rolls you could ever want to put in your mouth. He loved to bake, and his cinnamon rolls were humongous. He didn't spare any of Uncle Sam's sugar or cinnamon, either. His cinnamon rolls would melt in your mouth, and we actually cried when he went home.

I worked in the kitchen for a few weeks during basic training at Fort Benning in Columbus, Georgia. I had a crazy buddy I met on the train from Shreveport, Louisiana, and he told me he had the answer to all of our worries about being in the army.

"Hey, we volunteer for everything," he said.

"Look," I said. "Everybody I've talked to told me not to volunteer for nothing. People have warned me about doing something stupid like volunteering."

During our first week of basic training, one of the sergeants walked up to my platoon and said, "I need two volunteers for KP."

I knew KP was kitchen patrol, and I didn't want any part of it. But before I could even move, my buddy had not only his arm up but also mine.

"You idiot," I told him. "This better work out."

Hey, it might have been worse. When I was in Vietnam, one of the sergeants asked my platoon if any of us had experience in radio communications. I nearly raised my hand because I thought I might finally get to see some serious action, but then I thought better of it. Some sucker from Indiana, who was an amateur radio operator, raised his hand instead.

"Good," the sergeant said. "You can dig the hole for the new telephone pole."

For two weeks during boot camp, I helped in the kitchen, mostly peeling potatoes and washing pots and pans. I received a behind-the-scenes look at how the food was prepared and cooked. Hey, it wasn't pretty. Surprisingly, we actually had good meat come into the kitchen. The steaks we were fed were some of the best-looking beef I'd ever seen—at least until the cooks got their hands on them! What the army cooks did to the meat was criminal. Hey, you haven't chewed on a two-dollar steak until you've eaten a New York strip in the army! But the rest of the chow they cooked in the mess hall didn't taste that bad for the most part.

After I was finished with KP, I made the mistake of offering our company cook some advice.

"Hey, if you put a lid on the pan there will be less dust and dirt in your soup," I said.

"You mind your business," he told me. "Your job is to defend South Vietnam."

"That's right," I told him. "My duty is to defend South Vietnam—not eat it!"

Even some of the combat rations the army fed us were pretty edible. Our rations were actually called Meal, Combat, Individual (MCI), but everybody called them C-rations, which was what the army had been feeding its troops since the end of World War II. The MCI was introduced in 1958 and came to us in a cardboard carton, which contained one small flat can, one large can, and two even smaller cans. The cans were stacked on top of each other, so they were easy to carry in your pack.

The M-unit can was a meat-based entrée, which might have been something like beefsteak with potatoes and gravy, beans and wieners, chicken and noodles, chopped ham and eggs, ham and lima beans, or spaghetti with meatballs. The spaghetti was probably my favorite. Crackers, chocolate, hardtack biscuits (everybody called them "John Wayne cookies"), processed cheese, peanut butter, or jam was usually in the B-unit can, and the D-unit can was a dessert, typically something like apricots, peaches, pears, fruit cocktail, pound cake, or applesauce. If you were really unlucky, the D-unit can only contained a couple of pieces of white bread. That was a bad day, Jack!

The army also gave us an accessory pack with each meal, which included a spoon, salt, pepper, sugar, instant coffee, a couple of pieces of chewing gum, and toilet paper, as well as a four-pack of cigarettes and book of twenty matches. I started smoking cigarettes in high school (I have since quit, but I'll tell you more about that later), so I was happy to find them in my accessory pack. Eventually, the U.S. military figured out smoking wasn't healthy for its troops, so the army took cigarettes out of MCIs in 1975. I'll be honest: I was not a happy camper at the time.

Hey, army food wasn't exactly Miss Kay's cooking or fine dining, but you could survive on it and it was better than going hungry.

Of course, I never would have survived twelve months in Vietnam without Momma sending me care packages from home. In one of the first boxes, she mailed me a pair of work boots. There was a Tupperware iced tea cup and a couple of cans of jalapeño peppers in one boot, and a couple of cans of Spam and beans and wieners in the other boot.

I had a small electric cooktop in my hotel room in downtown Can Tho, so I cooked myself late-night meals whenever I was hungry. Shortly after Momma sent me the jalapeño peppers, one of my buddies came into my room. Of course, he'd been drinking whiskey all night and was three sheets to the wind.

"Oh, man!" he said. "Whatcha cookin', Robertson?"

"Hey, get you some of the pork and beans and Spam," I told him. "But you don't want any of these peppers."

"I love hot peppers," he said. "Give me a couple of 'em."

"You don't want any of these," I said. "These are from Louisiana. They get jalapeño in your business!"

He grabbed a couple of peppers anyway. A few seconds later, he ran out of my room looking for water.

Somehow, Momma's iced tea cup stayed with me all the way through Vietnam, and I've carried it with me in my back pocket ever since. I guess if it can make it through the napalm, mustard gas, and rice wine of Vietnam, I'll probably take it to my grave.

Iced Tea Glass

Everywhere I go, I carry a gallon of iced tea and my light blue Tupperware cup. Now my cup even has its own Facebook page and Twitter account. Some people might even say my cup has a better personality than my nephew Jase.

Some people might even say my cup has a better personality than my nephew Jase.

Now, there are plenty of duplicates of my blue Tupperware cup, but there's only one original. It never leaves my sight. One time, a guy handed me a blank check and wanted to buy my iced tea cup.

"Fill in the amount," he said. "Whatever it takes—I want that Tupperware cup."

"It's not for sale," I told him.

I told the guy to go buy his own Tupperware cup, but he insisted he wanted mine. I told him A&E TV wouldn't let me part with it.

During our first season of *Duck Dynasty,* I walked into the Duck Commander warehouse, and one of the workers told me there was a big box for me in the back.

"Are you sure it's for me?" I asked him.

"Oh, yeah, it says Si Robertson on it," he said.

"Hey, put it on the back of the truck," I said.

I took the box home and opened it up. Inside, there was a stainless steel saucepan with a lid, a big boiling pot, and a really nice set of steak knives. I looked at the bottom of the box and there were twelve Tupperware cups.

There was also a letter to me from the chairman and CEO of the Tupperware Brands Corporation in Orlando, Florida.

Apparently, Tupperware cups are making a comeback.

And they have the lovely Merritt Robertson to thank.

DUCK COMMANDER

"Today, with computers,
if you're dating some little ol' girl online,
you can't even smell her.
Girls smell nice."

Christine and I pose in front of one of our first houses. I probably asked her to marry me two hundred times before she finally said yes!

The Woman of My Dreams

After I left Vietnam on October 17, 1969, the army transferred me to Fort Devens in Shirley, Massachusetts, which is about fifty-five miles northwest of Boston. I was stationed at Fort Devens for about two years and worked in medical supply. Hey, you want to talk about living in a foreign land. I grew up in the South, and it took me a long time to get used to living in the cold, harsh winters of the Northeast. I'd rarely seen snow in my life, and it seemed like it snowed at Fort Devens eight months out of the year.

Hey, have you ever listened to someone from Boston talk? It sounds like their elementary school teachers went straight from Q to S when teaching them the alphabet. They don't know how to use the letter R! During a weekend pass, I visited Boston with a buddy of mine who was from there. He didn't have a car, so I drove mine. After we visited his parents, he took me to nearby Cambridge, Massachusetts, which is the home of Harvard University. He wanted me to go bar hopping with him to find some college girls. Hey, I figured the Ivy League and I went together like shrimp and grits. I dropped him off outside a bar and he told me, "Pahk the cah at Havad Yad." Of course I had no idea what he said, so I drove around in circles for hours. And some people think *I* talk funny!

People from Boston also used words I'd never heard before. Hey, they refer to shorts as clam diggers and headaches as bangers! They even refer to rubber bands as elastics. Do they use rubber bands to keep up their trousers? I walked into the barbershop on base, and the barber told me he was going to give me a whiffle.

"Are we playing baseball?" I asked him.

The first time I walked into my barrack, I asked a sergeant where I could find some water to drink.

"The bubbler is down the hall," he said.

"The what?" I asked him.

It took me a few minutes to realize he was talking about a water fountain!

Living in the Northeast was definitely a change in scenery for me, but I believe God has a purpose for everything. It didn't take me long to realize he'd sent me to Fort Devens to meet the woman who would become my wife. I met the former Christine Raney for the first time when I was hitchhiking to an off-base nightclub in November 1969. Christine was riding in the car with two of her friends, one of whom I already knew, and they saw me walking down the road. They couldn't have missed me. I was wearing a black leather jacket with a big dragon on the back of it. The dragon practically glowed in the dark. I'd picked the jacket up in

Vietnam. If Christine's friend hadn't recognized me, they probably would have thought I was some rock star.

From the start, Christine didn't like me very much. She thought I was arrogant and full of myself. She even told me, "You think you're the rooster of the walk!"

Christine had been married once before; her husband left her because they didn't think she could bear children. They'd tried to have a baby for a couple of years, but she couldn't get pregnant. Doctors told her she couldn't have children because of an underlying medical condition. Her husband wanted a family, so he left her. When Christine met me, she was still pretty leery about dating men. My buddy had been trying to set her up with some of his friends for months, but she had a long list of demands she wanted in her next boyfriend.

"Well, describe to me the kind of man you want," my buddy told her.

"Okay, here you go," she said. "He has to be six feet to six feet three inches tall with a slender frame. He has to have blue or green eyes and a beautiful smile with dimples. Most importantly, he also has to be smart and have a keen sense of humor and a warm heart."

"I've got just the person for you," he told her.

"There's no way you know anyone with all of those attributes," she said.

Hey, Christine Raney didn't know the real Silas Merritt Robertson. I was eight for eight, Jack!

My buddy set us up on a blind date. Well, at least she was blind going into the date. I knew who I was taking out, but my buddy didn't tell her she was going out with me. He knew how she felt about me after they picked me up hitchhiking. I decided to take Christine to our company's Christmas party at Fort Devens on December 12, 1969. She picked my buddy and me up at our barracks. As soon as Christine saw me, she was convinced it was going to be the worst night of her life. She couldn't remember my name, but she remembered my face. How could anyone forget a face like mine?

Of course, I turned on my charm and we had a great time. Christine said she'd never laughed so hard in her life. I amazed her with my dancing skills, of course, and we started dating regularly pretty soon thereafter.

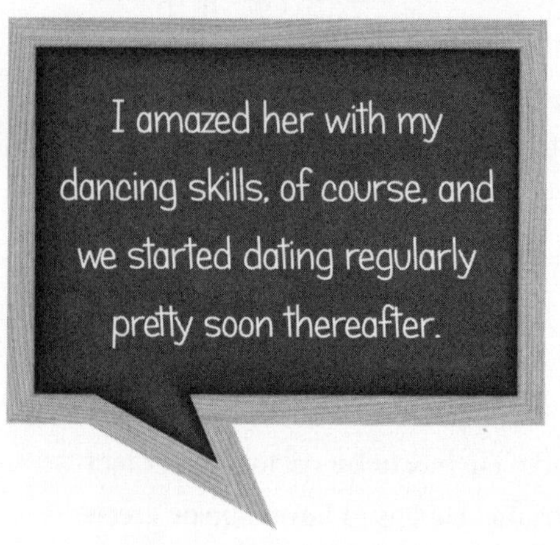

Christine was born and raised in Kentucky, where her father was a farmer. She loved living in Massachusetts. She'd moved there when she was twenty-one and was working as a seamstress in a factory that made furniture upholstery.

After a couple of years of dating, I was ready to pop the big question. I knew she was the one. My enlistment in the army was about to expire, and I knew I was moving back to Louisiana. I wanted to take Christine with me.

Before I proposed to Christine, I called Momma to tell her the news. I knew Momma and Daddy wouldn't be happy that Christine had been married before. My family didn't believe in divorce. We believed that when you made a vow of marriage, you were supposed to spend the rest of your life with your spouse. I was taught that when you chose a husband or wife, you were making a commitment for the rest of your life. But it wasn't Christine's decision for her first marriage to end.

"Hey, I've got a little news," I told Momma. "I'm fixing to get married. Her name is Christine. She was married before, so I want to make sure you will accept her as your daughter-in-law."

There was a short pause on the other end of the telephone. I was getting a little anxious.

"Yes, I'll accept her," Momma said.

"Good," I said. "This is the woman I'm going to marry. If you can't accept her, I'm not going to be around, either."

"You ought to know better than that," Momma said. "I will accept her."

On April Fools' Day, 1971, I told Christine's best friend that I was going to ask her to marry me. Of course, I was only kidding at the time. Five days later, on the same day I was released from the army, I asked Christine to marry me. Much to my surprise, she told me no.

And then she told me no again—and again and again and again.

Christine didn't want to marry me because she knew she couldn't have children.

"I can't be your broodmare," she said.

"Hey, I'm not like your first husband," I told her. "There are other doctors out there. If God wants us to have children, we'll have children. If he doesn't want us to have children, we'll adopt some kids. I want to marry you."

Finally, after I'd pestered Christine for nearly a full day, she agreed to marry me. We went to see the justice of the peace the next day.

On April 7, 1971, we were married at the courthouse. Because I was leaving the army, the judge even waived the state's requirement of having a five-day waiting period, marriage license, and blood test before a couple could be married.

When we were standing in front of the judge, he said to me, "Son, you just got out of a three-year commitment. Are you sure you want another one?"

"Yes, sir," I told him.

I knew this commitment was for the rest of my life.

Christine and I exchanged our vows and became husband and wife.

DUCK COMMANDER

"There's some people who got it.

And some people who don't.

Hey, I've always had it!"

My first impression with Christine wasn't much, but I knocked her socks off once she realized I was a modern-day Fred Astaire!

Chapter

21

Newlyweds

As soon as Christine and I were married, we jumped into my 1966 Plymouth Fury and drove straight to her parents' home in Kentucky. We were headed to Louisiana, but we stopped there so her parents could meet me. On the way to the courthouse the morning we were married, Christine said I wouldn't stop talking. But she said I barely said a word during the drive from Massachusetts to Kentucky. I guess I was in shock from actually going through with marriage.

We arrived at her parents' home late at night, and I didn't meet them until the next morning.

"Boy, y'all must have been tired," her momma said.

"What were you expecting to hear, Momma?" Christine asked her. "The bedsprings squeaking?"

Thankfully, her parents' house had thick walls.

Hey, Christine was in for a rude awakening when we arrived in Louisiana. I told her she was going to meet my family at a get-together at my brother Harold's house in Ruston, Louisiana. I don't think she realized she was going to meet my entire family. It wasn't like, "Hey, meet Momma and Daddy." It was more like, "Hey, meet my entire family and all of the in-laws."

My grandparents, parents, aunts, uncles, cousins, and second cousins were there, along with practically anyone else who had a spot on our family tree. Christine is a very shy person, and she was worried about meeting my parents, let alone everyone else. There were more than twenty people at the impromptu reunion. She was really taken aback at how loud and competitive we were while playing games like dominoes and solitaire. She barely spoke a word the entire day—not that she had much of a chance to say anything.

Hey, welcome to the Robertson family.

Fortunately, Christine won over my momma pretty easily. She actually wrote my mother letters thanking her for me. Christine thought she'd gotten the best of the bunch of Momma's boys. Was there ever any doubt? In our first year of marriage, Momma told Christine how happy she was that I'd married her. Momma thought Christine was the perfect wife for me. I was really happy Momma liked her.

Christine thought she'd gotten the best of the bunch of Momma's boys.
Was there ever any doubt?

In April 1971, Christine and I moved to Junction City, Arkansas, which is where Phil and Kay were living at the time. It was during Phil's struggles with alcohol and drugs, so it was really a wild time to be around him. As I said earlier, I quit drinking alcohol shortly after I came back from Vietnam. Once I met Christine, I stopped drinking altogether. But Phil was operating a honky-tonk and was drinking all the time.

Christine did not like Phil very much in the beginning. In fact, she despised it when I went hunting or fishing with him, which was usually every day. She didn't like the fact that Phil was taking other women on his fishing and hunting trips while he was married to Kay. Phil was my big brother, and I still loved him. But it was very difficult for me to see him go through his struggles. To be honest, Phil was not a very good person until he found Jesus Christ when he was twenty-eight years old. But he repented his sins and is spending the rest of his life sharing God's Word.

Much to my surprise, I had a difficult time after I left the military. When I was in Vietnam, I couldn't wait to get back to the United States. When I was in Massachusetts, I couldn't wait to get back to Louisiana. But once I was closer to home and around my parents, brothers, and sisters again, I was bored out of my mind. I was different from a lot of guys in the military. I put a uniform on every morning when I went to work, but I took it off when I came home. It was more of a job to me than a career. But I liked that I had a lot of free time in the military, which allowed me to hunt and fish. After we moved to Arkansas, I worked a nine-to-five shift in a particleboard factory, and I didn't make much money. I was usually too tired to do the things I liked doing in the outdoors.

In August 1971, Christine and I moved to Ruston, Louisiana. For whatever reason, I decided to go back to school on a GI Bill, which paid my tuition and helped pay for our living expenses as long as I was in college. I took classes at Louisiana Tech University—the administration was more than happy to welcome back one of its honor students—and worked from three o'clock to midnight five days a week. I worked in a broom factory for about two months, but then the owner fired me because his nephew needed a job.

Since I was married, I needed a job to support my wife. The GI Bill didn't cover everything. Fortunately, the Ruston police department was looking to hire a radio operator. Back then there was no such thing as 911, at least not in Ruston, so I was in charge of handling all the emergency calls at night, as well as being a dispatcher for the police officers who were on patrol. You wouldn't believe some of the calls we received! One time, a guy called me and told me his wife was in labor.

"Her contractions are only two minutes apart," he said.

"Is this her first child?" I asked.

"No, you idiot, this is her husband!" he told me.

Hey, another time a guy called me from a pay phone and told me he was having trouble breathing.

"Sir, where are you located?" I asked.

"I'm at the corner of West Kentucky Avenue and South Chautauqua Road," he said.

"Are you asthmatic?" I asked.

"No," he replied.

"Well, what were you doing when you started having trouble breathing?" I asked.

"Running from the police," he said.

It didn't take me long to realize I didn't want to pursue a career in criminal justice. It wasn't very long before I started losing interest in attending college, too. I was enrolled at Louisiana Tech for more than a year, but I just couldn't see myself staying in college for three more years. Five days a week, I was attending classes in the morning, working at night, and studying before and after I went to work. Hey, I figured out I was working a lot less and making a lot more money when I was in the military!

Before too long, Christine could sense my frustration. I'm not an angry person and really don't have much of a temper, but she could see that I wasn't the same happy-go-lucky guy I was when I was in the army. One night after work, she sat me down in our living room.

"Are you happy going to school and working at night?" she asked me.

"No, not really," I said.

"Well, I have a question," she said. "Were you happier in the military than you are here?"

"Yeah, I really enjoyed the military," I said.

"Well, why don't you go back into the army?" she said.

In November 1972, Christine and I drove to the army recruiter's office in Shreveport, Louisiana. They agreed to take me back, and I enlisted that same day. When I signed my contract to go back into the army, I made the recruiter specify that I would spend at least sixteen months at Fort Knox, which is about thirty-five miles from Louisville, Kentucky. I figured Fort Knox was pretty close to Christine's parents, and it would also ensure that the army wouldn't send me back to Vietnam or another foreign country.

Uncle Sam kept his word. We stayed at Fort Knox for sixteen months. On the first day of the seventeenth month, I got my orders to go back overseas.

"This is just the icing on the tip of the iceberg!"

Hey, the Germans required me to dress pretty sharp for our hunts. Can you imagine me wearing these duds in Phil's duck blind?

God's Blessing

ONE OF THE FIRST things I did when I arrived at Fort Knox, Kentucky, was make an appointment for Christine to see a fertility doctor. The military doctor started working with us in December 1972, and he eventually told Christine that he could fix it to where she wouldn't experience any more pain, but he still wasn't sure if we could have children.

A few years earlier, Christine had been diagnosed with Asherman's syndrome, which is a rare condition that causes scarring on the uterus; more than 95 percent of her uterus was covered in scars. The condition can cause infertility and miscarriages and is sometimes very painful. When Christine was working, she often missed at least a couple of days of work every month because she was in excruciating pain.

Christine had surgery in July 1973 to remove the scarring

from her uterus. Fortunately, the procedure eliminated her pain, but we still weren't sure whether we could have children. The doctors told us to keep trying to get pregnant for a year, and we had to closely monitor when she was ovulating. Well, nothing happened in the first nine months after her surgery. The doctors thought everything was fine with Christine, so they wanted to examine me to see if everything was okay. Hey, I didn't want to go see a doctor.

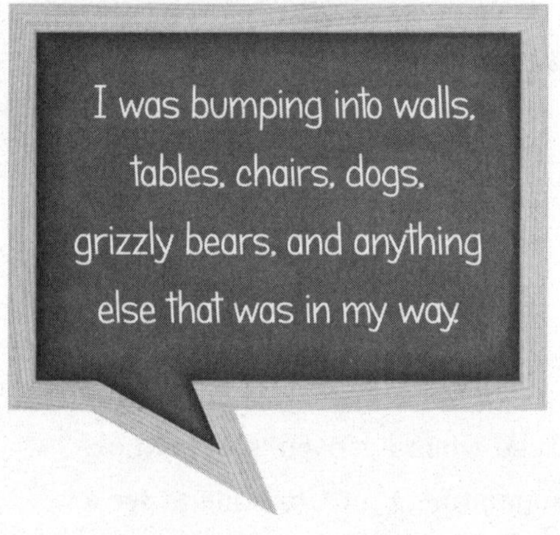

Doctors and I go together like peanut butter and Dijon mustard. We don't get along, Jack! I remember when Momma took me to the doctor for the first time because I was having trouble with my eyes. For a few weeks, everything was really blurry, and I was bumping into walls, tables, chairs, dogs, grizzly bears, and anything else that was in my way.

"Mrs. Robertson, your son needs to stop drinking iced tea," the doctor said. "It's bad for his vision."

"Hey, I love iced tea," I said. "I don't care if I go blind. I'm drinking tea, Jack!"

"Well, at least take the spoon out of the cup before you drink it," he said.

Christine was ready to have a baby, so she really wanted me to visit the doctor to find out what was going on. I wanted to have children badly as well, so I agreed to go. After an examination, the doctors thought my sperm count might be low. They handed me a glass jar and told me to bring back a specimen the next day. Now, I'm not going to lie. I didn't feel comfortable doing it. Despite my embarrassment, I agreed to come back with a specimen. The next day, I returned to the doctor's office.

"Where's the sample?" the doctor asked me.

"Hey, I tried to do it," I told him. "But no matter how hard I tried, I couldn't do it. I asked my wife for help, but I still couldn't do it. Then I asked my neighbor to help me, and I even asked my army buddies for assistance. No matter who helped, I couldn't do it."

I looked at the doctor and his face was bright red.

"Hey, none of us could get the lid off the jar," I said.

We found out that my sperm count was very low. Hey, they were Grade A sperm, but there weren't enough of them. The doctors discovered that my body temperature was too warm because I was always wearing tight shorts, kind of like the low-cut ones football coaches used to wear on the sideline. I liked to wear them because they really showcased my legs. To fix the problem, I started wearing boxer shorts and sweatpants. Christine and I went back to trying to have a baby.

In April 1974, when my sixteen-month enlistment at Fort Knox was about to expire, the army notified me that I was being deployed to Baumholder, Germany. The Baumholder post was an old Nazi garrison located in southwest Germany, just east of the French border. Before World War II, the Nazis displaced hundreds of families to build a military training ground that covered nearly thirty thousand acres. During World War II, Baumholder was also the site of a prisoner-of-war camp that housed prisoners from the Soviet Union, Poland, and other countries.

In March 1945, Baumholder surrendered to the Americans

without a fight, and it became a French military outpost. In 1951, the U.S. army took over the outpost and built schools, houses, churches, and warehouses for more than four thousand troops and their families. Until recent military cutbacks, Americans outnumbered the Germans living in Baumholder by nearly three to one. It really was a beautiful area. Rolling hills surrounded Baumholder, and it had bars, dance halls, and music halls from its medieval roots. It was located in the middle of Germany's wine country, and Austria, Belgium, France, Holland, Luxembourg, Switzerland, and the Bavarian Alps were within a few hours' drive. Hey, it was a lot different from Louisiana and Vietnam!

I left for Germany in May 1974, and Christine joined me there about three months later. In December 1974, Christine became very ill. She thought she had the flu. Sharon Sawyer, the woman living next to door to us on the military base, encouraged her to take a pregnancy test.

"I know I'm not pregnant," Christine said. "There's no need to go."

"Do it for me," Sharon told her. "Please do it for me. You never know."

Sharon persuaded Christine to go to the military hospital and take a pregnancy test. Later that day, Sharon asked her to call the hospital to find out the results.

"I'm not even going to call," Christine told her. "I know I'm not pregnant. I know it's going to be negative."

Without Christine's knowing, Sharon called the doctor's office and pretended to be her.

After a few minutes, Christine heard her say: "What do you mean do I want to keep the baby? Of course I'm keeping the baby!"

God's Blessing

Sharon walked into the living room of our apartment and shouted: "We're pregnant! We're pregnant!"

When I found out Christine was pregnant, it was one of the happiest days of my life. I always knew if God wanted us to have children, He would make it happen. If He didn't want us to have kids, we wouldn't have them. I have always left those kinds of things up to the Almighty, and I've always known I've had no control over them.

When I first asked Christine to marry me, she told me, "No, I won't marry you. I've seen you around children and you love them. You need to have kids. You want to have kids."

Even though I would have been perfectly happy adopting kids or living with Christine without them, I'd always wanted children of my own. I loved being around Phil's boys when they were babies, and I really wanted a chance to spread our love with children of our own. As it says in Psalms 113:9: "He settles the childless woman in her home as a happy mother of children. Praise the Lord."

Hey, the next eight months were the most anxious days of my life as I waited for my baby to arrive.

"We are fixing
to have a hootenanny
like you ain't seen in your lifetime!"

Christine and I pose with Trasa when she was only a toddler. After we had tried for so long to have a baby, her arrival was one of God's great blessings.

Chapter 23

Trasa

ONE OF THE HAPPIEST days of my life was August 30, 1975, when my daughter, Trasa Robertson, was born at a military hospital in Landstuhl, Germany. After going through so many struggles to have a child, Christine and I couldn't have been more excited. We named Trasa after Christine's father, Asa Lee Raney, and she actually has dual citizenship because she was born in Germany while I was stationed there.

From the time Trasa was born, she was Daddy's girl. When Trasa was old enough to crawl, she sat in the foyer of our house every day waiting for me to come home for lunch. She'd sit in my lap while I ate, and then she was waiting in the foyer again at the end of my workday. Her eyes lit up every time I walked in the door, and I don't know that I've ever seen a more beautiful sight.

When Trasa was only a toddler, Christine and I realized that she was an exceptional child. She was an absolute angel until she was three years old, but then she turned into a little devil. Christine took her to the pediatrician on the military base, and the doctor talked to Trasa without her mother in the room. The pediatrician came out and told Christine to put Trasa in preschool because she was bored to death. We put Trasa in preschool for two hours a day, and it really made a difference in her behavior.

Trasa could read before she went to kindergarten. Hey, I told you my stock was Grade A! One day in preschool, the teacher told the class something that wasn't factually correct. My three-year-old daughter stood up and said the right answer. Needless to say, the teacher didn't like being corrected by a toddler.

Trasa was always a very curious child. When we lived in Germany, I still liked to go squirrel hunting. I'd kill five or six squirrels and bring them home to cook. Trasa was probably only five years old at the time, but I had her hold the squirrels' legs while I skinned them. As I was gutting the squirrels, she would always ask what the organs were.

"What's that?" she asked.

"That's its kidneys," I told her.

"What's that?" she asked again.

"That's its heart," I said.

She was fascinated by the anatomy of a squirrel, while most girls her age would have been completely grossed out. Squirrels are my favorite game to eat, and Trasa loves eating them, too. When she started dating her future husband in college, they were sitting on a park bench, watching squirrels run around in the grass.

"Oh, I'd love to have a rock and hit them and then take them home and cook them," Trasa said.

Trasa's boyfriend looked at her like she was nuts and asked, "What are you talking about?"

"That's the best meat you'll ever eat," she told him.

Hey, that's my girl. She's a chip off the old block.

When Trasa was eight years old, a military psychologist on the base tried to tell us how to treat her because she was so intellectually gifted. But we wanted our daughter to be normal, so we treated her like any other kid. To this day, Trasa thanks us for not treating her like she was different.

When Trasa was growing up, if Christine or I needed to punish her, we would take her books away. She always begged us to take away something else, like the TV or dessert, but we took her books away because we knew how much she loved to read and learn. Eventually, we even had to put a time limit on how long she could read. If Trasa didn't have a book in her hand, we thought something was wrong with her. Sometimes I would ask her, "Hey, why don't you have a book in your hand? Are you sick?"

Because Trasa was so intellectually gifted, she never had many friends growing up. In fact, she was very isolated and kind of a loner until middle school. But then Trasa made two friends in the sixth grade, and the girls made a world of difference for her. One of the girls knew how to wear makeup, and Christine asked her to teach Trasa how to use it. The girls went shopping together, and Trasa started buying clothes that the other teenagers were wearing. She never worried about her appearance as much as she did about her brain. More than anything, those girls taught Trasa how to be a teenager.

Along the way, I learned that raising a teenager is about as hard as trying to nail Jell-O to a tree. I tried to do the best I could do and offered Trasa and her friends advice whenever they needed it. Hey, I'd rather they learned from me than from their friends or somebody on TV. I remember one of the girls' mothers asking me if I minded her daughter being at our house all the time.

"Hey, I better ask you this: do you mind her being over here all the time?" I said. "Because if they bring up a topic, there is nothing taboo in this house. If they want to ask me about sex, I'm going to tell them how it is."

One night, I warned the girls about the dangers of drinking alcohol.

I called the three girls into our kitchen, where I filled one glass with water and another one with whiskey. Then I placed a worm in each of the glasses. The worm in the water lived, while the worm in the whiskey shriveled up and died.

"What does that tell you?" I asked them.

"Well, I won't have worms like a dog if I drink alcohol," Trasa said.

It wasn't exactly the lesson I was going for.

Sometimes Trasa's sleepovers didn't go so smoothly, either. One night, Christine left me with a handful of ten-year-old girls while she went to a friend's house to play bridge.

"Whatever you do, do not let these girls leave this house," Christine said.

A couple of hours later, one of Trasa's friends came downstairs.

"I need to go home," she said.

"Nope, you're not going anywhere," I told her. "Go back upstairs."

A few minutes later, the girl was standing in the living room again.

"Mr. Robertson, I really need to go home," she said. "I was supposed to be home an hour ago."

"Hey, I'm under strict orders from headquarters," I said. "Nobody leaves this house."

About an hour later, there was a knock at the front door. It was a lady who lived down the street.

"Is my daughter here?" she asked.

"Nope," I said. "I haven't seen her."

Then the little girl stuck her head around the corner.

"Momma, I've been trying to come home," she said. "But he won't let me leave!"

In October 1992, the army transferred me back to the United States. Trasa was in her senior year of high school, and we made the difficult decision to leave our seventeen-year-old daughter with coworkers and friends in Germany. I didn't want to be away from my daughter for a year, but I knew it was the best thing for her. We'd always talked about what happened to me during my senior year of high school, when my parents moved from Dixie, Louisiana, to Gonzales, Louisiana. I had to move schools during the middle of my senior year and graduated with people I didn't know. I was determined not to do that to my children. We talked to Trasa about it, and she understood the situation and was very grateful we were leaving her behind. It was a very long year without her.

Trasa was attending Zweibrucken American High School in Zweibrucken, Germany, which was located on a United States Air Force base. The school also served the children of troops stationed at two nearby army facilities. It was an exceptional school, and she received a fantastic education. When Trasa graduated from high school in 1993, she received a Presidential Scholarship to Texas

A&M University in College Station, Texas. In high school she was named a student delegate to the United Nations and visited the Hague in the Netherlands. As a National Merit Scholar she was invited to the White House in Washington, DC, where she met First Lady Hillary Clinton. We couldn't have been more proud of her.

She also excelled at Texas A&M. During Trasa's sophomore year of college, one of her close friends was working as a fashion model. She invited Trasa to attend one of her photo shoots, and the modeling agency became interested in Trasa. She eventually became a model in advertisements around the country. I was so happy for her. Until Trasa was fifteen, she never felt like she was pretty. But she really blossomed by the end of high school. As a child, Trasa wore Coke-bottle eyeglasses. When Trasa was eight years old, we were told she would probably be blind by the time she was twenty-one. I told her we wouldn't worry about it, and God would take care of everything. It was a hereditary condition. Christine's father was legally blind in one eye until he had laser surgery when he was much older. Fortunately, Trasa's vision gradually improved, and she was able to wear contact lenses by the time she was fifteen.

Trasa graduated from Texas A&M in 1997. She took a year off from school between her junior and senior years because she was starting to get burned out. She spent a year working as a model and waitressing and really enjoyed it, then returned to Texas A&M the next year to finish her bachelor's degree. She was offered a scholarship to attend law school at Southern Methodist University in Dallas, but turned it down; she had other plans for her life.

Trasa met her future husband, Kyle Cobern, during her freshman year at Texas A&M. He is nine years older than Trasa, and they've been married for seventeen years now. Kyle is perfect for our daughter, and that's really all any parent could ever want. Trasa now has four sons—Brady Silas, Caden, Jaxon, and McCrae—and she absolutely loves being a mother. She teaches middle school in Hurst, Texas, and loves what she's doing. I couldn't be more proud of and happy for her.

Looking back now, it's amazing how much the good Lord has blessed us. For the first four years of our marriage, Christine and I weren't sure we could have children. But as I said earlier, I put it in God's hands. I knew I had to have faith in the Lord. As it says in Matthew 21:21, "Jesus replied, 'Truly I tell you, if you have faith and do not doubt, not only can you do what was done to the fig tree, but also you can say to this mountain, "Go, throw yourself into the sea," and it will be done.'"

A couple of months after Trasa was born, Christine returned to her doctor for a routine checkup. She asked him if we could have another child.

"If I'd seen you before your first child, I would have told you that you could never have children," he said. "If you had one, I don't see why you can't have another one."

I knew if the Lord wanted us to have another child, then Trasa would soon have a brother or sister.

"You can't tell by looking at me, but I'm a comedy man!"

I was a big fan of muscle cars when I was younger.
This beauty required nearly as much oil as gas!

Chapter 24

Like Father, Like Son

CHRISTINE WASN'T PREGNANT FOR ten days before she started having problems with our second baby. I like to joke that our son, Scott, was trouble before he was even born. Scott was born at a military hospital at Lackland Air Force Base in San Antonio, Texas, on December 18, 1977.

After we returned to the United States from Germany in July 1977, I was stationed at Fort Lee, which is near Petersburg, Virginia, and Christine and Trasa went to stay with her parents in Kentucky. When the army transferred me to Fort Polk in Leesville, Louisiana, in September 1977, Christine's parents brought them down to live with me. Two weeks later, Christine started having serious problems.

One morning, I woke up to go squirrel hunting. Hey, it was the first time I'd been back in Louisiana in a long time, and I couldn't wait to go shoot the long-tailed critters! But for whatever reason, Christine didn't want me to go hunting. "Why not?" I asked her.

"I don't have a reason," she said. "I just have a feeling that you're not supposed to go."

"That's not good enough," I said. "I'm going to shoot me some squirrels."

When I came home from hunting, I found a note on our front door. Christine was at the hospital because of complications from her pregnancy, and Trasa was down the street at the preacher's house. Doctors told Christine there was a serious problem with her pregnancy and broke the devastating news that her fetus would probably die. But a month went by and Christine didn't miscarry, so the doctors took another ultrasound in October 1977. The fetus was still alive, and the doctors decided that when Christine was seven months pregnant, they would hospitalize her until our baby was born.

On the day after Thanksgiving Day 1977, Christine was admitted to the military hospital at Fort Polk, where she was supposed to stay for the next three months. But on December 8, 1977, Christine started having contractions. The next day, she was flown to San Antonio because there was an experimental drug there that doctors believed might be able to stop her contractions. Our baby wasn't due until February 5, 1978. If the baby was born in December, there was a good chance he wouldn't survive.

On December 17, Christine started hemorrhaging and doctors couldn't stop the bleeding. They delivered our son, Scott, the next day. I was at Fort Polk when Christine started hemorrhaging, and the doctors called me and told me I needed to jump on the next flight to San Antonio. When I walked off the elevator at the hospital, I saw Christine walking down the hall. I looked at her and figured she hadn't delivered the baby yet.

"I've already had the baby," she said. "Come on, let's go down and see him."

"Hey, get out of here," I said. "You haven't had the baby."

"Trust me," she said. "I had the baby. Let's go see your son."

Scott was in critical care because he was seven weeks premature. You couldn't really see him because there were so many tubes and wires sticking out of him. For years, Christine joked that Scott was the ugliest baby she'd ever seen! When Scott was born, Christine kind of went into a shell because she was convinced he wouldn't survive. It was a very scary time for us. The doctors told us the biggest factor on Scott's side was that he weighed five pounds, thirteen ounces when he was born. Even though Scott was born nearly two months premature, he was still a pretty good-sized baby.

When Scott was only three days old, I left to spend the night at a friend's house. Before Christine went to bed, she liked to go down and see him in the neonatal intensive care unit. She liked to rub his stomach and tell him she loved him. But on the third night, she walked into the ICU and the nurses told her she needed to go back to her room. All of the nurses were around Scott. She knew something was wrong, so she called me and told me to come back to the hospital.

Before I got to the hospital, doctors operated on Scott because his liver wasn't functioning properly. His bilirubin levels were critically high, and the doctors didn't discover the problem until he was three days old. Bilirubin is a brownish-yellow substance found in bile. It is produced when the liver breaks down old red blood cells. Bilirubin is then removed from the body through feces and urine. When bilirubin levels are high, jaundice causes a baby's skin and the whites of its eyes to turn yellow.

Scott was given a blood transfusion, and thankfully the Lord healed him.

When I arrived at the hospital that night, a doctor apologized to me for operating on my son without my permission.

"Hey, did he need it?" I asked.

"If we hadn't operated on him, he would have died," the doctor said.

"Then no apology is necessary," I said.

Well, we found out a few years later that Scott's high bilirubin levels had damaged part of his brain. Scott was suicidal from the time he was about five years old. His behavior was really erratic as a child. When Scott would get tired, he would throw his arms out and fall backward. When we were hunting hogs in Germany one time, Scott fell on the ground, which concerned the Germans who were hunting with us. "Hey, he does that all the time," I told them. Scott would fall down wherever we went; he did it in stores, in school, and while we were walking down the sidewalk.

I never realized my son had serious problems. I don't know if I'm hardheaded, I'm stubborn, or I just wanted to overlook it, but Christine kept telling me Scott had real problems.

"Well, hey, then I had problems, too," I said. "All kids have problems."

It took me a while to realize Scott needed help. When Scott was angry, he was out of control and did a lot of damage. The tipping point came when he was eleven years old. He came home from school, and Christine could sense that he was very tense. His bedroom was his safe haven. He had to learn to never get angry outside of his bedroom. Well, Scott walked into his bedroom that day, closed the door, and proceeded to destroy everything. When it was finally quiet, Christine went into the room. Scott was getting ready to jump out a second-story window. I don't know if the fall would have killed him, but it was straight down. Christine grabbed Scott and pulled him back into his room.

"I can't go on," Scott said. "I can't do it. I just can't. You're my mother. You're supposed to help me. Make the pain go away."

It broke our hearts. Christine called the military hospital and we took him there the next morning. We met with a new military psychiatrist, and Scott was his very first patient. The psychiatrist told us there was a new drug on the market, and he wanted Scott to take it. The psychiatrist diagnosed Scott with having an attention disorder, hyperactivity, and a behavioral disorder.

The psychiatrist told us we wouldn't see the effects of the new drug for ten to fourteen days. But on the third day, Scott got himself out of bed and walked into the kitchen for breakfast with a big smile on his face. We didn't know who he was! From that day forward, Scott became a typical child. He never lost his temper and rarely had mood swings. He continued to see a psychiatrist until he was seventeen years old, but he never had serious emotional or behavioral problems again. We eventually figured out Scott was suffering from Asperger's syndrome, which is a form of autism.

The military psychiatrist saved my son's life. There's no doubt in my mind that God had a hand in our finding the doctor who could control Scott's disorders. It was another example of God taking care of us. It always seemed like when we desperately needed someone to help us, like when we were trying to get pregnant, God pointed us in the right direction and put people in our lives who could fix our problems. As it says in Proverbs 3:5–6, "Trust in the Lord with all your heart and lean not on your own understanding; in all your ways submit to him, and he will make your paths straight."

Eventually, Scott became a good student and graduated from Paint Rock Valley High School in Princeton, Alabama, in 1996. From the time Scott was a young boy, all he ever wanted to do was join the army. Christine and I tried to talk him out of it and told him he could find a better career, but he wouldn't listen. Christine even pointed out things about the military he wouldn't like, such as authority and obeying orders. Even though Scott was a good student, he liked to argue with his teachers. We told him he couldn't argue with his superior officers in the military.

We never thought the army would accept Scott because of his medical history. When the military recruiters came to Scott's high school, he talked with representatives of the navy, marine corps, and air force. He didn't talk to the army. As soon as Scott told the recruiters about his behavioral conditions, they told him he wouldn't pass the physical exams to join the military. We thought that was the end of it and Scott would find something else to do with his life.

As soon as Scott graduated from high school, he left to visit Trasa in Texas. Scott called his mother about a week later and told her he'd enlisted in the army.

"I have one question," Christine said. "How did you manage that with your medical history?"

"Don't ask, don't tell," he said.

"Scott, that doesn't apply to your medical history," she said.

"Well, they didn't ask, and I didn't tell them," he said.

Scott joined the army and went to basic training at Fort Jackson in Columbia, South Carolina, in November 1997. He completed advanced individual training at Fort Eustis in Virginia. It was the same exact training I had when I joined the army. When Scott tells me things about the army, it's like I'm reliving my experiences. He even had a superior officer named Doc just like me! I always tell him, "Scott, didn't you learn anything? I always told you, don't be like your dad!"

Scott and his wife, Marsha, have four boys—Ethan, twins Connor and Logan, and Wyatt—and live at Fort Eustis. They had Wyatt in July 2013, giving Christine and me eight grandsons. I'll have my own baseball team if Trasa or Scott has one more child! Ethan was Marsha's son from her first marriage, but Scott adopted him last year. Ethan was signing his name as Ethan Robertson at school, and his teachers kept telling him he couldn't do it. "Oh, yes, I can," Ethan said. "Scott Robertson is my dad."

One night, Ethan asked Marsha what would happen to him if anything happened to her.

"Well, Connor and Logan will stay with Scott, and Scott would have to go to court to get you," she said.

"I don't like the sound of that," Ethan said.

Last Christmas, Scott and Marsha wrapped a birth certificate with Ethan's name change and a duck call engraved with his new name and put it under the Christmas tree.

Christine and I received another grandson that Christmas, and it was the best present of our lives.

"Work hard, nap hard.

Hey, that's what I always say, Jack!"

Chapter 25

Sleepwalking

After Scott was born, we spent four more years at Fort Polk, where I worked with the Fifth Aviation Battalion, which is an air ambulance detachment of helicopters. Hey, I learned that flying a helicopter is really no different than riding a bicycle. It's just a lot harder to put baseball cards in the spokes. My kids really liked living at Fort Polk, and I was happy to be back in Louisiana. But Christine was never very fond of the place. The base was located in the middle of a swamp and the mosquitoes were bad. When Christine came to pick me up from work on the base one day, there was an alligator sitting in the middle of the road. That might have been the straw that broke the llama's back. In 1982, the army transferred me to Zweibrucken, Germany. When we boarded a plane to fly to Frankfurt, Germany, Christine told me, "You'll never get me to live in this state again!" I knew she was serious. I loved being closer to my parents, brothers, and sisters, but Christine was never very close to her siblings. Her family wasn't as close as mine, so she didn't realize how important living in Louisiana was for me.

During the first two years we were living back in Germany, Christine became very depressed and was really battling her emotions. Scott was about three years old at the time—before we'd gotten him help—and I think Scott's problems were weighing on her mind. She felt guilty because she didn't know how to help him. She was always upset. I didn't yet understand the gravity of the situation. I don't think I wanted to accept that my son had serious emotional problems; I wanted him to be like every other kid. But Christine knew something was wrong with Scott, and she wasn't a very happy person for two years. Finally, I came home from work one day and told her, "Get help or I'm gone. I'm not going to live like this."

After we both calmed down, Christine told me that whenever she pictured herself being old and gray, she thought of herself sitting in a rocking chair with me sitting next to her. Christine told me she couldn't see herself living without me, so she agreed to go to a psychiatrist to get help. In order to get the help Christine needed, she had to move back to the United States with our kids.

In 1984, Christine and our kids flew back to the United States and moved in with Christine's parents in Kentucky. We shipped our furniture back with them, so I lived in the barracks on base. It was like I was in boot camp all over again, living like a bachelor in the military. Christine started seeing a psychiatrist, and thankfully the doctor was able to help her. During their sessions, Christine revealed that a relative had sexually molested her when she was younger. Christine never told her parents about it and internalized the painful memories for many years.

Talking about her past and getting the issues out in the open really helped Christine. It was like a great burden had been lifted from her shoulders, and it helped me understand what she was dealing with. The psychiatrist told Christine that any relationship with God as its center has a better chance of being mended. We each knew we needed one another. As it says in Ecclesiastes 4:9–11, "Two are better than one, because they have a good return for their labor: If either of them falls down, one can help the other up. But pity anyone who falls and has no one to help them up. Also, if two lie down together, they will keep warm. But how can one keep warm alone?"

Christine wasn't the only one with problems when we were moved to Germany for a second time, although my issues seemed trivial in comparison. I was having a lot of problems at work; one of the colonels in Germany just didn't like me for whatever reason. For an entire year, I sat behind my desk and did nothing. I did not have a specified job, but I still had to show up for work every day. Somehow, I upset a bunch of my superiors by doing my job, so they took my job away from me. By exiling me to a desk, my superiors thought I would quit, request a transfer, or do something wrong that would enable them to get rid of me.

What they didn't know about Silas Merritt Robertson is that I'm perfectly content doing nothing.

But what they didn't know about Silas Merritt Robertson is that I'm perfectly content doing nothing. I showed up every day wearing spit-shined boots, a pressed uniform, and a big smile on my face. I kicked my feet up on my desk and rubbed it in their faces for eight hours a day for twelve months. On most days, I put my head down and slept for a few hours. Hey, I can sleep anywhere. Look here, napping is just like hunting. If I walk through the warehouse when I'm at work, I look over, and there's the perfect spot. Boom! I'm asleep.

I learned to sleep and ignore my surroundings when I was young. When I got past my bed-wetting stage, I moved into the bedroom with my three brothers. There was always a lot of noise in the bedroom because there were four boys sleeping in the same bed. I never slept with a pillow over my head because I was afraid the fairies would take all of my teeth! Sometimes I slept in a sleeping bag on the floor; I was a human tortilla. I tried to sleep with an electric blanket one time, and I even plugged it into a toaster to make it warmer. But then I kept popping up out of bed all night!

I've always loved to sleep. Hey, like I always say: work hard; nap hard. Napping is my favorite thing to do. In fact, I believe it should be our national pastime. Hey, when I'm napping, I might be dreaming about ducks, beavers, squirrels, Stevie Nicks, or anything else. When I'm asleep, it's just my mind and me. Everybody should take a nap once a day. It's a medical fact. Work! Work! Work! Nobody takes time to stop and smell the roses anymore. Hey, doctors have proven that daytime naps improve your memory and help you remember important facts. I guess that's why my mind is like *Encyclopaedia Britannica*.

Look, I've never had a problem falling asleep or staying asleep. When I was younger, I was asleep in my bed at my parents' log house. Phil was in the bed with me, and he heard something scurrying outside. Phil grabbed his rifle, opened the window, and laid the rifle across my chest to steady it. He fired a shot at a squirrel and missed. He missed the squirrel two more times, but I never woke up. Phil said I lay there snoring, while he fired three shots out the window!

Sleepwalking

When I was a little bit older, my sister Judy started dating when she was in high school. One night, Judy came home with her boyfriend, who was a football player at North Caddo High School. When Judy and the boy opened the front door to our house, I was standing in the living room, looking right at them. I was sleepwalking! Then I bolted out the front door and took off running down the road. The boy realized I was asleep, so he took off running after me. He chased me for two miles before he caught me. The next day, the boy came to our house. He told me, "Man, I thought I was fast. But I couldn't keep up with you!"

It's amazing what some people can do when they're sleepwalking. There is a nurse in North Wales who draws and paints works of art while he's sleeping. A woman in England woke up one night at two A.M. and found her husband mowing the grass while he was naked! Tragically, an electrician in Wisconsin sleepwalked out of his house wearing only his underwear and a shirt and froze to death before he woke up. Hey, I do all sorts of things while I'm sleepwalking. I've run marathons, washed the dishes, vacuumed the house, cleaned my rifles, and prepared a big pot of gumbo. Christine never wakes me up when I'm sleepwalking because she says it's when I'm most productive! Hey, what do you call a sleepwalking nun? A roamin' Catholic, Jack!

Obviously, it didn't take the army very long to figure out that I wouldn't have any problems sleeping through twelve months on the job. Fortunately, I was able to get back into the good graces of Uncle Sam when a new colonel was assigned to our unit. I was transferred back to the U.S. in 1985 and rejoined my family at Fort Bragg in Fayetteville, North Carolina. Being reunited with Christine and my kids was one of the happiest days of my life.

And I couldn't wait to climb into my own bed again.

“These boys packed so much stuff, hey, they could survive a zombie nuclear a-poca-liss.”

Serving in the Army for so long allowed me to hunt all over the country and the world. I dropped this buck near Fort Bragg, North Carolina.

Chapter

26

Mass Murder

ONE OF THE BEST things about being in the military is that I was able to hunt all over the world. I've hunted in Germany as well as Alabama, Kentucky, Louisiana, North Carolina, and Texas. Hey, you haven't hunted until you've sat in a deer stand with artillery shells firing over your head! That's exactly what happened to me at Fort Bragg, and it didn't take me long to find another deer stand, Jack! Believe me, it's a sound you'll never forget!

When I was stationed in Zweibrucken, Germany, I had a buddy who was the hunting instructor for the area. If you were in the American military and wanted to hunt in Germany, you had to go through eight weeks of classes to learn the German traditions and hunting regulations. Until you were certified, you weren't allowed to hunt there. When my buddy went back to the United States, he talked me into taking over as the hunting instructor. I couldn't speak German very well, but a lot of the local hunters liked me and allowed me to hunt on their land.

Hunting in Germany was a little different than how we do it in the United States. Most hunting clubs in the U.S. lease land to hunt for ducks, deer, birds, and other game, but in Germany you actually lease the animal rights for a certain piece of property. A lot of the hunters sold what they killed to restaurants to recoup some of the money they were paying to hunt. If an American soldier killed a deer or hog on someone's property, we had to pay the rights holder money to keep the meat. We hunted for roe deer, wild hogs, foxes, birds, and German *hasen,* or hares.

German hunts were more like a big party. They were very big events, including an elaborate posthunt meal and, of course, a lot of beer drinking. Sometimes I was in charge of bringing the noon meal. I usually had the mess hall cook a big pot of chili or beef stew, but sometimes I'd cook the Germans barbecued pork or another American dish.

The first year I taught the hunting course, seven Americans were in my class, and I took them hunting when the course was over. On our first hunt, six of the Americans killed a roe deer, which is a lot smaller than the deer we have over here. Roe deer typically weigh between thirty and seventy-five pounds, and they have reddish bodies with short, erect antlers. They're good to eat, but they're just not very big. Germany is about the size of Oregon, and they kill over six hundred thousand roe deer every year. They're everywhere!

One of the great things about hunting in Germany was that it didn't get dark until about ten o'clock at night. If you went deer hunting, you hunted all day long. On the first hunt, one of the Americans who killed a roe deer wanted to keep the meat, but he wanted me to clean it because he didn't know how. We paid for the deer and gutted it in the woods. By the time we got back to the apartment complex where I lived, it was close to midnight.

"Well, it's late and I don't feel like fooling with it tonight," I told him. "I'm going to hang it up in the basement."

I tied a rope around a water pipe and hung the deer from the ceiling. I put a plastic tub under the deer so blood wouldn't drip all over the floor. It was cold in the basement during the wintertime, so I decided to go to work the next morning and then clean the deer when I came home.

Hey, when I came home from work the next day, there were four military police cars and another five German police cars sitting outside my apartment complex. There was even an emergency medical wagon sitting in the parking lot. "What in the world is going on?" I asked myself.

When I walked up to my apartment, one of my neighbors told me, "Hey, there's been a mass murder in our apartment building!"

"Get out of here!" I told him. "A mass murder?"

"Hey, I'm serious," he said. "There's blood everywhere!"

Immediately, I ran to my apartment to make sure Christine and the kids were okay. They were fine, so I went back downstairs to see what was going on. I saw a German doctor I'd been hunting with the day before.

"What's going on?" I asked him.

"Oh, they found a roe deer in the basement," he said.

"All of this for a roe deer?" I said. "What are you doing here?"

"They called me here to determine the cause of death," he said.

"Well, what did you tell them?" I asked.

"I told them it looked like a thirty-aught-six to me," he said.

"You're exactly right," I said.

Well, a woman in my apartment building had gone down to the basement that afternoon to do her laundry. She saw the deer hanging from the ceiling and freaked out. The crazy woman ran out of the basement screaming, "Mass murder! Mass murder!"

Fortunately, I was able to talk my way out of the predicament. The police even let me keep the evidence.

Hunting roe deer was a lot of fun because they would appear out of nowhere at any time. They're so small that they love hiding in tall grass. You would be walking through a field and roe deer would start popping up everywhere.

One time when we were hunting, one of my buddies killed the first wild hog on the property in about twelve years. It was near the end of the day, and there were three of us hunting. I put one guy in the stand and told him he couldn't shoot anything but a fox or pig. The other guy and I went down to a different stand to find a deer. The guy with me hadn't been hunting before, and I kept telling him he was making too much noise.

"Hey, you have to be still," I told him. "If you'll be quiet, we'll kill a deer in about fifteen minutes. I'm listening to the deer eat corn right in front of us. When they're done eating corn, they're going to walk out here and eat some grass."

Well, he never sat still and the deer never walked in front of us. Right before dark, I heard gunfire. Boom! Boom! Then I heard something big fall to the ground.

"Well, either that's a giant fox or that sucker has killed a pig," I said.

We climbed out of our stand and walked toward him. He'd killed a one-hundred-and-fifty-pound pig.

"You haven't gutted him?" I asked.

"No, I was afraid I'd mess it up," he said.

"Boys, here's rule number one in hunting: if you're going to shoot something, you have to learn to clean it," I said.

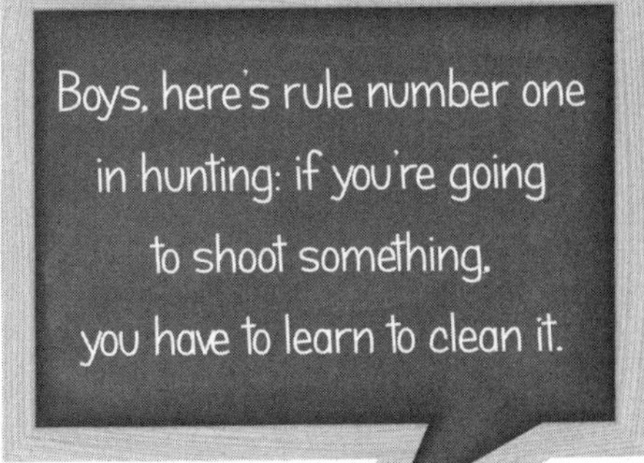

I gutted the hog in the woods and we carried it back to my Mitsubishi Montero. We drove to the landowner's house and knocked on the door. His wife answered and told us he wasn't there. He was at a guesthouse on the north side of town. When we found the owner, he couldn't believe we'd killed a pig on his property. Being in Germany, we had to discuss the hunt over a couple of pitchers of beer. The owner kept the hog, but he gave my buddy its teeth as a trophy.

The landowners in Germany were very particular about what you could shoot on their property. They didn't like us shooting the biggest hogs. During one hunt, I noticed a hole that looked like a big horseshoe in the middle of tall brush. It was actually a trail where hogs had been running. A few minutes later, I heard dogs barking and it was getting louder. The dogs were running toward me! All of the sudden, the big hole in the brush was gone. A hog stuck its head through and kept running right at me. I didn't think it was going to stop, so I grabbed my gun. The hog came within about three feet of me, but then it turned around and ran back into the hole. My sergeant major was with me and was yelling, "Can I shoot him? Can I shoot him?"

"No, he's too big," I said.

The hog probably weighed more than three hundred pounds and had huge tusks sticking out of the sides of its snout. It was pretty, but it was too big to shoot. A few minutes later, guns started going off, and I saw a forty-pound hog running my way. I looked through the scope of my rifle and saw two big oak trees. If the hog ran between the trees, I thought I had one chance to shoot it—if someone else didn't get it first. When the hog hit my scope, I fired and the hog flipped in the air. The Germans blew their horns, signaling that the hunt was over. One of the Germans came down and asked everyone who shot it. About five guys claimed it, but I told him I was the last one to shoot when it fell. They gave the hog to my colonel, which was probably a good thing.

It was always fun to see the spread after a German hunt. There was such a variety of game. There was usually an elk, four or five roe deer, twelve hogs, a couple of pheasants, and a bunch of rabbits. You have to understand that a German *hase* isn't much smaller than a roe deer. They're the biggest rabbits I've ever seen! Whenever we went rabbit hunting, the Germans always warned us not to confuse a roe deer with a rabbit. But it was easy to do because they are so similar in size.

The first time I went rabbit hunting, I was convinced they had bulletproof fur! The Germans liked to shoot over-under shotguns, and I watched four of them fire at the same rabbit. Every time one of them shot twice, I saw fur fly, but the rabbit kept running. As the rabbit got closer, I told myself the rabbit wasn't going to get by me. When it got close to me, the dogs were just about to catch it. The Germans were screaming, "Don't shoot the dog! Don't shoot the dog!" I fired my gun. Boom! It was a head shot and the rabbit flipped. The dog was so close it caught the rabbit in the air.

I'm not sure what would have happened if I'd accidentally shot the German's dog. Those Germans loved their dogs. I've never had much success with hunting dogs—except for standarad poodles—but the Germans train their dogs meticulously. Sometimes when I walked into a restaurant in Germany, dogs would be sitting next to a table while their masters ate steaks. The dogs didn't move and didn't have an ounce of slobber on their mouths. That wouldn't happen in Louisiana. At Phil's house, Miss Kay's dogs usually eat steak before we do!

One of the most ferocious dogs I've ever seen was in Germany—and it weighed only ten pounds! It was only a puppy, but it had razor-sharp teeth. Before we went hunting one morning, a couple of dogs started fighting. The little dog had latched on to a German shorthaired pointer's ear and wouldn't let go. I thought, *Man, that dog's tough. He's a buzz saw with teeth!* When the hunt started, dogs and pigs were running everywhere. All of the sudden, I saw a two-hundred-pound hog running toward me. The pig kept shaking its head. The little dog had latched on to its ear and wouldn't let go! A couple of hours later, the little dog ripped the ears right off of a rabbit!

It's a good things rabbits have good eyesight from eating so many carrots. If that rabbit had needed glasses, it would have been in trouble!

"I live by my own rules
(reviewed, revised,
and approved by my wife) . . .
but still my own rules."

Trasa poses with one of her prom dates.
Once she lost her glasses and gained some confidence,
my daughter was a beauty!

Chapter
27

Semiretirement

I WAS STATIONED IN GERMANY three times for a total of nearly eight years while I served in the army. During my last deployment to Germany, the army informed me it didn't need me anymore. In 1992, Congress trimmed the military budget by more than $278 million, and I was part of the cuts. After serving for more than twenty-four years, Uncle Sam forced me into retirement on January 31, 1993. The army told me to hit the road, Jack!

Christine and I moved to Hollytree, Alabama, which is located in the northern part of the state, not far from the Tennessee border. Christine and I really enjoyed living in the mountains in Germany, and the Appalachian Mountains in north Alabama were beautiful as well. We rented a house from an army friend of mine for about a year, and then we bought a place of our own and lived there for four more years. Trasa was in college, but Scott was still living with us and attended high school in Alabama.

Hey, you know what I didn't do after I retired from the military? I didn't shave. After shaving my face for more than two decades while I was in the army, I threw away my razors, Jack! Phil already had a long beard, and most of the Duckmen who were hunting with him on a regular basis had long, thick beards. Facial hair helps hide your pale skin from ducks. You might as well be wearing spotlights if you get into a duck blind with a clean-shaven face. The ducks will see you from a mile away! I've learned over the last several years that a beard helps camouflage your face and keeps you warm during the winter. Hey, you want to talk about fifty shades of gray? I have an entire range of hues in my beard nowadays. Hey, it's tough being this good-looking.

Our house in Alabama was located in the mountains, and our property actually had about four levels from where rock had busted through the earth. It was a great hunting ground. There was an abundance of game and so many places to hide. I could walk on an upper level of rock and look down and see everything. One day, I was deer hunting and thought I heard a buck rubbing its antlers on a tree. But when I looked down, I saw about forty turkeys. I crawled closer to get a better look, but the scout saw me and started chirping. The turkeys took off running! I never figured out where the turkeys came from or where they went! Turkeys also liked to climb into a pine tree in my yard. Four turkeys climbed the tree, with one facing east, one west, one north, and one south. The rest of the turkeys slept under the tree, while the four in the tree stood guard.

We also had two giant pear trees about ten yards from our house. One day, a doe with two fawns walked into our yard to eat pears that had fallen to the ground. The deer gorged themselves on the pears for about thirty minutes. Every time one of the deer moved, it farted! The deer ate so many pears it looked like their bodies were going to explode! Their bellies were so bloated. I'd never seen a deer with so much gas! Christine, Scott, and I sat on the front porch laughing at them. When the deer finally left, they sounded like a train leaving our yard!

Now, I told you I don't like snakes, and I don't care if they're venomous or nonvenomous. If you bring a snake close to me, you're going to get hurt! I had a garden in our backyard in Alabama that was surrounded by waist-high grass. One day, I was out picking tomatoes, cucumbers, and peppers from our garden, and our wiener dog ran into the weeds. As soon as the dog yelped, I knew what had happened to it. A rattlesnake had bitten the dog. I took the dog inside our house, and I saw the fang marks while Christine was holding it. We took the dog to the vet, but he said he couldn't do anything because it was too much venom for such a little dog. The vet ended up putting our dog down.

About two weeks later, I was driving back to our house and saw a bunch of people gathered around a barn by my driveway. I looked and saw a big rattlesnake lying in the middle of the road. I drove my truck over the snake about ten times. I put it in reverse, slammed on the brakes, and made sure the snake was as flat as a pancake! When it was dead, I saw that the snake had about ten rattles and a button. It was huge! I knew it was the snake that killed my dog. One of my neighbors asked me if I wanted the rattles.

"No, you can have them," I told him.

My neighbor slit the snake open with a knife and then cut off its head. He cut off the rattles, put them in his pocket, and walked down the road. I told Scott about the snake when he got home from school. Of course, Scott wanted to see it, so I took him down by the road. When Scott stepped on the snake's body, it popped him even though its head had been cut off! There was a bloody mess all over his boot.

"Good grief," Scott said. "Can you believe that?"

"Yeah, I can believe it," I said. "That's the only thing that snake is designed to do—strike you!"

Several years later, Phil and I went back to his house after a fishing trip. He saw a copperhead sitting on the front steps and killed it with a hoe. Phil chopped the snake into about ten pieces. Well, Jesse, who was Miss Kay's prized rat terrier dog, grabbed the snake's head and took off running. When the dog grabbed the snake's head, it struck him. The dog staggered off into the woods, and when it came back its head was swollen like a basketball! Somehow, Jesse survived the snakebite.

After I left the military, I wasn't really sure what I was going to do for the rest of my life. I was receiving a military pension, but I needed to find something to keep me busy. So I started working as a groundskeeper at a golf course near our house. Hey, there were snakes all over the golf course! One of the guys who worked with me killed a huge cottonmouth and was chasing everybody with it. When he started coming my way, I grabbed an iron stake. One of the other guys told him, "Hey, he will hurt you."

"What are you talking about?" the guy asked.

"Hey, he will wrap that iron stake around your head," the other guy said.

"The snake is already dead," he said.

"Hey, if you bring that snake any closer, you're going to be dead with him!" I said.

While I worked at the golf course, I nearly drove the superintendent slap insane because I kept asking him if I could fish for crappie in the ponds.

"You can't fish on the course!" he told me. "We have golfers out there."

"Hey, I'm not going to bother the golfers," I said. "When they come up to the green, I'll walk away and they won't even see me."

One day, the superintendent finally relented and let me fish in the ponds. I caught so many fish that I filled up the back of a golf cart cargo bed with bass and crappie. Some of the bass weighed between five and seven pounds! I must have caught thirty crappie, and they weighed about two pounds each.

The superintendent drove by me while I was fishing. "Good grief!" he said. "Where did you catch all those fish?"

"Duh," I said. "In the pond! It's a gold mine!"

After that day, the superintendent knew he wasn't going to keep me from fishing in the ponds. Before too long, I was also begging the superintendent to let me hunt deer on the golf course. Whenever we mowed the fairways, I kept seeing eight- and ten-point bucks! I chased the deer with my lawn mower all over the golf course.

"Look, are you going to let me hunt deer out here?" I asked the superintendent.

"No!" he said. "You can't deer hunt out here! There are golfers all over the place. You'll shoot one of them!"

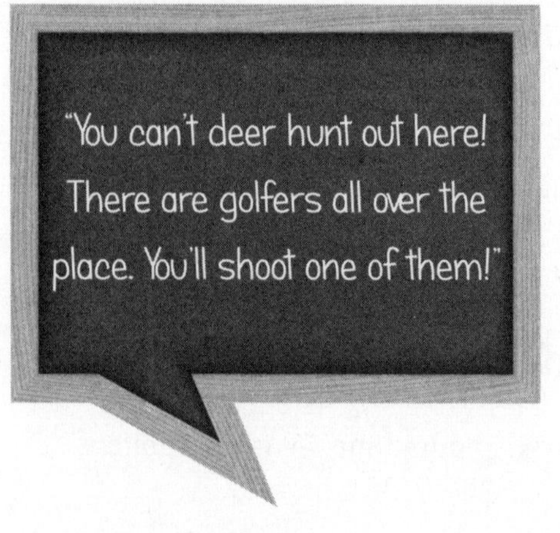

"Hey, I'll be careful," I said. "Did you look at the pond on the third hole this morning? There were sixteen deer down there. This place is like the Graceland for whitetails!"

A few months after I quit working at the golf course, one of my buddies called me and told me he shot a sixteen-point buck on the seventeenth fairway.

"They're letting you hunt out there now?" I asked him.

"Yep, as soon as you left," he said.

I could have filled up seven freezers with venison!

I worked at the golf course for about a year, and then one of my buddies and I left to go work for Hewlett-Packard in Huntsville, Alabama. I worked in the warehouse and backed the trucks up so we could load them up with computers. I worked there for about a year, until they started talking about layoffs. Then I went to work with my neighbor, who owned a home-repair business. We remodeled houses, built decks and barns, and completed other construction projects. It was good work, but I wasn't sure I wanted to be doing manual labor for the rest of my life.

One day in the winter of 1999, I called Phil to see if they were killing any ducks in Louisiana.

"Hey, when you going to come work for me?" he said. "This Duck Commander thing is really starting to take off."

"Nah, Christine told me she doesn't want to live in Louisiana," I said. "I don't think it's going to work."

"Suit yourself," Phil said. "Building duck calls is a heck of a lot more fun than repairing roofs."

Phil wasn't kidding.

"I'm so dope,
I'm illegal in fifty-five states!"

Chapter 28

Homecoming

REMEMBER WHEN I TOLD you Christine said she would never live in Louisiana again? When we were living in Alabama, I came home from work one day, and she stopped me in my tracks.

"You know what I think we should do?" she said. "If we can sell our house, we should move back to Louisiana so you can be closer to your brothers and sisters."

"Are you sick?" I asked her.

Hey, I thought Christine was terminally ill. My children and I really thought she was going to die! After we left Fort Polk near Leesville, Louisiana, she told me she would never live in the state again—no matter what! I didn't think there was any way she would ever move back to Louisiana, but she knew how much returning home meant to me. I called Trasa to tell her the news about our moving.

"Momma's dying, isn't she?" she asked.

"I think so," I said.

Christine was actually fine, but she was willing to make a sacrifice so I would be happy. I was ready to start working for Duck Commander, and Phil's business was really starting to prosper. Every time I went back to Louisiana to go hunting with Phil, he was always trying to get me to work for him. I knew Phil needed some help, and I figured helping him build duck calls would be a heck of a lot better than what I was doing for a living at the time. Christine had been working for the U.S. Department of Defense for about ten years, and she was working about ten hours a day and six days a week. We didn't have much of a life outside of work, which was really what we'd been doing our entire lives. Christine was getting ready to retire and needed a break.

Well, God must have been watching over us again. After Christine and I seriously talked about moving to Louisiana, we agreed to call a real estate agent the next Monday and advertise our house in the newspaper. Hey, we never even had to put our house on the market. We talked about it on a Friday and Saturday and went to church on Sunday morning. We told some of the people in our congregation that we were going to move to Louisiana if we could sell our house. One of the women in our church overheard us talking, and her eyes immediately lit up.

"Hey, you want to sell your house?" she said. "My daughter wants to buy it. That's her dream house."

We found out later that we had actually outbid her daughter for the house when we'd purchased it a few years earlier. I came up with a sale price that would pretty much allow us to break even or make a little bit of cash, and the lady's daughter agreed to buy it a couple of days later. There was no negotiating or haggling over the price, probably because there weren't any real estate agents involved. I probably could have asked for more money, but I was ready to move to Louisiana.

Hey, as soon as the girl signed a contract to buy my house, I packed my bags and jumped in my truck.

Hey, as soon as the girl signed a contract to buy my house, I packed my bags and jumped in my truck.

"Okay, baby, I'll see you later," I told Christine. "You can find me at Phil's house."

I drove straight to West Monroe and started working for Phil the next day. Well, we actually hunted and fished for a few days, but Christine doesn't need to know that. I left her behind to pack up the house and handle the details. She wasn't too happy about my leaving, but she was used to doing it, since we'd moved so many times while I was in the military. A few weeks later, Christine called me and said I had to come back to Alabama to sign the closing papers for our house.

"You can't do it without me?" I asked.

"No, honey, legally you have to be physically present to sign it," she said.

We moved to West Monroe and bought a house a few miles down the road from Miss Kay and Phil. From day one, I was the reedman at Duck Commander, which is what Phil wanted me to do. He said I made reeds better than anyone else, because nobody else took the time to do them right. Whenever Jase, Willie, Jep, or someone else built reeds, you could never build a duck call quickly because you were always fixing the reeds.

When I built the reeds, if you looked at one hundred of them, they all looked the same. They were uniform. I figured out exactly how short to cut the reeds and determined that the top reed has to be just a little bit shorter than the bottom one for the calls to sound right. After I bend two reeds and put a dimple and rivet in them so they'll stick together, you don't even have to blow the calls to make sure they sound right. Of course, Jase, Godwin, Jep, Martin, me, and other Duck Commander employees blow every duck call to make sure it sounds like an actual duck. I don't know how many reeds I've built over the years. At one point, I'd made four hundred thousand reeds, which were put into two hundred thousand duck calls. We only have one duck call that doesn't use reeds.

Of course, I didn't realize what I was getting into when I took a job with Duck Commander. I figured I'd build duck calls for a few years, and hunt and fish on most days. But when Willie bought the company from Phil, he had much bigger dreams for it. I had no idea Hollywood and cable TV were part of his plans!

Phil had been making hunting videos for several years, and eventually I had a regular role in them. At first, whenever they pointed the cameras at me, I told them, "Hey, y'all don't have to film me. Film somebody else." I really didn't want to be on the video; I was only out there to hunt and shoot ducks. But then they started filming me on the sly, and I never saw them doing it. Jase or Willie would do something in the blind to make me angry, or I'd start telling them a story from Vietnam, and I wouldn't even know that they were filming me! Well, the people who were buying our hunting DVDs loved hearing my stories. They started calling and writing to Duck Commander, telling us they wanted to hear more Uncle Si stories.

When we went to Outdoor Channel and then A&E TV, I didn't even know how big of a role I was going to have in our shows. Willie asked me if I wanted to be involved, and I told him, "Hey, whatever y'all want me to do." Well, when A&E launched *Duck Dynasty,* I was only supposed to appear in the show occasionally. After we filmed two or three episodes of *Duck Dynasty,* they showed them to a focus group in Los Angeles. For whatever reason, the people loved watching me. They said I was the star of the show, and I wasn't even supposed to be in it! I'm not sure why I struck a nerve with so many people, but I could have never imagined people's reaction to me.

Duck Dynasty has really changed my life. It's hard to go anywhere now without being stopped for a photograph or autograph. I'm happy to do it, but nowadays it takes a lot longer to go to the gas station or grocery store. I'll do almost anything a kid asks me to do, and I know our show wouldn't be where it is today without our fans. It's amazing how many people send me free stuff at the Duck Commander warehouse. A car dealer in Arkansas even gave me a free truck to drive. The dealer put its name on the doors, and they asked me if I wanted anything else on it. I told them to put "Hey, Jack" in the back window and "The Duck Man" on the tailgate. Wouldn't you know it? I worked my entire life and never had a new truck, and now someone is giving me a free truck to drive when I'm retired.

Hey, only in America.

"One time I stopped
and smelled the roses
and a big bumblebee went
and stung me on the nose.
So, hey, from then on,
look here, you smell the roses,
but you smell them quick."

Broken Heart

I STARTED SMOKING CIGARETTES WHEN I was in high school. Hey, back then nobody really knew that smoking was bad for you. Both of my parents smoked, and so did most of my friends' parents. All of the Hollywood actors of the 1960s smoked, whether it was Steve McQueen, Burt Lancaster, Paul Newman, or James Coburn. Hey, if those guys were smoking cigarettes, I figured it had to be cool. And, hey, there wasn't anyone cooler in Dixie, Louisiana, than Silas Merritt Robertson.

Well, I eventually figured out that a cigarette is nothing more than a pinch of tobacco rolled in paper—with fire at one end and an idiot at the other! Hey, what's the result of too much smoking? Coffin, Jack!

I smoked for more than thirty years. It was hard to quit while

I was in the military because the army gave you four cigarettes with every meal; when they stopped giving them to us, I just bought them myself. I tried to quit many times over the years. I even used tobacco alternatives like water-vapor cigarettes and electronic cigarettes. Hey, they never warned me that I could electrocute myself when I smoked them together. You want to talk about a high. Good grief!

> I eventually figured out that a cigarette is nothing more than a pinch of tobacco rolled in paper—with fire at one end and an idiot at the other!

I smoked cigarettes in Vietnam to occupy my time more than anything else. One night, a sergeant ordered a buddy and me to deliver supplies to a camp on the other side of a jungle. It was a dangerous mission, which was made even worse by a driving rainstorm. As we made our way down a dark road, I heard a tap on the passenger-side window of our Jeep.

"Hey, there's somebody knocking on my window!" I told my buddy.

"Well, open it and see what he wants," he said.

I rolled down the window. A Vietnamese man was staring at me. I didn't know if he was a civilian or with the Vietcong.

"Do you have a cigarette?" he asked.

"Hey, he wants a cigarette," I said. "What do I do?"

"Give him a cigarette and let's get out of here!" my buddy said.

I handed the man a cigarette and rolled up the window.

"Step on it," I said.

I was a little freaked out by the incident, so I lit up a cigarette of my own. Now we were really in a hurry to finish the mission, and I figured we were probably driving sixty miles per hour through the jungle. Then I heard another knock on my window.

"Good grief," I said. "He's knocking on my window again."

"Well, see what he wants," my buddy said.

I rolled down the window again.

"Do you have a light?" the Vietnamese man said.

"Light his cigarette!" my buddy said. "Make it quick!"

I lit the man's cigarette, and my buddy put the Jeep's gas pedal to the floor. We were probably going ninety miles per hour now!

Then I heard a knock on my window again.

"What in the world?" I screamed. "He's back! How is he doing it?"

I rolled down the window again, expecting him to shoot me.

"What do you want?" I asked.

"Hey, would you like some help getting out of the mud?" he said.

After I left Vietnam and quit drinking alcohol, I figured smoking wasn't the worst vice for me. I never really noticed the toll smoking was taking on my body. Even though I was smoking Winston cigarettes, I was still able to complete the mandatory training runs and any other kind of physical activity the army required of me. I even smoked when I played high school football, although the coaches probably would have killed me if they'd ever found out.

I didn't realize secondhand smoke was bad for you until I went deer hunting when I was in my forties. I was hunting on a friend's property in Germany, and he walked me to a deer stand at the start of the hunt. I climbed into the stand and lit a cigarette. A few seconds later, I heard someone coughing. I looked around for my buddy, figuring he'd come back to tell me something. But then I looked down and saw a spike buck standing next to the tree. It was coughing from the cigarette smoke! Who knew secondhand smoke was even bad for deer?

Well, eventually the cigarettes caught up with me. Near the beginning of January 2005, I knew something was wrong with my health. I was eating antacids constantly, even though my stomach was never upset by anything I ate. Growing up in Louisiana, everything we ate was spicy. I put hot sauce and pepper sauce on nearly everything—even my Fruity Pebbles. I had a cast-iron stomach. When I started feeling ill, I thought I was having heartburn or acid reflux, but the antacids weren't helping. Christine kept telling me I needed to go see the doctor, but duck season was almost over, so I wanted to keep hunting. I kept putting off a doctor's visit.

Christine knew I absolutely hated going to the doctor or visiting a hospital. Whenever Christine had surgery over the years, I tried to visit her, but she knew how anxious it made me. She always sent me home because I made her nervous. I visited her as soon as the surgery was over, and then I went back to get her when she was released. I figured it was the least I could do for her. It's not that I hate visiting doctors or going to the hospital, it's really more of a deeply rooted phobia. When we were kids, a mobile doctor's clinic visited the rural areas of Louisiana. Momma always took us to the clinic to get tetanus shots and other vaccinations we needed for school. Well, the first time Momma took me, I took off running through a cornfield! I don't like needles and I don't like shots, Jack!

Well, on the next-to-last day of duck season in 2005, we were sitting in a blind and killed about four or five ducks. Jase noticed a big flock of ducks flying to another part of Phil's land. They decided to pick up a few decoys and move to the other spot.

"Hey, y'all go ahead," I said. "I ain't feeling too good. I'm going to sit here and see if I can get me a couple more ducks. Y'all come back when you're done hunting."

After they left, I saw a mallard drake and mallard hen fly into the woods. I decided I was going to slip into the woods and whack 'em. I killed the mallard drake and retrieved it, but then my chest started hurting as I walked back to the blind. Suddenly, I was overcome with severe chest pains. I sat on a log and tried to catch my breath. When the pain finally abated, I walked back to my truck and drove home. I went straight to bed. I was absolutely exhausted and slept all day.

Throughout the night, Christine kept checking on me to make sure I was still breathing. She feared something was seriously wrong with me. I got up at four o'clock the next morning to go duck hunting again. When I leaned over to put on my boots, the pain in my chest took my breath away. I woke up Christine and told her I needed to go to the emergency room. She knew something was very wrong. After the nurses checked my vital signs, they admitted me to the hospital.

The doctors sent a camera scope down my throat to look at

my heart. They told me I was having a heart attack and needed open-heart surgery. Hey, I told you I was a heartbreaker!

"Are you sure I need it?" I asked the surgeon.

"Yeah, you need it," he said. "You'll die if you don't."

"Well, I've been healthy all of my life," I said. "If you say I need it, then I guess I need it."

Since it was a Saturday, the heart surgeon decided to wait to do my surgery until his regular team was on duty on Monday. I kept having heart attacks, but the doctors and nurses were monitoring me around the clock. They took really good care of me. On Monday, I had open-heart surgery. When the surgery was over, doctors told Christine that overall I was pretty healthy. They took a vein from my leg and used it to bypass a blockage and get blood to my heart. After I woke up, the surgeon told me it was a privilege to operate on me because he didn't have to do any work to find my heart. When the surgeon cracked me open, he couldn't find an ounce of fat. My heart was sitting right there. They didn't even have to put me on a heart-lung machine to pump my blood during surgery; the surgeons repaired my heart between beats!

I knew I was lucky to be alive. The surgeon told Christine I had what they called a "widow-maker." My left main coronary artery was almost completely blocked. Medically, the doctors told me, I should have died. A widow-maker can kill you within a matter of only ten to twenty minutes. It was another of God's miracles. Thankfully, the Lord was watching over me again and sent me to good doctors, nurses, and surgeons who saved my life.

My recovery from surgery was pretty rapid. It was around the time I usually helped Phil work on his land, which I really enjoyed doing. I liked being out in nature and loved spending time with my brother. I paced myself for six weeks and when I received the all clear from the doctors, I went back to my normal routine. I had shortness of breath and got tired easily for a while, but before too long, I was back to being regular ole Uncle Si.

After my heart attack, I never picked up another cigarette. I promised Christine, my children, and my brothers and sisters that I would never smoke again—and I haven't. My heart attack really woke me up, and now I cherish every day I'm on this earth. Before my heart attack, I hadn't been to the doctor since 1993. Now I get a checkup every six months. Sunrises and sunsets are a lot more beautiful now, and I even take time to smell the roses. Hey, I still smell them quick, because you never know when a bumblebee might sting you on the nose!

"Never insult a man's beard.
You get either thunder or lightning."

Chapter 30

Faith

HEY, I DON'T USE the term "religious." A lot of people say they're religious, but then you watch how they act or listen to how they talk. Their actions and language say otherwise. I don't really care about the names on the front of a church building, either, because I don't believe in denominations. You're either a Christian or you're not.

My faith is pretty simple: I believe that God is the Father and his Son is Jesus Christ. I believe Jesus Christ came to this earth and became flesh for us because we have two problems. We have a sin problem and a death problem, and, hey, we can't solve either one of them. Jesus left our Father's side, came to this earth as flesh, and died on a cross for the things Silas Robertson does wrong. I deserve to be on a cross and would be guilty as charged for some of the things I've done in my life. Jesus was innocent of all charges and did not belong there, yet he willingly went there and accepted my punishment.

Hey, that's not the end of the story. A little girl watched her mother kill her father. The little girl went to church with her grandmother, and a Sunday school teacher showed her a picture of Jesus on the cross.

"Does anyone know who this is?" the teacher asked.

"I don't know his name," the little girl said. "But he didn't stay on the cross."

"What are you talking about?" the teacher asked.

"I know he didn't stay on the cross because the night my mother killed my father, he was holding me in his arms," the little girl said.

Jesus Christ dying on the cross wasn't the end of the story. They took his body down from the cross and buried him in a tomb. Before Jesus was crucified, he told everyone that if they ruined the temple—they thought he was referring to a religious temple, but he was actually talking about his body—he would raise it in three days. Three days after they hung Jesus on a cross and killed him, he fulfilled what he said. He rose from the dead and spent forty days and forty nights with five hundred people to prove his resurrection. Some people even watched his body ascend into the heavens.

It was all part of God's plan. Jesus came to earth of his free will and knew what he had to do. He paid for my sins and then ascended into the heavens. Right now, Jesus is sitting next to our heavenly Father. When I mess up, I say, "Lord, I'm sorry, I have sinned again because I'm weak." They look down at me, and Jesus turns to the Father and says, "Remember the cross. I have him covered."

Hey, my faith is what my momma and daddy raised me to believe. I watched them live it. They didn't only talk the talk, but they walked the walk that matched the talk. When people ask me where I go to church, I tell them I'm a follower of Jesus Christ. I'm a Christian. I believe that he is who he said he was. Jesus said he was God's son, and I believe him. I believe he died on the cross for me. I believe he beat the grave, and that's a promise he has given me. He said, "If you trust me, even if you die, you shall live."

Hey, if anyone has a better offer for me, in which my sins will be forgiven and I can beat the grave, I'm willing to listen. But I don't think I'll ever hear a better offer for everlasting life.

It's what I live by, and it's the great hope the Bible gives us. As Jase likes to say, the Bible is a love letter from God to mankind. In the Bible, God tells us how much He loves us and that He sent his Son to die for us. Some people have asked how Jesus was able to live on this earth and not sin. Some people claim Jesus really wasn't a man. Hey, Jesus was a man. He proved it to the Apostle Thomas, who doubted Jesus was resurrected until he could see and feel the wounds Jesus received on the cross.

As it says in John 20:24–29:

> *Now Thomas (also known as Didymus), one of the Twelve, was not with the disciples when Jesus came. So the other disciples told him, "We have seen the Lord!"*
>
> *But he said to them, "Unless I see the nail marks in his hands and put my finger where the nails were, and put my hand into his side, I will not believe."*
>
> *A week later his disciples were in the house again, and Thomas was with them. Though the doors were locked, Jesus came and stood among them and said, "Peace be*

with you!" Then he said to Thomas, "Put your finger here; see my hands. Reach out your hand and put it into my side. Stop doubting and believe."

Thomas said to him, "My Lord and my God!"

Then Jesus told him, "Because you have seen me, you have believed; blessed are those who have not seen and yet have believed."

Thomas believed Jesus was the Father's Son because he could touch and feel his wounds. Jesus was of flesh and blood, but he was also deity. If he wasn't, he couldn't help me because he wouldn't be able to understand. Jesus died on the cross because he loved perfectly. When Jesus was in excruciating pain and was dying on the cross, he told the Father, "Forgive them. They don't know what they're doing." There isn't a more painful way for a human to die than being crucified on the cross, but Jesus still forgave those who killed him.

Hey, if you're a Christian, racism is out. God made mankind from dust and then He made woman. We don't even know what color Adam was. When I was growing up in Dixie, Louisiana, there were probably only six or seven white kids in the entire town. Most of my friends were African-American. If I had chores to do, I'd get my friends to help me paint a fence, clean the barn, or cut the grass. Then I'd take them to the water hole and teach them how to swim. I probably taught twenty African-American kids how to swim.

When Daddy fell from an oil rig and broke his back, we didn't have very much money because he wasn't working. Momma told some of the ladies in the neighborhood that we weren't going to have a Christmas that year because she didn't have any money to buy us presents. Well, the black families in town took up a donation and raised about two hundred dollars for us. We had a memorable Christmas because of their generosity, and nobody even asked them to do it. The Bible tells us to love everyone, regardless of race or religion.

Hey, I believe in Jesus Christ and he is God's Son. He came to this earth as flesh and died on a cross for our sins. He loved us enough to die for us, even his enemies.

That's a fact, Jack!

Letters to Si from His Family

A Letter to Si from His Wife, Christine

When I first met you, I knew you as "Rob." In the military, names were usually shortened, and the first name was never used. We had been together sixteen months when I was introduced to your siblings, their children, and your parents They called you "Si," not "Rob," so I did the same when we were with your family. But when we were alone, it was back to "Rob." But after you became a household name, I decided I might as well join the crowd.

When I met your family that first time, I wanted to run in the opposite direction. You know how shy I am and that I don't open up to people easily. It has always surprised me that you and I were able to talk as easily as we did from the very beginning.

You wanted to live near Phil, so we stayed with Phil, Kay, and Alan until we found an apartment not far from them. I understood that you had missed the hunting and fishing with Phil, but every time you went out with him, I worried. He was drinking by then, and I didn't trust him. After about a year, you realized he was beyond your help, and we moved to Ruston, Louisiana. I knew how that hurt your heart, but I was concerned about you. When you reenlisted in the Army, I thought it was a great idea. Even though you are strong (and stubborn), I worried about Phil rubbing off you.

Do you remember the first year you were able to duck hunt in 1971? You and Phil had killed eight, but when you cleaned them, there were only seven. Jason was now three. When he came out of the bedroom the next morning, he had the duck under his arm. Evidently he had slept with it. Phil said, "There is a duck hunter in the making!" Look at Jason now!! Alan, at such a young age, told everyone he would be a minister when he grew up. And that's exactly what he did.

When we couldn't have children, you had so much faith! In my heart, I never believed I was worthy of children. But when I became pregnant, I knew it was a special gift from God. I was only sick twice, and everything went fine. When my contractions started and were coming every fifteen minutes, you took me to the clinic. After the exam, they told you to get me straight to the hospital. It usually takes forty minutes;

you got me there in twenty. All the way there, you kept me laughing. When we were waiting for a nurse to open the door, I was still laughing. When she opened the door, she said we didn't belong there. Both of us were shocked! She finally said, "No one who rings this bell is laughing."

This was in the time before ultrasounds, so I had to have an X-ray. I ended up having an emergency C-section. You were there when I woke, but the only question you were able to answer was "What was the sex?" I wanted to know how much she weighed, how long she was, and what color was her hair was. You are such an observant person. NOT!! Trasa was born on Saturday night, but you were in the midst of a huge inspection, so you had to return to base. I'm a military wife, and I understood that spouses have to do some things alone. You were allowed to return to the hospital to sign some papers; then you had to return to base. Trasa and I were discharged on Friday, but you were not allowed to come get us.

Our home was always full of love and laughter, but with the addition of our beautiful daughter, it was even more so.

Mom had always told me to be careful how I worded prayer. When we prayed for patience, we had no idea how God would answer. You always say that God has a sense of humor. We sure learned patience when we had our son. Due to complications in my pregnancy with Scott, our family was split up. Trasa was sent to my parents in Kentucky, you were at Fort Polk, and I was in

Texas. We had so many people praying for us from three different states.

In our time together, we have seen God's work in so many ways. Before I knew you, my dad was the only man I loved and respected. Girls often marry men like their dads. God was first in Dad's life. He also loved Mom and didn't care who knew it. I have been so blessed by having you in my life. Because of you, I have reached the brass ring! Life with you has never been boring or mundane.

May God continue to keep you in the palm of His hand. I love everything about you and would never change anything. I'm also proud that you are now sharing your laughter and love of God with many, many people. You are awesome!

A Letter to Si from His Daughter, Trasa

When I think of you, the first word that springs to mind is "faith." You have always been so committed to God and the Church, and that definitely rubbed off on me. The years of attending church three times weekly never seemed a burden, because you made sure we knew it was the right thing to do. I learned Scripture, first by hearing it from you and then by reading it on my own. I learned so much from God's Word. I used to wake up early some mornings and memorize pieces like the Sermon on the Mount so I could be an educated Christian. That habit has continued into my adult life, and I often turn to the Bible in times of trouble and of thanksgiving. That basis, that rock, which you gave me during my childhood, has led me to be the strong Christian woman I am today.

The second word about you that wells up is "nature." You love the outdoors and all the natural gifts the world has to offer. Because of your family's background, hunting and fishing are like breathing to you. But many were the times that we would sit together and you would point out the wildlife all around us—a bunny rabbit there, here a hawk with talons extended to catch a meal, sometimes a deer as its eyes reflected green in the passing headlights. I enjoyed those times immensely as you shared your wisdom about nature.

Of course, I couldn't forget to thank you for my great love of food! As anyone who knows me will attest, I am an eater. And I'm not one of those dainty, waifish girls, either—despite my history of modeling. On our first official date, when my future husband Kyle asked me if he could cook me dinner, he asked what I'd like. He expected me to say, "Oh, a salad," or "Whatever you'd like to make." Instead, I definitively stated, "I'd love a steak and a baked potato." That part of me surely comes straight from you—as well as my love for all kinds of meats. Yep, I'm quite the carnivore. As I told a friend recently, squirrel is still the best meat I've ever eaten—but the stinkin' critters are just too small! It takes a dozen just to feed two people!

Seriously, though, a lot of my political perceptions were formed at your knee. I still believe in gun rights for hunters and also for constitutional guarantees against governmental recklessness. I believe that people are more important than things or animals. And I believe that the right to life is sacred, from conception to natural death.

Thank you for helping form me into the person I've become. I am a physically confident, emotionally mature, intellectually gifted human being, and am so blessed by God in this life with my adoring husband and beautiful sons. I could not be happier in my life.

I love you, Dad.

A Letter to Si from His Son, Scott

When I think back to my childhood, I have so many memories. I remember watching you and Trasa clean squirrels and helping y'all once I got big enough. I remember you dressing up in costumes like the big rabbit. I remember you taking me deer hunting with you in Germany. I must have driven you crazy that day with all my fidgeting. You so wanted me to get a deer and maybe share that experience of your childhood. I simply loved the fact that I got to spend a day with my dad. I watched you and listened to you more than you knew. I picked up your love of the land and being in the woods simply from watching how you moved and the different trees you pointed out.

I remember when you took me along on the wild boar hunt in Germany. I found out later I was going to be a beater, and not with you. So there I was crawling around this thick brush on the side of a mountain making a lot of noise (which I have to say I enjoyed) to drive the animal toward the hunters. The gentleman with me had a pistol, which got me thinking, What happens if the boar doesn't beat it like he's supposed to? The gentleman with the pistol said I shouldn't worry about that, as it's very rare that the boars come at the beaters. I have to say I was not very reassured. When we finally got to stand up, I was relieved, only to find that, after walking a short distance, we had to do it again at a different location.

I remember you taking me with you for your duck

hunting vacation in Louisiana when I was in the fifth grade, and fishing at night with cane poles and a lantern on the Ouachita River.

I remember when we took a family trip to Bavaria and Mom and Trasa got lost. You remained quite calm, in spite of all my questions of "What if?" I remember you reviewing the short sermon that I gave at the church we attended in Pirmasens and helping me get over my first-time jitters.

I look back at the conversations we had when I was a hardheaded teenager. I remember the heated discussions we had where you were just trying to steer me in the right direction, maybe away from mistakes you made. I remember that you wanted me to go to college, and I wanted to join the military. I thought I had my points all lined up for the discussion and that you would understand. Needless to say, the conversation didn't quite go as I'd planned, and we agreed to disagree. I can't describe to you how I felt when I came back from AIT as a soldier, and you told me that I had made the right choice. I remember you telling me that the only things I can control—something I came into this world with and will leave with—is the value of my word.

Dad, there are so many things I remember, and you are threaded through them all. I remember you telling me how much smarter your father got as you got older. I have to say I never thought you didn't know what you were talking about, though I can't say I understood as a child what I understand now as a parent myself. I look back to your words then and find myself applying them now when I hit a bump in the road of life. I have to say I am amazed at the level of patience you possessed then and now. I consider myself blessed that I had the parents I did. No one is perfect, but y'all are the perfect ones for me.

You are and always have been the rock this family holds to. Your faith in God as I grew up showed me that we might not always have the answers and that was okay, because God was in charge and would always take care of us. I love you, Dad, and will consider myself lucky if I grow up to be half the man you are.

> *Blessed is the man who does not walk in the counsel of the wicked or stand in the way of the sinners or sit in the seat of mockers. But his Delight is in the law of the Lord, and on his law he meditates day and night. He is like a tree planted by streams of water, which yields its fruit in season and whose leaf does not whither. Whatever he does prospers.—Psalms 1:1–3*

THANKS TO MY MOM and dad for raising me and introducing me to Jesus Christ and for encouraging my love for hunting and fishing. Thanks to Mark Schlabach for taking my stories and putting them all together to show my journey so far. Thanks to Philis Boultinghouse, Amanda Demastus, and our friends at Howard Books. Thanks to Phil and Kay and their family for being there for all of my life. Thanks to Alan for helping with the book. Thanks to John Howard for his help. Thanks to my poker buddies for keeping me sane. Thanks to Trasa, Kyle, Scott, and Marsha for making me proud and giving me eight wonderful grandsons. Finally, thanks to my wife, Christine, that redhead who has kept life interesting for the past forty-three years.